WRITTEN BY DAVID S.J. HODGSON & TRACY ERICKSO … **GAME GUIDE**

Layout: In Color Design
Design: Jody Seltzer and Bryan Neff
Copyeditor: Asha Johnson
MP Maps: David Bueno
Manufacturing: Stephanie Sanchez

Prima Games would like to thank the following people for their help and support throughout this project: Nik Karlsson, Kevin Brannan, Kirk Somdal, Laura Campos, Chris Tomassian, Jared Beauchamp, Jared Kortje, Steve Malandra, Chris Cross, Christopher Chaparro, Jeremy Greiner, Simon King, Hayden Mulholland, David Votypka, Erin Daly, Jason Priest, Martin Raymond, Zachary Wilson, Simon Deal, Matthew Bromley, Rob Donovan, Rachel Maille, Albert Meranda, Benjamin Johnson, Ryan Hanscom, Patrick Haslow, CJ Kershner, Rex Dickson, Jason Deaville, Breck Campbell, Ron Janzen, Simon Orr, Ryan Baker, Jeff Dicker, Richard Carrillo, Daniel Matlack, Evan Hort, Paul Callender, Brian Holinka and Paul Oribine.

Important:
Prima Games has made every effort to determine that the information contained in this book is accurate. However, the publisher makes no warranty, either expressed or implied, as to the accuracy, effectiveness, or completeness of the material in this book; nor does the publisher assume liability for damages, either incidental or consequential, that may result from using the information in this book. The publisher cannot provide any additional information or support regarding gameplay, hints and strategies, or problems with hardware or software. Such questions should be directed to the support numbers provided by the game and/or device manufacturers as set forth in their documentation. Some game tricks require precise timing and may require repeated attempts before the desired result is achieved.

David S. J. Hodgson
Originally hailing from the English city of Manchester, David began his career in 1995, writing for numerous classic British gaming magazines from a rusting, condemned, bohemian dry-docked German fishing trawler floating on the River Thames. Fleeing the United Kingdom, he joined the crew at the part-fraternity, part-sanitarium known as GameFan magazine. David helped launch GameFan Books and form Gamers' Republic, was partly responsible for the wildly unsuccessful incite Video Gaming and Gamers.com. He began authoring guides for Prima in 2000. He has written over 80 strategy guides! He lives in the Pacific Northwest with his wife Melanie, and an eight-foot statue of Great Cthulhu.

We want to hear from you! E-mail comments and feedback to **dhodgson@primagames.com**.

Contents

PRIMA GAMES
AN IMPRINT OF RANDOM HOUSE, INC.
3000 LAVA RIDGE COURT, SUITE 100
ROSEVILLE, CA 95661

WWW.PRIMAGAMES.COM

ISBN: 978-0307-89017-7 ★ Printed in the United States of America ★ 11 12 13 14 LL 10 9 8 7 6 5 4 3 2 1

BASIC CAMPAIGN >> TRAINING

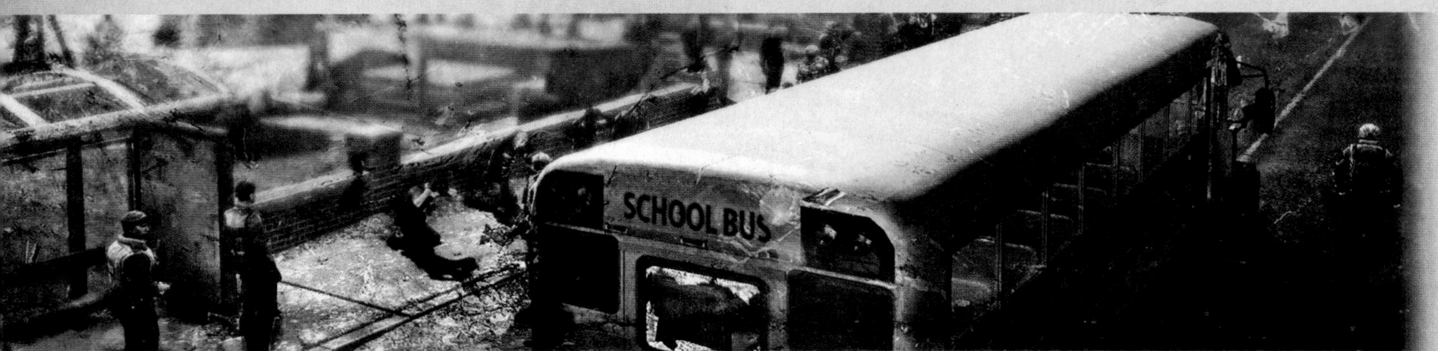

BASIC TRAINING

America is in tatters. The Korean invaders stand poised for ultimate victory. Yet there are those who refuse to yield. Count yourself among those resisting the Korean People's Army. The following chapter details the basic survival skills you need to thrive in this hostile environment. Welcome to *Homefront*.

The following information details basic survival techniques, serves as a primer to all of the available weapons in the Single Player Campaign, and introduces the Campaign Walkthrough.

TIP 영리한

Are you looking for Multiplayer Training? Then consult that chapter, which comes after the Campaign Walkthrough.

Game Difficulty

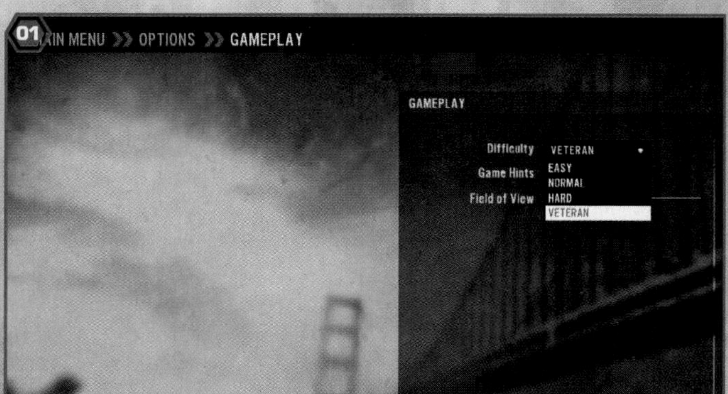

At the main menu, or during your Single Player Campaign game, you may elect to change the difficulty setting **[01]**. The four difficulty settings relate to the following game attributes:

Ally Accuracy: How well your teammates fire when attacking the enemy.

Enemy Accuracy: How precise the enemy is at hitting you, or your team.

Player Health: How much damage you can take. This does not change dependant on difficulty.

Enemy Health: How much damage an enemy can take before dying.

NOTE 알아두세요

Player health is noted because you effectively have "less" health at higher difficulty due to enemy competence and teammate incompetence.

Normal Difficulty is the default setting, and all four game attributes are measured based off this. The following table shows how the difficulty ramps up, compared to Normal.

Game Attribute	Easy Difficulty	Normal Difficulty	Hard Difficulty	Guerrilla Difficulty
Ally Accuracy	Better	Standard	Worse	Much worse
Enemy Accuracy	Worse	Standard	Much Better	Devastating!
Player Health	Worse	Standard	Much Tougher	Extremely Tough!
Enemy Health	The same	The same	The same	The same

For example, if you play on Guerilla Difficulty, your allies are 70 percent less effective than normal, and the enemies' accuracy is four times better than normal.

NOTE 알아두세요

Certain Achievements or Trophies depend upon the difficulty setting. Consult the Walkthrough or Appendix for further information.

Single-Player HUD and Loadout

Heads Up Display Data

During the Campaign, you access a constant data stream of information. The adjacent picture shows the various aspects of your HUD.

1. **Weapon:** The weapon you're currently using.
2. **Scope or Sight:** Some weapons you pick up have an attachment that allows scoped or trace dot aiming over an enemy.
3. **Target Crosshairs:** This pulses when you're firing at an enemy, and closes considerably when you're aiming. It also changes when you're crouched or prone. It changes color depending on whether an enemy (red) or friend (green) is in your reticle. The smaller the crosshairs, the more focused your shot will be. See "Aiming," below.
4. **Damage Marker:** A curved red mark shows the direction you're taking damage from. Turn and take down that threat when you can. A grenade marker is also shown when one is thrown; step away from where it's pointing!
5. **Ammunition:** This shows your current weapon's remaining ammunition, in icon and number forms.
6. **Explosives:** The number of grenades and C4 (up to four) is shown here.
7. **Actions:** Prompts to climb ladders, reload, or perform other pertinent actions are mentioned here.
8. **Objective:** Your current objective appears here when given. After it disappears, find it in your Pause menu.
9. **Compass:** This allows you to situate yourself. For example, if you remember which direction you were facing when you started a checkpoint, you're less likely to get lost. The Guide Walkthrough refers to compass directions, too.
10. **Compass Data:** Whether you're following a teammate or finding an objective point, any relevant icons are shown here, along with a distance (in meters) to that target.

Single Player Loadout

You can carry two weapons, a knife, up to four frag grenades, and up to four C4 explosives at a time, as shown in this fully equipped player's HUD **[02]**. Aside from the knife, which is only used to inflict melee strikes, all other weapons are found during your adventure. Additional weaponry is available, but only in Multiplayer games. Follow your game instructions for swapping between your two weapons, which can be any combination of Assault and Sniper Rifles, SMGs, LMGs, or even Rocket Launchers. The Walkthrough continuously updates you on recommended weapons to use in specific situations.

Crosshairs and Scopes: Aiming

From the Hip

The crosshairs that you see when using a weapon vary in size depending on a number of factors. If you aren't targeting a specific foe using your weapon's iron-sights or scope, you are firing "from the hip." This is generally inadvisable at medium or long ranges (and indeed, is almost impossible while using a Sniper Rifle). However, for weapons designed for closer gunfire (such as SMGs and the Shotgun), firing from the hip is a good idea. It allows instant shots, rather than taking time to aim through a scope or sight. Note the different sizes of crosshairs depending on the chosen weapon **[03]**, **[04]**.

Zoomed, scoped or sight aiming (the terms are interchangeable) uses the attachment at the top of your weapon. The crosshairs width diminishes as you take more careful aim, and the bullet spread therefore is diminished. Bullet spread also depends on the weapon.

Sight Aiming

Taking the time to look down your weapon's sight is more accurate than firing from the hip, but it takes longer. If you have this luxury, and your weapon is designed for such action, this is the recommended takedown tactic because your weapon's bullet spread narrows, and you use fewer bullets.

During the Campaign, you can pick up a variety of weapons, and the way they function when you're carefully aiming can vary depending on the type of sight attached. In these three examples, the same Assault Rifle is fired using zoom aiming, but with one of the three types of attachment:

Iron Sights [05]: A weapon without an attachment has the rudimentary sight that came with the weapon, which allows you to draw your eye down the weapon to the target.

Sights [06]: Certain sights allow a more enhanced view of the target, and sometimes come with a dot to pinpoint the foe; this makes lining up headshots a lot easier.

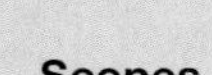

Scopes [07]: The finest weaponry comes with a scope. Scopes allow you more accuracy, as well as a zoomed-in perspective, enabling even more precision tagging. This is the recommended tactic that veterans employ.

TIP 영리한

Your crosshairs also diminish if you're crouching or prone, as does the weapon's "kick back" (how much it shudders when fired), which can knock your aiming off-target.

NOTE 알아두세요

One of your game options is Auto-Aiming. When you trigger your aiming, this automatically shifts the weapon onto a target and "locks" onto it, quickening the time it takes to shoot it. Turn this off if you want a challenge. Turn it on if you're getting decimated.

TIP 영리한

Fire from the hip when you're using SMGs or the Shotgun. Use sight aiming when employing Sniper Rifles. With all other weapons, try both before deciding on a preference, both generally and for the specific combat situation you find yourself in.

Spray and Pray

This is the act of holding down the trigger of your automatic weapon, and tagging as many foes as you can before your ammunition runs out **[08]**. SMGs and LMGs are better-designed to take advantage of this technique, which can clear a room of enemies (and your ammunition) in seconds. Use this in panicked situations, if you have plenty of ammunition, or when facing a large number of foes. This is usually done from the hip.

Fluttering

A much more focused technique, "fluttering" your weapon means taking a (usually semi-automatic Assault Rifle) weapon and pressing the trigger repeatedly, as quickly as possible **[09]**. Also known as "burst firing," this conserves ammunition and keeps your crosshairs tight as it limits kick back, but it takes longer to line up your shots and may only wound (and require further shots to kill) an enemy. Use this if you like to conserve ammo, or want to perfect your accuracy. This is usually done from a down a sight.

Headshots

When you're aiming at enemies, unless you're using high-powered Sniper Rifles, which inflict a killing blow no matter where you target a foe, the majority of your kills should be headshots **[10]**. This takes more accuracy, but less time, so practice and become adept at cranial takedowns.

Going On Maneuvers

Standing, Crouching, Prone

Standing [11]: Standing makes you a bigger target, but allows you to maneuver more quickly. Stand around 50 to 60 percent of the time, such as when moving between combat situations, breaking for cover, or following teammates.

Crouching [12]: This allows you move (albeit slightly slower), while staying less of a target to enemies. You can move to certain types of cover mostly without being seen, you receive a slight accuracy bonus when firing, and you can quickly go prone or standing depending on the threat level. Expect to spend around 20 percent of your time in this position.

Prone [13]: Unless you're spraying and praying, a more sedate pace is called for. Going prone allows you to crawl (extremely slowly) under gaps in walls, and to stay behind even the shortest of scenic cover. The accuracy bonus you receive is high, and you can sometimes confuse a foe by crawling and ambushing them as they round a corner trying to find you. Spend around 20 percent of your time in this position, for the accuracy and cover benefits.

Jumping, Climbing, and Sprinting

Jumping **[14]** is rarely-used technique employed when you wish to vault over a low wall or up to a location to stand on.

Climb ladders with a context-sensitive button press; step to a ladder, press the button, and you automatically climb.

Sprinting **[15]** allows you to cover distances at a swift pace, but sacrifices the ability to fire or turn abruptly. Use this when scurrying between cover points without the enemy seeing you, or toward an area you need to reach. Sprint and Jump to cover longer distances; this handy Multiplayer tactic isn't really used during the Campaign.

Strafing and Sidestepping

Strafing is the movement from side to side, or in a circle around a point (usually an enemy). This allows you to keep targeting (and usually firing) at an enemy without taking your aim away. Perfect this technique so you can move and shoot, without looking where you're going, but getting there just the same. Sidestepping (such as in the example images **[16]**, **[17]**) from cover is the best way to quickly ascertain a battle situation before returning to cover, or firing and stepping back into cover while remaining unscathed.

Outflanking

Because you have teammates, you can use the environment to your advantage and rush the outskirts of an area so you can attack from the sides or behind **[18]**, a technique known as "flanking" or "outflanking" if you've gained the upper hand. A direct approach to combat works, but sometimes a more subtle weaving around a group of foes is called for.

Adrenaline Event

Sometimes, time slows to a crawl, usually in a high-stress, panic situation where your military training comes into play. You know exactly what to do: shoot the enemies causing you distress **[19]**.

Being Environmentally Conscious

Taking Damage

When you're struck by enemy fire, immediately return fire—ideally killing the foe who shot at you—or run to cover, or both. If you don't, damage from an initial winging attack **[20]** becomes a much more dangerous condition **[21]** where your vision blurs, and everything turns black and white... and then red... and then fades to black. Seek cover and recover your composure and health.

Enemy Grenades

Never ignore a grenade symbol appearing on your HUD **[22]**. Back away from the grenade's location (indicated by a red grenade icon), or face high damage or death.

Cover Opportunities

Your enemies tend to search for cover, and you should do the same. Cover consists of scenery you can fire over **[23]** or around **[24]**. Stepping out from complete cover is easier than standing up from a crouch and having bullets whiz by your head. Some cover is destructible as well, so seek items that are toughened, such as KPA armored crates or larger containers. Once behind cover, you can recover from damage taken, quickly peer out to see what your foes are doing, and lob grenades.

Explosive Barrels

Avoid taking cover near explosive barrels **[25]**. It's worth spending a few rounds detonating them, either when foes are near them, or before you reach them so enemies don't shoot them and damage you in the process.

ARMORY

Main Weapon Types

You are encouraged (and due to the lack of ammunition to pick up, *strongly* encouraged) to switch your weapon loadouts continuously during the Campaign. Weaponry is found in the following ways:

Firearms are (rarely) given to you by a member of the Resistance, such as Connor.

You can find weapons propped up against a wall, or in a cache.

Weapons dropped by enemies are your primary source of ordnance.

Unique Weapons are placed throughout the Campaign, usually down side alleys or in out-of-the-way locales. These are usually weapons with powerful scopes or other attachments that are excellent during battles occurring immediately after finding them.

Enemies almost always drop Assault Rifles, Submachine Guns (SMGs), or more powerful LMGs (Light Machine Guns). Occasionally, a Sniper Rifle (or Shotgun) is found, but these are deemed appropriate for specific offensive actions, as detailed in the Campaign Walkthrough.

NOTE 알아두세요

Information on Close, Medium, and Long Ranges

- **Close range is anywhere from actual melee combat range to 15 feet or so from a foe.**
- **Medium range is farther than 15 feet, but less than 35 feet or so from a target.**
- **Long range is farther than 35 feet.**

Melee Strikes

When you're extremely close to an enemy, you can elect to step forward and stab them with your knife (which you always carry) **[26]**. Usually a desperate measure, this is an instant kill, but only at hand-to-hand range. Use this if you're ambushed, you know an enemy is around a corner that you're coming to, or after charging them and running out (or almost running out) of ammunition. Don't expect to survive if you miss that swipe!

Submachine Guns

SMGs (PWS Diablo shown **[27]**) are effective at close range takedowns, with a rapid rate of fire that overwhelms an enemy. You can "spray and pray" to clear a chamber of foes before they even have a chance to fire back. The SMG's biggest downfall, however, is the number of bullets you'll expend using this tactic; which forces you to scramble for

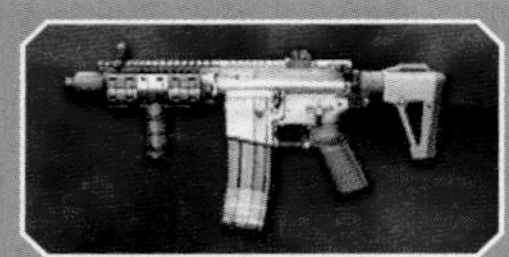

more SMG ammunition (from fallen foes using the same weapon), or to swap the weapon for a longer-lasting Assault Rifle or Light Machine Gun. But do not overlook the SMG, as it out-performs the other gun classes, albeit briefly.

Assault Rifles

ARs (M4 shown **[28]**) are the "middle" class between SMGs and LMGs. They have a slower rate of fire than SMGs, but inflict more damage. This allows you to "flutter" the trigger more adeptly, allowing you to pump a surgical three-round burst into individual enemies to kill them while conserving ammunition. Also note that some ARs (such as the M16) are single-firing, which conserves ammunition still further, and are a more tactical option than the semi-automatic M4, which continuously fires when you hold down the trigger. Play with both types before deciding which you prefer. ARs are excellent at medium range, and still effective at longer ranges; especially if the weapon comes attached with an ACOG or Holo Scope (so look for these as a matter of urgency). You can make your AR last a lot longer than an SMG due to these ammo conservation techniques; which is handy if you have a favorite AR weapon.

Assault Rifles are also the only weapons that support the under-barrel attachments, such as the Grenade Launcher **[29]**, or the Shotgun attachment, but these are generally uncommon, and designed to provide vital help during a particularly spectacular firefight. Accurate firing is a must, as ammunition is limited to that which comes with the weapon.

NOTE 알아두세요

The M16 is a semiautomatic weapon, just like the M110 Sniper and the M9 Pistol. This is the best weapon if you're the type of person who likes to count (and account for) all your bullets.

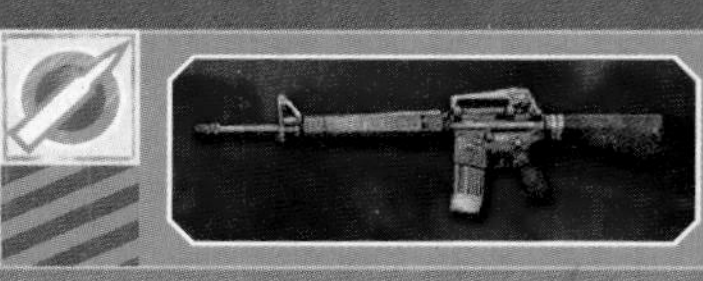

NOTE 알아두세요

The XM10 Rifle is available only during Multiplayer matches. Consult the MP Training chapter for further information.

Light Machine Guns

LMGs **[30]** are meat-grinders, designed to mince enemies. They inflict a ferocious amount of damage, and it only takes one or two bullets to drop a foe. A fair amount of ammunition and "overkill" is always wasted, but with a large amount of ammunition, the "spray and pray" approach is a viable plan. However, the rate of fire is quite slow, making a surgical strike (quickly aiming and tagging foes in focused bursts) approach another viable option.

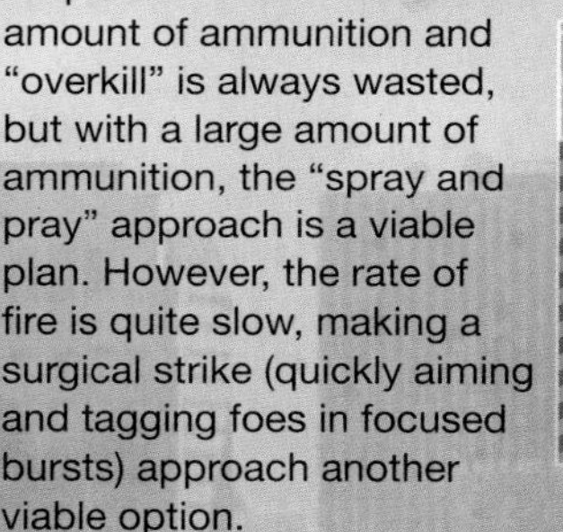

The biggest concern LMG users have is the lengthy reload and deploy times (the time it takes to find a foe and fire the weapon), so consider keeping a smaller, more agile weapon as your alternate firearm, and swap to it if you're surprised.

NOTE 알아두세요

The SCAR (Special Operations Forces Combat Assault Rifle) comes in AR and LMG variants, so be sure to read the pick-up message before you grab one!

TIP 영리한

Reloading with an LMG (especially the M249) is a lengthy affair; you may wish to expend your ammunition, and then flip to your other gun when you're almost ready to reload instead of waiting for the reload. Switch back in-between battles so you can reload at your leisure. Alternately, follow up bullet expenditure with a melee strike.

Specialized Weapon Types

M9 Pistol

Do not underestimate the power of the M9 Pistol! This **[31]** isn't just a sidearm to throw away when something two-handed lands in your lap; it is incredibly useful for picking off foes with precise and damaging shots. The pistol can be fired as quickly as you can pull the trigger, effectively making it the fastest firing weapon (if you're quick and adept enough!). Despite its small size, the M9 holds a lot of ammunition. Unfortunately, enemies do not drop the M9, meaning it must be found.

870 Express Shotgun

Rarely encountered, the Shotgun **[32]** offers devastating power at close range, and the closer edges of medium range, but the shots dissipate at farther distances. You're almost guaranteed a kill with a single blast, and the shotgun is fantastic for stepping around corners to ambush foes. But this weapon has serious drawbacks: the amount of time between shots and the lengthy reload time, which usually allows the enemies to rake you with faster-firing firearms. Don't attack groups with this, but do blast away if you're comfortable with the weapon's slower rate of fire.

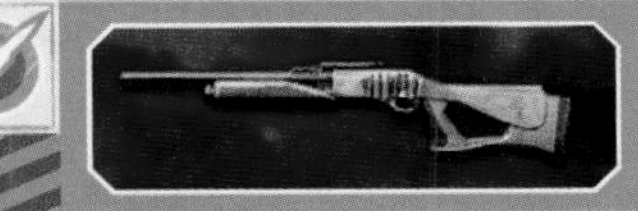

Sniper Rifles

For those who like to do their killing through a scope, and from a distance, these weapons are your one-shot wonders. The M110 Sniper **[33]** is an excellent choice as a secondary weapon, when the enemy you're facing is at medium range. It is semiautomatic (the faster you fire, the more shots you'll make) and has a reasonable clip size, so use this to bring down foes on the perimeters or back line of a fight, or those behind cover or on balconies that are otherwise inaccessible.

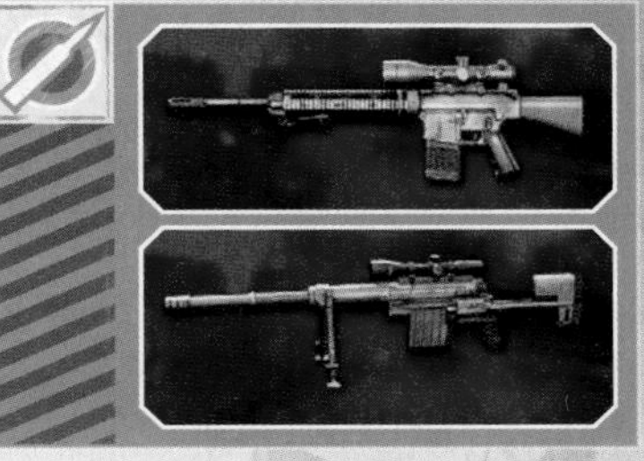

The M200 is a bolt-action infantry cannon. It's useful in medium-range skirmishes but is really meant for long-range takedowns, ideally of foes that aren't within running distance of you. The lengthy reload time between shots is a problem, so really line up your enemies to ensure a kill. The M200 is also the only weapon with a double-zoom feature, for when you want extra detail of a foe's face before you pull the trigger.

Unfortunately, Sniper Rifles are only accurate when shot through the scope. Firing from the hip is possible, but you have to be practically at melee range, and lucky, to hit.

RPG Launchers

Appearing at specific points during your Campaign missions, these weapons destroy heavy (and usually mechanized) targets **[34]**. It is usually advisable to discard the weapon after the vehicle takedown, because at closer quarters the splash damage can be deadly.

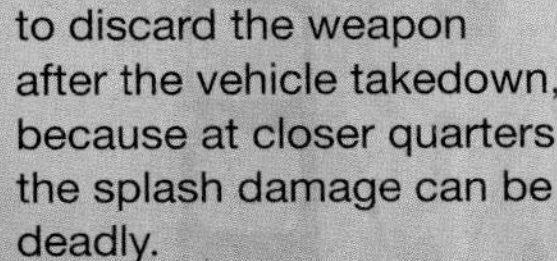

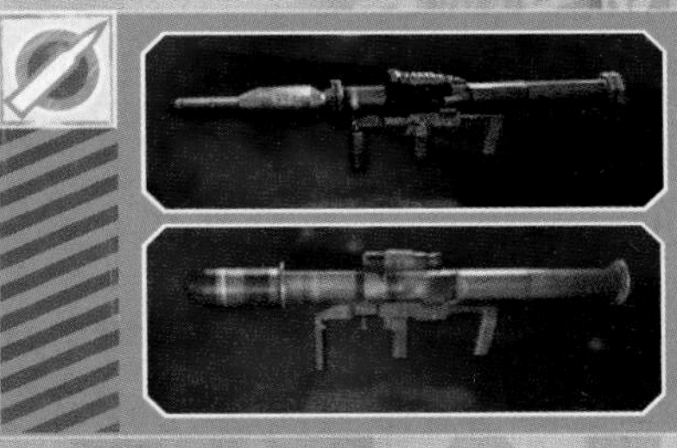

Explosives

You can carry four Frag Grenades **[35].** They're usually thrown to destroy a group of foes close together, although there's a more cunning plan: lob one at a foe behind cover, and he usually moves, allowing you to "flush out" enemies that are dug-in or otherwise inaccessible to your other ordnance. Remember you can "cook" (hold onto) your grenades—ideally for around 2-3 seconds—before throwing them, so they explode immediately. Otherwise, they detonate after a few seconds, giving the enemies precious time to retreat out of the blast radius. Don't keep holding a grenade though; overcook one, and you're done!

C4 explosives **[36]** are available only on rare occasions. Drop them around corners or in the paths you know foes will take. They are usually reserved for destroying a vehicle when you have no RPG Launcher.

The rarely seen Grenade Launcher attachment is as effective as a "cooked" grenade, so utilize it in the same way.

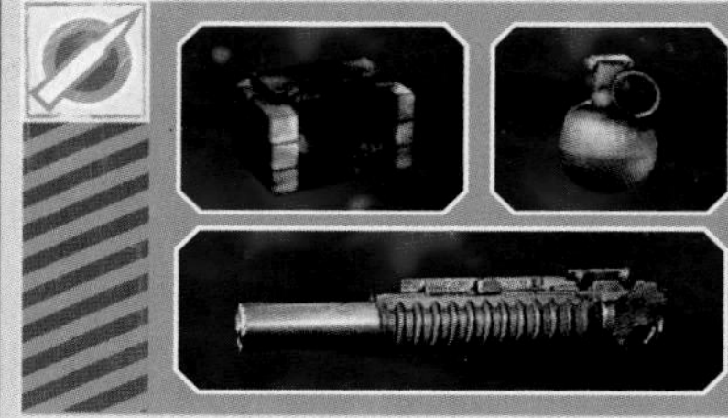

 Weapon Ratings 

The following tables show the relative strength of each main gun (explosives are excluded because they kill infantry instantly), as well as their practicality.

Weapon Damage Per Second and Effectiveness

This list shows the weapons ranked in the effectiveness of the killing power of a single bullet from each weapon, where one is "most effective" and 13 is "least effective."

Rank	Weapon
1	M200 Sniper
2	M110 Sniper
3	870 Express Shotgun
4	M249 LMG
5	SCAR-H LMG
6	M9 Pistol
7	T3AK AR

Rank	Weapon
8	ACR AR
9	M16 AR
10	M4 AR
11	SCAR AR
12	Diablo SMG
13	Super V SMG

What does this mean? Well, when facing an enemy, a single bullet (in this case, a shell) from a M200 is the most devastating way to dispatch them. Bullets from a Super V SMG are the least effective, but the weapon fires a great many of them, which lessens the problem considerably.

Practical Effectiveness

This list shows the relative effectiveness of each weapon during a normal, medium-range combat encounter, where one is "most effective" and 13 is "least effective."

Rank	Weapon
1	ACR AR
2	M16 AR
3	SCAR AR
4	T3AK AR
5	M9 Pistol
6	M249 LMG
7	SCAR-H LMG

Rank	Weapon
8	M4 AR
9	Super V SMG
10	Diablo SMG
11	870 Express Shotgun
12	M110 Sniper
13	M200 Sniper

What does this mean? Although other circumstances factor in, such as ammo levels, teammates, location, types of enemy, if you're choosing a weapon to use in a "regular" combat encounter, make it the ACR Assault Rifle. The M200? Not so much.

WELCOME TO THE RESISTANCE

 Walkthrough Overview 

Your subservient existence under the jackboot of the Korean-controlled invaders ends now! Once you've met the major players in the Resistance, in the next chapter of this guide, you can begin to peruse a highly detailed Walkthrough, noting every event that happens during your time with Connor Morgan, Boone Karlson, and the other members of the Montrose Resistance. Here's what all this information means:

Checkpoints and Maps

Each of the seven missions is broken up into a number of checkpoints. The Walkthrough details these individually, and notes (in great detail) the different possible plans for defeating the enemies in each location. Each begins with a map. The map has a compass, and the following icons:

 Where you start

 Where you usually finish

 Waypoint

 Hidden History

 Korean Kodex

 Unique Weapon

 Weapon Pick-up

Friendlies and Enemies

Connor

Enemies

Soldier (Scout)

Every checkpoint has a picture and name of every friendly (first encounter) and enemy (each encounter) you meet. These allow you to know who is active in your current theater of war. These portraits include vehicles.

Waypoints

Each checkpoint has a number of chokepoints or other areas of interest, collectively known as "waypoints." An occurrence of note happens here, so it is noted on the map, and the same general location shown in picture form. The waypoint is always mentioned in the text, so you know exactly what to expect, when to expect it, and what action to take.

Objectives

Objective: Exit the Bus

Every time your on-screen prompt updates your objective, it is updated in the Walkthrough text.

Hidden History (61)

HIDDEN HISTORY >> 1 (1/61)

Your first news pick-up is around the left corner from the White Castle entrance. Pick it up before the KPA helicopter gets you in its targets.

12/3/2013

WILD FLUCTUATIONS IN OIL MARKET LEAD TO INSTABILITY, UNCERTAINTY

Throughout the Walkthrough, there are various discarded news pick-ups to find, usually hidden away in an alcove, or a low-trafficked area. The checkpoint map shows the location of each one, and an image helps you further pinpoint the pick-up location. The news report is also reprinted, so you may learn of the past atrocities perpetrated on this great nation!

TIP 영리한

Once you pick up a Hidden History news pick-up, it doesn't reappear when you replay a mission. Keep a running total by checking this walkthrough every time you find one (you may wish to place a check mark across the "R" icon every time you pick one up). Did you miss a news pick-up? Then replay the checkpoint to find it.

Korean Kodex (10)

KOREAN KODEX >> 1 (2/10)

On the board next to the drinks machine, in the gas station service area.

The Xbox 360 version of the Campaign allows eagle-eyed Resistance members to spot special "QR" codes spray-painted on easily overlooked walls. Your instruction manual has the first one of these. The other nine are located (and shown) throughout the Campaign Walkthrough.

Unique Weapons (17)

Unique Weapons Detail: 1/17

WEAPONS >>
Desert M16 Rifle [Mk1 ACOG Scope]

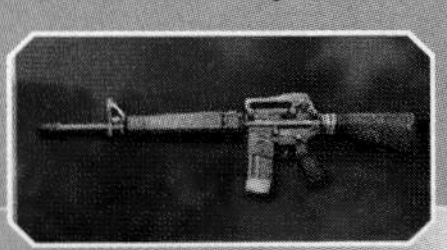

This desert-camo variant of the M16 has the optional scope.

Seventeen individual weapons have been deemed "Unique," and are noted on the map and in the Campaign text. These usually come with a handy sight or scope, silencer, or other attachment, and are usually the ideal weapon for the subsequent few checkpoints. Find them before you progress too far from them.

Other Weapons

WEAPONS >>
M9 Pistol

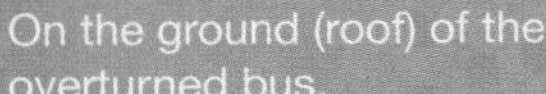

On the ground (roof) of the overturned bus.

Whenever a particularly useful weapon cache is spotted, it is noted in one of these box-outs. Although weapons are dropped by foes, and some weapons aren't noted (due to the abundance of firearms), be sure you find the weapons noted here if you're low on ammo. The weapons you begin each mission with are also listed.

Mettle of Honor

Mettle of Honor

Award Chronicler | Rating 10 | Trophy Bronze

You receive this reward when you first obtain a News Pick-up; one of 61 documents detailing the Hidden History of this conflict. This is the first opportunity to earn this reward.

If there is a particular Achievement (Xbox 360 or PC) or Reward (PS3) available in the walkthrough, the first time you can obtain it is noted in this type of box.

YOUR INTRODUCTION TO THE RESISTANCE BEGINS NOW!

MEET THE FOLKS »THE MONTROSE RESISTANCE

The quartet of like-minded patriots that you're working with consists of disparate sorts, but all are unquestioningly loyal. Here, we delve a little deeper into their backgrounds.

Connor Morgan

Hometown: **Charlotte, North Carolina**

Age: **37**

Morgan is a legend of the Resistance. He's a hard bitten, enigmatic, fearless Resistance fighter from North Carolina, dedicated to eradicating the homeland invaders. His reputation precedes him, mainly from his experiences in the Oil Wars and through his victories in Montrose.

Heroic, but still a wild card with a violent undercurrent, he holds everyone to his extremely high standards and does not believe in tact, diplomacy, or half-measures of any kind. His morality is very black and white: you're either with him or against him. He is the kind of man who is absolutely essential in leading an uprising, but who has no place in the peace that follows.

Boone Karlson

Hometown: **Montrose, Colorado**

Age: **39**

Karlson is the leader of a small resistance cell in Montrose, a natural but also uncompromising leader. Once a Montrose County policeman, Boone was among the first to escape the detention camps and organize fighters.

He is the principal architect of the squad's compound/living quarters, a collection of three houses with shared backyards called "The Oasis," where he engineered all of the post-peak-oil systems. He dreams of living in peace in the free zone. He's a level-headed leader, but still a ferocious soldier. Somewhat beaten down by all the fighting he has done, Boone has a world weariness to him. With the squad all younger than him, Boone plays the role of father figure to the group.

Rianna

Hometown: **Parts Unknown, Northern Colorado**

Age: **27**

Rianna (last name unknown) has been waiting for the opportunity to make a difference all her life, and the Resistance has finally given her that opportunity. She developed survival and weapon skills growing up in the backwoods of Colorado. Prior to the Occupation, Rianna was surviving in post-peak-oil America as an accomplished hunter, going on treks into the forests and mountains surrounding Montrose to shoot elk and deer for their meat and skins. She learned about weapons from anyone who would teach her.

Because Rianna is not former military, and not a battle-hardened combat vet, cracks in her exterior resolve show at times. She is a humanitarian, and she has feelings that she needs to deal with and control in the line of duty. She'll never feel good about everything the Resistance has done and will continue to do, but she'll also never let those emotional struggles destroy her ruthless resolve to win at all costs. There is no other option.

Hopper Lee

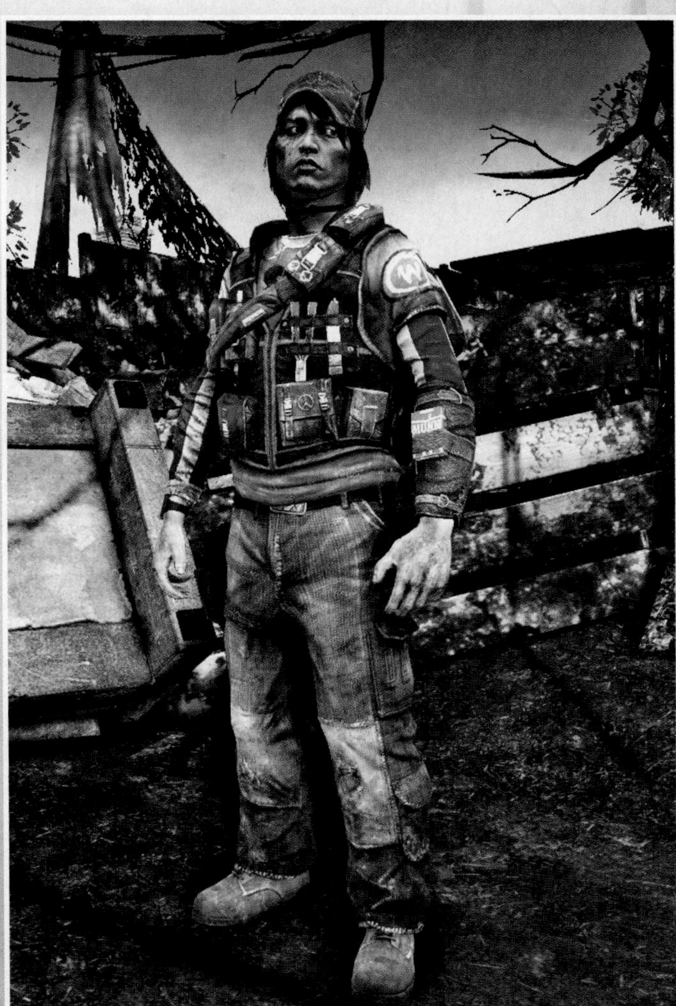

Hometown: **San Francisco, California**

Age: **32**

Lee is a third-generation Korean American. Because of his ethnicity, Hopper had a hard time during the early days of the Occupation, and his face is badly scarred from the Oakland Race Riots. To this day, he finds his loyalties questioned. Working in Resistance cells in SF, he kept getting the worst, most dangerous, assignments.

Hopper is an expert mechanic and is proud of his driving expertise. He can fix almost anything, making him extremely useful in a resource-strapped world. He's the squad's go-to man for setting up explosives or otherwise jerry-rigging equipment. He has a close attachment to Goliath and is his prime handler.

No one is a prouder American than Hopper, and he is appalled that his "homeland" has invaded the country and taken away the freedoms he holds so dear, having heard stories of the oppression in the homeland that caused his great grandparents to flee North Korea in the 1960s.

MISSION SELECT >>01 >>WHY WE FIGHT

Welcome to 2027. It's been two years since the KPA attacked the United States. You are a former Marine pilot just trying to keep a low profile. A week ago, you received a draft notice: the Koreans want to recruit you. But they're not the only ones.

HIDDEN HISTORY >> 10 (10/61 total)

KOREAN KODEX >> 1 (2/10 total)

UNIQUE WEAPON >> 4 (4/17 total)

CHECKPOINT A: HOME FROM NOWHERE

Friendlies

Connor

Rianna

Enemies

Soldier (Scout)

Soldier (Commander)

Soldier

Military Police

Soldier (Heavy)

Military Police (Scout)

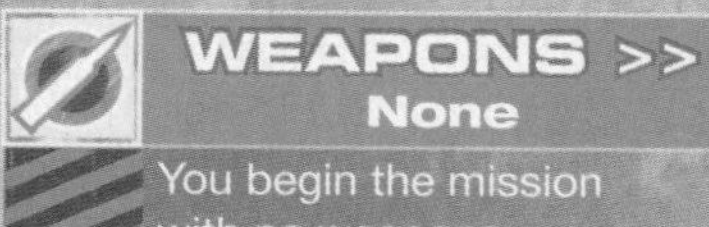
WEAPONS >> None

You begin the mission with no weapons.

Objective: Answer the Door

Another Beautiful Day in the Colorado Territories

A.01

A.02

You waken with the radio on, and bright light streaming through the windows. As the announcer and the Korean translation burbles away in the background, you can check your surroundings **[A.01]**: a stove, rations, candles for light, and a flyer about a job the KPA wants you to perform for them. There's a knock at the door; the occupational police are attempting to locate you. You can watch a KPA Humvee race down the deserted street outside **[A.02]**. Ignoring the door only delays the inevitable, so open it.

A.03

Two KPA soldiers and an Occupational Police Commander burst through the door, and you're pinned against the wall. The officer questions your patriotism to the new cause **[A.03]**, and your vision fills with blood after you're beaten with a rifle butt, dragged to the top of your apartment stairs, and thrown down to the ground below.

When you come to and attempt to shake your concussion, you're dragged across the main street. The KPA is out in force, rounding up inhabitants with a vicious degree of force. You're bundled onto the bus **[A.04]**, pushed forward, and pressed into your seat, with the shouts and screams echoing inside your bruised head.

Look to the left. A citizen protests his innocence **[A.05]**. He doubles over from a rifle butt to the guts, and a bag is placed over his head. The bus sets off, as you pass more inhabitants, kneeling with their hands behind their heads.

A struggling man is separated from his shrieking wife **[A.06]**. He'll be sent to the shale mines. Or worse. A line of citizens slowly walks down the sidewalk under armed guard.

You pass the drugstore. A man is being brutally beaten. More inhabitants of Montrose are being shackled to the metal roof of an army truck. Another round-up is underway at Jankovic's Farmers Market **[A.07]**.

The passenger in front of you strikes up a conversation. He's been forced into serving with the KPA, otherwise his family will suffer.

A citizen tries to run from his captors and is executed **[A.08]**; his blood splatters across the bus window.

The bus turns, and you watch as a man and wife are executed on the street corner **[A.09]**. A weeping child, no more than five years old, runs over to his dead parents as the soldiers walk away.

The nearby passenger murmurs that "this shit" is happening all across the state of Colorado. Out the window, corpses are being dragged along the sidewalk **[A.10]**. Any time the Resistance gains some ground, the KPA takes it out on the innocents. You pass a row of bodies half-covered in hoods and sheets.

A large number of citizens are slowly walking to a checkpoint guarded by a KPA tank and a large, automated Sentry Tower **[A.11]**. More fodder for the labor camps. Most of those folks won't ever be seen again.

As you leave the checkpoint **[A.12]**, you see what happens to those without proper identification: they are thrown into an increasingly large corpse pile. Your friend mutters about mass graves, and sticking together. The man hatches a plan....

"You Can Thank Me Later."

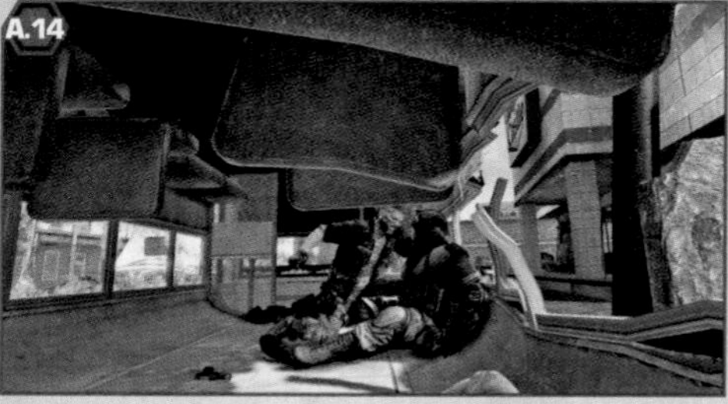

Quickly glance to the left, and you spot a big-rig cabin driving straight at the side of the bus **[A.13]**. It strikes the bus, sending it barrel-rolling, killing your passenger friend. A man sprints out of the cab, and with a woman guarding the front of the bus (which is now upside down), executes the driver, and then stabs the still-woozy guard in the chest **[A.14]**. He comes over to you, and checks that you're okay.

Objective: Pick up the Pistol

The man has ordered you to pick up the pistol the guard was carrying. Grab it **[A.15]**.

WEAPONS >>
M9 Pistol

On the ground (roof) of the overturned bus.

NOTE 알아두세요

This is your first weapon. You can carry a maximum of two. Keep this, or swap it for a more powerful weapon when you come across one.

Objective: Exit the Bus

Edge toward the broken windshield at the front of the bus, and step through. Rianna **[A.16]** greets you and gestures to Connor; the man who "saved" you. Step out onto the parking lot.

CHECKPOINT B: PISTOL IN HAND

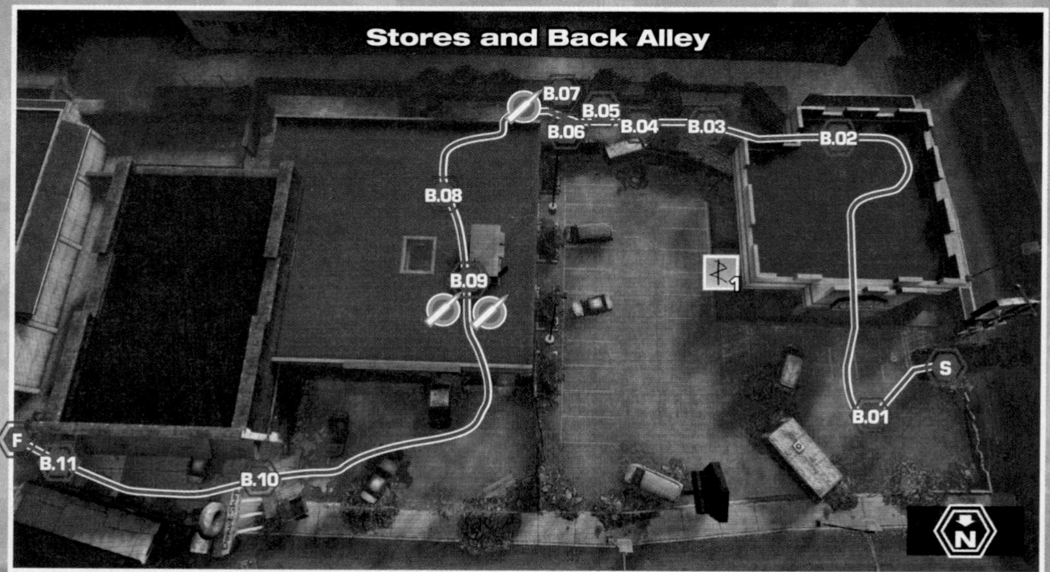

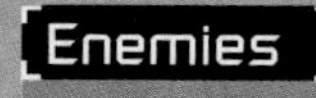
Enemies

Transport Helicopter

Soldier

Military Police

Military Police (Scout)

Here Comes the Cavalry!

After scrambling out of the overturned bus, Connor yells "here comes the cavalry!", and flees inside the White Castle with Rianna quickly following, as a KPA attack helicopter drops down to survey the daring rescue **[B.01]**. The KPA insists that you surrender, but doing so (or even staying outside the building by the bus, or out of cover) results in the helicopter soldiers gunning you down. The only safe route is to follow Rianna into the store, move to the Exit doorway **[B.02]**, and head east, out into the back alley. However, quickly inspect the parking lot around the left (southeast) side of the building to find an item of considerable interest. Pick this up, and check out an old newspaper article; one of 61 pieces of Hidden History. The contents of each pick-up are noted throughout this guide.

HIDDEN HISTORY >> 1 (1/61)

Your first news pick-up is around the left corner from the White Castle entrance. Pick it up before the KPA helicopter gets you in its targets.

12/3/2013

WILD FLUCTUATIONS IN OIL MARKET LEAD TO INSTABILITY, UNCERTAINTY

Although the first decade of the 21st century is the "poster boy" for fluctuating oil prices, the sudden shifts of the past few years suggest that this decade may yet break that record. A series of reforms aimed at stomping speculation in the sector, enacted after the wild price spikes in 2008, temporarily appeared to smooth out fluctuations in the market. However, a cascade of unforeseen events (including a strike in Venezuela and ongoing political instability in Nigeria) have caused analysts to question the global market's ability to keep pace with demand. "This year, we've seen oil prices as low as $70 a barrel and as high as $200," commented Goldman Sachs analyst John Rice. "It's difficult to say how a market as essential to global economic health will weather any additional instability."

Rice and other analysts fear that as demand returns and supply cannot be met, prices will skyrocket out of control, further depressing the global economy. Already, major American automobile manufacturers are feeling the crunch as demand for personal vehicles has bottomed out. "The US auto manufacturing sector is dead in the water," Rice stated in no uncertain terms. "It remains to be seen what will happen to other petroleum dependent sectors."

NOTE 알아두세요

These newspaper pick-ups can only be picked up once (they won't appear once removed). If you didn't spot one or more of them during your investigating, simply replay the campaign and search for any that remain, which you've missed.

Mettle of Honor

RESISTANCE

Award	Chronicler	Rating	10	Trophy	Bronze

You receive this reward when you first obtain a News Pick-up; one of 61 documents detailing the Hidden History of this conflict. This is the first opportunity to earn this reward.

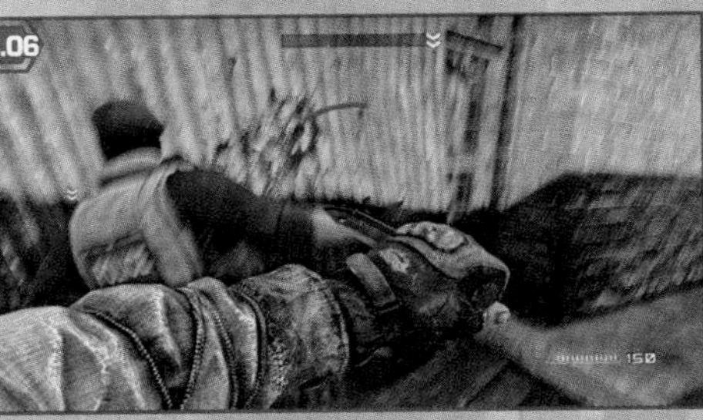

As you reach the back alley **[B.03]**, Rianna shouts that two KPA Military Police have scaled the fence, and while your new friends provide covering fire, you get to utilize your new pistol. There are a variety of ways to dispatch these foes:

You can follow instructions and aim down the pistol's sights, expertly tagging each foe in the head, dropping them **[B.04]**.

You can fire in the general direction of the foes, with or without a sighted aim, winging the enemies before they fall **[B.05]**. Don't worry about your ammunition; you'll find plenty of weapons during combat to come!

Or, you can rush the foes in a dangerous sprint, pausing behind cover to avoid being struck, and then execute either foe with a melee attack **[B.06]**.

You can also crouch behind cover, take careful aim, and drop either foe from one side of the alley; it doesn't matter which.

CAUTION 조심하다

Be careful if you're moving close to the foes, as they can pistol whip you with a melee strike if you're too near them!

NOTE 알아두세요

Depending on the system you're playing this on, the controller or keyboard presses to perform particular actions vary. Consult your game's instruction manual, or the game's Control Settings menu. Do this any time you're not sure how to attempt a particular action. At this point, you should be perfecting the art of:

Sprinting: To cover distance quickly, at the expense of not being able to shoot.

Crouching: To drop behind cover, so you're not as easily shot, at the expense of fast maneuverability.

Aiming Down Sights (Zoom-Aiming): To quickly and accurately take down foes.

Melee Attacks: If you're caught by a foe while reloading, or at close quarters. Remember that foes can melee attack too!

TIP 영리한

The game automatically defaults to "Aim Assist," which makes zoom-aiming using your weapon sights a whole lot easier. For additional challenge, turn this off!

Mettle of Honor

Award Pistol Whipped | Rating 10 | Trophy Bronze

Now that you have a pistol, you can complete this task: kill 25 foes using the pistol between now and the end of the mission. You can switch to other weapons during this time, but to ensure completion, do this as early as possible. You can return to this mission after finishing it to focus on this task.

Mettle of Honor

Award Give Him the Stick | Rating 10 | Trophy Bronze

With the melee attack learned, you have an additional optional task: to finish 25 foes using just this technique. This means getting up close to them, and is best reserved for groups of three or fewer, or when you're finishing stragglers. You can return to this mission after completing it, and try to claim this reward.

Objective: Get the Assault Rifle

B.07

With Korean blood on your hands, you're now a member of the Resistance whether you like it or not. Check the body of one of the KPA MPs you just took down **[B.07]**, and scavenge the T3AK Assault Rifle from close to the corpse. You now have that, and your pistol to use. You switch to the T3AK now.

CAUTION 조심하다

Don't fire at the helicopter above, it will fire back and kill you.

WEAPONS >>
T3AK Rifle

By the corpse of one of the fallen KPA soldiers.

NOTE 알아두세요

Fallen enemies usually leave behind an automatic weapon of some description, and scavenging them constantly is an excellent way to avoid running out of ammunition. Many weapons have augmentations (such as sights or grenade launcher attachments), and there are varieties of weapons (such as rifles, automatic rifles, and SMGs), so it is always worth checking the ground for a better armament. The Armory chapter of this book lists all the weapons, along with their strengths and weaknesses.

Objective: Follow Connor

KPA Street Takedowns

B.08

Connor kicks open the back door and enters the remains of a store. Sidestep right, around the wall and Rianna yells that more KPA forces are coming in from the store's skylight **[B.08]**.

Face north, and take a split-second to survey your scenery before reacting. The optional plan is to rake the foe descending from the roof with assault rifle fire so he's dead before he hits the ground. Then use any of the store shelves, optionally crouching, and dispatch the two red beret–wearing MPs without being winged **[B.09]**. While Connor barks orders about the route to take, swap your pistol for a dropped SMG; ideally one with a sight.

WEAPONS >>
PWS Diablo SMG [Mk 1 Red Dot Sight]

WEAPONS >>
PWS Diablo SMG

Near the corpses of one of the fallen KPA soldiers.

NOTE 알아두세요

From this point in the Walkthrough, only weapons of considerable merit, usually recommended over usual armaments, will be noted, because each foe drops ordnance.

Exit the second store, swinging right as Connor spots a trio of KPA hiding close to an abandoned bus near the Donut Shop sign **[B.10]**. Use the burned-out vehicles as cover and attempt some long-range tagging of these foes, although you can sprint around and attack from the right wall, at closer quarters. As the KPA chopper continues to harass you, follow Rianna and Connor and sprint past the fallen foes (now is a good time to fully arm yourself for the next checkpoint), then jump over the remains of the wall **[B.11]** as you enter the gas station.

CAUTION 조심하다

The constant buzzing of the KPA helicopter during this daring escape may annoy you into firing at it. Don't, because you're simply wasting your ammunition. Also be careful of remaining in the open for too long, as the KPA helicopter will fire on you and kill you!

CHECKPOINT C: INTO THE GAS STATION

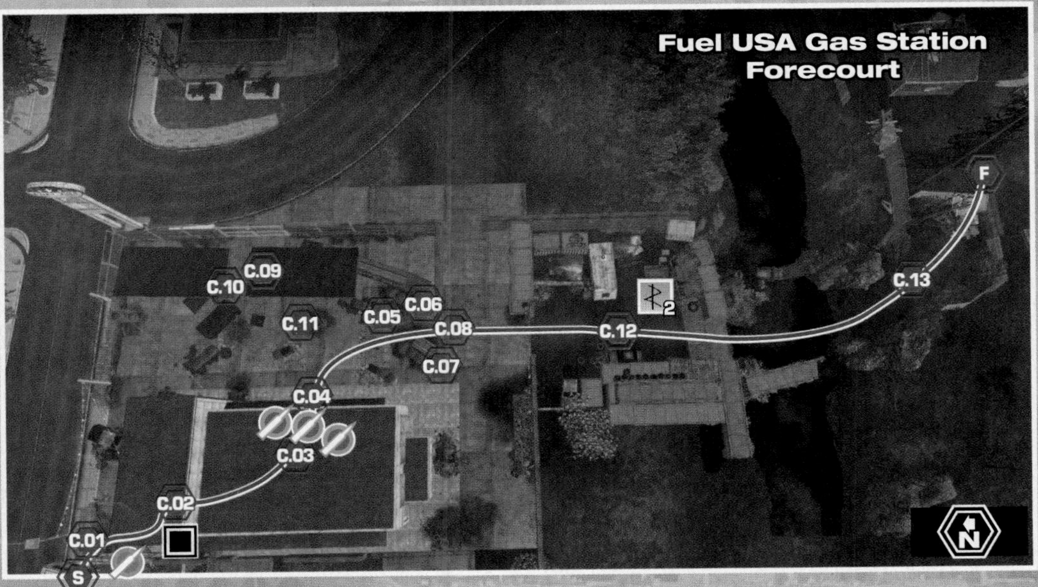

Enemies

Transport Helicopter

Transport Truck

Soldier

Military Police

Military Police (Scout)

 Surviving the Firestorm

Connor and Rianna dash into the service department building across from a Fuel USA gas station sign **[C.01]**, avoiding the relentless searching of the KPA helicopter. Optionally check the alley just right of the building's entrance, to secure your first Unique Weapon. Then follow Rianna inside, passing a drinks machine near a board with an odd square message on it (your first Korean Kodex) and check the shop to the right that your teammates are standing on either side of **[C.02]**. The KPA appears to have lured you into an ambush, and the first of many epic firefights begins now!

KOREAN KODEX >> 1 (2/10)

On the board next to the drinks machine, in the gas station service area. These QR codes are available in the Xbox 360 version of the mission only. The first Kodex is in your instruction manual that came with the game.

Unique Weapons Detail: 1/17

WEAPONS >>
Desert M16 Rifle [Mk1 ACOG Scope]

This desert-camo variant of the M16 has the optional scope. This exceptional one-shot weapon inflicts serious damage to foes as long as you remember this is single-fire, not an automatic weapon. There are no bursts, but rapid trigger-finger prowess allows you cut down foes as fast as you want. Check the alley to the right, before you enter the gas station, to accrue this recommended rifle.

Tactical Planning: What's in Store 

Threat Assessment: KPA Forces

After the two initial MPs, expect foes dug in between the gas station pumps, with a transport truck arriving on the right (south) side to off-load more infantry troopers as the fight progresses, and a second troop transport skidding in toward the end of the ambush, on the left (north) side, under the gas station overhang. You are seriously overwhelmed, and extreme caution (along with cunning planning detailed to come) must be taken!

Objective: Survive Ambush

Plan A: Methodical and Measured 

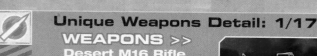

The optimal plan is a confident, but self-aware strategy of dealing with the closest threats first, listening to (and acting on) your teammates' yelled instructions, and not putting yourself in too much danger. Either from the shop entrance, or after using the scattered shelving as cover, bring down the beret-wearing MPs so they drop to the floor by the gas station doorway **[C.03]**. This is the perfect introduction to the Unique M16 Rifle you may have just picked up. A third foe also charges in from the left; cut him down **[C.04]** while enemies begin to rappel down from the chopper.

An optimal takedown would be to step over the corpses of the first two foes you cut down, just inside the store, and automatically pick up a quartet of Frag Grenades. Then lob one so it lands at the bottom of the rope the three infantry are descending, wounding or taking out most of them **[C.05]**. Then quickly cut down any remaining stragglers as they dive behind the sandbags and cover below the gas station forecourt **[C.06]**.

TIP 영리한

Although you can use previously scavenged automatic weaponry for this fracas, if you're (extremely) quick, you'd do well to grab the ACR Rifle one of the initial foes drops; it has a good rate of fire and a scope.

WEAPONS >>
Fragmentation Grenade (12)

WEAPONS >>
PWS Diablo SMG

WEAPONS >>
ACR Rifle [Mk 1 ACOG Scope]

Dropped by the initial KPA enemies, on the shop floor.

TIP 영리한

The best place to stand inside the store varies during combat, but near the corrugated sheet just left of the entrance is good; shoot the windows out so you can lob grenades. The raised area inside the store on the south wall isn't a great place to fire from, because you're more exposed than you think and less able to sidestep fire.

A second later, Connor yells that a troop transport has arrived; it screeches to a halt on the right (south) side of the forecourt **[C.07]**, and around four enemies disembark from the rear, with a few more appearing soon afterward. With an adept flourish, arc a grenade in to explode just before the enemies spread out, and then deal with the remaining foes moving from right to left **[C.08]**.

Sharp, expertly aimed bursts of rifle fire (optionally using your scope) should cut them down fast. Aim to remove most of the threats by the time the second troop transport crashes through into the gas station forecourt.

This truck stops between the pumps, and you can lob in a grenade to catch three or four foes as they run around the side of the vehicle **[C.09]**. Or, train your weapon on the right of the transport, and cut down four or five before they can spread out. More enemies are coming in from both sides, swarming the area; no matter how adept you are at firing, there will be more enemies to shoot. Stay put, inside the building as a fire starts to rage by the pumps. Moments later, the KPA are engulfed in a huge gasoline explosion **[C.10]**, which rages through the forecourt, and detonates the second troop transport.

Moments later, the first transport explodes too, killing all the remaining enemies, and leaving your team shaken.

Plan B: Chaotic and Doomed

You face overwhelming odds, so don't try any outlandish plans of attack, or you'll end up dead. For example:

Straying outside the store front and into the courtyard gets you cut down in seconds **[C.11]**.

Firing on the pumps before they explode, or into the transport vehicles doesn't shorten the combat.

Fiddling with different weapons, or waiting for your team to handle most of the enemies elongates the fight.

Attempting to remain in the entrance area simply lengthens the time you'll spend fighting.

TIP 영리한

Once this battle is over, you should now be proficient in lobbing grenades. Note that the distance you throw is based on how high (vertically) you aim.

Objective: Escape Through Suburbs

"Count Your Pieces Later!"

Connor radios a man named Boone regarding the acquisition of "the pilot" (you). Follow Connor and Rianna into a small container yard **[C.12]**, and pause for a moment. On the ground near a small corrugated tire shack is another old newspaper. Pick this up, then rush up the small hill **[C.13]**, and cross over the broken fence, following your new brethren.

HIDDEN HISTORY >> 2 (2/61)

On the ground in the small container yard between the gas station and stream.

KIM JONG-UN PROMISES TO PROTECT KOREANS WORLDWIDE *8/23/2017*

The following is an excerpt from a statement to the nation of Korea by Kim Jong-un, President of Korea, broadcast on state television on Thursday:

"In ancient Rome, just three words were enough to protect any citizen: 'Civis Romanus sum': I am a Roman Citizen. So great was the power of Rome that an attack on a citizen of Rome was considered an attack on Rome itself. This is the message I am sending out to the world: anyone who carries a Korean passport, anyone born in our great country has but to utter these words: 'Na n'un (Chosun) shi-min in-mi-da' — 'I am a citizen of Korea'. If you can speak those words, know that you will be protected."

"Our countrymen are under attack on the island nation of Japan. Because of their Korean heritage we have seen their property destroyed and their persons assaulted, and in some cases they have been murdered. Simply because they are Korean. My message to them is simple: we will protect you. If we cannot protect you, we will avenge you."

CHECKPOINT D: A TANK

Enemies

T-99 Main Battle Tank

Soldier (Scout)

Objective: Crawl into House

More Haste, Less Speed

Drop down from the fence, and secure another hidden historical document from under the remains of a bay window, and then follow Connor's barked instructions; go prone so you crawl through the hole in the structure of a dilapidated house **[D.01]**.

Stand up on the other side as both teammates take cover against a ruined wall section, and watch as a KPA tank rumbles past **[D.02]**, accompanied by a squad of soldiers.

TIP 영리한

You should now have learned how (and when) to go from standing, to a crouch, to a prone position and back again.

HIDDEN HISTORY >> 3 (3/61)

On the ground below the blown-out bay window of a ruined home, just before you go prone.

PENTAGON: NORTH KOREAN MISSILE TEST FAILS

7/6/2006

Despite ongoing talks to convince North Korea to give up its nuclear programme, the isolationist country staged a series of missile tests that began at 3:30 am local time (2:30 pm ET) and lasted for five hours. The Taepodong 2 missile (a variant of the Soviet-era Scud) failed 40 seconds into its launch, officials reported.

The US, Japan and the UN strongly condemned the tests, which they say violated a commitment on the part of Pyongyang to a long-standing moratorium on missile tests. The moratorium went into effect after the failed launch of a Taepodong 1 missile over Japan in 1998.

CAUTION 조심하다

Although your trigger finger may be itching to unload on the Korean forces, even the most impressive display of carnage [D.03] is soon nullified as the tank's cannon swings around and shells you into submission!

Objective: Sprint Across the Street

Wait for Connor's mark, and when he yells at you to run, oblige him by sprinting across the street **[D.04]**, once the patrol has passed. Don't turn right and cut down any foes with your fire; you're supposed to be stealthy! Once across, step over the broken fence. As Rianna confirms that the team is clear, continue your escape. Before you follow your team onward, however, check the backyard to your left for another newspaper article.

TIP 영리한

Remember the distinct difference between walking and sprinting: you can't sprint and fire, for example, and your weapon is carried to your chest during the run. Be sure you master this technique, and use it whenever you need to cover ground quickly, or catch up to a friend, or race to execute a foe with a melee attack before they do the same to you.

HIDDEN HISTORY >> 4 (4/61)

Propped against the boarded-up window in the backyard of the first house on the left, after the sprint to escape the tank.

GKR PEACEKEEPING MISSION IN NIGERIA A SUCCESS

10/3/2023

Representatives from the Greater Korean Republic and the United Nations monitored the first democratic elections in Nigeria since the start of ethnic strife last year, with both groups declaring the process a "success." The GKR intervened late last year after civil war marred the Nigerian landscape and widespread ethnic violence led to what is now officially recognized as a genocide, resulting in the death of nearby 300,000 people.

Ambassadors and officials around the world are lauding the KPA's intervention as a "true peacekeeping mission" and "a selfless act of humanitarianism." Along with aid missions to Sri Lanka and relief efforts in Cuba following last year's devastating hurricanes, what was formerly international suspicion of the Greater Korean Republic appears to be transforming into a more positive opinion.

The GKR has also offered on several occasions in the last two years to help the United States with material and military support, but the US has flatly rejected all offers of aid from outside North America. Although the situation in the US has begun to stabilize, many are questioning what place the former superpower has, if any, in a world now led by East Asia.

CHECKPOINT E: TREEHOUSE

Enemies

Objective: Escape Through Suburbs

Treehouse of Horrors

While Connor explains the topography and rants about the danger his escape plan put the Resistance in, follow Rianna past the landing gear of a large passenger plane, jutting oddly out from a clump of grass close to the next house to infiltrate. Your teammates watch as a couple of KPA transport helicopters fly over **[E.01]**, before passing the gear, and enter the house via the open back door. Once inside, check the interior of the dwelling for two newspaper pick-ups. As you exit from the dwelling, you're urged to climb the treehouse in the backyard **[E.02]**.

HIDDEN HISTORY >> 5 (5/61)

Resting on the edge of the fireplace, inside the dwelling between the tank and the treehouse.

AIRCRAFT CARRIERS DECOMMISSIONED, NAVY TO DOWNSIZE

9/2/2015

The aircraft carrier USS John C Stennis joined the USS Theodore Roosevelt as being the second ship of its type to be decommissioned this year. Part of a broad goal on the part of the military to downsize and re-focus its efforts on fourth generation warfare, large capital ships have come to be regarded as redundant, expensive and inflexible. A brief, but moving ceremony accompanied the handoff from the captain of the ship to the shipyard commander at Puget Sound.

The USS John C Stennis was contracted in 1988 and commissioned in 1995. The carrier has participated in operations all around the globe including exercises in the Persian Gulf, and with the Japan Maritime Self Defense Force and the Republic of Korea. The last two years have seen a series of announcements regarding the re-focusing of the military's priorities, as combat trends toward a more agile, "digital" army of the future.

HIDDEN HISTORY >> 6 (6/61)

Halfway up the (blocked) staircase, inside the dwelling between the tank and the treehouse.

GLOBAL ECONOMY BITES BACK

8/27/2014

The continuing decline of the global economy is visible everywhere. In Elizabeth, New Jersey, container ships arrive less frequently, only partially filled or sometimes not at all. In Singapore those same containers, once destined for the US and other ports, lie empty in massive stacks near once bustling ports. And all over the United States, people wait in lines for supplies that were once plentiful and easy to come by. In some area, nerves are beginning to fray as tensions grow.

A riot broke out at a Wal Mart outside of Phoenix on Tuesday after supplies failed to arrive on schedule. An unthinkable circumstance only two years ago, consumers were forced to wait in lines as long as 8 hours in the hot sun for simple goods that never arrived. “Is it so hard to get asthma medicine from one warehouse to another?” asked Janet Evans, a former legal assistant and mother of two. “I desperately need this medicine for my son, who suffers from uncontrollable asthma attacks. The whole time I stood in that line I was worried sick that he might be having an attack.”

Representatives from Wal Mart did not respond to inquiries about their supply chain, save for a generic press release that described their shipping and supply chain as the “envy of the developed world.”

Objective: Climb up into Treehouse

While the team vaults over the fence, you take stock of a grim (but relatively ancient) plane crash site **[E.03]**. It’s now an area of increased enemy activity, including KPA soldiers and reinforcements rappelling down from a helicopter. The ruined houses and broken sections of wings and fuselage have KPA teeming across them like ants. You can try some long-range sniping (ideally the foes on the wings, as they are more difficult to tackle in the combat to come). However, once a transport helicopter heads by, a KPA soldier with an RPG spots you, and fells the tree with an explosive chop **[E.04]**. You tumble onto the ground, and must face numerous KPA in this patrol zone.

TIP 영리한

Before you’re forced to the ground, take a good look at the layout of the ruined houses and plane sections, so you’re aware of the routes to take during the next checkpoint.

CHECKPOINT F: PLANE CRASH

Enemies

Military Police

Military Police (Scout)

Objective: Fight Through the KPA Patrol Zone

You get to your feet **[F.01]** behind some partial cover; the remains of a building that the crashed plane hit on its way down to its final resting place. The area is now extremely dangerous, and it’s worth taking stock of exactly who you’re facing, and the best methods of defeating them.

Tactical Planning: Fracas at the Fuselage

Threat Assessment: KPA Patrol Forces

KPA forces are crawling over this aircraft; expect at least 10 to contend with as you push through, and more if you take your time. There are well-armored MPs, and red beret–wearing commanders; both fall to short, sharp bursts of automatic rifle fire. They use their vantange on one of the aircraft's wings to rain fire down on you from above, and hide behind sections from the debris field. Expect automatic gunfire in your direction, and at least a grenade or two. This is a sizable force, and you are more open to attack than in previous encounters. Plan accordingly:

Plan A: New Weapon Over There (Outflank to the Right)

F.02

F.03

Although you can scrabble in the dirt for a dropped SMG where Connor fought off an attack, and locate an M4 Rifle propped up against the shell of a nearby house section while you fight the enemy **[F.02]**, there's a unique (and potent) weapon in this area that's well worth locating. Keep along the right side of the combat arena, moving along the shell of the house heading southward. Round the corner when you see the landing gear **[F.03]**, and locate the Desert Camo SCAR-L Rifle with a scope.

F.04

F.05

Either before or after you find this Unique Weapon, attempt to bring down the opposition forces from either the shell of the house (the remains of the windows provide some cover and firing opportunities) **[F.04]**, or the area where you located the desert camo weapon **[F.05]**. The latter offers excellent line-of-sight opportunities for foes both close and rushing, as well as those milling about the ground near the broken fuselage, or on the wings. Mix up quick, scoped blasts with grenade throws and melee attacks if you're charged.

F.06

Finish the foes in this vicinity by pushing forward between the engine part and the seating on the rough ground, especially when Connor yells that there are reinforcements on the wing. This is the direction the reinforcements come in from, and this location provides perfect line-of-sight and partial cover so you can easily massacre and mop up the rest of the patrol **[F.06]**.

TIP 영리한

This plan offers minimal exposure, an excellent weapon, and enables you to back up your team while they take the brunt of the damage. It is recommended.

WEAPONS >> M4 Rifle [Mk1 ACOG Scope]

Propped up by graffiti reading "RIP" in the shell of a ruined house.

Unique Weapons Detail: 2/17

WEAPONS >> Desert SCAR-L Rifle [Mk1 ACOG Scope]

This desert-camo variant of the powerful SCAR has an excellent scope augmentation. With swift zoom-targeting, this can drop foes in one or two quick, automatic bursts. Thoroughly recommended.

Plan B: On a Wing and a Prayer (Flank to the Left)

The main route, where Connor and Rianna fight their way down, is in and around the remains of a brick house, using the remains of the walls to crouch behind **[F.07]**, and then the main thoroughfare where most of the foes are milling about. Follow their lead if you want to press the attack from the same direction; the foes will know where the fire is coming from, but they'll have more targets. You're much more easily spotted if you try to hold this area, optionally using the plane engine as cover, or to scramble atop of, which is only necessary if you have a deathwish, or want to easily aim and drop foes scrambling over the wing **[F.08]**, and you're rushing in as quickly as you can.

Other recommended cover opportunities include the corrugated metal section of fencing **[F.09]** to the left (east) of the brick ruins, which offers excellent views toward the two sections of fuselage **[F.10]**, and all foes. This is an excellent place to aim grenades from. You can also easily react by aiming left (southeast) and blasting enemies off the wings. Save your grenades for those on the ground, and slowly advance as the enemies are whittled away. Before entering between the main fuselage sections, be sure to check for stragglers to the right (west).

CHECKPOINT G: LAV

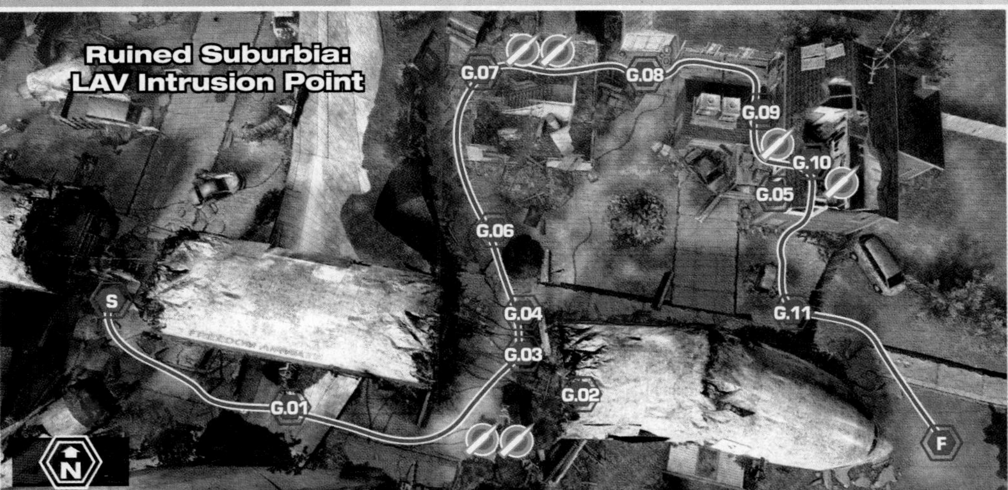

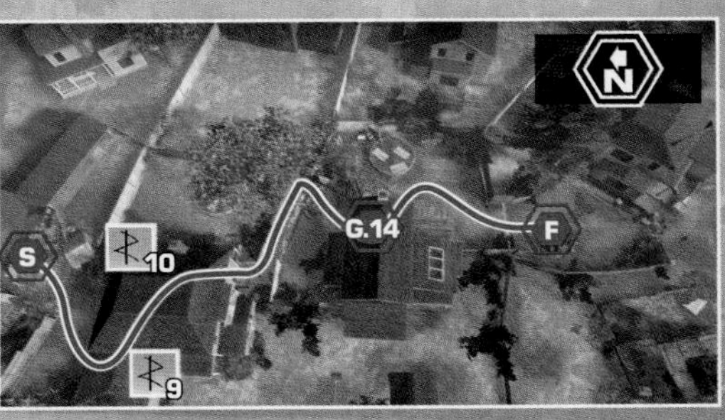

Military Police

Military Police (Scout)

Piranha Light Armor Vehicle

Soldier (Heavy)

Norks in the Fuselage!

G.1

Connor and Rianna press the remaining foes and move between the pieces of plane. Follow them in, and quickly drop two KPA targets around the corner, by the concrete barricades to the left (east) **[G.01]**. If the one behind the seating falls, crouch so he has less chance of hitting you as you edge toward the piece of wing the seats are resting on.

G.2

G.03

As you move toward the edge of the wing, two "Norks" (as Rianna calls them) dash up the fuselage section ahead (east) of you **[G.02]**. Line them up and drop both with a single burst of your rifle. Or bring them down one at a time. If you're lacking a weapon, wait for them to drop to the ground, so you can scavenge their armament. However, there are two scoped T3AKs; grab one as you drop down if you need it. Then head into cover **[G.03]** looking into a small open area dominated by the remains of a home, and the ruins of others, where the KPA is still very active.

WEAPONS >>

T3AK Rifle [Mk1 HOLO Scope] (2)

Leaning against the burned-out pickup truck, by the front fuselage section.

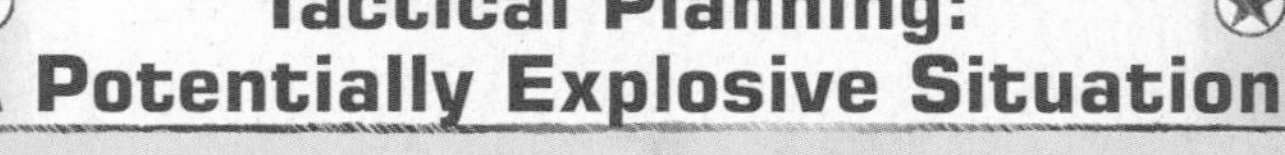

Tactical Planning: A Potentially Explosive Situation

Threat Assessment: KPA Patrol and LAV

The KPA forces are dug in at this location; expect foes behind concrete barricades and firing down from the ruins of a two-story structure to the east. Expect around six enemies, with a further entity near a cache of weapons in the northern corner. Once you've severely weakened these foes, an LAV (Light Armored Vehicle, which Connor also refers to as an "APC" or Armored Personnel Carrier) crashes through the fence. It fires RPG shots and can kill with a single strike. Therefore it's imperative to take cover (and orders from Connor) to avoid an explosive end to your adventure.

Plan: Optimal LAV Takedown

G.04

There is one overall plan for survival against the foes in this sector, although there are slight variations (which are mentioned, too). As Connor and Rianna enter the clearing, lob in a grenade across from the concrete barriers you're ensconced behind **[G.04]**, and try to take out two foes on the ground, behind the burned-out car. Alternately, drop them with gunfire. Do this before you fully expose yourself and exit from behind the fuselage.

G.05

Stay at the corner of the plane wreckage. Watch the window in the structure across (east) of you; quickly target and drop the foe at the window **[G.05]**, and then train your weapon on the window immediately left. Drop the foe who clambers out.

There are another couple of foes. One may be clambering over the fence at the opposite (east) end of the clearing. Sidestep out, ideally to cover behind the burned-out truck, and strafe them both with gunfire until they fall **[G.06]**. Then expect the KPA LAV to crash through the fence, and begin a series of devastating salvos.

At this point, there are two directions you can run:

To the north, following (or passing) Connor and Rianna, and reaching a KPA weapons cache **[G.07]**. You or your team need to dispatch a foe. Then turn right (east), after optionally grabbing any of the weapons scattered in the armored crate, and sprint for the orange-red ladder.

Sprint to the northeast, directly toward the orange-red ladder propped up against some scaffolding **[G.08]**, near the garage of the two-story house. Expect to be shot at, and possibly killed by the LAV or any KPA stragglers; this is almost certain if you don't sprint.

WEAPONS >>
T3AK Rifle

WEAPONS >>
T3AK Rifle [Mk1 ACOG Scope]

Scattered in and out of the armored KPA weapons cache.

Objective: Flank the LAV

CAUTION 조심하다

Although you can quickly kill any KPA infantry close to the LAV, don't step out to engage the LAV itself, or face a rocket barrage and instant death.

Climb the ladder, and look right (south), training your (ideally fast-firing) weapon on the window with the makeshift boards connected to it. Bring down the KPA foe who exits the window **[G.09]** before he draws on you. You can pick up his L249 LMG if you wish. Then get in the window, as Connor commands.

Objective: Destroy the LAV with C4

Drop into the small upstairs office, which is now a KPA weapons storage and lookout post **[G.10]**. Fortunately, one of the armored cases is stocked with C4 explosives. Grab four, and check the LAV under one of the windows. Lob two C4 packets onto the armor of the LAV **[G.11]**; one charge is not enough to destroy it. Then follow the on-screen instructions and activate both explosives at once with one flick of your remote detonator. The LAV is consumed in a massive fireball and so are you if you're leaning out of the window when the C4 combusts! Step back before pulling the trigger!

CAUTION 조심하다

You can also drop down and lob C4 from ground level, or view the explosion from a different angle, with minimal differences in the outcome, and major differences in danger; this isn't necessary or advisable.

NOTE 알아두세요

You should now be adept at using (and detonating) C4. You can restock afterward, and use C4 for the remainder of this mission, although few opportunities exist to effectively do so.

Objective: Head to Civilian Neighborhood

Connor makes his pleasure felt with a special, profanity-laced thank-you. Drop down and advance past the smoldering husk of the LAV, into a cul-de-sac of boarded-up properties **[G.12]**. The route continues to the south; simply follow your teammates (or their radar blip). However, before you do, quickly search the cul-de-sac for two more newspaper articles plus a Unique Weapon.

HIDDEN HISTORY >> 7 (7/61)

In the northeast area, in the rubble and thicket to the right of the yellow, foreclosed property.

VIOLENCE AND PROTEST SWEEPS CHINA AS MANUFACTURING JOBS DISAPPEAR

5/18/2012

Workers at a Taiwanese facility near Beijing clashed with authorities on Thursday, resulting in one dead and fifty injured. The protest comes after a wave of firings resulting from the falling demand for Chinese-made goods. The year has seen a loss of 15% of jobs in the manufacturing sector in China thus far, and many experts suspect that the trend will continue.

China's primary market for exports has changed radically in the last few years, said Arthur Brooks, an analyst for Morgan Stanley. "Consumers in the United States no longer seem interested in purchasing luxury goods from labels like Gucci and Louis Vuitton. Even mainstays like personal electronic devices have seen a pronounced dip in sales."

Many expect the trend to continue as the recent crash in the housing market continues to ravage the American economy. "We're not talking about 'green shoots' anymore," said Brooks. "I think everyone has started to become a lot more pragmatic. Many are now trying to guess where the bottom is and what we do when we get there."

Unique Weapons Detail: 3/17

WEAPONS >>
Digital Circuit M249 LMG [Mk1 ACOG Scope]

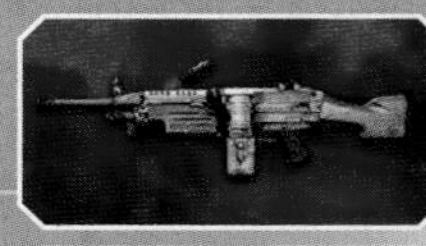

Featuring all the rapid-fire devastation of a regular M249 (which you first encountered moments ago on top of the garage roof), but in an attractive metalic hue, with attached scope for more accurate swath-cutting. Find this at the foot of the tree near an overturned fridge, in the southeast part of the cul-de-sac.

HIDDEN HISTORY >> 8 (8/61)

On the side porch of the yellow house in the southeast area of the cul-de-sac.

US INFRASTRUCTURE CRUMBLES AS DEBT BECOME UNMANAGEABLE, TAX REVENUES DECLINE

6/21/2017

In the middle of the 20th century, Route 66 was considered the crown jewel of the United States' transcontinental highway system. Once called the "Main Street of America," it's now a barely navigable stretch of treacherous potholes and dangerously deteriorating bridges. It's no surprise either; at more than a million dollars a mile, many highways and superhighways are simply too expensive for Federal and State Governments to maintain and repair.

Other parts of the national infrastructure are starting to crumble and collapse as well. Much of the Northeast has been crippled by intermittent blackouts as portions of the energy grid prove to be too unstable and interconnected. While the National Guard has been deployed to help repair the aging systems, there are lengthy waits for replacement parts.

Governments around the world have seen a sharp decline in tax revenues as global trade cools off. Faced with an almost insurmountable debt, many policy makers are being forced to slash the budgets of even essential services.

Ideally with your new LMG, follow Connor past the car, graffiti-daubed house, and over some wooden planks **[G.13]**, into another backyard. Pass the shed on the left, and enter the house after Connor kicks open the door. Just inside is another news pick-up. Enter the main floor of the house, checking one of the corners for another article, and then head out the door that Rianna opens to a narrow alley between

two picket fences, with a chest of drawers at the far end. Turn right (south), and follow your team into (and quickly out of) another dwelling **[G.14]**.

HIDDEN HISTORY >> 9 (9/61)

On the floor of the garage of the house you enter, en route to Boone.

AMERICAN GAS PRICES RISE TO RECORD HIGHS AS GREAT ARAB WAR ESCALATES

9/18/2016

Rising demand from across the globe, coupled with instability in the Persian Gulf region, have caused gas prices in the US to skyrocket. Up 79.1 cents from last month and up three dollars from this time last year, the week's average gas price in Southern California was at $12.61 for regular, $12.81 for premium and $12.77 for diesel.

"Markets are incredibly vulnerable to a variety of influences at this point," said Chris Winters, manager of the Consumers Network Gas Tracker. "It's difficult to predict how the market is going to react to further pressures." Winters went on to say that although May is typically the month with the highest gas prices during the year, the political situation in the Gulf could throw standard calculations and expectations out the window.

The state government has reacted to the situation by implementing a rationing system, the details of which will be announced this coming Tuesday. It is expected to focus on interstate shipping with an emphasis on food and medicine, and to discourage using gasoline for personal transportation.

HIDDEN HISTORY >> 10 (10/61)

In the northern corner of the main, ruined living room of the house you enter, en route to Boone.

JAPANESE CAPITULATES TO KOREAN OCCUPATION

4/7/2018

Reeling from the shock of the destruction of one of its largest nuclear power plants and the subsequent fallout ravaging much of their southern coast, Japan capitulated to Korean control on Thursday. The Japanese Diet passed an emergency measure on Wednesday night as Korean troops moved toward Tokyo, acceding to all of Kim Jong-un's demands.

A spokesman for the Korean Department of Defense stated that "the government of Korea has no interest in further violence," and "applauded the Japanese government in its swift decision to surrender." Korean officials stated that their goal was to prevent further violence against Korean citizens, and that every effort would be made to create a smooth transition.

CHECKPOINT H: SUBURBAN NATION

★ "We Had Nowhere Else to Go!" ★

Friendlies

Boone

Enemies

M1114 Humvee

Hop over the fallen fence, and you spot a man with a State Police flak jacket, placating a group of concerned citizens about the heat the Resistance is bringing to the area **[H.01]**. After Boone requests them to disperse, he turns his anger on Connor; Boone isn't happy with the less-than-subtle manner of your escape. After some chest-puffing, Boone separates Rianna and Connor, and introduces himself to you **[H.02]**.

Objective: Take Cover in the House

Boone's explanation of why you're here (a plan of reaching San Francisco and locating fuel for a daring raid) halts as two enemy Humvees screech into the neighborhood, firing their cannons at the civilians **[H.03]**. As they scatter and are raked with gunfire, step away from the carnage, turn around, and follow the Resistance members into the adjacent house to your left (south) **[H.04]**. Prepare to return fire from this dwelling.

CHECKPOINT I: HOUSE DEFEND

Objective: Defend Front of House

A Place to Stay

Inside the dwelling **[I.01]**, the cries of a startled baby and its terrified mother cause Boone to shout for you all to take defensive postures behind cover and defend the residence. Connor yells for the mother to shut the baby up. You'll be spending some of your ammunition keeping the KPA out of this dwelling. Locate a Unique Weapon lying by the kitchen sink, and grab it if you want something fully automatic. There are a few places to stand when repelling foes. You can:

Stand by the breakfast bar **[I.02]** to the right of Boone, between the screaming baby and screaming Connor. This is perhaps the best place to fire from, as you can crouch or duck to avoid damage if you're wounded, and you have a great line-of-sight to the front door and side window, where enemy intrusions stem from.

Enemies

M1114 Humvee

Military Police (Scout)

Stand by the front door and window. This allows you to easily target and drop the infantry in the street **[I.03]**, as you can see them through the window, and kill them before they advance. However, you need to physically turn right to spot foes jumping in through the side window **[I.04]**, making this a more dangerous place to stay.

Or, you can move to the entrance leading into the garage, facing right (northwest), looking at the front door **[I.05]**. Your main plan is to remove threats from the side window. This is a safer plan, but one that won't win any awards for bravery.

Unique Weapons Detail: 4/17

WEAPONS >>
Desert T3AK Rifle
[Mk 1 Red Dot Sight]

Although it lacks a scope, the T3AK more than makes up for this shortfall with an excellent sight. It's fully automatic, allowing you to remove any infantry threat easily. Watch that ammo consumption, though!

Combat continues until the KPA tire of your refusal to die, and lob in some noxious gas to smoke you out **[I.06]**. Everything goes green.

CHECKPOINT J: ESCAPE HOUSE

Friendlies

Hopper

Goliath

Enemies

M1114 Humvee

UCAV Drone Bomber

Military Police (Scout)

Objective: Escape the House

A Place to Leave

When your vision turns green, it's definitely time to leave. Follow Boone through the door into the garage, and eastward out into the backyard **[J.01]**.

CAUTION 조심하다

Spend too long in the house once the gas starts to flow, and you die of asphyxiation. Stand around just outside the garage for too long (optionally taking potshots at the KPA on the street through the gaps in the fencing), and the KPA comes through the garage, outflanking, and eventually killing you. Although you can defend for a while, this results in a stalemate. Push on!

Objective: Follow Boone

Boone lifts the woman and child over a fence **[J.02]**, and tells her to hide; they'll return for her once the situation is under control.

Then Boone turns and runs across the open backyard. Follow the team past a small vegetable patch, and a house, and into another garage **[J.03]**.

Objective: Meet up with Hopper

The situation is looking grim as you step through into another dwelling. There's no time to greet Hopper; the guy in the baseball cap is attempting to stem a downed colleague's bleeding with Rianna's help **[J.04]**. She shouts for "Goliath," and you're instructed to pick up the targeter for what you surmise to be some kind of automated machine. You soon come to realize it is so much more than that!

CAUTION 조심하다

The KPA is still in the area, which is periodically visited by Korean drone aircraft, and more reinforcements. Without Goliath, simply firing from your stronghold will eventually mean running out of ammunition and becoming overwhelmed.

Objective: Pick up Goliath Targeter

Locate Hopper's backpack, and snag the targeter from inside. A second later, "Goliath" crashes through from the backyard **[J.05]**; it appears to be some kind of autonomous wheeled fighting vehicle, with a targeting system you control!

CHECKPOINT K: FOLLOW GOLIATH

Friendlies

Goliath

Enemies

M1114 Humvee

Military Police

UCAV Drone Bomber

Military Police (Scout)

Transport Truck

Objective: Target Enemy Vehicles

With Goliath trundling into play, the previously impenetrable KPA defenses are now much weaker. As Goliath rumbles out of the hole in the front of the house **[K.01]**, look through the adjacent window, and begin to take the fight to the KPA.

Tactical Planning: Keep on Trucking

Threat Assessment: KPA Forces

The KPA's forces would be insurmountable without Goliath. Infantry runs in from up the street and across yards to the west, backed by five Humvees. Four are initially in the theater of war, while the fifth arrives once a stationary KPA cargo truck blocking the road is destroyed. With all these enemies, resort to your main weapon to tackle them.

Goliath: Targeted Takedowns

You may have missed Hopper's rather garbled explanation of how Goliath works, but this robotic wheeled entity uses its machine guns independently, and moves of its own accord, based on threats in the immediate vicinity. The targeter operates the main salvo of rockets fired from its central turret. Simply hold the targeter like a pair of binoculars, and when the targets flash red **[K.02]**, press your fire trigger **[K.03]**.

Note that infantry is instantly targeted, and you can make small "sweeps" to catch three or four foes with a single strike. However, vehicles take slightly longer to lock-on, so don't fire too quickly. You can target foes as much as you wish, or until Goliath explodes (which fails your objective).

Plan A: The Rockets' Red Glare

Battling the KPA is a lot easier with a hulking war machine. From the window, target either of the initial Humvees, and have Goliath fire on it **[K.04]**. The Humvee explodes, and the other Humvee moves up the street. At this point, a KPA drone aircraft swoops low over the battlefield.

Immediately bring out your targeter, and hit the Humvee that just passed Goliath **[K.05]**, before or as it parks close to a third Humvee, to the right (north) of a stationary truck.

> **TIP** 영리한
>
> **You can stand just outside the house you emerged from, to the left. This allows you to step back into cover easily. Or, you can stand in the street behind Goliath, or next to Connor behind cover. But if you're adept with the Goliath targeter, the foes won't get a chance to hit you!**

If KPA infantry are swarming your location, immediately use Goliath to target six or seven of them with a single rocket barrage **[K.06]**. This is much quicker, and less dangerous, than using your carried weapons.

Now take down the Humvee parked to the right of the truck **[K.07]**.

Then target the Humvee parked on the left (south) side of the street, on a front lawn **[K.08]**. KPA stream in from this location, so you may need to wipe out infantry reinforcements at this time, too.

Now destroy the stationary truck **[K.09]**. This causes a final Humvee to screech down the road; target that to complete the combat **[K.10]**. Remove the other Humvees first, before you target the truck, to minimize enemy fire from vehicles.

Plan B: The Red Mist Descends

Although you may be tempted to utilize a mixture of other methods, such as throwing and attaching C4 explosives onto Humvees (you only have four packets, meaning you can take down only two of Humvees, and that takes some luck), or using firearms plus grenades against enemy soldiers as they run at you from the south **[K.11]**, this is both dangerous and unnecessary. The longer combat takes, the more foes arrive, the more damage Goliath takes, and the less chance you have of surviving. Plan A is your better bet!

The Bombs Bursting in Air

When the final Humvee has been destroyed, your celebrations are short-lived. A KPA drone swoops in from the west **[K.12]**, and carpet-bombs the entire street! Everything fades to black, as the Resistance scatters. You lose consciousness....

Mettle of Honor

Award: Why We Fight | Rating: 10 | Trophy: Bronze

Completing this mission earns you this particular reward. Difficulty level, or how many times you restarted a checkpoint, do not matter.

Mettle of Honor

Award: Why We Fight—Guerrilla | Rating: 25 | Trophy: Bronze

Completing this mission earns you this individual reward. However, you must complete this on the hardest difficulty.

Mettle of Honor

Award: Iron Man—Why We Fight | Rating: 25 | Trophy: Bronze

Completing this mission without dying once or restarting a checkpoint earns you this reward. Lessen the difficulty if you're having problems completing this task.

MISSION SELECT >> 02 >> FREEDOM

After the airstrike on the cul-de-sac, you were carried to your new home: a self-sustaining community hidden in the suburbs. Your next mission is to steal tracking beacons from the nearby labor camp, but there are things inside that can't be unseen.

 **HIDDEN HISTORY** >> 16 (26/61 total)

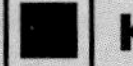 **KOREAN KODEX** >> 3 (5/10 total)

 **UNIQUE WEAPON** >> 4 (8/17 total)

CHECKPOINT A: WORLD MADE BY HAND

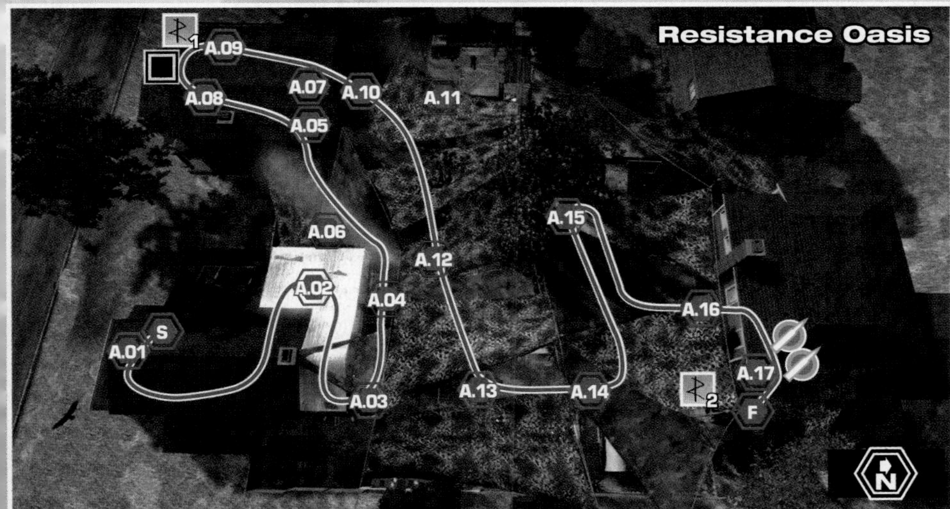

Friendlies

Boone Connor Settler

WEAPONS >> None

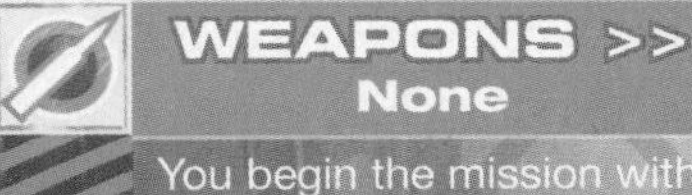

You begin the mission with no weapons.

 **Objective:** Follow Boone

Our Own Little Piece of America

You wake to the sounds of propaganda on the radio. Boone quickly switches it off, and tells you to head outside when you're good and ready **[A.01]**. A KPA patrol helicopter heads over the desolate suburban foothills. Peer out of the window for a closer look at the deserted streets if you wish. Then step through the remains of the safehouse, passing the makeshift cultivation greenhouse, resplendent with tomato and flower sprouts **[A.02]**. Boone is on the radio, letting others know you're up and about. Then follow Boone out of the plastic-wrapped greenhouse, and into the backyard: the Resistance's own little piece of America.

Look out across the merged backyards of the surrounding properties; the Resistance has come together to preserve some sense of community **[A.03]**. It's certainly a lot better than the shale quarries. To the KPA patrols on the outside looking down, this looks like just another section of boarded-up suburban failure, but inside is a safe haven. Boone explains the camouflage keeping the KPA away **[A.04]**. But vigilance is always necessary. Boone confirms that Rianna has prepped "the playground," motions to the various ways the Resistance claims power, and beckons you to follow him into a nearby home.

Enter the home (you will have an opportunity to talk to the Oasis settlers in a moment), so you can listen in on Connor and Boone's conversation **[A.05]**. Connor isn't happy about the time it's taking to secure some tracking devices, and lets Boone know, loudly. Boone keeps order, and tells you to look around the place if you want. He'll meet you out back.

[Optional] Settling In: Part 1

Head back outside if you want a closer look at the home-schooling area, and the settler tinkering with some circuit boards. Speak to him and he tells you there's no shortage of parts to fix **[A.06]**. Keep conversing until you exhaust topics.

NOTE 알아두세요

Talking to the Oasis settlers is important to acquire an Achievement or Trophy, so make sure you speak to everyone in the camp once.

Head back inside the home, and speak to the woman Boone called Sally **[A.07]** who is cooking leftovers for lunch, at seven. She tells you Connor and Boone are always like that.

Pass the two kids sleeping by the fire, and speak to the woman Boone saved during the previous mission **[A.08]**. She is nursing her child on the couch. She is appreciative, but she wants to be alone with her baby.

Into Boone's Office

Head through the nearby doorway to a small office. Plastered across the walls are various maps, newspaper clippings, and schematics **[A.09]**. Study them closely; included is a map of the United States showing the various pockets of resistance west of the Radiation Zone.

KOREAN KODEX >> 1 (3/10)

On the wall between the metal filing cabinets is a code you can access; under the whiteboard map of the "Fuel Raid."

HIDDEN HISTORY >> 1 (11/61)

On the floor in the corner of Boone's planning office, at the foot of the two corner filing cabinets.

JUCHE IDEOLOGY

2/18/2007

Created by Kim Il-sung and based off classic Marxist-Leninist dogma, the Juche ideology of self-reliance was created in the sixties as a check against proxy control by other prominent communist nations. Focused on North Korea's contemporary goals of an independent foreign policy, a self sustaining economy and a self reliant defensive posture, it has also served to create an autocratic regime completely under the control of Kim Jong-il.

While the Juche ideology is focused on self-reliance and manifesting the will of the people, the North Korean government has been forced to accept food aid from the outside and implement a number of market reforms. Famine resulting from Kim Jong-il's policies has resulted in widespread starvation, and numerous governments including the United States have given aid to North Korea through the UN World Food Program. While this has weakened the foundation of the ideology, it has not stopped the North Koreans from attempting to re-unite the peninsula on their terms, using erratic displays of military power to threaten its neighbors.

Many critics and human rights organizations contend that the North Korean political environment bears no resemblance to the Juche ideology. Based on reports from defectors, the people have no actual part in the decision making process, and the country relies on aid for more than a quarter of its food. It remains to be seen how long Kim Jong-il can maintain absolute control over the country.

Head out of the other entrance and meet up with Boone again **[A.10]**. There's time to introduce yourself to the remaining settlers before you dodge the Korean patrols, so explore the main exterior part of Oasis as thoroughly as you wish.

Objective: Meet Up with Boone Outside

[Optional] Settling In: Part 2

Your next stop is an optional talk with the settler working on the rudimentary communications array near the fertilizer vats **[A.11]**. The receiver he's building should allow the Resistance to listen in on radio chatter. Continue to converse with him. His colleague on the roof above doesn't say anything, and you can't climb up there.

Visit the soup-canning operation close to the giant central oak tree, and speak to the settler **[A.12]**. He recognizes you as the pilot. After hiding out here for two years, he hopes to build the land back into a country. Leave him and his pincers alone, and continue past the small child merrily swinging.

Over in the corner are two settlers tilling the soil amid the tomato plants, and whispering about you; apparently you're part of Boone's "San Francisco plan." They clam up when you talk to the woman **[A.13]**, who exchanges (slightly nervous) pleasantries with you.

Nearby is a man on a stepping machine, which is attached to some rain barrels **[A.14]**. Hopper has ingeniously rigged this so that Oasis is irrigated without the settlers needing to carry water. Now inspect the upper allotment to the right of the building Boone is standing near.

HIDDEN HISTORY >> 2 (12/61)

Close to the mesh fence and locked gate, to the left of the upper tomato allotment.

UNITED STATES BEGINS PHASED WITHDRAWAL FROM MIDDLE EAST

10/5/2012

In a joint press conference with his British counterpart, the President announced that both governments will begin withdrawing troops from Iraq as early as this month. The phased withdrawal calls for reducing the force level to around half its current strength by June, culminating in a complete withdrawal by December. The announcement comes on the heels of a statement from the Iraqi Prime Minister that he no longer feels that US forces are needed in most of his provinces.

The withdrawal is officially being described as a "transition," focusing on US-trained Iraqi security forces taking control of the country. Although there have been more than 5,000 US servicemen lost since the war began in 2003, there has been a sharp decline in fatalities in the last few months, with only two deaths occurring in the last thirty days. A spokesman for the Defense Department said that 70 percent of the Iraqi army was expected to be in control of its own sectors by the end of the year.

The final settler to speak with is the older man milking one of his goats, Nancy **[A.15]**. He isn't too keen on you lingering longer than is necessary at the goat pen.

Mettle of Honor

Award	Welcome to Freedom	Rating	10	Trophy	Bronze

Access this by speaking to all the settlers mentioned in this checkpoint area, as described previously.

Objective: Pick Up Assault Rifle

After meeting the settlers, check back in with Boone at the porch on the upper side of the yard. Hopper radios in to let him know the KPA patrol has moved on, giving you a window of opportunity that shouldn't be wasted. Follow Boone into the house **[A.16]**, and agree to contribute to the mission Boone has already underway (you have no other choices!). Connor indicates a weapons crate with some grenades, a pistol, knife, and assault rifle on it. Step over and gather these items up. Then follow Boone down the trapdoor Connor holds open for you. You climb down into a tunnel. Follow Boone along the tunnel **[A.17]**, which the Resistance dug during the early days of the occupation.

CHECKPOINT B: NIGHTFALL

Friendlies

Hopper

Enemies

Sentry Tower

Objective: Meet Hopper

Objective: Recon the Area

Preparation for the Tower Takedown

When you reach the end of the tunnel, climb back up to the surface, following Boone. Dusk is painting the backyards of Montrose in a thin haze of gloom. Hopper is waiting as you emerge from the tunnel **[B.01]**, and thanks you for your help with Goliath. You and the three Resistance fighters move to recon the area, stopping behind the shed **[B.02]**, and peering around. Hopper informs everyone that the Gunnison Cell delivered the van and mortar, but there's a Sentry Tower between you and the playground, where the van is parked. Boone wants the tower taken out. You can spot the tower in the distance.

HIDDEN HISTORY >> 3 (13/61)

Before following Boone, turn and inspect the bushes in the southwest corner.

IRAN, SAUDI ARABIA TEST NUCLEAR WEAPONS

11/14/2014

Just 24 hours after Iranian state television showed grainy footage of the country's first nuclear weapons test, Saudi Arabia conducted a successful test of a similar thermonuclear device, which it claimed demonstrated a yield of 13.5 megatons. Iran and Saudi Arabia have been engaged in an escalating race to accumulate arms ever since the United States vacated the area last year. Analysts from the Pentagon confirmed the success and yield of both tests.

After stooping to read the news pick-up, move around the shed to the backyards where the rest of the team ran.

HIDDEN HISTORY >> 4 (14/61)

Before rejoining them, quickly step into the shed, and secure another piece of historical data.

US MILITARY TO SCALE BACK, REFOCUS

7/21/2014

Facing increased pressure from policy makers, the Pentagon has announced its plan to rescope the military's procurement priorities. "The United States is no longer fighting the Cold War," a spokesman for the Defense Department said, "and it's time the composition and strategies of our forces reflects that." The plan, as outlined in a 200 page report titled "Agile Warfare for the 21st Century" focuses more on Special Operations teams and the use of unmanned vehicles, and less on fleets of capital ships and large-theater military conflicts. "The modern nature of asymmetric warfare demands that the United States respond in kind if it intends to stay on the frontline of armed combat," the report states. "The future military of the United States will be light, fast and heavily automated, featuring drones and relying primarily on the strength of our digital infrastructure.

Boone shifts the remains of a refrigerator out of the way, allowing access through an abandoned house **[B.03]**. Hopper reels off the Sentry Gun's statistics, before being shut up by Connor. Boone's advice is more relevant: make your way up the street, waiting for the spotlight to pass, before moving. Inside the house, the side rooms have nothing of value, so wait for Boone to edge out, and follow him **[B.04]**.

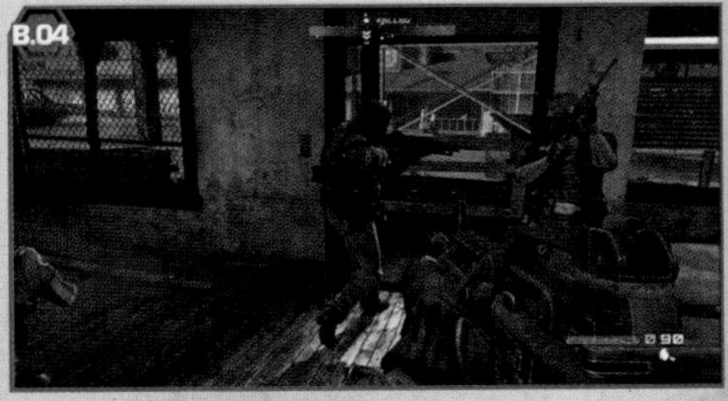

CHECKPOINT C: SCOUT THE SENTRY

Enemies

Sentry Tower

Objective: Use a Grenade to Destroy the Sentry Tower

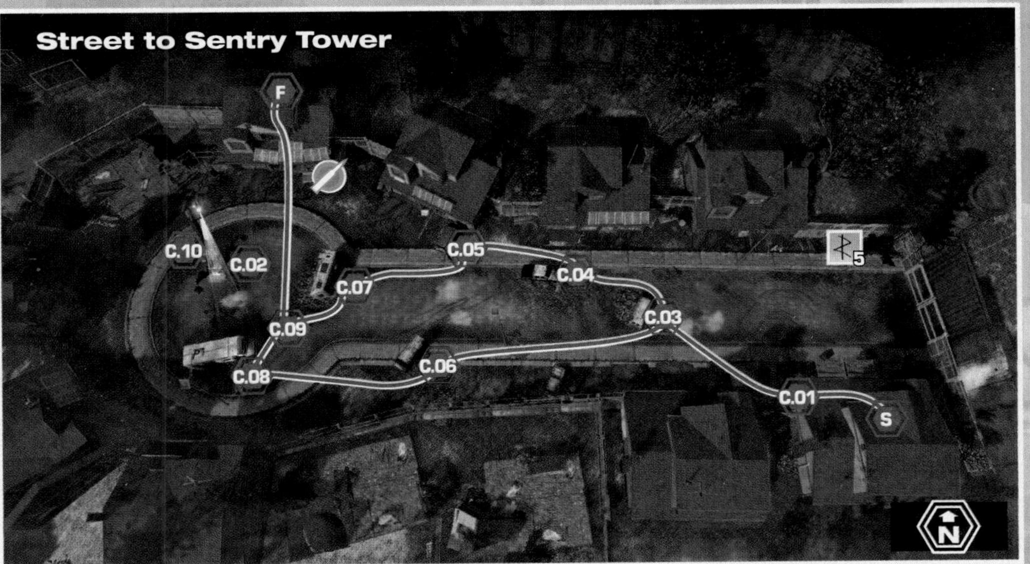

TIP 영리한

Have you been overly free with your grenades? Then step up to Boone (in this area) or Connor and Hopper (after this area) to receive additional supplies.

Running the Gauntlet

Boone vaults over the porch fence **[C.01]**, and you should follow; jumping and landing on the cracked tarmac. While Boone makes a dash to the parked van, hide by the corrugated metal to the left by the tree, and study the Sentry Tower's swiveling gun appendage **[C.02]**.

The searchlight attached to it pivots around; wait for the beam of light to pass from right to left, and then sprint to the van, either before or after your teammates **[C.03]**. From the van, follow Boone's lead (or head up first), and sprint to the vehicle lodged up on the red-striped concrete barricade **[C.04]**, as the car on the left side of the road offers less cover. From here, you have a choice of routes.

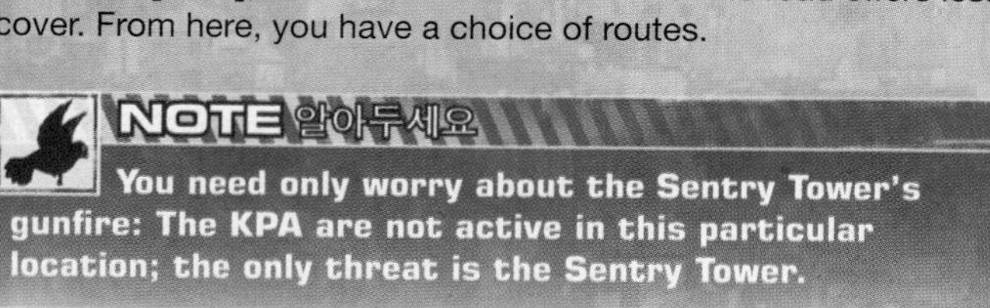

NOTE 알아두세요

You need only worry about the Sentry Tower's gunfire: The KPA are not active in this particular location; the only threat is the Sentry Tower.

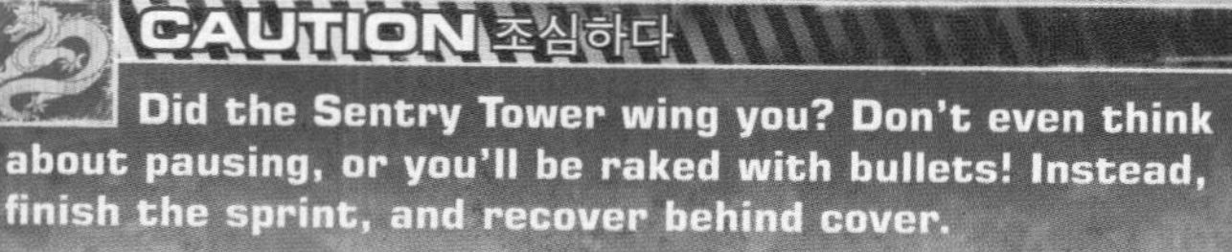

CAUTION 조심하다

Did the Sentry Tower wing you? Don't even think about pausing, or you'll be raked with bullets! Instead, finish the sprint, and recover behind cover.

When you reach the van, and other cover opportunities, be sure to crouch to avoid any stray bullets. Before leaving cover, watch the sentry's searchlight, and sprint up between gunfire bursts, or just after the light beam passes you.

Threat Assessment: Sentry Tower

Armed with a 20mm Auto-Cannon linked Kayoo-Band Radar, the fire-control systems of this autonomous fighting unit are impressive and devastating, with a full 360-degree field of fire (aside from the appendage arm the auto-cannon hangs from). The field of vision is somewhat more restricted; it reacts to movement caught in the beam of its searchlight. Seek cover, rushing between defensive positions when the searchlight isn't in your vicinity. Destroy it with a carefully aimed grenade into its weakly armored rear under-carriage.

Step out to the right, and sprint up along the right side of the street, ducking down behind the remains of the minivan **[C.05]**. This is shorter, and safer.

You can move to the left, heading west toward the parked yellow van **[C.06]**, but this is longer and puts you at greater risk.

Either way, rush for the overturned camper trailer directly in front of the Sentry Tower **[C.07]**, and recover for a moment. The motor home to the left isn't necessary to inspect, although it's a better place to run to **[C.08]** if you're dashing in from the yellow van. Instead, step out to one side (ideally the left, as it's easier to aim at the rear of the tower's base), and lob a grenade at the red-lit area **[C.09]**. Moments later, the grenade explodes, and the Sentry Tower topples over **[C.10]**. With the threat gone, you can secure a well-hidden news pick-up, before following Boone to the exit. Before heading through the door of the house, check the crate outside the porch for an impressive Unique Weapon.

CAUTION 조심하다

Or, if you threw the grenade too far, or not far enough, the explosion misses the tower. Step out, and try again!

Mettle of Honor

Award	Good Use of Cover	Rating	10	Trophy	Bronze

Stepping competently between the abandoned vehicles is as important as correct timing; avoid getting hit by any Sentry Tower bullets to receive this reward.

HIDDEN HISTORY >> 5 (15/61)

In the northeast corner of the street where the first Sentry Tower is located, close to the KPA wall, on a pile of refuse near a security fence and tree.

OPINION: THE THREAT OF EMP ATTACK

8/15/2014

A little known fact about nuclear weapons is that in addition to the concussive, thermal and of course radioactive forces, there is also an intense release of electromagnetic energy. Despite the fact that it's the least visible and least well known component of a nuclear blast, it has the potential to be the most devastating.

While most nuclear nightmares focus on the sudden destruction of a city, those in the know have nightmares of a much different flavor. A specially tuned nuclear weapon, detonated in near space would have a devastating and final effect on our national infrastructure. Simulations performed by the military suggest that a device triggered at a distance of only 200 miles from the surface of the earth would permanently disable nearly all modern electronic devices and deactivate the national electrical grid.

While our new military has been described as "agile" and "digital," there's another word that could be used to describe it—"fragile." This administration needs to take seriously the threat of an EMP attack, by generating emergency plans, hardening key sites like power plants, and ensuring that our military is capable of withstanding such an attack. It's a challenge that in order to face we must have imagination and courage and the willingness to sacrifice in order to protect our future.

Unique Weapons Detail: 5/17

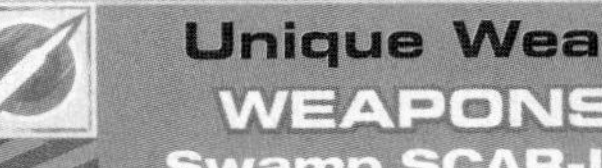

WEAPONS >>
Swamp SCAR-L Rifle

Inside the crate by the exit house is a green and mean SCAR-L rifle. Although it lacks a scope, it is incredibly effective at dropping enemies with a single burst of fire (which occurs each time you pull the trigger).

Objective: Follow Boone

CHECKPOINT D: SENTRY DOWN!

Enemies

Military Police (Scout)

Military Police

KPA Private Property

House-to-House Skirmish

Enter the house to the right of the Sentry Tower, where Boone and Connor are yelling, and survey a sloping backyard, teeming with KPA. It seems a patrol is early, and they're milling about in the yard. The soldier on the porch roof looks to be particularly troublesome, and although they haven't seen you yet, they'll attack as soon as you fire a shot. Peer through the partially boarded up window to the right of Boone **[D.01]**, and take your shot; line up the head of the foe on the porch. A firefight now begins, as your team storms the yard **[D.02]**.

Objective: Clear the Back Yard

WEAPONS >> KPA Infantry Ordnance (Various)

By the corpses of the recently deceased.

T3AK example shown

Tactical Planning

Threat Assessment: KPA Patrol

Expect around a dozen infantry and military police in this backyard, armed with the usual weaponry, such as the M4 Rifle, PWS Diablo SMG, SCAR-L Rifle, and T3AK Rifle. Beware of troops dug in behind cover, especially after the majority of the foes are defeated; they can pop up and ruin your day. Pay particular attention to foes inside the house, on the upper floor window to begin with, and inside once you push up to the upper building.

Plan: Staying Put

You can remain inside the lower building, using the gap in the window to tag foes, although you're easily caught by return fire. A better plan is to remain just inside the back door, firing at all available targets **[D.03]**, and sidestepping to cover if you're winged. This can continue as long as you wish; the door only closes and locks once you reach the house at the opposite side of the yard.

TIP 영리한

This plan also allows you to easily target and bring down the couple of foes that appear at the upper windows, and on the porch if you missed him before the fight began. You can also lob a grenade up and behind the upper defenses.

Plan: Left Flank

D.04

D.05

This is a recommended route to take, ideally after you've culled as many KPA as possible from inside the lower house. Use the cover of the concrete wall halfway up **[D.04]**, and check for foes at the upper window of the house you're assaulting. Optionally lob a grenade as you step out from the concrete wall cover. Then duck behind the crates as you and your team clean out the stragglers **[D.05]**.

Plan: Up the Middle, or Right Flank

D.06

Far less impressive is charging straight up the middle of the yard, because you're an easy target **[D.06]**. The right flank is blocked by sections of concrete wall, so you have to head left, around the tire defenses and into the middle of the yard anyway. Dive behind cover and encroach upon the foe, lobbing in a grenade or two if needed. Or scoot across to the KPA's less-defended left flank.

CAUTION 조심하다

D.07

When it all goes quiet, don't let your guard down; combat isn't over until Connor shouts "That's the last of 'em!" If he hasn't yelled that out, carefully enter the upper house [D.07], and prepare for a foe to attempt to melee at your current position. Swiftly return the favor before continuing.

Objective: Meet up with Rianna

CHECKPOINT E: MEET UP WITH RIANNA

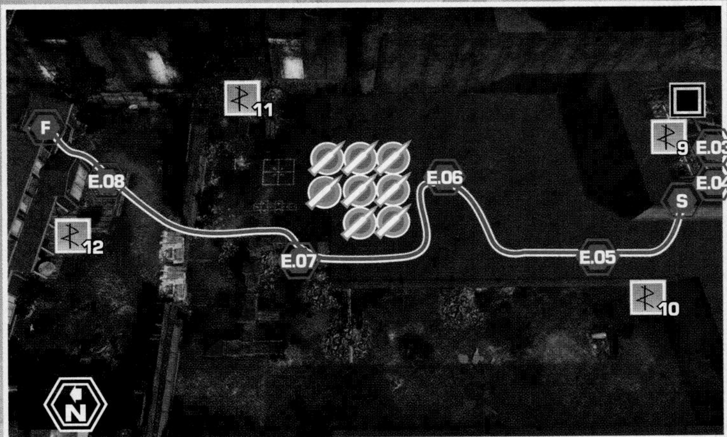

Friendlies

Rianna

School's Out

There's little but the remains of a survivalist's tent inside the house. Boone and Connor kick open the front door. The drop-point is an abandoned school, and the team begins to cross the exterior entrance **[E.01]** to the front doors. You can opt to follow them, but a brief reconnoiter beforehand is advisable. You can grasp the solidity of the KPA's concrete walled entry points **[E.02]**, and more importantly, check the area for news snippets.

HIDDEN HISTORY >> 6 (16/61)

Look around the house you emerged from, near the first school bus. The article is in a corner on a small pile of garbage.

OPINION: HOW SOON WE FORGET

12/18/2015

Anyone with any knowledge of history will tell you that the various Nobel Prizes are a sham. Based on some of the winners, it's clearly an award that carries all the gravitas of a Cable Ace Award. For one of the more egregious examples, consider that a Nobel Prize was awarded to Henry Kissinger, a man responsible for more deaths in Asia than Pol Pot.

Despite his laudable efforts to craft a lasting peace between the two Koreas, Kim Jong-un has yet to answer for the crimes of his father; the mass imprisonment and forced impoverishment of millions of innocent civilians justified only by an insane ideology. For 50 years, his country represented the greatest humanitarian crisis in the world and now they've been rewarded for it. I hope that humanitarian groups across the world will join myself, Amnesty International, and others in demanding that he be stripped of his prize, and that the full extent of his government's crimes be published for the world to see and judge. Korea may be on the road to peace, but its threat to the world remains undiminished.

HIDDEN HISTORY >> 7 (17/61)

Before entering the school, inspect the war memorial with the flagpole for another news pick-up.

SOUTHERN STATES ENACT STRONGER BORDER CONTROL POLICIES

11/26/2016

California joined Texas and Florida in enacting strict border control policies with the states along their northern borders. Meant to curb the influx of starving, freezing Americans from the north, the policies have been met with controversy and outrage. California has seen hundreds of thousands of citizens flocking south looking for work and food, and have been met with rejection and in some cases violence.

"We're stretched beyond capacity all over the state," said Kathy Griffiths in a statement to the national press. "California has to worry about its own citizens, the majority of whom are without work and are forced to go hungry. We don't like turning our backs on American citizens, but our backs are to the wall here. We have to protect Californians." Griffiths called on the federal government to aid in California's quest to put an end to illegal border crossings. The National Guard has been used on several occasions to beef up security at checkpoints along the state line, but the federal government is also stretched thin as it tries to send aid to the beleaguered and freezing northern states.

HIDDEN HISTORY >> 8 (18/61)

Then check the school bus at the northern end of the road. Climb inside to procure the following missive.

ROOFTOP GARDENS A WAY OF LIFE FOR SOME URBANITES

7/2/2017

Frustrated by an inconsistent food supply, some enterprising individuals in downtown Rochester, New York have embraced an old fashioned way of life. Reminiscent of the 'victory gardens' from World War II, more and more rooftops and balconies are speckled with patches of green bearing fruit and vegetables.

"I have a three year old boy," Amanda Kratzert told me as we toured the extensive garden on the roof of the three-story building she rents a floor of. "I want to make sure that he has fresh, healthy vegetables year-round and isn't forced to rely on government rations." Mrs. Kratzert shares the roof with the other two families that live in the building. "We all work together to provide food for our families and all take an equal share. It's worked out really well."

The Kratzerts aren't alone in their agricultural endeavors. All across upstate New York, families are building gardens and miniature farms to supply fresh food to eat and barter with. In many towns and cities, local governments have thrown out regulations banning livestock, which has led to an explosions of backyard chicken coops and goat pens. Pleasant as these personal farming operations are, they are a reminder of just how much America has changed since the Great Arab War disrupted global energy supplies.

With all the immediate news gathered, rejoin Boone, Connor, and Hopper as they bust open the door to the school interior. Boone sounds winded, but the true extent of his wounds isn't revealed until he collapses in the gymnasium **[E.03]**, where Rianna is waiting with a shipment of white phosphorus mortar rounds.

The Sentry Tower clipped Boone, and he can't go on without medical attention. He hands over his badge to Connor **[E.04]**, and Rianna elects to take him back to Oasis while you, Hopper, and Connor finish scouting the area. Before joining them, be sure to thoroughly check the gym:

KOREAN KODEX >> 2 (4/10)

Below the left foot of the Montrose Beaver basketball mascot, on the whitewashed gym wall.

HIDDEN HISTORY >> 9 (19/61)

Below the codex, on the gym floor below the painting of the Montrose Beaver basketball mascot.

8/2/2017

EAST COAST BLACK MARKETS LIGHT UP

P J Cooper left his home in Chevy Chase, Maryland at 6 in the morning on Tuesday, hoping to beat his neighbors to a local gas station. When he arrived he was shocked to see a line of more than a hundred people, many of whom had waited in line overnight in the bitter cold.

Gasoline has become increasingly scarce in recent months, which many blame on the ongoing unrest in the Middle East that began last year. Cooper remembers a time when gas was cheaper than a gallon of milk, but now the 23 year old pays a hundred dollars for five gallons of gas.

Some Americans avoid the lines by purchasing gas from dealers on the street. Marked up by as much as 30 dollars a gallon, it's sometimes the only way to get gas when you need it. Many dealers aren't interested in dollars either—they're trading for medicine, fresh or canned food and even weapons and ammunition. Although local authorities have tried to stamp out the practice, setting up a black market gas dealership is as simple as a plastic can and a 25 dollar bribe at the right time.

Objective: Recon the Labor Camp

Follow Connor and Hopper through the "Exit" doors, into a school corridor, and past the abandoned tents **[E.05]**. In the distance, you can hear muffled shouts and coughing, but can't locate the source. Pass through the ransacked classroom (labeled "Mr. Kalb"), and into a secondary room where Brooks (from another Resistance cell) has left a variety of weapons to choose from **[E.06]**. Connor tells you to pick one you like. Choose from the following, and optionally test any out on the mannequins standing on the far side of the room. Don't forget to make the Unique M16 one of your weapons, as it outshines the others.

WEAPONS >>
Fragmentation Grenade (4)

WEAPONS >>
SCAR-H LMG
[Mk1 Red Dot Sight]

WEAPONS >>
Super V SMG
[Mk2 Holo Scope]

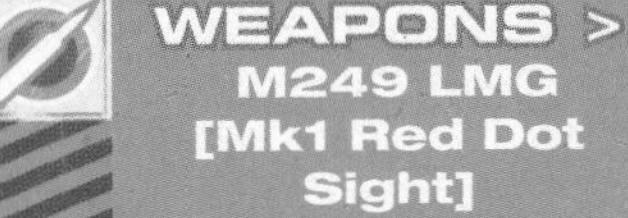

WEAPONS >>
M249 LMG
[Mk1 Red Dot Sight]

WEAPONS >>
ACR Rifle
[Mk3 Holo Scope]

WEAPONS >>
SCAR-L Rifle
[Mk2 Holo Scope]

WEAPONS >> PWS Diablo SMG [Mk3 Holo Scope]

All weapons are in the elementary school cache.

Unique Weapons Detail: 6/17

WEAPONS >> Swamp M16 Rifle [Mk 1 HOLO Scope] [Silencer]

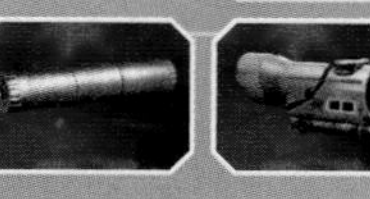

Aside from the natty camouflage design, this is an excellent, single-fire armament that can take down a foe with a single, well-aimed shot. Line up the sight with your enemy's head, pull the trigger, and he goes down. The faster you fire, the more shots are expelled. Excellent for the precision tactician.

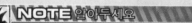

NOTE 알아두세요

This is likely to be your first exposure to a large cache of firearms, and choosing the correct two isn't vital, but is recommended. Simply cross-reference the adjacent list to the statistical information contained in the Campaign >> Armory chapter of this guide. Remember to switch out both weapons (even if you're comfortable with what you're currently carrying, these armaments are fully loaded).

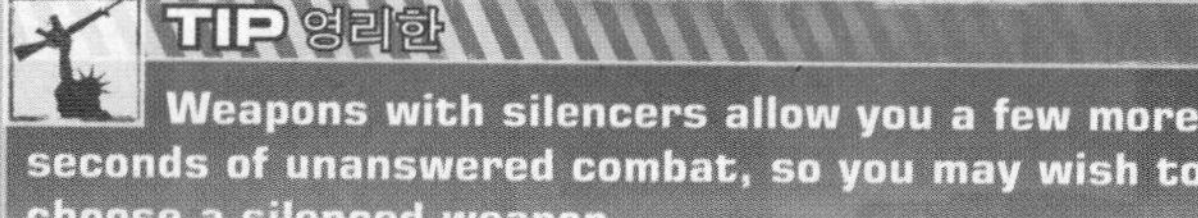

TIP 영리한

Weapons with silencers allow you a few more seconds of unanswered combat, so you may wish to choose a silenced weapon.

TIP 영리한

If you're still unsure of which weapons to pick, a combination of the PWS Diablo SMG and ACR Rifle (with their scopes), or the Unique M16; these work well in the immediate combat to come.

Connor breaks open the exterior door, and stumbles out into a playground **[E.07]**. While rendezvous point nomenclature dawns on him, search the surrounding area for newspaper articles, which are listed nearby. When you've made a thorough sweep of the school quadrant exterior, playground, and refuse-strewn porch with the two recently dug graves, close to where your team is waiting, move toward them **[E.08]**, and the large concrete wall, ready to engage the enemy.

HIDDEN HISTORY >> 10 (20/61)

In the southeast corner of the exterior quadrant, by the steps of the locked double doors.

INTERNATIONAL REACTIONS TO KOREAN OCCUPATION OF JAPAN DIFFER

9/13/2018

Korea on Tuesday called America's call of sanctions against its occupation of Japan "hypocritical" and blamed the United States for the spread of chaos and discord around the globe. Korea, which claims it is occupying Japan in an attempt to stamp out an attempted genocide against its citizens, taunted the US from Pyongyang, saying "How can a regime that can barely feed its citizens or heat their homes gain the respect of the rest of the world?"

Ahmad Jannati, a leading Iranian Cleric, offered his country's congratulations to Korea on national radio. Iran has taken strides in recent months to align itself with Korean interests in East Asia, providing weapons and fuel at reduced rates.

Other East Asian nations also pledged support for Korea's mission in Japan. Mahathir Mohamad, the Prime Minister of Malaysia, has provided two elite Renjer battalions for counterinsurgency operations in Japan.

HIDDEN HISTORY >> 11 (21/61)

At the far eastern end of the playground climbing frame.

KOREAN GOVERNMENTS DEMANDS INTERNATIONAL CONDEMNATION AGAINST JAPAN

9/23/2017

Violent protest spiraled out of control on Saturday in Tokyo as a renewed wave of demonstrations hit the streets. Although Japan has publicly condemned the attacks, Korea alleges that the protests are supported and in some cases supplemented by Japanese soldiers. Photographic evidence presented by the Koreans at the United Nations Headquarters in Brussels appears to offer circumstantial, but compelling evidence that Japanese police are involved in systematic attacks against ethnic Koreans.

As tensions escalate, many Koreans have made high profile exits from the country and returned to the mainland. Others are not so lucky. Official estimates indicate that at least a thousand Koreans may have been murdered at the hands of Japanese nationalists. Unofficial estimates claim that as many as ten thousand may have already been killed.

HIDDEN HISTORY >> 12 (22/61)

In the blue child's paddling pool, on the detritus-strewn porch of the home across from the playground.

NORTH KOREA SUSPECTED OF DEVELOPING NUCLEAR WEAPONS IN JAPAN

2/2/2019

French authorities presented evidence at the United Nations today that appears to prove that Korea is using existing Japanese infrastructure to develop nuclear weapons. The evidence included satellite imagery that showed the Korean Military operating in and around Rokkasho Reprocessing Plant in Amori Prefecture. Owned by Japan Nuclear Fuel Limited, the facility is one of the prime sites in Japan that is separating and enriching nuclear fuel for use in weapons. French intelligence also provided evidence that Korean troops were operating around the Japan Aerospace Exploration Agency, where the M-V rocket is developed and maintained. The rocket is based off the American Peacekeeper ICBM and can be used to deliver payloads, nuclear or not, anywhere in the world.

Although Japan has maintained a strong anti-nuclear stance since the end of World War II, the tiny island nation has long been considered a "screwdriver's turn away" from being a nuclear power. They have a well funded ballistic missile program, battleships capable of delivering the payload and facilities to enrich the fuel. All that is needed is to assemble the parts, which—depending on whom you ask—would take as long as a month or as little as 24 hours.

CHECKPOINT F: A COUPLE OF TROOPS

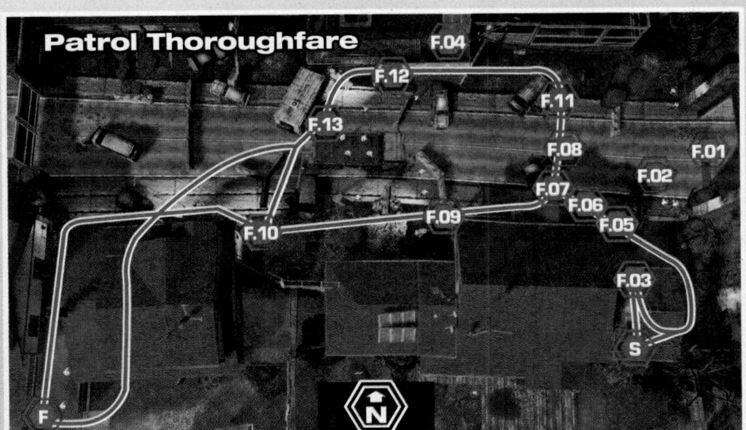

Enemies

Military Police (Scout) | Military Police | Sentry Tower

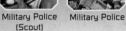

CAUTION

Don't be over-eager when you spot the enemy; let the transport truck pass through the gate, or it stops, lets out its troops, and you have further MPs to combat.

F.01

F.02

Intel in the area hasn't been as accurate as Hopper had hoped, and he expresses his frustration before Connor orders him to "stick to the plan." A truck with troops passes through the walled thoroughfare **[F.01]**. Stay in your hiding place without firing for a moment. Don't engage them, because you want to attack as few KPA forces as possible. When the gates close, begin to battle up the street. As the truck passes, you're left with around four enemy soldiers to dispatch in your immediate area **[F.02]**, and another high up on the balcony to the left (northwest).

Tactical Planning: Initial Contact

Threat Assessment: KPA Forces

Face at least 10 infantry and police forces from the KPA as you battle up the street. They are armed with their usual weapons (like the M4 Rifle, PWS Diablo SMG, SCAR-L Rifle, and T3AK Rifle). Of particular threat are foes dug in on upper balconies or windows of the structures on the opposite (north) side of the street. As you near the far (west) end of the street, expect an attack from a Sentry Tower, which you can't incapacitate yet.

Plan A: Fragging from Height

You can remain on the upper lean-to shed, which gives you more height than following your team to the sandbag defenses on the right (east). This allows you to lob a Frag Grenade at the four initial soldiers before they spread out **[F.03]**, and remove at least three of them without firing a shot.

Then quickly swing left, and target the foe on the upper balcony, just left of the telephone pole **[F.04]**. He's a particular nuisance if you don't catch him early, but he's easy to tag from this vantage point. Pick off any foes that appear, then rejoin your team to push up the street.

Plan B: Staying out of Sight

The other option is to follow your teammates around, and (ideally using a silenced weapon) start to take down the four troops in the immediate vicinity, as well as the foe on the opposite balcony, from your lower position **[F.05]**. Most of the forces are farther up the street to your left (west), so staying behind the sandbag crates is an excellent idea. Back up or flee to the left, staying behind cover, if a grenade is lobbed your way.

Tactical Planning: Street Combat

Plan A: Left Side of the Street

With initial threats abated, you must attack the main forces streaming down from the opposite end of the thoroughfare. You have at least 10 more kills to attempt, so remaining tucked in behind the sandbags is an excellent defensive posture **[F.06]**. It also allows you to cut down enemies encroaching your line-of-sight, such as foes stepping behind the burned-out car, or behind the van on the opposite verge. Be sure you prepare a melee attack (or SMG raking fire) for one or two KPA that may attempt to storm your position; dispatch them before they strike you down **[F.07]**.

There's no need to rush this, and impatience usually results in you becoming overly exposed and peppered with enemy fire. Instead, remain at the edge of the sandbag defenses and sidestep out to the right **[F.08]**, bringing down foes as they advance toward you, and lobbing a grenade if you see foes bunched together, or want to smoke out a foe behind the concrete defenses farther up the street. From here, you can choose to dash across to the right side, or continue up the left.

Assuming you push up the left, expect fewer cover opportunities, and a Sentry Tower gun targeting you as you progress **[F.09]**. Either step up to the trailer to the right, or dash to the porch light on the house to your left. From here you can take down the half-dozen or so KPA troops remaining here **[F.10]**. Another option is to dive into the open garage on the other side of the porch light, and use the inside cover to launch attacks from. Don't push too far up though, or you'll reach the next checkpoint.

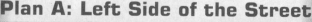

Plan B: Right Side Meet and Greet

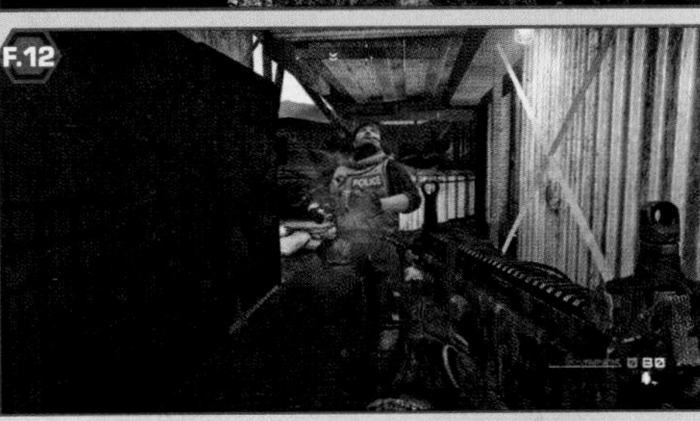

Between rounds of gunfire, you can shrug off enemy shots and sprint across to the opposite (north) side of the street, and hide behind the van **[F.11]**. Crouch down at the corner of the van, and start to drop KPA foes from up the street while your teammates push up along the left side. This helps split the KPA's fire, and allows you another angle from which to strike them. Beware of foes coming down along the covered defense corridor **[F.12]**; be sure to catch them before they overwhelm you.

Rushing up the left side of the road leaves you exposed, so an alternate route is to dash up through the covered corridor to the right, step left to avoid Sentry Tower fire, and hide behind a motor home. From here you have good cover and can mow down the half-dozen or so KPA troops milling about here **[F.13]**.

> **TIP** 영리한
>
> **No matter which route you take, be sure to double-check the upper windows and roofline for possible foes as you progress. Move on to the next checkpoint as soon as all the infantry troops in the street have been nullified. Before attempting the next objective, you may wish to gather weapons or ammo.**

Objective: Flank the Sentry Tower

CHECKPOINT G: FIGHT UP THE STREET

Backyard and Upper Street Defenses

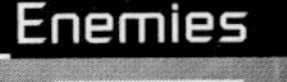

Enemies

Military Police (Scout)

Sentry Tower

Soldier

When you reach the alley between the houses on the left side of the street **[G.01]**, Connor yells about moving around to avoid the Sentry Tower by using a backyard. Mop up any stragglers before meeting up with Connor and Hopper. You may have entered the garage of the previous residence, and can reach your team from the backyard itself **[G.02]**, but be careful not to alarm another KPA group ensconced inside another house; you want the element of surprise.

NOTE 알아두세요

You're about to engage the enemy, and then stow your weapons when you reach the labor camp. Conserving ammunition or grenades isn't necessary, although don't be overly wasteful.

Objective: Destroy the Sentry Tower

Tactical Planning: Backyard Barbecue

Plan A: Hanging Back

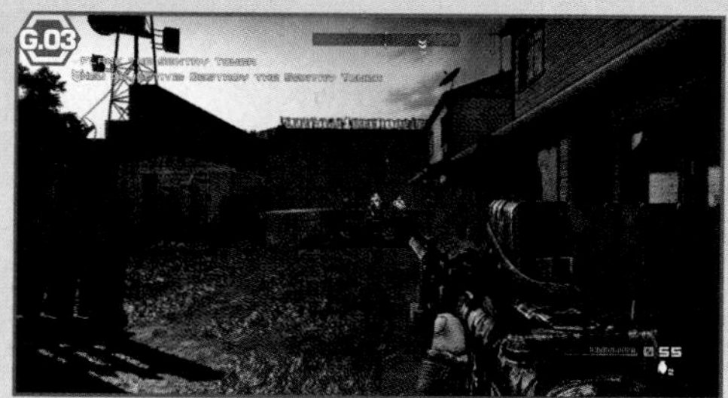

This is usually attempted from the gap in the fence from the backyard of the previous house. From this relatively defensive position **[G.03]**, lob in a grenade to soften up the quintet of enemy troops, and then carefully tag as many as you can from long range. You can easily dodge any incoming grenades, and use patience and sharpshooting to remove as many threats as you can see before rushing in.

Plan B: Rushing In

Whether or not you've engaged the troops, you can opt to rush in and bring the fight to the foes. Start by lobbing a grenade over the far fence **[G.04]**, and while the foes mill about, sprint diagonally to the left, heading for the open shed to the southwest **[G.05]**. From either entrance near the pile of tires on the near or far side of the shed, continue your culling. Connor yells that there's a foe at the second floor window, which is another target to acquire, but not instantly. Instead, keep in cover, and take down foes one at a time from the cover of the shed **[G.06]**, sweeping from left to right, before quickly stepping back behind

cover to ensure you aren't struck. With one or two stragglers left, drop the foe from the upper window **[G.07]**. Then focus on any remaining enemies behind the sandbags.

TIP 영리한

Once foes are defeated, check the dead-end side yard for a Unique Weapon on the barrel. It's a little out-of-the-way to be used in this combat, but grab it for later, because you're about to lose all your automatic weapons.

CAUTION 조심하다

Although you can creep up the right side of the backyard, and use the corrugated sheeting and fence as cover, the enemy is more difficult to hit from this position; the shed is a better bet than aiming for the gap in the final fence.

Unique Weapons Detail: 7/17

WEAPONS >>
Dragon Ice Pistol

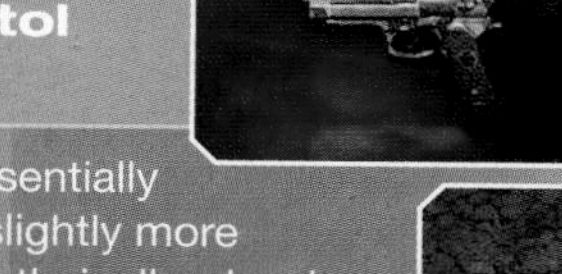

Essentially a slightly more aestheically-pleasing version of the regular pistol, this would normally be ignored. However, in a forth-coming clandestine skulk around the labor camp, a pistol becomes your only armament, so take it if you wish.

Tower Takedown

When all the foes behind the sandbags have been nullified, carefully edge into the house. One or two more KPA may still be inside this building, so concentrate on them, slowly securing the building **[G.08]** before moving around to the staircase. Ensure you have grenades on your person before you ascend the stairs (take some from Connor or Hopper if you're out), and duck as you reach the top **[G.09]**, moving to the cover beside the broken window in the middle of the wall.

With the mesh fence preventing you from taking out the Sentry Tower on the ground floor, quickly peer out of the middle upper window **[G.10]**, and step back if you're caught in the Sentry Tower's searchlight. When the light passes (use the broken window on the right to watch for the searchlight beam so you know it has passed your location) step up to the window, and lob a grenade down to the rear of the Sentry Tower, where indicated. Moments later, an accurate throw results in the tower falling **[G.11]**.

Objective: Enter the Labor Camp

Head back downstairs. Connor realizes the KPA will be mobilizing after your fireworks, so leap the porch fence, meeting up with Connor, and follow him and Hopper past the closed KPA gate **[G.12]**, and the "private property" sign. Drop down the service tunnel hole after Hopper.

CHECKPOINT H: ENTER THE CAMP

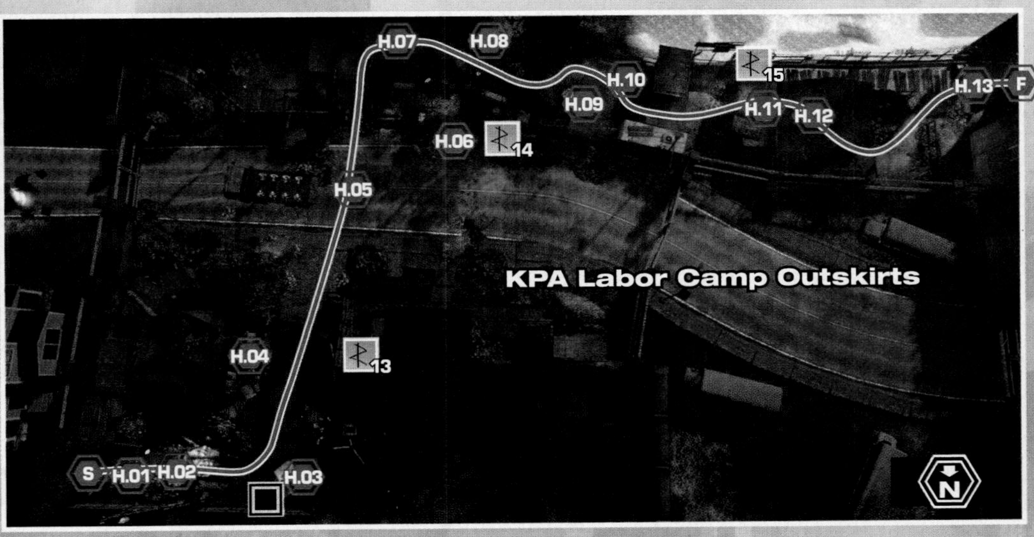

Blending In

The plan appears to be working; while the KPA send out armored trucks and troops to investigate your handiwork, the three of you enter the labor camp via the small connecting side tunnel **[H.01]**. Follow Hopper up the exit ladder. Connor disarms, and throws his, Hopper's, and your weapons into a trash bin, so you attract as little attention as possible **[H.02]**. You're only carrying a pistol now. Find Arnie by spreading out, and asking around.

Objective: Find Arnie

NOTE 알아두세요

You can simply follow Connor to Arnie's location, or do some optional investigating yourself, as detailed below:

As Connor watches, speak with the man pinning his desperate hopes to find his relatives on a wall of lost souls **[H.03]**.

KOREAN KODEX >> 3 (5/10)

On the right side of the wall of lost souls, at the start of the labor camp.

You can witness a heated discussion between Hopper and labor camp inhabitant tinkering on a circuit board **[H.04]**, before speaking to her directly and getting an earful of offensive comments. You're not well-liked, it seems.

You can follow Connor and Hopper up the steps of the raised viewing platform, or spend a few moments checking the immediate area. Step onto the road **[H.05]**, blocked by gates at each end. In-between the steps is El Rey **[H.06]**, a scum-bag dealer with a couple of customers lying comatose on makeshift bedding on either side of the street. You can converse (without much success) with all of them. But the main reason to check this area is for the two newspaper articles. Grab them before heading up the steps.

TIP 영리한

Just as with the inhabitants of Oasis, keep coming back to talk until there's no more to say.

HIDDEN HISTORY >> 13 (23/61)

Behind the clothesline, to the right of the house on the north side of the street, up the steps from the sleeping vagrant. Crouch to access it.

ANARCHY IN THE US AS NATIONAL GUARD FAILS TO RESTORE ORDER *7/7/2019*

Faced with a lack of food and a looming winter, many Americans have decided to take matters into their own hands. Promising food, clothing and protection, warring gangs have taken over many urban centers and continue to fight with elements from the National Guard.

Originally deployed to distribute aid and restore order, the National Guard has fallen under criticism for its perceived ineffectiveness. "We're simply stretched too thin," a spokesman for the Guard told me earlier today. "We're simply not equipped to deal with gang warfare on this scale. At any one time, there are multiple conflicts in a dozen cities going on simultaneously. We just can't deal with them all effectively."

The president called his staff into an emergency session earlier this week, the main topic at hand being the deployment of military personnel into the hardest-hit cities. Although this action would violate the Posse Comitatus Act that has stood since the end of the Civil War, many believe that a broad deployment of the US military inside the country is the only way order can be restored.

HIDDEN HISTORY >> 14 (24/61)

Among the rubble and refuse to the right of El Rey's patch, against the mesh fence.

KOREAN OFFICIALS PROVIDE DETAILS OF IRAQ OPERATIONS

10/18/2020

Korean Special Forces have been participating in operations in northern Iraq, working side-by-side with the Iranian Coalition to help restore order. In Farah province, Koreans detained a group of suspected insurgents based on information provided by the ISS. The force was able to locate a cache of mortar shells and a large quantity of bomb making components.

Using American-designed V-22 Osprey tilt-rotor aircraft, Iranian and Korean forces captured two Iraqi insurgent commanders. As the aircraft approached the target compound, the two men attempted to escape on foot but were captured without the use of violence.

Korean forces also conducted several precision air strike operations, targeting an arms dealer who was supplying the insurgency with rockets and bomb-making materials. After careful planning to minimize collateral damages, Korean Special Operatives called the air strikes on a series of targets. The Korean military uses the Shenyang J-5 unmanned aerial vehicle to deliver airstrikes, which is a copy of the American MQ-9 Reaper.

Labor Camp Overlook

Connor and Hopper survey the main camp from this vantage point, overlooking a football field now filled with dilapidated shacks and an air of despair punctuated by KPA transport helicopters and piercing stadium lights **[H.07]**.

Pass by "Steve" and his cohort, who (if you speak with them) mentions the exploits of the Resistance in a voice that's a little too loud for this clandestine operation **[H.08]**.

Through the gate and down the steps is a campfire, and a labor camp worker who doesn't take kindly to Hopper's Korean nationality **[H.09]**. Hopper keeps walking to avoid further confrontation, and the workers don't want to speak with you when you try to talk to them.

Around the corner, Connor's coat is tugged by an emaciated child desperate and hungry **[H.10]**. Connor pushes him aside with a callousness you had previously only suspected of him. The child shuffles away, disappearing over a refuse pile.

Arrival at Arnie's

Follow Hopper and Connor as they reach a concrete structure and request the presence of Arnie. When the guard responds with a less-than-pleasant retort, Connor knees him in the happy-sack, and finishes with a head-butt **[H.11]**. Arnie quickly calms the situation down **[H.12]**, beckoning you in and agreeing to lead you to the beacons and the bus depot, but only if you follow his orders precisely. Leave the guard groaning, and keep up with the team.

Objective: Follow Arnie

While Connor explains the virtues of Arnie's teenage daughter arming herself for the current predicament, follow the three of them toward the turnstiles of Secure Area 1 **[H.13]**. Before heading through, check behind you for another newspaper report.

HIDDEN HISTORY >> 15 (25/61)

At the opposite (east) end of the entrance to Security Area 1, on a table by the fence overlooking the main camp.

GREATER KOREAN REPUBLIC GROWS

4/7/2021

Malaysia became the fifth country to join Kim Jong-un's "Greater Korean Republic" on Tuesday, joining Indonesia, the Philippines, Thailand and Korea. The Prime Minister of Malaysia joined Kim Jong-un at the GKR Parliament Building in Pyongyang for the flag-raising ceremony. The ceremony included the national anthem of Malaysia and a signing ceremony, followed by a lavish banquet. Over the next several days, representatives are expected to focus on trade talks between member nations as well as a decision on whether to allow Cambodia and Vietnam to join the Republic.

The GKR is an economic and military alliance with the mission of growing the strength of the East Asian region through a united monetary policy and a central military command. The GKR Central Bank, the economic headquarters of the Republic, is based in Seoul and is tasked with setting and enforcing monetary policy among the member states of the GKR. The military capital, the GKR Strategic Command, is located in Pyongyang and is responsible for coordinating defense and training of the militaries of all member states.

Push the turnstile open, and enter a holding area for the prisoners, before they're shipped to the shale mines. Connor is a little suspicious about the lack of security, but Arnie reassures him that he's taken care of it. That certainly appears to be the case as you step through the second turnstile, and you're grabbed by the jacket as Arnie double-crosses the team **[H.14]**!

In the haze of combat that follows, KPA forces storm the area, grabbing both Connor and Hopper. Time seems to slow down as Connor grabs one of the KPA's submachine guns and turns it on Arnie. Splattered in his brain fluid and gore, you have just enough time to turn your pistol on two more KPA hurriedly charging you from the stairs on the left **[H.15]**. As the red mist fades, you find yourself in the middle of a one-sided gunfight, with the odds stacked heavily against you.

CHECKPOINT I: ARNIE

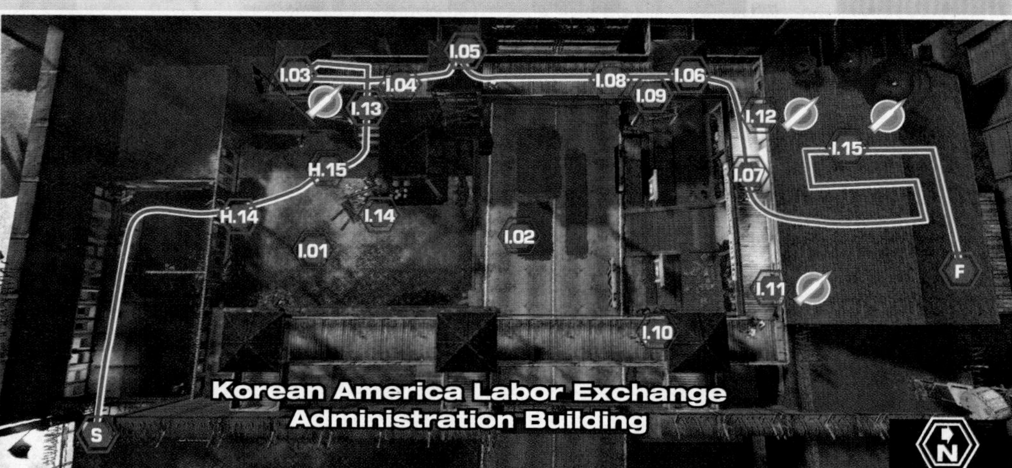

Enemies

Arnie

Soldier (Scout)

Soldier

Soldier (Heavy)

Objective: Clear the Administrative Building

CAUTION 조심하다

You have limited time and only quick-witted decisions to save you and your team. Be certain of your actions, and learn what to do, and what not to attempt:

Tactical Planning: Outgunned, Not Outmatched

Threat Assessment: KPA Checkpoint Forces

Enemies are both numerous and aggressive. Note the four foes along the platform above and behind the initial stairwell, and more teeming out of the Labor Exchange building at the far end of the courtyard. Expect a couple of foes inside the structure itself, once the exterior balconies have been cleared out; which is your next plan!

Plan A: Overwhelmed and Under Fire

The only way to secure this area is by ascending the steps to the left of Connor and Hopper (who are pinned down behind a concrete barrier). Other options, such as ineffectively shooting your pistol up at the foes on the walkways from down below **[I.01]**, or charging the admin building from the ground **[I.02]**, usually result in a quick death. However, if you're more cunning with your hiding spots, you can attack between floors; see Plan C.

Plan B: All Along the Walkway

This is the "usual" way to storm the admin building: Scale the stairs as quickly as you can, and face fire from your right (across on the opposite walkway), as well as a soldier firing down ahead of you **[I.03]**. Quickly dispatch him with your pistol, and as he drops, grab either his weapon or one of the two identical rifles propped against the reinforced section of walkway (with the extra metal fencing) at the top of the stairs. Alternately, take one of the M4 Rifles, and then cut down the nearest foe.

WEAPONS >>

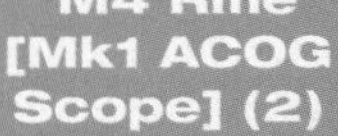

M4 Rifle [Mk1 ACOG Scope] (2)

Propped against the reinforced walkway at the top of the stairs.

TIP 영리한

The zoomed scope of the M4 Rifle, coupled with quick bursts of well-aimed gunfire, is the key to targeting and removing all nearby KPA threats during any of these three plans.

At this point, remain behind the reinforced fence to your right, so foes can't wing you from the opposite side of the walkway. Train your aim (remember to zoom and fire) at the advancing foes heading toward you from the admin building's upper exit to the north. Crouch down, so no gunfire from the right hits you. Now quickly lay waste to the foes **[I.04]**.

TIP 영리한

Should you receive a grenade, immediately back up, diving down the stairs if the grenade lands too close to avoid on the walkway. Or sprint forward and step left into one of two alcoves on the left side of the walkway.

During a lull in the bullets whizzing at you from the north end of the walkway, head toward the admin building, and then immediately step into the first alcove **[I.05]**. Stay crouched, and deal with any threats to the north; expect foes streaming out of the exit, using the guard tower supports and alcoves to the left as cover, and return fire, quickly zooming in and dropping them **[I.06]**. As you step over the bodies of those you killed first, swap out your pistol for one of their more rapid-fire weapons, and use that as backup to the M4.

TIP 영리한

Keep a constant check on your grenades. You begin with none, but you may automatically pick up one (or more) as you check each enemy corpse you've dispatched. Should you find a grenade, you can easily (and expertly) lob it across to the four soldiers on the opposite walkway, and remove them with a single projectile strike.

Halfway along the walkway, begin to tackle the foes firing on your teammates (and you) along the eastern walkway opposite. Although you can crouch by the tower fencing, you're prone to more attacks from KPA coming up from the north admin building. Instead, stay in the alcove, firing across the walkway and strike the foes from long range **[I.07]**; if any KPA head up from the north, you'll see them round the corner (or react to them with periodic checks to your left), and can melee or shoot them before they do the same to you **[I.08]**.

Continue with this plan until you've exhausted the enemy infantry, leaving only two foes within the building. They are firing at Connor and Hopper from inside the building, and there are two ways to take them down. The first way is to lean over the side of the walkway, and aim a zoomed shot at the foe, removing them easily **[I.09]**. Then repeat this from the opposite walkway (that you haven't been on yet), aiming at the foe dug in on the opposite (western) side of the building **[I.10]**.

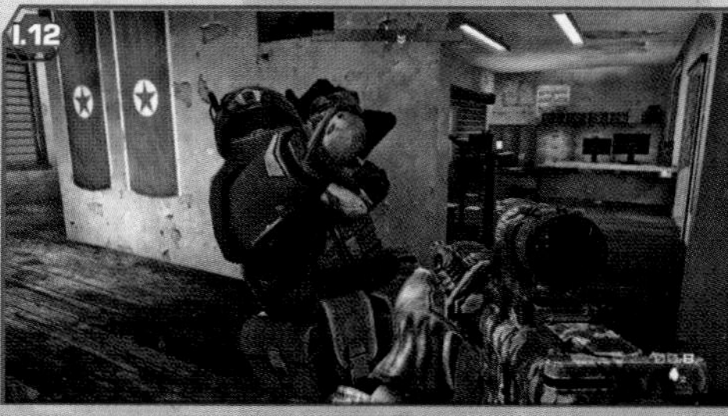

Or, you can enter the building, switching to an SMG if you wish, and head halfway down the stairs, quickly looking down and left and removing the first KPA threat near the computer desk **[I.11]**. This alerts the other foe, who is inside the open doorway at the bottom of the stairs, on your right (west) **[I.12]**. Quick shots or a melee strike ends his life before he does the same to you. This secures the admin building.

Plan C: Halfway up the Stairway

A slightly longer possible method of clearing the area in and around the admin building is possible once you've scaled the stairs and acquired the M4 Rifle. Bring down the first foe close to the weapons cache, before retreating halfway down the stairway, and crouch so you're not struck by bullets coming in from the building itself **[I.13]**.

Now you can quickly dispatch the foes on the far walkway, before intermittently wiping out the enemies pouring out of the top floor of the admin structure. Remember to check for foes coming down the steps to your right (there's usually one early on), and then continue to snipe from this protective position, bringing down both the foes inside the building, and then emerging and tackling any stragglers on the walkways from the courtyard below **[I.14]**, where Arnie double-crossed you.

CAUTION 조심하다

This is more dangerous, as foes do make the journey around the walkway and down the stairwell, so be vigilant when you're down on the courtyard. Also, you need to dash back up and along the walkway, as the admin building entrance isn't accessible until you enter from the upper floor.

TIP 영리한

Before you go, search the corpses of the two foes who were firing from the doorway; they were carrying an M249 LMG. The Unique T3AK is of particular note:

Unique Weapons Detail: 8/17

WEAPONS >>

Swamp T3AK Rifle

[Mk 2 Holo Scope] [Grenade Launcher]

This rapid-fire rifle has an excellent scope and boasts a grenade attachment. Remember to switch between regular bullets and grenades depending on the forthcoming situation!

WEAPONS >>

M249 LMG (2)

On the bodies of the fallen KPA guards, inside the administration building.

❯ Objective: Retrieve the Beacons

Aside from some translations and a wanted poster of Connor, there are limited items inside the admin building, with the exception of the beacons on a computer desk on the west side of the building **[I.15]**. Grab them as Connor radios in to Rianna, who has some good news about Boone (he'll pull through), and the next plan; to exit the building, and locate the baseball field.

❯ Objective: Cut Through the Baseball Field

CHECKPOINT J: GOT THE BEACONS

Atrocities on the Mound

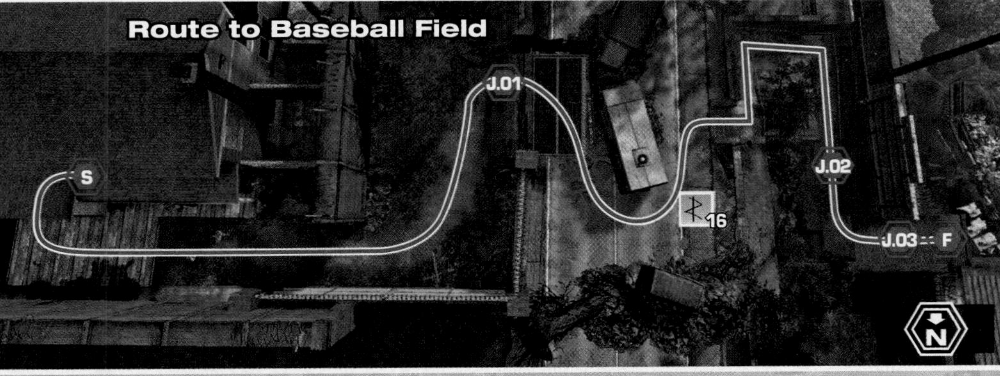

After grabbing the beacons, proceed along the unkempt streets of cracked concrete and earth, as Connor fills you in on the plan to attach the beacons to KPA convoy trucks, and hijack them for their jet fuel; and you'll be piloting the helicopter when the hijack takes place. But first, head to a corrugated metal fence that Connor kicks apart **[J.01]**.

An uneasy gloom shrouds the baseball field in the distance as you round the corner of a blocked road. Pick up the next news item on the pathway, and then follow the concrete stairs down to where Hopper kneels, peering around a corner. Connor has gone on ahead to investigate the sound of digging equipment **[J.02]**....

HIDDEN HISTORY >> 16 (26/61)

On the path near the minivan road blockade, between the admin building and the baseball field.

5/6/2024

NORTH KOREA LAUNCHES FIRST GROUP OF NEXT-GEN GPS SATELLITES

Kim Jong-un joined the heads of state from the Greater Korean Republic member countries at the Kagoshima Space Center on Kyushu Island in Japan to observe the launch of an M-6 rocket bearing the first of many "Starry Messenger" class GPS satellites. Meant to replace the US military's aging GPS system, the launch marks Korea's first foray into space travel.

Many countries have begun to work with the Koreans to supply the parts and materials necessary to create the network of satellites that will form the backbone of the system. "GPS was one of the greatest accomplishments of the United States," a spokesman for the Korean Space Program said. "And like the Americans we want to share this technology with the world in the hopes that it will improve the lives of all and help bring new light to the waning global economy."

After massive defense cutbacks and ongoing internal turmoil, the US was forced to stop supporting the GPS system that it created, an advanced system which decayed rapidly without the stream of financial support necessary to keep it afloat. The system is now starting to collapse, with many high-profile satellites crashing into the sea over the past year.

Connor and Hopper can't quite believe what they're seeing. A bulldozer has scooped up the twisted, putrid remains of dozens of executed Americans, and is dropping them into huge pits dug around the field. While Hopper kneels agog, Connor is consumed by rage **[J.03]**, and fires into the field, alerting the KPA troops to your position. Two Sentry Towers activate, meaning a dash across the field is both dangerous and foolish. But the KPA must pay!

Objective: Cut Through the Baseball Field

CHECKPOINT K: NOSEBLEED SECTION

Enemies

Soldier (Scout)

Soldier (Heavy)

Soldier

Sentry Tower

Objective: Destroy the Sentry Tower

Tactical Planning: Behind the Bleachers

Threat Assessment: KPA Population Management Forces

This is the largest concentration of KPA forces you've faced. Four to six squads appear at various sections as you traverse the baseball field's perimeter toward two Sentry Towers to the north: your final destination. Slow, methodical clearing is recommended over running and gunning.

Plan A: Connor's Carnage

Connor is a loose cannon—almost literally—as he indiscriminately rakes the field with assault rifle fire until the two Sentry Towers activate. Although you can attempt to tag enemy troops as they cross the field **[K.01]**, you risk being struck by Sentry Tower fire. However, a well-aimed grenade (ideally from your T3AK's attachment) can remove two or three threats before you enact Plan B.

CAUTION 조심하다

Foolishly sprinting onto the bleachers, into the field, or moving around in front of these structures allows the Sentry Towers to easily cut you down. Consult Plan B instead.

Plan B: Behind the Bleachers

While Connor continues to believe yelling and compromising your position is the key to success, follow the more measured Hopper, and sprint along the alley behind the bleachers **[K.02]**, to the viewing tower behind the batting cage, and stop behind either of the small sections of fence cover. Expect initial KPA infantry along the perimeter wall, and around the left side of the next bleacher as you face west. Bring these foes down quickly **[K.03]**, before heading behind the next bleacher.

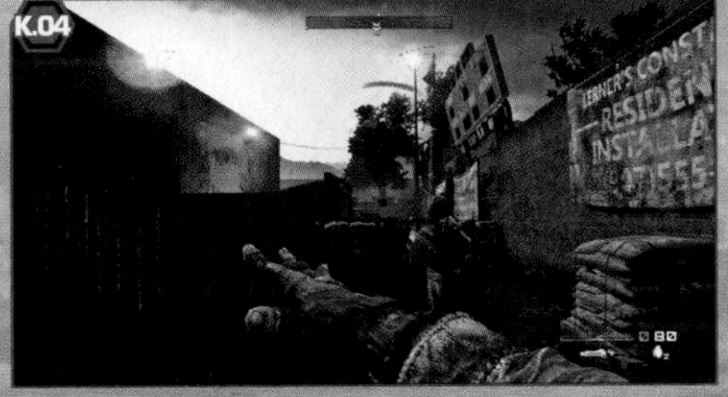

Begin an attack on around half a dozen foes, looking for grenade-lobbing (or punting from your T3AK) opportunities if the foes haven't spread out yet **[K.04]**. Remain behind cover, sidestep out and quickly target (optionally zoom-targeting) an enemy, and drop them with short, sharp bursts.

Edge forward to the next cover spot (fencing or sandbags) and repeat this process **[K.05]**. Back up if a grenade is lobbed your way.

Time your sprint between the bleachers so you're not spotted by the Sentry Towers, although there's a slight delay due to distance. Combat continues in exactly the same manner as you cross behind a final bleacher, lobbing a grenade in if you can catch more than one foe in the explosion **[K.06]**, and clearing the area ahead of foes from behind cover before advancing. Be sure nothing survives before you reach the far end of the last bleacher **[K.07]**. You're now about to attack foes at the corner of the field before turning south.

Plan C: In Front of the Bleachers

Once you reach the building behind the batting cage, you can optionally take your life into your hands, waiting for the Sentry Tower searchlights to swing away from your position, and then sprint toward the path between the dugout huts and the bleachers **[K.08]**. Dive and crouch behind this cover (if you make it; you're likely to be winged by the Sentry Towers), and then sprint behind the huts and cover on your left, with the bleachers on your right. It is now possible to try the following:

Pause between the final bleachers and mow down the enemies attacking Hopper and Connor, to your right (north) **[K.09]**.

Head to the front corner of the final bleacher, and gun down foes near the two parked buses (Checkpoint L).

Circle around and attack the foes behind the bleachers from the rear.

All plans are incredibly dangerous, but possible with enough luck and chutzpah.

CHECKPOINT L: GROUND RULE DOUBLE

Enemies

Soldier (Scout)

Soldier (Heavy)

Soldier

Sentry Tower

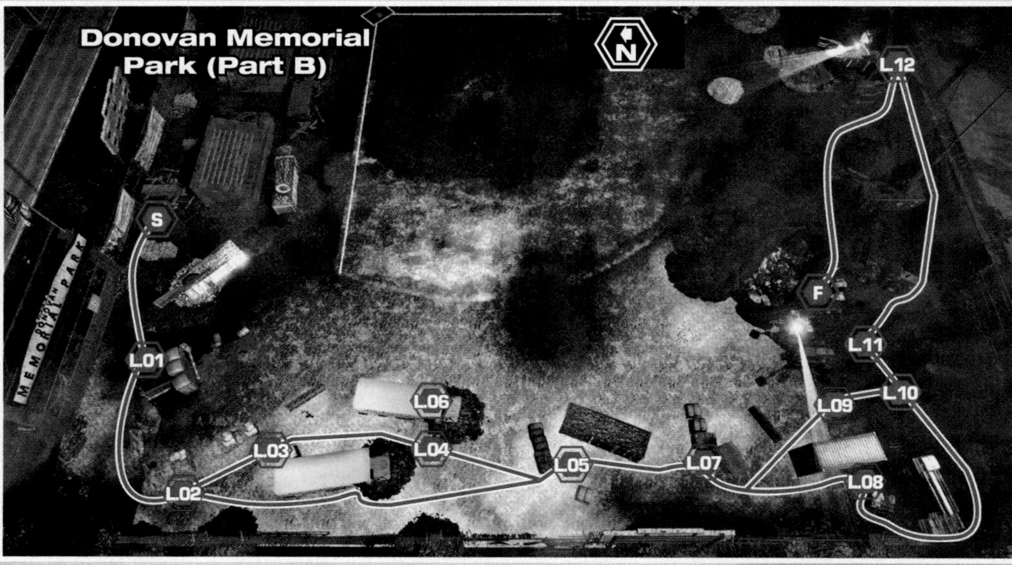

Tactical Planning: Behind the Buses

Combat continues with a similar pace and danger all the way up the field from north to south as you encroach closer toward the two Sentry Towers, mopping up the remaining KPA forces. Slow but methodical takedowns are favored, with a constant vigilance regarding the Sentry Towers' searchlights and auto-cannon aiming.

Plan: Beeline for the Buses

Step from the last bleacher and move toward the chemical toilets and variety of barricades and fencing in the corner of the field. Expect three to four enemy soldiers in this area. You can elect to remain at a distance **[L.01]**, allowing you a good vantage point

to take down all the foes from long range. The advantage here is you can aim for the foe inside one of the school buses, without needing to deal with him later.

CAUTION 조심하다

This is a better plan than rushing the area and moving around to the buses [L.02], as the enemy and the Sentry Towers can both locate and fire on you.

TIP 영리한

Concrete barriers behind the buses can be destroyed, which makes them less ideal for cover. Always keep something metal between you and the roving searchlights of the Sentry Towers, or face a quick death.

Approach the buses **[L.03]**. The one on the right may still have an enemy inside; fire through the open rear of the vehicle to remove the threat, before moving up to the front of the buses. You have slightly more room to maneuver if you stand between both buses, but you're closer to the Sentry Towers.

Plan A: Off the Buses

When you reach the front of either bus, stop and take stock of the foes across the field, nestled behind the cargo containers and sandbags **[L.04]**. These are normally a nuisance, but each time you sidestep out to cut them down, you risk additional damage from the Sentry Towers. Therefore, use nimble sidesteps, focusing on quick bursts of well-aimed gunfire to tackle a single foe at a time **[L.05]**, and then duck back behind cover. Lob a grenade to soften the foes up, too. Back away from incoming grenades.

Plan B: On the Buses

What was possibly a good idea at one stage turns into a motorized mausoleum if you attempt to board either of the buses and use the height it offers to your advantage **[L.06]**. Although you can aim down on the foes, you're simply too exposed and don't have enough room to move or dodge if you're inside this vehicle. Hide behind the driver's seat to avoid being peppered with Sentry Tower fire, and return to ground level when you can.

Plan A (Continued): Cornering the KPA

Rush to the cover on the right side of the metal containers, and then deal with the remaining infantry in the southwest corner of the field. Rushing forward too quickly is dangerous, because there may be three or four foes, plus the ever-present Sentry Towers. Instead, sprint to the pallets **[L.07]**, dropping any foes you see. You can let Connor deal with the enemies, or move to the next metal containers and finish off the foes behind cover here **[L.08]**, and on your left.

Plan B (Continued): Ignoring the KPA

Or, you can leave the KPA to your teammates to deal with, and make a dangerous and manic run from the pallets, around the left side of the containers, toward the bulldozer and the Sentry Towers **[L.09]**. From here, you can complete your objective, or outflank any KPA in the corner from this area **[L.10]**. However, you're likely to face Sentry Tower fire, so hide in front of the bulldozer, pallet stacks, or Sentry Tower itself. This is dangerous and non-methodical, but it works sometimes.

Sentry Tower Takedown

You've had practice destroying Sentry Towers before, so these last two automated monstrosities shouldn't be difficult to tackle. Use the bulldozer or pallet stacks to shield you from the second one, and lob a grenade into its rear **[L.11]**. You can also use one of your T3AK's grenades if you have any left. For the second Sentry Tower, sprint to cover behind the bulldozer, then the KPA communications trailer, and finally bring the final target down **[L.12]**. Everybody's dead; Connor is happy now.

Objective: Regroup with Hopper and Connor

CHECKPOINT M: WHY THIS WAS NECESSARY

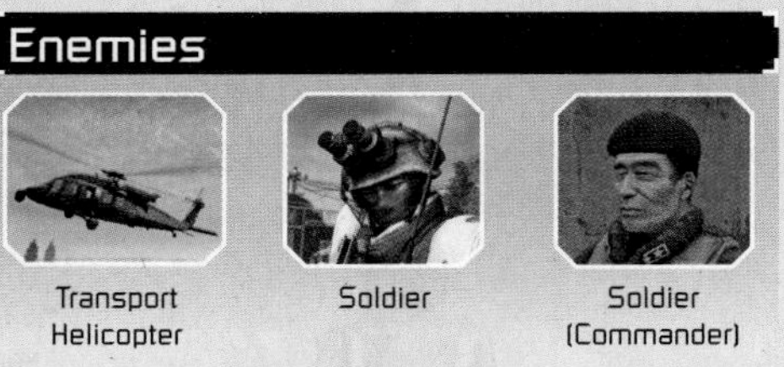

Tactical Planning: Between the Corpses

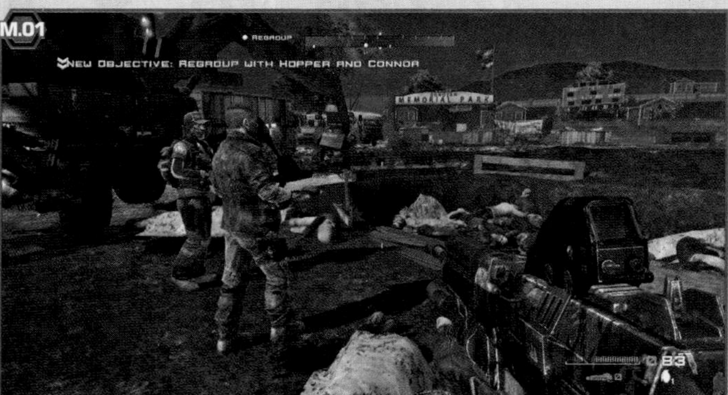

With both Sentry Towers destroyed, rejoin Hopper and Connor as they look over the pit of decaying bodies with a sense of shocked disgust. Your team's malaise fades with the sounds of rotor blades **[M.01]**; a trio of KPA transport helicopters is incoming! Connor makes the decision to hide, and unfortunately chooses the corpse pit....

Objective: Hide in the Mass Grave

CAUTION 조심하다

Refusing to drop down with the dead means being raked with gunfire from the KPA choppers, which eventually kills you.

While Connor orders Hopper to lie down, and moves the dead away to cover his teammate **[M.02]**, the choppers begin to descend. Drape a cold, dead arm across you, while the three of you brave the mental torment, the flies, and the smell as one of the helicopters touches down. KPA troops come over, peer into the pit, and begin indiscriminately shooting **[M.03]**. Satisfied that their inhumane plan has been effective, they return to the chopper, just as Rianna radios in. It looks like you're going to be late for that rendezvous....

Mettle of Honor

Award	Rating	Trophy
Freedom	10	Bronze

Completing this mission earns you this particular reward. Difficulty level, or how many times you restarted a checkpoint, do not matter.

Mettle of Honor

Award	Rating	Trophy
Freedom—Guerrilla	25	Bronze

Completing this mission earns you this individual reward. However, you must complete this on the hardest difficulty.

Mettle of Honor

Award	Rating	Trophy
Iron Man—Freedom	25	Bronze

Completing this mission without dying once or restarting a checkpoint earns you this reward. Lessen the difficulty if you're having problems completing this task.

MISSION SELECT »03 »FIRE SALE

Resistance cells are preparing an assault on the abandoned TigerDirect.com®, which now serves as a KPA fuel depot. The tankers will only be in town for a few hours and, if the squad hopes to capture them later, the beacons have to be in place tonight.

 **HIDDEN HISTORY** » 8 (34/61 total)

 **KOREAN KODEX** » 1 (6/10 total)

 **UNIQUE WEAPON** » 0 (8/17 total)

CHECKPOINT A: THE CALM BEFORE THE STORM

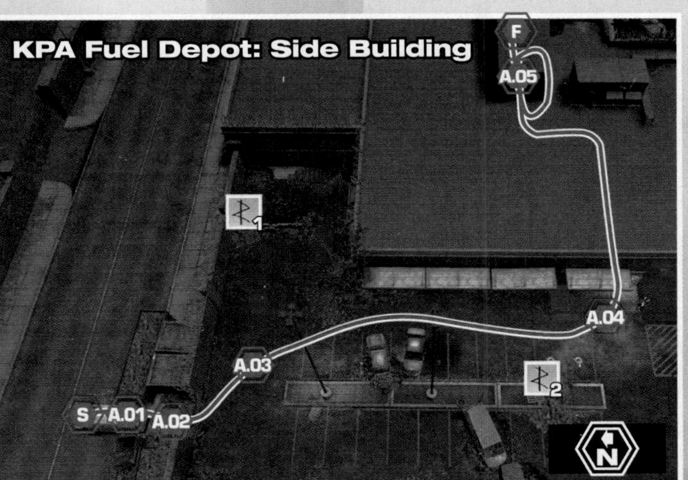

WEAPONS >> M4 Rifle [Mk1 HOLO Scope]

WEAPONS >> M110 Sniper

WEAPONS >> Fragmentation Grenade (4)
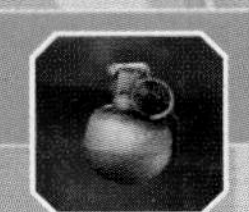

You begin the mission with these weapons.

"White Phosphorous? Worse than Napalm."

Friendlies

Connor

Rianna

Hopper

Resistance

Enemies

Soldier

You clamber inside the back of the Resistance-secured van, nodding to Hopper in the driver's seat. Rianna tells Boone to let the wound he suffered heal, and gives him a hug. Boone offers some words of encouragement before closing the rear doors **[A.01]**. Hopper pulls up to the wall outside the KPA fuel depot while Rianna and Connor have a little talk about the dangers of white phosphorous. Outside the van, Connor tells Rianna that you and she should be covering the ground attack while Connor clears the way for Goliath **[A.02]**.

Objective: Follow Rianna

Drop down onto the parking lot. Rianna meets a Resistance member who tells you the exterior of the overlook building is secure, but there may be troops inside. Check the area for two news pick-ups, and then follow the Resistance member (and Rianna) past the car wrecks **[A.03]**, and more Resistance forces checking on a corpse. Scour the area for a news pick-up, and approach the door Rianna is standing near **[A.04]**. Don't step too far to the right (south) around the side of the building, or the KPA may spot you, and you don't want the operation going "tits up."

HIDDEN HISTORY >> 1 (27/61)

In the small parking lot where Rianna meets the first Resistance member, in refuse behind a barricade, northeast corner alcove.

6/3/2009

KIM JONG-IL APPOINTS SUCCESSOR

Kim Jong-il, the eccentric and brutal leader of North Korea has officially appointed his son, Kim Jong-un, as his intended successor. Kim Jong-un was born in North Korea and attended the International School of Berne, where he became friends with Americans attending the school and became fluent in several western languages. Kim Jong-un attended the school under a pseudonym and was described as "shy." He was an avid skier and player of basketball, and reportedly idolized American sports icon Michael Jordan. It is unclear when Kim Jong-un will take power, but reports of his father's failing health indicate that it may be sooner rather than later.

HIDDEN HISTORY >> 2 (28/61)

In the small parking lot where Rianna meets the first Resistance member, in refuse in a small pile by the handicapped parking spaces.

3/16/22014

KOREAN INTEGRATION CONTINUES

After 3 years of intensive talks, the first steps towards integrating the economies and militaries of the two Koreas have begun. The plan calls for an opening of the border between the two nations, a dismantling of the Demilitarized Zone, and an audit of the prisoners in North Korea's notorious labor camps. North Korea's new leader, Kim Jong-un has been proactive in releasing prisoners from his father's system of labor camps and allowing officials from Amnesty International and the Red Cross to examine both the prisoners and their living conditions.

"What we found in those camps was both horrifying and encouraging," said Dr. Steven Haldeman, an American doctor working with the international organization Doctors Without Borders. "The fact that so many lived in such terrible conditions for so long is truly horrifying. But the fact that aggressive steps are being taken to fix the problem fills one with hope." Haldeman is part of an international aid group working with the UN to provide relief to the bedraggled, but recovering nation.

Follow Rianna into the building, and down a long corridor leading to a stairwell, and follow Rianna up two floors. You don't have access to your weapons yet (you're running silently at the moment). Wait (anywhere you wish) as Rianna quickly grabs and strangles a KPA guard, throttling him, dropping him to the floor, and cracking his windpipe **[A.05]**. Those executions never get any easier.

CHECKPOINT B: THE ASSAULT

Friendlies

Resistance

Enemies

Soldier (Scout)

Soldier (Heavy)

Soldier

Soldier (RPG)

A Hunk of Burning Love

Rianna finishes off the KPA guard, and carefully opens the door to the roof overlook. Quickly inspect the area from your vantage point **[B.01]**, noting three guard owers (one northeast, one east, and one southeast), and the discount computer store to the south, which is your destination. Also note the Hooters restaurant to the southwest. A few seconds ater, drop down to join Rianna on the concrete lip of the overlook and pick up the newspaper near the sandbags. Connor checks in, and starts to roll the vehicle in.

HIDDEN HISTORY >> 3 (29/61)

On the concrete corner of the overlook, in the southwest corner near the sandbags and barbed wire.

1/17/2013

KIM JONG-UN RECEIVES NOBEL PRIZE

North Korea's young president, Kim Jong-un, won the Nobel Peace Prize on Friday for his efforts to end the Korean War and bring a lasting peace to the Korean Peninsula. The result of more than a year of intensive negotiations, the governments of the two sister nations were finally able to carve out a peace treaty and have reportedly begun discussing re-unification under what has been described as a "one nation, two-system solution." Born in North Korea and educated in Switzerland, Jong-un cites his overseas education and exposure to the west as the driving force behind his desire to see the reconciliation of the two nations. North and South Korea have been divided for nearly 70 years, and for his efforts Kim Jong-un is being hailed as "The Great Unifier."

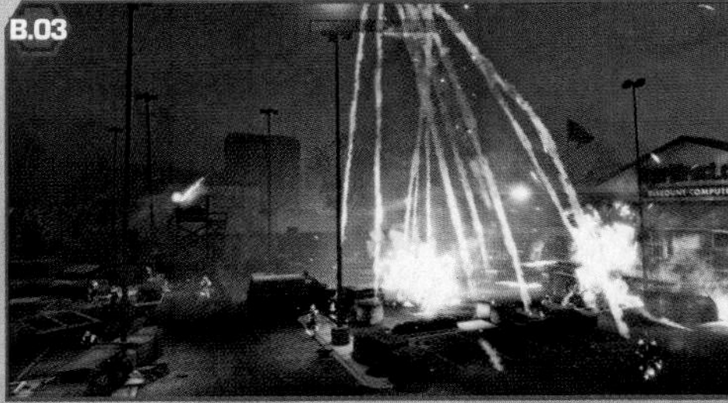

Check the gates to your left (northeast). Seconds later, with an Elvis tune blaring, the van smashes through the gates, and continues into the sandbag-filled parking lot, crashing into a barricade. Moments later, the KPA swarms the van **[B.02]**. They're just beginning to think it's a trap when Hopper launches the first white phosphorous. The missile arcs up into the sky, and then splits apart, raining molten death down on the KPA below. The parking lot erupts into a hellish blaze **[B.03]**.

Objective: Engage the Enemies

Plan A: Camping at the Overlook

Bring out your M110 Sniper, and immediately check the northeast and east towers, as enemies with RPGs may be still alive on them. Drop both those foes first **[B.04]**, or face a barrage from them. Then continue your sharpshooting, quickly tagging KPA foes in the parking lot, and dropping them amid the confusion. Watch for:

Your own teammates, who are storming through the north gate, moving from left to right **[B.05]**. They're the ones not wearing KPA uniforms and helmets, and are easily distinguishable.

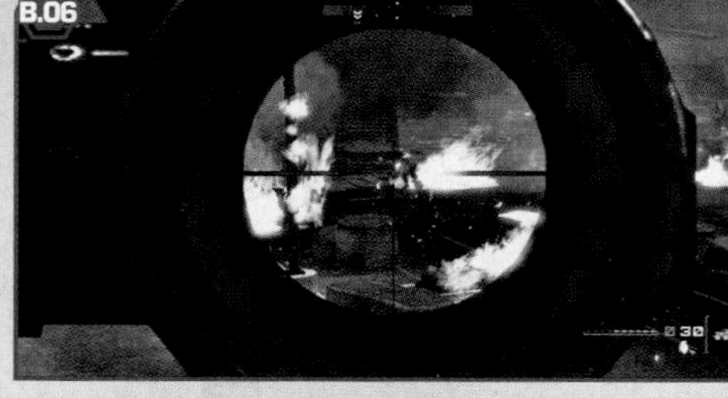

Enemies swarming up from the right (south), up the middle of the parking lot **[B.06]**. Bring them down with more well-aimed shots.

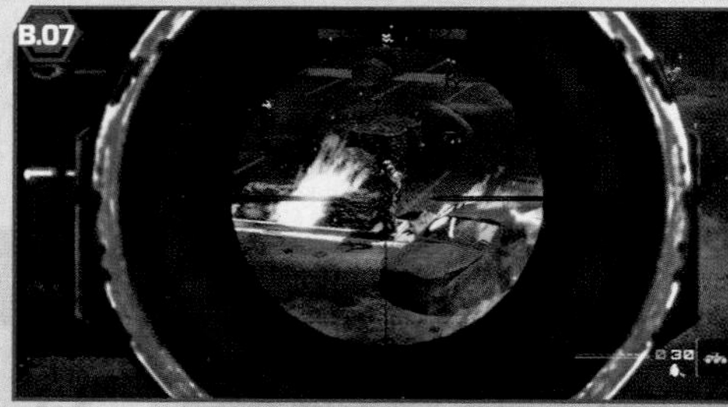

Foes milling around at closer ranges, below you **[B.07]**. Some may spot you, so concentrate on those first, then lengthen your range. Continue to bring the pain on any foes you see behind the partial cover of the vehicles or sandbags.

The combat continues; you can let Rianna get some shots off **[B.08]**, and sit back and tag any foes you may have missed in the guard towers. KPA takedowns continue until Hopper lights up the wrong part of the sky.

Plan B: Other Ordnance

Although it is recommended that you wield the M110, you also have an M4 Rifle, which you can switch to at any time **[B.09]**. It is quicker for mopping up closer enemies on the ground. Far-away foes, such as those in the guard towers, are harder to hit. You also have grenades, but lobbing them in usually isn't recommended (unless you catch a group running up from the discount computer warehouse); save them for later.

NOTE 알아두세요

Or you can save your ammo, and simply wait for Hopper's next salvo. This doesn't help your team out much, though.

Mettle of Honor

Award	Rating	Trophy
Mercy	10	Bronze

During this checkpoint, attempt to shoot five foes who are on fire before they die on their own. Quickly choose only those enemies close to the van, just after the white phosphorous explodes.

Mettle of Honor

Award	Rating	Trophy
Let 'em Burn	10	Bronze

During this checkpoint, don't shoot any KPA soldiers who are panicked and on fire.

Oh Shit! Misfire! Misfire!

Hopper's next communication is somewhat troubling, as he launches a salvo without proper trajectory aiming **[B.10]**. The missile flies too far to the west, and explodes directly above your head! Rianna screams as white phosphorous explodes and coats the area around you in roaring fire. You leap from the overlook **[B.11]**, and land with a thud on the boiling tarmac.

CHECKPOINT C: HOT RAIN

Friendlies

Member

Enemies

Soldier

Z-10 Chimera

Objective: Follow Rianna

Everything's Pretty Far from Okay

You see Rianna frantically shouting at you to move **[C.01]**, and head for the guard tower. All around you, the parking lot is ablaze in thick, liquid fire. Because the white phosphorous exploded directly on top of you both, you escaped a deadly coating. However, other Resistance members are not so lucky. Run east in a discombobulated fashion, passing a screaming Resistance member staggering to a fiery demise **[C.02]**.

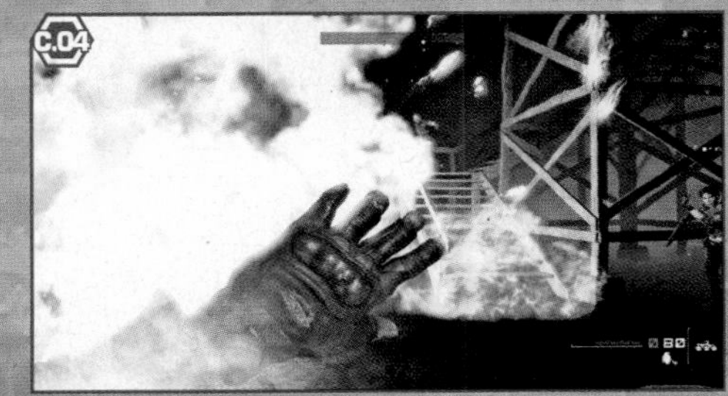

You pass another burning man, as Hopper asks what's happened, and whether everything is okay. Your blazing ex-colleagues and an exploding vehicle stop you both from answering **[C.03]**. Pick yourself up (again), and run east, passing another doomed friend, watching another vehicle detonate close by **[C.04]**. Pass Rianna as she frantically beckons you up the steps. Follow Connor up to the top.

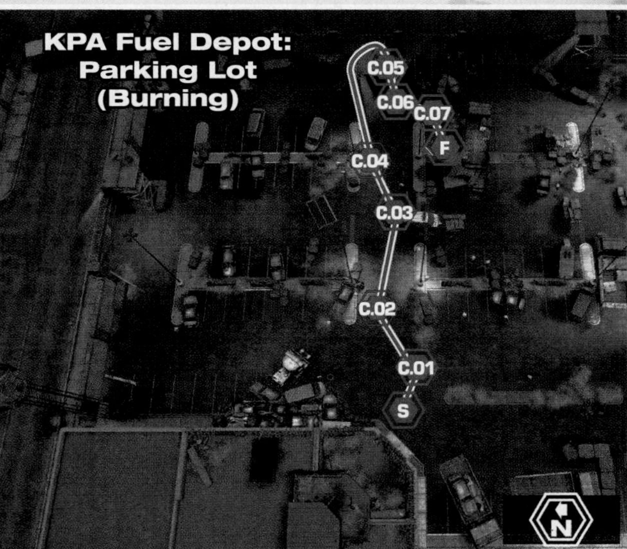

> **CAUTION** 조심하다
>
> **Rianna is correct. If you stay in the parking lot or venture into the fire, you become just another charred freedom fighter.**

This Shit Just Keeps on Getting Better and Better!

Hopper had kicked the jammed launcher, causing the accident. As Connor and Rianna yell stern words at the top of the tower **[C.05]**, you can continue to tag enemies on the ground, helping the remaining Resistance forces, until a KPA helicopter appears. Keep an eye on it as Connor coaxes Rianna back from the brink of despair. Moments later, the helicopter launches a rocket strike, crippling the tower, which slowly creaks, and topples over **[C.06]**. You're sent tumbling toward the tarmac yet again....

Connor and Rianna are sprawled nearby. The white phosphorous has burned off now, and a KPA trooper walks over to check whether you're really dead…and is run over as Goliath careens into the combat zone **[C.07]**. Connor lets out a chuckle as he gets up off the ground, then barks orders; it's time to assault the store.

CHECKPOINT D: GOLIATH ON DECK

Friendlies

Goliath

Connor

Rianna

Member

Enemies

Soldier (Scout)

Soldier

Soldier (EMP)

KPA Fuel Depot: Parking Lot (Store Frontage)

"We're Hitting the Store!"

Connor gathers the survivors of the firestorm, and points them in the general direction of the TigerDirect.com® building, forcing them forward (south), lining up behind Goliath (you now control its missile barrage). A second later, while you rush to a flatbed truck with some cover **[D.01]**, Goliath is hit by a sizable EMP blast from the building's rooftop. This isn't good.

Objective: Eliminate the EMP Soldier

Tactical Planning: Everything Must Go

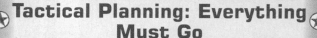

Threat Assessment: KPA Infantry Forces

Foes are all to the south of you, mainly streaming out of the store's front doors (although some come in from behind the cover to the far left and right), and utilizing the sandbags and trucks as cover. You may encounter the odd enemy to your right (west), attempting to outflank, and lurking on the left, close to the fortified flatbed where you'll be spending most of this next round of combat. Periodically, EMP soldiers appear on the store's roof, on either side of the signage. They are your primary targets.

Plan A: Guarding Goliath 

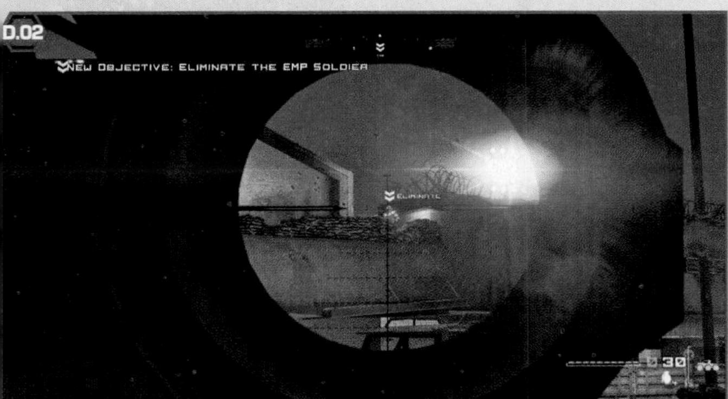

The optimal plan is to immediately target the first EMP foe (who is flagged and easily spotted) on the roof **[D.02]**, and drop him using your M4 Rifle, or your M110 Sniper Rifle (as shown) after zooming in to target. Moments later, the EMP blast disperses, and Goliath becomes fully operational. During this takedown, move and situate yourself on top of the fortified flatbed.

The second the EMP soldier is killed, switch to your Goliath targeter, and focus on the store's two main doors **[D.03]**. When you have four or more infantry targets selected, let Goliath rip them apart with a rocket barrage. Continue this ceaseless battering from Goliath's main gun until a second EMP soldier appears.

This soldier may step out on the same side as the first, or on the opposite side **[D.04]**; he appears in one place or the other. Quickly remove the enemy using your M4 Rifle or (as shown) your M110 Sniper Rifle, and then return to culling foes as they step out from the store's doorways. Expect a third (and final) EMP soldier once your barrages have dispatched more foes.

TIP 영리한

Now that you know where the EMP soldiers are, and when they are likely to appear, keep a keen eye open for movement in these locations, and bring the foes down before they are flagged by your HUD; this way you can keep Goliath active as much as possible.

Plan B: Other Options 

Although the M4 Rifle is the fastest way to quickly find, target, and shoot an enemy EMP soldier, you can utilize the M110 Sniper Rifle if you wish **[D.05]**, although it is slightly more cumbersome.

You can also lob grenades at the clusters of enemies streaming out of the store **[D.06]**. Usually, this would be extremely effective, but grenades should be saved for the assault on the store's interior, and Goliath's rocket barrages are far more dangerous to the enemy.

You don't need to use the fortified flatbed as cover all the time, but it helps. Venturing forward, or attempting to flank to the left or right means navigating around Goliath, and attacking enemies without the benefit of cover **[D.07]**. With this many foes, it's a foolish option.

Goliath is on deck [D.08]: Attempting to nullify an EMP soldier using Goliath's rocket barrage is possible, but you need to be extremely quick, firing off the salvo before your HUD even flags the foe to be eliminated. It is usually better to quickly switch to a carried weapon.

Objective: Target the Humvee

"Their War-Machine Is Too Powerful!"

Listen for Connor's orders as an enemy Humvee trundles in from right (west) to left. You should have your Goliath targeter already acquiring this foe, and locking on just as it stops in front of the store **[D.09]**. Finish, and Goliath rips through the vehicle, causing KPA survivors to lament the strength of your machine.

Objective: Regroup

Connor yells at the team to form up outside the store. Keep Goliath targeting foes that storm out, just after the Humvee explodes, and then peer over your fortified location. There are likely to be a few stragglers to the left (especially near the guard tower), as well as between you and the storefront. Take care when you vault over to the ground and rush to the store **[D.10]**; take time to ensure the coast is clear before you move. Goliath, or M4 Rifle fire, is a preferred plan here, usually before you leave the safety of the flatbed. Meet up by the smoking remains of the Humvee.

CHECKPOINT E: REINFORCEMENTS

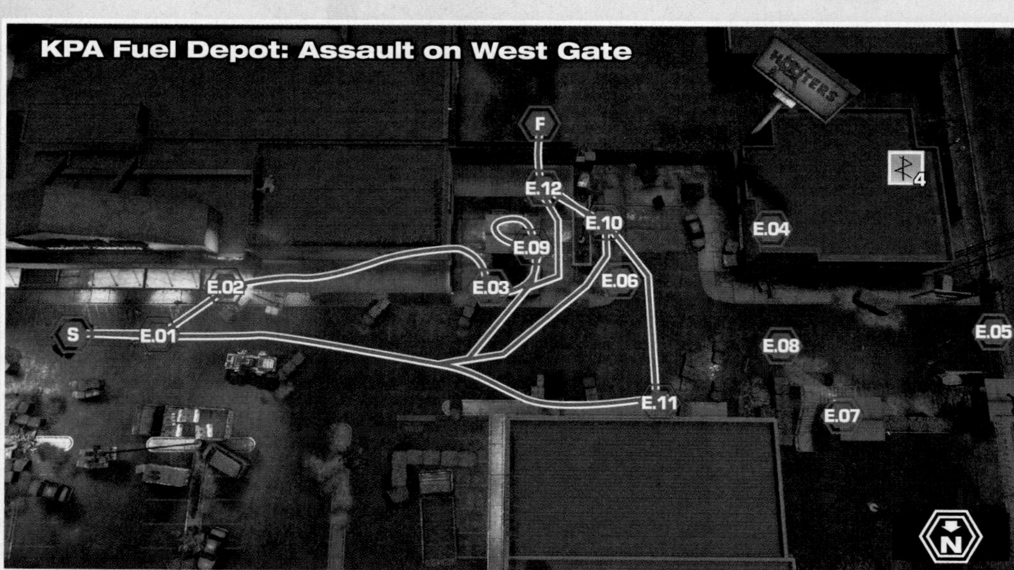

Enemies

Chimera

Soldier (EMP)

Soldier (Scout)

Humvee

Soldier

Piranha Light Armor Vehicle

Soldier (Heavy)

Objective: Follow Goliath

Objective: Target the Assault Helicopter

Fighting Fire With Fire

Hopper sends Goliath off down the parking lot, toward a coffee shop and Hooters, by the west gate in the parking lot's southwestern corner. Your remaining forces are just about to join Goliath when the enemy attack helicopter is spotted. Connor yells, but you should already know what to do.

The chopper flies from the right (north), and over the TigerDirect.com® building, before swinging around to launch another rocket strike from the west, heading east over Goliath and straight toward you **[E.01]**. Let the first blast hit Goliath, and dodge the second salvo (or you'll die) by sidestepping, or moving near the forklift on the left or truck and sandbags to the right. Or, head beneath the store awning, and completely avoid the enemy rockets **[E.02]**. With the chopper hovering above Goliath, let your autonomous tank blow the chopper out of the sky. It takes the full barrage, spins uncontrollably, and explodes on top of the store roof.

TIP 영리한

You can't target the chopper until it swings around, but you can finish targeting and fire as it shoots its salvo at you. Even if you're in cover, you're likely to take damage, so dodge (or take cover from) the rockets, and then retaliate.

CAUTION 조심하다

Got a sniper rifle? Grenades? Or an M4? Then save your ammunition, because none of them are effective against this attack helicopter.

Objective: Follow Goliath

Objective: Repel the Reinforcements

The moment the helicopter spins violently in the air after a successful strike from Goliath, sprint toward Goliath, or if you're under the awning, toward an adjacent guard tower overlooking the west gate **[E.03]**, which is being reinforced by both Resistance and KPA forces. Don't waste time shooting at your own forces (who run in from the right—north—near the coffee shop), and instead engage the enemy, who are gathering at the Hooters and west gate. Combat is ideally attempted from a dug-in location.

Tactical Planning: Keeping Abreast of the Action

Threat Assessment: KPA Reinforcements

The western gate is a hive of enemy activity: There's infantry inside the Hooters and around the gates, and more storm the area during combat. To the right is a guard tower and sandbags where more infantry troops tend to congregate. Periodically, an EMP soldier rushes up the guard tower and stands at the top, firing down crippling EMP launcher strikes to scupper Goliath. Expect three EMP foes (although these keep appearing the longer you take to complete the Checkpoint), along with light armor (an enemy Humvee), and one or two medium-armor vehicles (LAVs). Combat ends once the LAV is destroyed, and Connor yells at you to regroup.

The overall plan is to remove all of the threats, and Goliath is the only way you'll accomplish most of the enemy takedowns. Target the Hooters, gate, and sandbags near the tower, while keeping an eye open for the first of the EMP soldiers who scale the tower stairs and then situate themselves in the tower lookout itself.

Soldiers inside, and behind the cover at the perimeter of the Hooters, are easily removed using Goliath's targeting **[E.04]**. Do this as often as possible, gathering targets before the barrage is launched. Additional enemies usually appear from inside the restaurant shell.

Foes stream up through the west gate, and spread out into the Hooters, and to the right. Target them all in a collective target, and destroy them **[E.05]**.

The only time your regular weapons get a workout is if you venture too close to a foe, or one happens to make it to your vantage point **[E.06]**. As ever, you can lob in grenades, but Goliath is active, and therefore a preferable offensive tool.

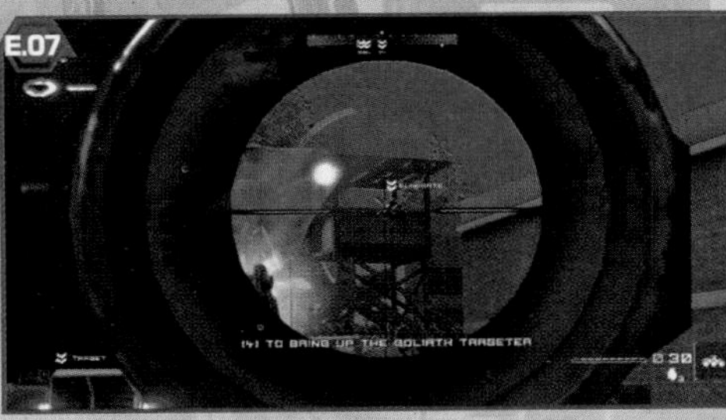

EMP soldiers and vehicles are more of a pressing concern, because both arrive around the same time. Obviously, having Goliath incapacitated with an enemy vehicle active can hamper your progress, so listen for your team yelling at you to take out the EMP soldier **[E.07]**. Better yet, watch for a soldier running up the guard tower steps, and kill him before he reaches the top. This is the only time you need to use conventional rifle fire. Target and blast each vehicle with Goliath **[E.08]**. Expect an EMP soldier quickly followed by a Humvee. Then expect an EMP soldier followed by a LAV.

TIP 영리한

Unlike the previous battle with EMP soldiers, Goliath can easily target and destroy the foe if you target him quickly enough, while he's still running up the guard tower stairs.

TIP 영리한

If Goliath is hit by an EMP strike, take down the EMP soldier, and then halt the enemy incursions with grenades and rifle fire. Hopper yells (and the targeter icon on your HUD changes color) when Goliath is back online.

Locations: Views to a Kill

The guard tower by the side entrance, adjacent to the storefront awning is by far the best place to be. Gradually ascend while finding infantry targets for Goliath to fire at **[E.09]**. You don't need to go all the way to the top, but you can if you wish.

At ground level, you can maneuver more easily, but you don't have the height advantage that allows for easier enemy targeting. The concrete barriers to the left (south) at the foot of the guard tower are safest **[E.10]**.

Or, you can stay around the sandbags by the brick wall of the coffeehouse on your right, pushing up to the defenses. This allows for easy spotting of the EMP soldier, but is a much more dangerous place to be. If you're feeling reckless, try heading here **[E.11]**.

CAUTION 조심하다

Don't stand here: Charging the Hooters, wandering around the tarmac where Goliath is, and sprinting at the west gate are all terrible ideas. Although you can (if you're lucky) run toward the gate, then step around the back of the Hooters and enter through the rear doorway, you have limited visibility to target the EMP foe. Spectacular failure is your only option here.

Objective: Regroup at the Side Entrance

When Connor comments on your "great goddamn work," this fracas is over. Locate the news pick-up inside the Hooters, then find the side entrance to the main store, which is flagged, and to the south of the tarmac courtyard, by a fence **[E.12]**. Go prone, and crawl under the gap in the fence. Now to flush the foes inside the store.

HIDDEN HISTORY >> 4 (30/61)

On the floor behind the counter near the popcorn machine in the southwest corner of the Hooters next to the west gate.

THE BIGGEST INDUSTRIAL COLLAPSE EVER: GM DECLARES BANKRUPTCY A SECOND TIME *11/1/2014*

For the second time in a decade, the largest auto maker in America declared itself bankrupt in a courtroom in lower Manhattan yesterday. Despite efforts by the US Government to prop up the automaker and save the jobs of nearly 235,000 Americans, the company's overall profitability has continued to spiral out of control.

Speaking on behalf of the White House, an aide to the president said that a second bailout was "unlikely." "The United States Government has worked with GM to restructure their operating process"; the spokesman noted, "however, they have been unable to keep up with demand for hybrid and high efficiency vehicles." With gas now averaging nine dollars a gallon, American consumers are beginning to value cars that are less status symbols and more machines of a specific quality and function.

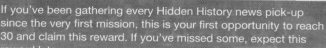

Mettle of Honor

Award: Archivist | Rating: 10 | Trophy: Bronze

If you've been gathering every Hidden History news pick-up since the very first mission, this is your first opportunity to reach 30 and claim this reward. If you've missed some, expect this reward later.

CHECKPOINT F: SHOP 'TIL YOU DROP

Enemies

Transport Helicopter

Soldier

Soldier (Scout)

Soldier (Heavy)

"Walk Softly. We'll Take 'em by Surprise."

After a discussion about how Connor came by the quantities of white phosphorous, your teammates halt flanking a side entrance into the big-box store. Check the wall to the right of this door for a news pick-up before rejoining your team. Connor pushes the door open, and Rianna steps through, spotting KPA troops immediately, over by the cash registers **[F.01]**. They haven't seen you yet. If you take cover, your team waits. If you move forward, or don't charge in first, Rianna opens fire, while Connor shouts that this is where the KPA have been storing some of their fuel.

Note the location of two new weapons: an 870 Express Shotgun, and an ACR Rifle with a shotgun attachment, a secondary-fire function. The shotgun is by the fallen drinks machine, and the rifle is on a pallet stack near a KPA generator. You may wish to pick up one, or both of these weapons, but be warned; the ACR is located in an area where the KPA can easily spot you, so consider one of the forthcoming plans before grabbing it.

CAUTION 조심하다

The shotgun (and attachment to the ACR) is a powerful, one-shot kill weapon. However, if you shoot and miss a target close to you, the time between shots and lengthy reload time mean you may be cut down before you can fire back. Use the ACR's main function, or keep your M4 for a rapid-fire response, although this is purely user preference.

WEAPONS >>
870 Express Shotgun

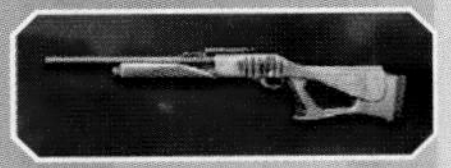

WEAPONS >>
ACR Rifle [Shotgun]

Propped up or on the crates just inside the side entrance.

HIDDEN HISTORY >> 5 (31/61)

On the ground near trash and a drinks machine, to the right of the side doors to the TigerDirect.com® big-box store.

2/13/2016

NEW KOREA FAR FROM A DEMOCRACY

American television has recently seen a wave of advertising from the new Korean Office for the Promotion of Tourism. Advertisements depict futuristic cosmopolitan cities juxtaposed with idyllic farm life, with the text "A pure expression of the ancient Korean culture." Posters, billboards and bus advertisements feature themes of "Mystery," "Romance," and "Relaxation," to name a few of the more popular campaigns. Based on reports from students and academics in the country, however, the advertisements are not showing the whole story.

Professors and students critical of the new regime have reported receiving threatening letters, been mobbed by angry protesters, and in some cases have seen their personal property vandalized. While the government has spoken out against these acts, it has not moved to protect these individuals. The Jong-un administration insists that "there have been no systematic violations of civil rights. This is clearly the work of a few extremists."

Once a shining example of modern democracy in the region of East Asia, South Korea appears to have been completely engulfed by the radical ideology and fervent nationalism of its Northern brother. After taking the country by seemingly peaceful means, Kim Jong-un has moved to quash all opposition to his "New Chosun Party." The party maintains a remarkable 81% majority in the Korean Senate, and includes statesmen from both South and North Korea. Members of the opposition party in the Korean Senate have reported incidents similar to those reported by academics and students; in one high-profile incident, a mob attacked a Senatorial vehicle as it toured a low-income area. The administration released a statement urging all Korean politicians to take appropriate measures to protect themselves.

Objective: Follow Connor

CAUTION 조심하다

Combat inside this giant warehouse store is both dangerous and confusing. Enemies may (or may not) be around every corner, and pushing forward too quickly or missing with an offensive attack can lead to your demise. Be careful out there.

Tactical Planning: Checking In, Not Checking Out

Threat Assessment: KPA Infantry Forces

You face at least two dozen KPA throughout the following three checkpoints, as you battle through—and eventually secure—this big-box store. All of the enemies are competent shots, work as a team, and use cover. Overstretching yourself and racing off to engage them results in a quick death; it's better to remain close to your team and methodically clear each section of troops before moving into the next. But the KPA threat is more dangerous than ever before. During Checkpoint G, expect two dug-in foes on upper display cases, and four foes rappelling down from a helicopter. During Checkpoint H, beware of larger congregations of foes, especially to the southeast, near the exit ramp up to the outside roof.

Plan A: The Waiting Game

Step inside and immediately move to the left (north) wall, standing close to Connor's eventual location **[F.02]**. Although Connor gets twitchy, your team doesn't usually make a move, but you can listen to Hopper relaying information about a KPA chopper. After it crashes through the building in the opposite corner thanks to Goliath's rockets, the KPA troops retreat slightly, into the middle of the building (and the next checkpoint). This leaves you three stragglers to tag as you step out from cover **[F.03]**. Blast them, or the explosive barrels they are standing near. Then run around and down between the first lane of checkout counters, and push through into Checkpoint G. This plan allows you to reach Checkpoint G with minimal combat.

Plan B: A Memorable Entrance

If you can't wait until the chopper explodes to cut down the KPA, you can begin firing, or step out from cover and let Rianna shoot off the first shot, while staying close to your teammates. You may want to step onto the low side wall and use the pallet stacks as cover, on the left side **[F.04]**, before moving onward. Keeping close (and slightly behind) your crew allows them to become the focus of enemy fire, while you step behind or drop to a crouch and avoid enemy gunfire, and provide covering fire. When Rianna and Connor advance, follow them [F.05], providing backup as they enter the checkout lanes. When Rianna and Connor advance, follow them **[F.05]**, providing backup as they enter the checkout lanes.

Plan C: The Direct Approach

Plans A, B, and C all feature the same general route, but C involves the most risk. However, you control when the action starts: immediately! When the doors open, wait a second for the foes to rush in from the right (south), and then lob in a grenade, or better yet, shoot the explosive barrels to the northeast, near a fallen drinks machine **[F.06]**. In the chaos you've started, rush to the small shelving stand **[F.07]**, or where the barrels were, and use this area as cover. Expect at least eight KPA to swarm up from the south; so lob in a grenade to soften them up, and take quick, measured bursts of M4 fire (or single shotgun blasts) and deal with most of them before advancing on the checkout lanes.

TIP 영리한

Throughout this combat, seek cover behind any of the metal shelving units; remaining in the open simply attracts enemy bullets.

TIP 영리한

You only need to reach the southern end of the checkout lane to start the next checkpoint, so technically you could sprint there (optionally firing), and then dive behind cover or face death, but at the start of Checkpoint G.

Plan D: Checkout Choices 

When you reach the checkout lanes, enemies continue to appear from around the shelves of the looted mobile phone department **[F.08]**. At this point, you have two options. You can:

Press forward so they retreat, and begin Checkpoint G.

Or stay at the northern end of the checkout area, and tag foes that appear (usually with a scoped M4), whittling down their numbers in a war of attrition, until only one or two remain. This removes many of the foes from Checkpoint G and minimizes your risk, but takes a lot longer to accomplish. If you value safety over spectacular takedowns, try this tactic.

NOTE 알아두세요

While you're engaging the enemies at the checkout counter, the helicopter Hopper was chattering about arrives and hovers above a hole in the roof. Troopers begin rappelling down before Hopper uses Goliath to knock the chopper out of the sky. It spins and crashes into the far (southeast) corner of the warehouse, setting it ablaze!

CHECKPOINT G: CLEANUP ON AISLE 9

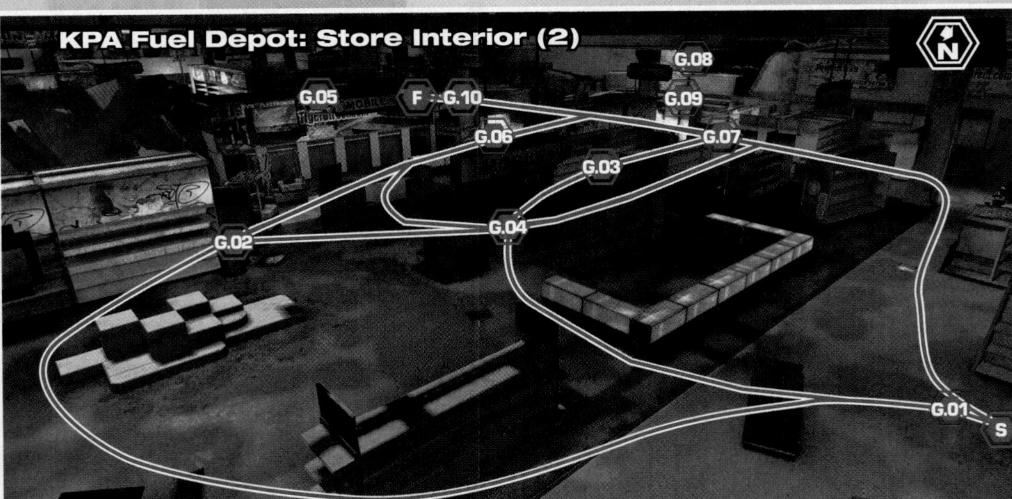

Enemies

Transport Helicopter

Soldier

Soldier (Scout)

Soldier (Heavy)

 Store Wars 

Push through to the main store floor, which is a maze of aisles, small fires, and partially collapsed shelving. Your overall task is to follow Connor, but you are welcome to split up and attempt to cull the intense KPA threats using various means. You begin at the end of the checkout lane, facing south **[G.01]**. This checkpoint ends once you've secured—or run past—the mobile phone department; the only exit into the other half of the store is to the southwest. Try one of the following plans:

TIP 영리한

Although you're supposed to follow Connor, you don't need to hang by him. Use him as more of a marker, in case you get lost.

Plan A: Left Flank Attack

Head around the display cases, to the left (east) side of the store, which is more open. Although this limits your hiding spots, it also makes it easy to spot and remove enemy threats. Run around to the empty display, near some shelving with explosive barrels, and shoot the barrels **[G.02]**. If you don't, the enemy will, and you don't want to be caught near them when that happens. Then look west, and watch for enemies scurrying between the shelves. Bring down as many as you see **[G.03]**. Then advance to the west, toward the middle of the store, joining the path in Plan B.

Plan B: Up the Middle

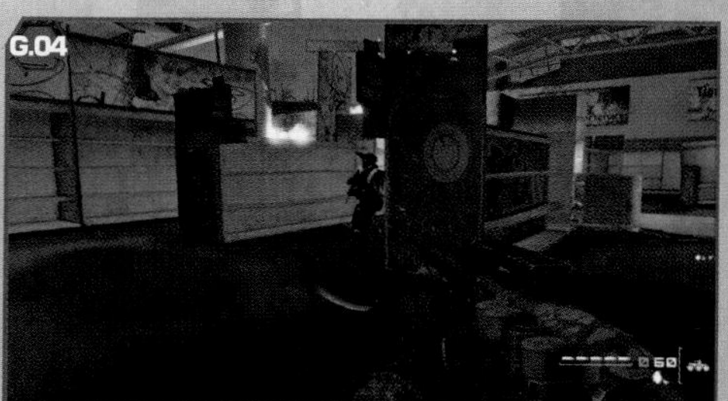

Watch for the explosive barrels in front of a large display case ahead of you, and tackle the foes milling around the display cases ahead and to the right of you **[G.04]**. You can investigate the shelving units to the right (west), but it is advisable to quickly sidestep, peering through and up from the fire, and tagging two foes dug in on top of the largest display case **[G.05]**, with the blue doors below the signage where the foes are located.

Plans A and B now merge, as you should check the three aisles on your right (west). Sidestep right to left, checking for enemy movement, before moving between the fires to the aisle by the large display area. Look for armored KPA crates to hide behind on the aisle where the display cases are **[G.06]**; these are great to use as cover while removing enemies on the store's west side. Listen for Rianna and the arrival of another KPA helicopter.

TIP 영리한

Continue to use grenades throughout this store battle, lobbing them to dissuade two or more foes from advancing at you, or groups you stumble across or spot at a distance. If you have the talent, try "grenade ricocheting." This is the fine art of lobbing a grenade at shelving so it bounces off (usually around a corner), landing at a foe you don't want to tackle directly.

TIP 영리한

Low on ammunition or grenades? Then be sure to step over the corpses of fallen foes, stooping to grab a new weapon if you need to. Grenades are automatically scooped up.

Plan C: Right Flank Fleeing (1)

Another idea is to head from the checkout lane up the right flank, or the main thoroughfare that runs the entire length of the store. If you're ignoring combat, you can clear Checkpoint G in seconds, because you can sprint the entire way, passing the sale signage that triggers Checkpoint H. In fact, you can rush all the way to the far (south) end, holing up in an alcove and letting your teammates do all the work. This concludes as Plan C: Right Flank Fleeing (2) in Checkpoint H.

However, if you're making a more measured series of maneuvers through the aisles in the west side of the store **[G.07]**, Rianna covers your left flank. Expect a slow but steady push toward the confrontation with the helicopter, although you're at a much closer location when the chopper arrives. For further tactics on dealing with foes along the western shelves, consult Checkpoint H's Plan B (below).

CAUTION 조심하다

If you try the sprinting tactic, or don't clear the area to the left (east), expect a few occasions of foes attacking from behind, especially during Checkpoint H.

Airborne Attack

When you clear the mobile department, Rianna shouts that a helicopter is above the roof. Be sure you've cleared the immediate area (and no foes are doubling-back to attack you from behind. Ignore the helicopter itself—you don't have an RPG that can damage it—and instead watch as four KPA troopers rope down to the ground **[G.08]**. A well-timed grenade, lobbed at their landing spot just before the first foe touches down, can kill all four at once **[G.09]**. Or fire bursts at the descending foes so each one is dispatched before they land. Otherwise, you need to stalk the shelving on the store's west side, but don't venture too far south.

Now meet Connor up at the "sale" wall where Checkpoint H starts **[G.10]**.

> **TIP 영리한**
>
> **Connor warns you about shooting the explosive barrels, but you can ignore his wariness; this building is coming down in an inferno no matter how many barrels you shoot.**

CHECKPOINT H: EVERYTHING MUST GO

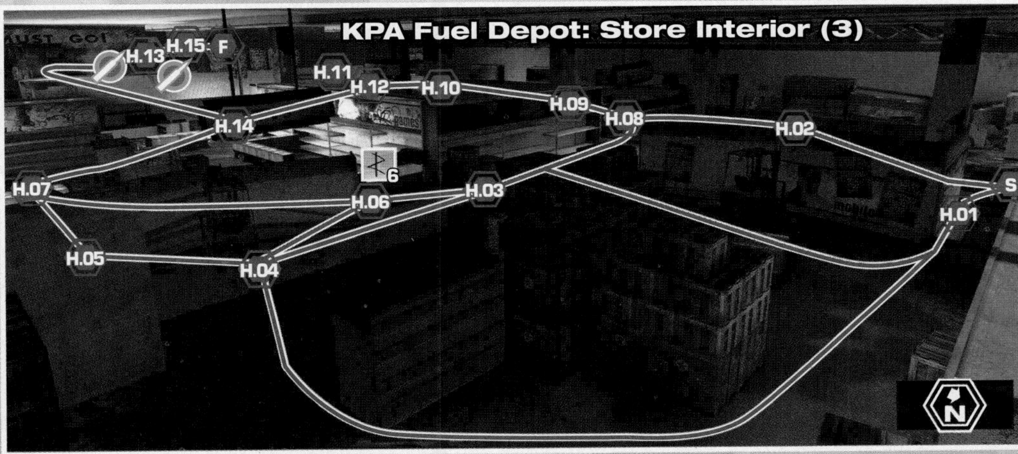

Store-Wide Clearance

The rest of this store looks like a maze of scattered crates and looted shelving, but it only consists of three main aisles, all to the left of the main corridor with all of the shelving ahead and right of you. You can choose to head down any of the three aisles at any time (which lead to the games displays), although Plan A presupposes that you step left at the "sales" sign where the checkpoint begins **[H.01]**, so you won't be attacked from behind and out-flanked. The other main route (Plan B) is a trek down the main corridor **[H.02]**, moving around any blockades into the shelving area. Both routes are filled with KPA threats. Use any remaining grenades during this time. The good news is that Rianna and Connor clear out the route that you don't take, so you don't have to execute everyone.

Plan A: Aisle Be Back

Most enemies lurk in an armored crate storage area in the middle of the store, and the games department south of that; all are accessed via aisles. The crate storage is a central cluster with three or four enemies on both sides of the crates, and a few more in the aisle beyond **[H.03]**. Drop them with head shots, or destroy the nearby explosive barrels (which ensures that you're not struck by later explosions).

On the far side of the storage area are two orange forklifts, allowing you to flank around and attack the enemies in this vicinity facing west **[H.04]**, while your teammates help out. This is marginally safer than running out into the aisle on the other side, as foes may be on either side of you. As always, check the aisles for enemies and react appropriately. Of course, you can vary your route and head to the main corridor aisle at any time, or if the games department is too hot.

Push through into the games department. You'll find a large number of enemies, so keep your distance; ideally at either side **[H.05] [H.06]** of the shelving one of the orange forklifts had struck. Lob a grenade (or two) into the mass of enemies, and pick them off one by one as they retreat to the store exit and conveyor ramp. Don't stand near the explosive barrel on the north side of this department. Shoot the barrels on the south side too, lessening the threats and pushing eastward toward the exit, staying on the left (east) side **[H.07]** so you can always step into cover.

TIP 영리한

You want to step out from cover, shoot a foe, and step back before you're winged by enemy fire. Head into the games department only once it's almost empty of foes. Crouch to utilize low cover. The shelving that was pushed forward by the orange forklift is a great place to attack from; vary the sides you peek out from to confuse the enemies, and then move in and outflank them.

CAUTION 조심하다

Display cases are too tall to jump on or over or use as an escape route; don't try it or you'll make yourself extremely visible!

Plan B: Corridor Carnage

Be sure you're heading south, clambering over debris as you head down the remains of the main corridor, with its numerous small fires and shelving units to navigate around. Expect KPA soldiers around every turn **[H.08]**, so keep a slower but steady pace. This plan involves closer combat, but is quicker and slightly safer. Each combat opportunity presents something different to try. You can:

Sidestep out, check for foes, quickly zoom and target them with your scoped weapon, or accurately blast them with a shotgun round or SMG fire [H.09] before stepping back into cover. Then advance, periodically checking the aisles to the left for incoming foes.

Double-back around shelving and attack a foe from the other direction.

Step up and stab him with a melee attack, which is useful if you just missed with your shotgun.

Lob in a grenade, or ricochet one off shelving, and remove a number of threats, or cause a disturbance to lure a foe out and then shoot them.

Shoot any explosive barrels you see.

H.10

Retreating can work, but foes will eventually attack from behind, so continuously push forward to the southwest corner of the store and a storage room garage doorway. This entrance, the nearby shelving, or the armored crates are great locations for cover **[H.10]** as you tag the last cluster of foes around a conveyor ramp. Lob in grenades from here, explode any barrels you see to weaken the foes and prevent them from shooting the barrels when you're near them, and cut down enemies that fire on you, all the while pushing east toward the store exit.

Plan C: Right Flank Fleeing (2)

A strange, but weirdly workable third option is available if you've fled the foes you're supposed to be firing at (killing only those that critically threaten your life). Race southward, and then around the blockade and shelves, back onto the corridor and straight down to the large storage garage door opening with a blown-out "Exit" sign **[H.11]**.

Hide in this location for the remainder of the battle, shooting only the enemies that have chased you down the corridor, or those approaching from the right (east). Either way, although you're in a dead-end storage room, there's more than enough room to dodge enemy fire or grenades, and the doorway is the perfect cover to step out and fire from **[H.12]**.

Store Closure

From Plan A: When you reach the exit corridor, if you're in the games department, stay on the left (east) side, using the shelving as cover. Shoot all the explosive barrels, and beware of two foes behind the conveyor ramp, under the upper exit. Two more enemies are on the upper storage overlook, too **[H.13]**; shoot barrels near them to weaken them, before finishing off with rifle fire (ideally from range), or a grenade. Wait for them to step out to fire, and then cut them down.

From Plans B or C: If you're approaching from the southwest corner of the store, moving up at a narrower angle heading east, expect enemies in this corridor area and destroy them with exploding barrels and grenades. For the foes under the upper balcony, sidestep right at the foot of the conveyor ramp, and attack them from the sides **[H.14]**. Your teammates should be close to defeating the two other enemies up on the balcony. If not, shoot out the exploding barrels and defeat them, or circle around and attack at a less obtuse angle (from the games department).

With all threats neutralized, search the games department for a news pick-up, and then climb the ramped conveyor belt structure, and check the upper balcony for the weapons the final enemies were carrying (as well as the ground for any grenades to automatically grab). Of particular interest (and help) is the M249 LMG, which should be up here. This is a very advantageous weapon for the next checkpoint. You may also wish to swap out your other weapon for armaments listed below, although the M4 is still a good secondary choice. When you've decided, head through the upper exit door **[H.15]** to the roof.

WEAPONS >>
SCAR-L Rifle

WEAPONS >>
M16 Rifle [Mk 1 Red Dot Sight]

WEAPONS >> M249 LMG

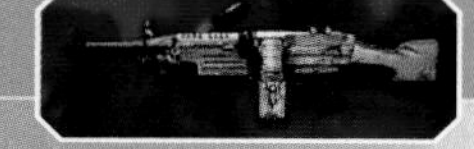

On the floor below, and on the actual balcony where your team exits.

HIDDEN HISTORY >> 6 (32/61)

Behind a display counter, in the northwest corner of the games department, below a "games" sign.

THE WINTER OF FREEZING DEATH

12/03/2016

Delaware has joined New York and Minnesota as the third state to report more than 10,000 deaths from freezing, hypothermia and extreme cold related illness. The cold snap that struck the northeast coupled with rolling brownouts has affected more than just the infirm, the very young and the homeless. Healthy, grown adults are dying in their homes simply from an inability to maintain heat.

A grueling, painful death, hypothermia slowly shuts down the whole body. Victims of hypothermia report a burning sensation in their extremities, followed by the gradual shutdown of the heart and respiratory system.

To combat this, the Federal government has taken over key facilities in the North, creating "National Heating Centers," large facilities that can keep groups of people alive who might otherwise freeze to death. Like the United Center in Chicago and The Palace in Detroit, Madison Square Garden is one such facility. Able to host over 20,000 high-risk individuals and run in concert with Cedar-Sinai Medical Centers, Madison Square Garden is now a rotating home for the elderly, the infirm, and the very young.

CHECKPOINT I: THE CHASE

Enemies

Soldier (Scout) | Soldier | Fuel Tanker

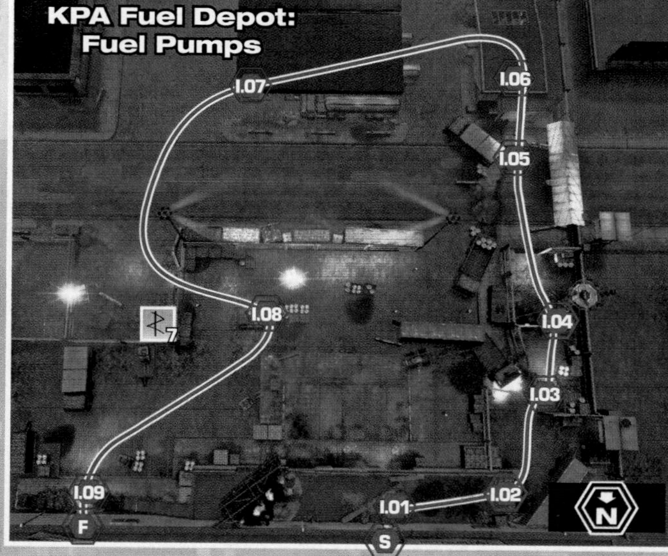

Keep On Tracking

Connor briefs you at the exit door, telling you in no uncertain terms, and with the saltiest of language, that failure isn't an option. You're to head out and locate one of the KPA fuel tankers, and attach a tracking device to it, so that the Resistance can locate and recover it, and continue Boone's San Francisco plan. Of course, as soon as Connor boots the exit door open **[I.01]**, things don't quite go according to plan.

Objective: Attach the Tracking Device

You have seconds to react as Rianna yells that the trucks are already moving. Peer over the side of the roof, and you'll see a few KPA in the rear parking lot below, which has walls and numerous storage crates dotted around it. If you simply stand there, you won't catch the truck, so immediately turn right (west), sprint, and drop off the side of the roof **[I.02]**.

As you land, look to the left (south) slightly, and you'll spot a KPA trooper stepping out from the jumble of fencing and crates. Rake him with your LMG, and he falls immediately **[I.03]**. The LMG is your preferable weapon because you don't need to zoom-aim it (which wastes time and slows you down), and it drops foes almost immediately. Otherwise, your preferred firearm is a good choice.

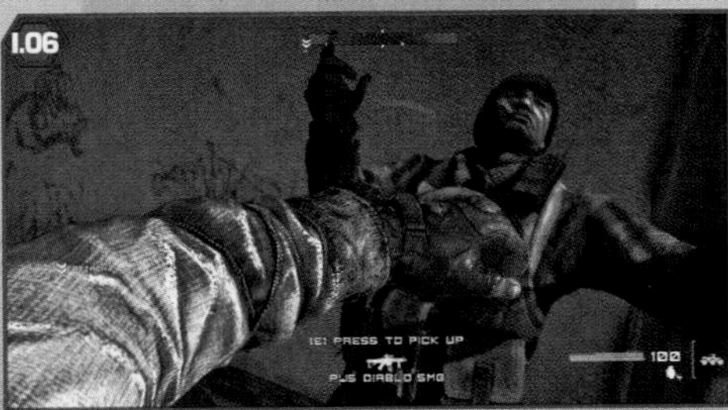

Continue down the perimeter of the fortifications, and a second enemy appears. Blast him with your LMG; the barrels behind usually go up, catching and killing him **[I.04]**. Sprint continuously as you head forward (south) toward the concrete doorway of a gas station **[I.05]**. Another foe rolls out a barrel, which explodes, catching him in the explosion. To be sure, fire on him as soon as you can, and run through the doorway. Lurking inside the derelict office is another foe, who may ambush you **[I.06]**. React with more LMG fire, or (if he's close enough) stab him with a melee strike. Then get back to sprinting!

The truck you need to tag is pulling out of the fuel depot! Sprint around the gas station desk and out the door to the left (east) and keep on sprinting as you see the back end of the tanker. If you don't sprint, the truck pulls away, failing the mission. If you run at an odd angle, the truck is usually too far away to reach, failing the mission. So run between the pumps directly behind the tanker, aiming just left of the left gas pump on the far (east) end of the station **[I.07]**, so you're traversing the minimum distance needed to reach the tanker. It slows slightly as it turns, so don't give up! Then attach the device and don't stop running until you're given the all-clear.

Objective: Regroup

Signal Broadcasting Five-By-Five!

Connor and Rianna remain on the roof, giving you a few moments to go north and then west, into the rear parking lot, where you find around six KPA stragglers **[I.08]**. The explosive barrels (and a thrown grenade) usually remove all of these threats in seconds, but you may need to cut down anyone surviving with your favored firearm. If you're low on ammunition, gather what you can, as your team has regrouped by the store doors **[I.09]**. While you check a small sentry hut for another news pick-up, Hopper radios in. The Resistance cells are getting attacked back at the initial parking lot; it's time to go! Connor shoves the door open, and you begin to head back into the store, which is now ablaze!

HIDDEN HISTORY >> 7 (33/61)

On the floor of a sentry hut, just right of the entrance to the rear parking lot, after you tag the fuel tanker.

18 MILLION DEAD AS KNOXVILLE COUGH BURNS OUT

8/19/2022

Federal officials allowed the Congressional "Declaration of a Public Health Emergency" to expire today, signaling an official end to the H5N1 influenza pandemic that has rocked the Midwest. The decision to let the declaration expire comes after several months of low flu activity and the vaccination of over 100 million Americans. The World Health Organization said that peak H5N1 activity had likely passed for most of the world, but the virus was still circulating in some regions.

The USA was particularly hard-hit by the disease, as its crumbling infrastructure and the high price of petroleum made the distribution of aid materials difficult and in some cases impossible. Official tallies estimate at least 18 million dead from H5N1, but that number is likely rise as hospitals file their final reports.

The US Military, previously charged with maintaining order as the virus spread, has withdrawn from a number of metropolitan areas and plans to continue a phased withdrawal. A spokesman for the Department of Defense stated that there will likely be a reduced but ongoing military presence in most cities for the next several months.

CHECKPOINT J: FIRE SALE

Enemies

Soldier (Scout)

Soldier

Objective: Follow Connor

NOTE 알아두세요

This part of the store hasn't been traversed before. However, there's only one route through the increasingly dangerous structure, now burning ferociously thanks to the exploding fuel and helicopters.

Korean Barbecue

As you enter the building, be aware of an enemy crashing through the window to your left (west) **[J.01]**. Immediately fire on the nearby barrel, catching it and him in a fiery explosion.

Or, you can lob in a grenade, shoot the enemy precisely and leave the barrel intact, or vault over the low crates and melee strike the enemy.

Two foes immediately appear behind the upper middle two windows ahead (north) of you **[J.02]**. Quickly retaliate, dropping them with well-aimed gunfire.

Or, simply avoid them by rushing through into the connecting room where the first foe rolled in from.

Around four foes attack from the store interior, on the opposite (west) side of the connecting room **[J.03]**. Simply fire a shot at the fuel barrels behind and slightly left of them, creating what Connor then refers to as a "Korean barbecue."

Or, you can target the foes individually, or throw in a grenade. Watch for the barrels detonating as you pass them if you haven't shot them already.

CAUTION 조심하다

Be on the look out for (and shoot at) explosive barrels, because they are everywhere. They usually cause a ceiling or structural collapse when you fire on them, but this is beneficial because you'll die if they detonate near you.

TIP 영리한

Lost in this inferno? Then remember the exit is always to the north, although the path isn't direct. When in doubt, follow Connor.

At the Movies

Press forward (northeast) past the armored crates to the movies department, where three foes await. One is to the left, behind a green crate **[J.04]**; shoot him easily and explode the barrels just behind him. The two others are on the right side of the pathway; one behind a crate and generator **[J.05]**, and the other just waiting to be singed, near a barrel just beyond the "Movies" sign **[J.06]**. Tag the latter with a headshot when he stands up, and explode the barrel near the other.

Let your team go on ahead, and they deal with these foes, as well as soaking up damage that you would otherwise take. You can also lob a grenade into the corridor so it lands between each foe and kills them. Finally, you can crouch and shoot the feet of the foe behind the generator; he isn't that well hidden.

J.07

J.08

The store is becoming engulfed in fire (thanks to the burning husk of a helicopter that crashed earlier), so keep heading north, shooting a foe in the distance by a forklift; a second later support girders falls on him, but this blocks your path **[J.07]**. The only way is forward and then right (east), around the burning shelves. Expect three KPA to attack at this corner **[J.08]** unless you land a grenade there or cut them down by sidestepping out with a favored weapon.

J.09

J.10

Step into the burning display area, and watch two foes run from right to left. You don't need to shoot them; you encounter them in a moment. First, watch a KPA soldier writhe in fire **[J.09]**; watch him die, shoot him before he falls, or melee strike him on your way to the perimeter corridor, turning left. In the distance, the two foes you just saw running have stopped to fire on you **[J.10]**. Blast either of them to explode an adjacent barrel. More supports come crashing down on them. If the explosion doesn't occur immediately, sidestep into the alcove of scenery on your left.

Roof Access

J.11

Head toward the blockage, and turn left (west), dodging around the aisle and back on the north corridor. Before you get there, look at another burning KPA on your right **[J.11]**; end his life or watch him burn!

J.12

You're nearing the exit, and a quartet of foes by the checkout lanes **[J.12]**. Advance and fire, and the ceiling collapses, forcing you through a fiery run to the right of the large support pillar. Shoot the barrels on the right, and ahead and to the left of you so they don't explode and kill you. Sprint so you aren't engulfed in flames.

J.13

Turn left (west); you're by the exit but the doors are blocked. Knife, shoot, or leave another burning KPA soldier, and meet up at the emergency stairs to the roof **[J.13]**. Waste no time following your compadres into the stairwell (although check below the first set of stairs for the mission's last news pick-up), and then ascend it as quickly as you can. At the top, near the graffiti with the "718" markings, Hopper radios in to let the team know transportation has been arranged. Wait for him to remove the cabinet blocking the exit door, and head outside.

HIDDEN HISTORY >> 8 (34/61)

On the floor below the first set of steps, in the store's emergency exit stairwell.

FAREWELL ADDRESS FROM THE PRESIDENT TO THE PEOPLE OF THE UNITED STATES

1/21/2025

The President is leaving office after serving for two terms. The following are excerpts from his farewell address: "The United States is a changed nation. Since I took office eight years ago during what many have described as the worst economic depression in the history of the country, coupled with the most vicious pandemic in human history, we have been forced to make some very difficult decisions in order to preserve our Union. Martial law, illegal for hundreds of years, became a necessity as we were forced to abandon our homes. Without the help of the fine men and women serving in uniform, many would have resorted to theft and murder under the threat of starvation and alienation. I have been called dictator by my opponents and a megalomaniac by my allies, but I have always promised you that the moment the necessity was gone our soldiers would leave our streets. Today marks the day that the Army turns over control of Detroit to civilian authorities, ending martial law for good in this country."

"It is a testament to the vision of our forefathers that this great country has been able to endure the trials and tribulations set before it, and come out stronger on the other side. It is a testament to the strength of the American people that they have been able to sacrifice and change and make do as we work together to rebuild our country. Much of our country is transformed beyond recognition, by disease and famine and death and resource depletion—but it is a truism that the only constant in this world is change. And it is important to remember that even though the physical appearance of our country has changed, her soul remains pure and bright, a shining light in a world gone dark. This peaceful transition of power is a testament to that fact."

"It is my deepest wish that my successor can take the work that we have done as a country and continue to grow us into a new nation, embracing change as a positive thing while remembering the foundations that our country is built on. I wish you all a fond farewell; it has been an honor to serve you in this darkest of hours. God bless you all, and God bless America."

CHECKPOINT K: EXODUS

Friendlies

Connor

Rianna

Goliath

Hopper

Member

Enemies

Soldier (Scout)

Humvee

Soldier

Chimera

Up on the Roof

Proceed along the rooftop between the large steel support and signs, toward where the attack helicopter crashed after your earlier barrage. Stop at the sandbagged edge of the building (where the EMP soldiers appeared earlier, next to the only Korean Kodex in this mission), and watch as Connor and Rianna leap over and drop to the tarmac **[K.01]**, heading for the transport trucks.

KOREAN KODEX >> 1 (6/10)

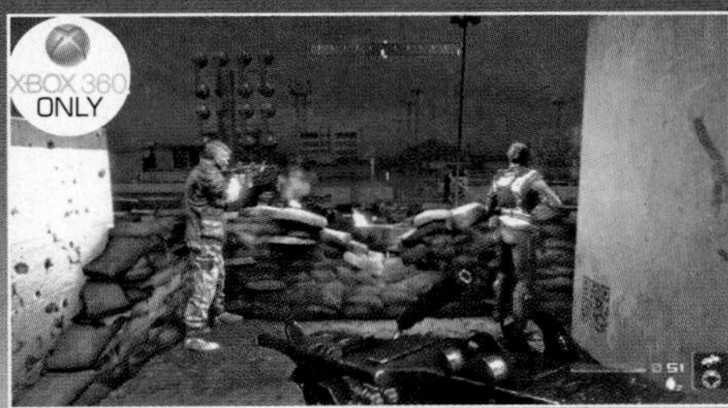

In the corner of the sniper spot where the EMP soldiers stood, at the base of the TigerDirect.com® sign, on the store roof.

Objective: Cover Your Squadmates

Objective: Vault off the Roof

KPA troops are coming in from the right (east), and it's your job to thwart them for a few moments. Although gunfire from your weapon is a possible help, it is far less effective than launching rocket barrages, courtesy of Goliath. The machine waits in the middle of the parking lot for your targeting data. Launch rockets at multiple infantry targets **[K.02]** until you're told to drop down to the ground. Immediately vault over the sandbags, and fall onto the tarmac.

Objective: Sprint to the Transport Truck

Hopper isn't slow in getting the truck started, and you're in danger of being left behind! Solve this by immediately sprinting as you reach the ground. Gunfire isn't necessary; just concentrate on shortening the distance between you and the back of the truck. Aim for the right corner of the truck, and cut the corner when the truck turns right (east) **[K.03]**. Then leap aboard.

Objective: Target the Assault Helicopter

"Kill... That... Chopper!!"

Immediately switch to Goliath's targeting as you sit in the back and watch Goliath trundle behind you. Your escape is soon noticed by KPA Humvees; as soon as one arrives, target it and launch a barrage, then do the same when a second Humvee appears **[K.04]**. As you race through the streets, listen for your team announcing the arrival of another attack helicopter. This is a primary concern, because its missile strikes can kill you if you don't immediately target it in a nice red box, and shoot it out of the sky remotely **[K.05]**. Regular weapons is as good as shouting: ineffective. Any other remaining Humvees are optional, but not vital to strike. After the chopper is hit and crashes into an overpass, your team limps out. Not exactly a job well done, but Boone is certain to be pleased....

Mettle of Honor

Award: Fire Sale | Rating: 10 | Trophy: Bronze

Completing this mission earns you this particular reward. Difficulty level, or how many times you restarted a checkpoint, do not matter.

Mettle of Honor

Award: Fire Sale—Guerrilla | Rating: 25 | Trophy: Bronze

Completing this mission earns you this individual reward. However, you must complete this on the hardest difficulty.

Mettle of Honor

Award: Iron Man—Fire Sale | Rating: 25 | Trophy: Bronze

Completing this mission without dying once or restarting a checkpoint earns you this reward. Lessen the difficulty if you're having problems completing this task.

MISSION SELECT »04 »THE WALL

After a bold raid, the squad heads home to meet with Boone and follow the tankers out of town. There are reports of KPA reprisals from the surrounding neighborhoods. To escape Montrose, you'll somehow have to get past the wall.

HIDDEN HISTORY » 8 (42/61 total)

KOREAN KODEX » 1 (7/10 total)

UNIQUE WEAPON » 4 (12/17 total)

CHECKPOINT A: HOME AGAIN

Friendlies

Connor

Hopper

Rianna

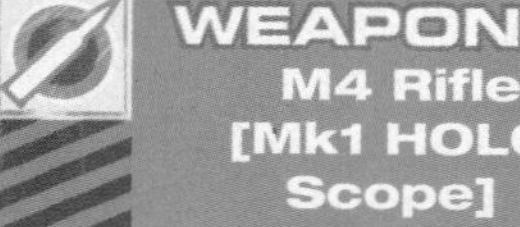

WEAPONS >>
M4 Rifle [Mk1 HOLO Scope]

WEAPONS >>
M110 Sniper

WEAPONS >>
Fragmentation Grenade (4)

You begin the mission with these weapons.

"Here's Your Badge Back, Old Friend."

Full of enthusiasm about a job well done, you follow your team up the ladder to Oasis. After shoving the stuck door open, you're greeted by chaos. The stench of death hangs in the air. Oasis has been ransacked. Burned. Violated. No one has survived. The KPA has killed everyone. Even the children. Rianna screams as she runs over to the swings; the ruined corpse of Boone is cut down **[A.01]**. Hopper sits on his haunches with

his head in his hands. Connor sets Boone's badge down on the old man's body. Helicopters are heard in the distance. The old oak tree has been defiled; branches and tarp netting still smoulder. Connor pulls Rianna away from Boone, and radios in to rendezvous with Brooks and the Gunnison resistance cell. It is time to pool resources, and push through the wall that surrounded Montrose. Shoving a blockade out of the way, you leave the tattered remains of Oasis **[A.02]**.

Objective: Follow Connor

You can search Oasis if you want. All you find are corpses with bags tied around their heads, and burning refuse. Head down the side yard, pausing only to look left (north) to find a news pick-up, and cross the street (there's nothing but rusting vehicles to inspect here), heading east down an overgrown side alley **[A.03]**. Hopper and a visibly shaken Rianna stand on either side of a door in some exterior fencing, and break the lock. Stand back, wait for Connor, and head through after him.

HIDDEN HISTORY >> 1 (35/61)

Among a pile of fence sections and a small bush, on the side alley of the Oasis house, across from a recycle bin.

PROFILE: KIM JONG-IL

8/4/2010

The official biography of Kim Jong-il deviates significantly from what is commonly accepted as the legitimate history. While Kim Jong-il's biographers will tell you that he was born in a log cabin inside a secret base on Korea's most sacred mountain, the real story is that he was born in an guerrilla camp in Russia while his father was hiding from the Japanese. He claims to have invented hamburgers and is, by his account, the greatest golfer in the world. He was at one point the world's largest consumer of Hennessey and once kidnapped a prominent South Korean director to create a Godzilla movie for him.

Although these stories are momentarily amusing, the reality is that Kim Jong-il is the center of a cult of personality, a vicious dictator that keeps his people in perpetual poverty. His erratic behavior and bizarre policies are impossible to judge from a distance—however, many who have met with him, including former Secretary of State Madeline Albright, regard him as informed and not delusional. No matter his psychological state, he is clearly a threat to his neighbors and to the west.

He currently exercises absolute authority in North Korea, but the future of his regime and his legacy remain in doubt. There are rumors that he has chosen a son to succeed him, and it's certain that we can expect that son to be fully indoctrinated into Kim Jong-il's vision of North Korean culture.

CHECKPOINT B: SUBURBAN ESCAPE

Objective: Follow Connor

"It's Too Quiet"

Step into a backyard, and follow Connor around to a section of fence that has fallen **[B.01]**, creating a ramp up and over to a cul-de-sac beyond. Before you step across the fence, make a thorough sweep of this garden. Aside from a covered above-ground pool, there's a news pick-up hidden in the clutter, as well as a Unique Weapon in the long grass, over in the northeast corner of the yard, next to a tree and log hutch. Grab the M16, and join your team across the fence.

HIDDEN HISTORY >> 2 (36/61)

Near the bush and overturned bench, close to the above-ground pool, in the backyard.

AS NATIONALISM SWEEPS COUNTRY, KOREA BLAMES ECONOMIC WOES ON US

2/19/2003

Despite a global economic downturn that many economists are blaming on a combination of factors, including fluctuating energy prices, the newly elected South Korean government is making waves by laying the blame squarely on the US. "Years of irresponsible financial practices have led the world to this point" said Chang Sung-taek, Korea's Minister of Finance. "Wall Street has stolen the Korea's hard earned money in the casino floor of exotic derivatives and other financial scams."

Many in the United States, however, do not share this opinion. "It's clear that the complicated and stressful process of re-integrating millions of poor, unskilled North Koreans into the regional economy has had a significant depressive effect on the South Korean economy," replied Princeton economist Saul Harris. Some critics in Seoul have even gone so far as to suggest that the US/North Korea military alliance has lost its value, and that the US military presence in the country is no longer needed.

Unique Weapons Detail: 9/17

WEAPONS >> Woodland M16 Rifle [Mk 1 ACOG Scope]

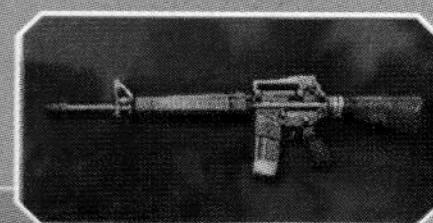

This exceptional single-fire armament can take down a foe with a single, well-aimed shot. Line up the sight with your enemy's head, pull the trigger, and he goes down. The faster you fire, the more shots are expelled. It's excellent for the precision tactician; perhaps swap out with the M110 Sniper Rifle you're carrying.

It Just Got Noisier

B.02

Once you step over the broken fencing, prepare for a well-orchestrated KPA ambush. An RPG-wielding enemy appears directly across (south of) the cul-de-sac you've moved into, and fires directly at you **[B.02]**. Sidestep and return fire at once; plenty of KPA pour out of the ground floor of the same house below, as well as to the left (east) and right (west) sides of the street.

TIP 영리한

Note that Goliath's icon has appeared in your inventory HUD, meaning you are moments away from employing this mobile killing machine. Ready yourself for its arrival.

Tactical Planning: Survival in the Cul-de-Sac

Threat Assessment: KPA Forces

You face at least 10 KPA infantry foes, including one with an RPG launcher, and they are more ferocious fighters than ever. They appear around the left side of the house across the cul-de-sac, out of that house (on the ground and upper floors), and from the house to the right (on both floors). Weathering this storm results in the KPA sending a Humvee crashing through to finish you, which is when your Goliath targeter comes in extremely handy.

Plan: "Kill 'em all!" Location

B.03

B.04

B.05

Following Rianna's emotional tactical considerations is the only option here, and with only minor differences in the tactics, such as where you're standing and which weapon you're using. Posture is important; if you remain between your team members in the middle of the fracas, close to the sofa and tree stump with Rianna, you have enough cover, but a slightly higher chance of foes targeting you **[B.03]**.

You need to keep this area clear for when Goliath comes to the rescue, so move to one side. This can be the car and furniture wreckage to the right (west), where Hopper is hiding **[B.04]**. Or, you can move to the speedboat where Connor is shooting from **[B.05]**; this is arguably the safest option because the boat is great to crouch behind, and you can step out to the left, with foes firing from a much narrower angle thanks to the barricade on your left (east).

Plan: "Kill 'em all!" Penetration

Choose a location and immediately target foes on the roof (especially if you're on the right side) **[B.06]**. Then (if you can), land an expertly lobbed grenade at groups of foes as they emerge from the houses (usually the one to the south where the RPG soldier fired from **[B.07]**). Catching multiple foes in an exploding blast augments your other main tactic: short, sharp, bursts of fire designed to bring down a single foe in a second, before you immediately switch to, and execute, the next foe. The M4 (which you began with), or the Unique M16 are both excellent choices here. The M110 sniper rifle is perhaps a little too unwieldy to use, but a good back-up option.

TIP 영리한

Having trouble aiming at all of the enemies in this maelstrom of violence? Then set your "Aim Assist" to "on" for some additional help.

CAUTION 조심하다

You can storm across the cul-de-sac, into the houses, or sprint to the cover (vehicles) across the road, but you're simply creating an easier target for the enemy. Staying with your team is the safest plan. On the off-chance that you make it into the house opposite, pick up the Unique Weapon.

Goliath Rolls In: "Target That Light Armor!"

Combat continues with no let-up from the KPA. If grenades are landing, step back or crouch down behind cover. Don't stop firing at foes though **[B.08]**, because they will swarm your location if you let them **[B.09]**.

Listen to Connor's yells, and react accordingly (for example, lob a grenade at the house entrance when he lets you know more are coming). As soon as a KPA Humvee careens into the cul-de-sac **[B.10]**, removing some of the barricade and allowing access further down (east) the street, watch the Goliath icon on your HUD.

When it changes to "Active," bring out the targeter, and immediately tag the Humvee. Failure to complete this task results in your eventual demise. As soon as the Humvee is targeted, step to the side and drop any foes causing immediate problems. Moments later, Goliath crashes into view and blasts the Humvee into smithereens **[B.11]**. Secure the Unique Weapon from inside the house to the south, where the majority of the foes came from, before you continue.

Objective: Protect Goliath from RPGs

Unique Weapons Detail: 10/17

WEAPONS >>
Shattered ACR Rifle
[Mk3 ACOG Scope]

With exceptional scope and rapid-fire bursts, this rifle is a must-have armament for the street combat to come. It can effortlessly target foes at whatever range is necessary, and drop them with quick clusters of shots. Use this on the RPG enemies to ease combat in the next two checkpoints.

CHECKPOINT C: GOLIATH RETURNS

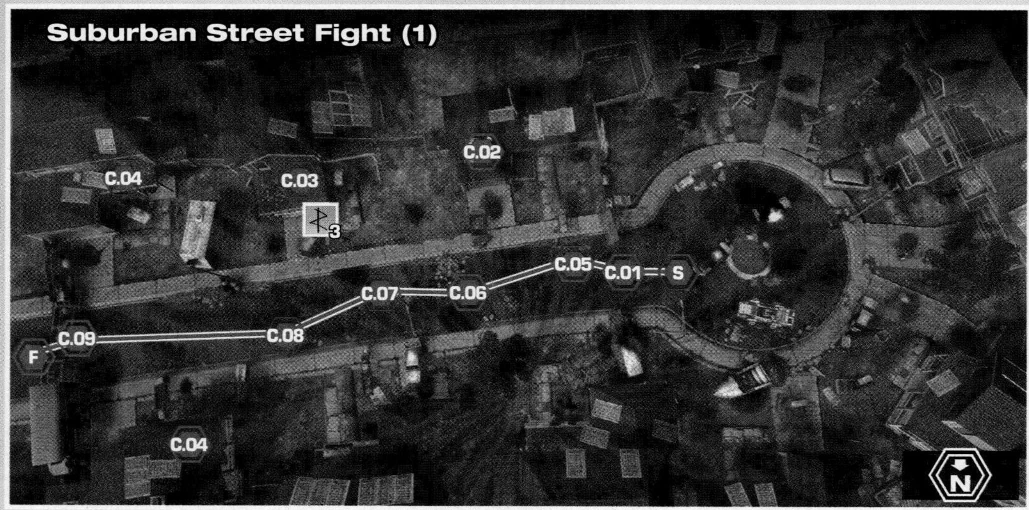

Friendlies

Goliath

Enemies

Soldier (Scout)

Soldier (Heavy)

Soldier

Soldier (RPG)

Objective: Eliminate the RPG Threats

"Jacobs, Take Out Those RPGs!"

The KPA's Humvee rampage was a blessing in disguise, because it cleared an area of street barricade **[C.01]**, allowing you to try to escape down this suburban war zone. The enemies are numerous, but you have a remote-controlled behemoth to help your cause. Reload, choose a primary weapon, remember that you're in charge of Goliath's main targeting, and push through.

Tactical Planning: Slaughter Down the Street

Threat Assessment: KPA Forces

Checkpoints C and D feature a multitude of KPA infantry, along with a nasty, mechanized surprise at the far end of the barricade-laden street. For now though, there are two types of enemy; primary targets with RPGs that appear on the porches or overhang roofs of the homes along each side of the street, and other infantry backing them up. The RPG targets are flagged with "Eliminate," and are easy to spot, but the trick here is to remove them before they cripple Goliath.

CAUTION 조심하다

Goliath is tough, but not indestructible; you must protect it from RPG enemies. Failure to do this results in Goliath's eventual explosion, and mission failure.

Plan: The Rocket Repellent

Remaining in good health yourself is your other main task, because plenty of KPA troops are shooting from the left and right sides of the street. Expect them to appear constantly as you push east down the street, toward a distant water tower. Unless you're being directly targeted by a foe on the ground, expect your teammates to engage them while you concentrate solely on defeating the enemies appearing on the roofs. Zoom in your aim, and drop each one. Around six of these RPG soldiers appear, on the second floor roof or balcony of each of the four main houses on the street (three are shown) **[C.02]**, **[C.03]**, **[C.04]**.

For cover, use the trees on the left or the car wreck on right. As Goliath progresses down the street, move up along either front verge or remain at the initial cover spots and target more foes at range. Keep tagging RPG foes unless you're spotted or shot at by enemies; drop any that threaten you before quickly switching back to your main task. Choose from multiple ways of bringing down the RPG enemies:

RPG Takedown Plan A: ACR, M4, or M16 Rifles

The optimal way to deal with these threats is to predict where a foe will step out from (the open windows in the locations shown above), and shoot before the foe even has time to aim his RPG **[C.05]**. For true takedown specialists, if the "Eliminate" tag has appeared, you're not being quick enough! Quickly zoom in, drop the foe, and move down the street until the next target appears. The Unique ACR Rifle you (should have) picked up in Checkpoint B is the best of the lot for this technique.

RPG Takedown Plan B: Goliath

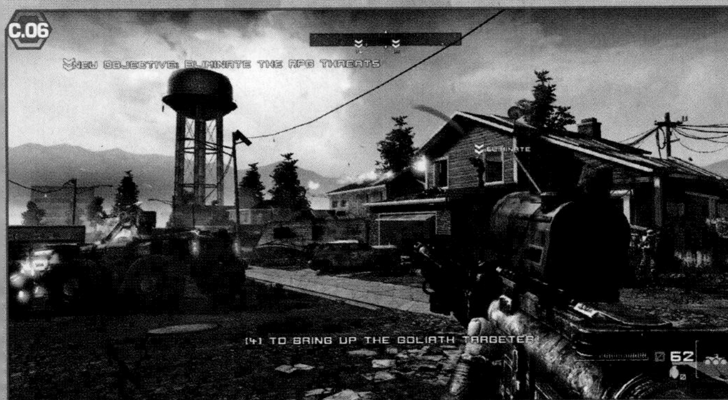

A secondary plan is to focus on the foe using Goliath's targeter system. When the target is flagged, let Goliath do the rest **[C.06]**. Usually, Goliath razes the area with explosive fire, taking multiple foes nearby. This advantage is tempered by the fact that the RPG wielder is likely to get one or two shots off before you target, lock on, and let Goliath fire. This is significantly slower than removing RPG threats using Plan A, so use this only if you're already targeting foes, and be sure the RPG foe is fully locked on, or Goliath's blast may miss.

RPG Takedown Plan C: Other Ordnance

The M110 Sniper Rifle (which you began the mission with) is an option for taking down enemy RPG wielders. However, the time it takes to target a foe, and the likelihood of other KPA attacking you, means you may be more susceptible to attacks while using this weapon. The M4 or M16 is a better bet **[C.07]**. Use Frag Grenades only as a last resort; grenades take time to explode, and landing one on a roof is time-consuming and tricky.

> **TIP 영리한**
>
> **Some houses have boarded-up windows, a sure sign that a foe may booting one out to reach a vantage point to fire an RPG from. Look for signs of that occurring, and react accordingly.**

Secondary Slaughtering

Ground troops are a consistent problem, and shooting all of them is both unnecessary and dangerous, because it takes you away from covering Goliath. Instead, use Goliath's targeting system and remove multiple threats with a barrage of rocket fire from the mobile weapon itself **[C.08]**.

The slow and explosive push down the street continues until your team reaches a bus and blockade, pausing along the way to retrieve a news pick-up by the garage of a house on the right side of the street. Goliath simply tears through this barricade **[C.09]**, and moves into a second area of the street, and to your next checkpoint.

HIDDEN HISTORY >> 3 (37/61)

Near the bushes on the right wall, outside the open garage of the second-to-last house on the right side of the street.

UNIFIED KOREAN MILITARY WILL INCLUDE MANY NORTH KOREAN SOLDIERS

4/7/2014

One of the major problems facing the governments of the two Koreas has been what to do with all the North Koreans. Lacking in any kind of technical skills, and in many cases any sense of personal identity, the utility of the citizenry remained a puzzle. The majority of the military, 4 million strong (2.4 million of which are in the reserves), will be integrated into existing South Korean military structure. It is expected that many North Korean officers will be discharged or demoted, posted under South Korean officers until their qualifications can be judged.

Many of the officers in the North Korean military got to where they are not through any particular set of skills, said a spokesman for the NK Military, "but through loyalty to the party and to Kim Jong-il. We're looking for the diamonds in the rough—the talented generals that genuinely want to rebuild our two nations." South Koreans reacted positively to this news; military service in South Korea is compulsory but unpopular—the hope is that this move will make compulsory service unnecessary.

CHECKPOINT D: THE BUS

Enemies

Soldier (Scout)

Soldier (RPG)

Soldier

T-99 Main Battle Tank

Soldier (Heavy)

Objective: Protect Goliath from RPG Enemies

Objective: Eliminate the RPG Threats

"Stand Back! Goliath's Coming Through!"

As Goliath rumbles through, you are presented with a further two foes with RPGs; one is almost immediately spotted **[D.01]** while the other kicks out a boarded-up window and steps on the lower roof of the next house on the right **[D.02]**. Bring them both down, while taking an interest in the incursion of foes to your left. A lobbed grenade can help, but after you finish off the last of the RPG threats, focus on utilizing Goliath's main missile weapons via your targeter instead.

Goliath rolls down the street to a much more sturdy blockade, which is reinforced by multiple incoming infantry foes. The only recommended course of action is to use Goliath's targeter, and continuously blast them [D.03] with bellowing fire until no more foes are present. Only then does your team hear the mechanized rumbling of a large enemy vehicle approach....

TIP 영리한

Hide behind Goliath's frame when you're targeting the foes on the barricade. You don't need to be close to the foes either; in fact, you're more likely to be wounded if so. Once the infantry enemies are culled, position yourself by the garage next to the last house on the left (north) side of the street, for a quick getaway....

Mettle of Honor

Award David Rejected | Rating 10 | Trophy Bronze

Use quick-thinking and an eagle-eye to remove all the RPG threats before they have a chance to fire on Goliath. Succeed in this task throughout Checkpoints C and D to receive this reward. No RPG shot must touch Goliath.

CHECKPOINT E: TANK!

Objective: Follow Goliath

Enemies

T-99 Main Battle Tank

"Through the House, Now!"

The rumbling crescendoes as a KPA tank crashes through the barricade, coming to a rest with its turret pointing at your team [E.01]. Instantly, Hopper reacts and controls Goliath as it rams into the adjacent house, smashing through the ground floor and out into the backyard. You are encouraged— in no uncertain terms—to follow Goliath through the newly created hole [E.02]. The alternative is to shrug off a tank shell, which is as impossible as it is pointless and foolhardy.

CAUTION 조심하다

Staying outside near the tank is a problem. The shells it fires can kill you. Although you can position the car between you and the tank (to absorb its shots), you can't destroy the tank. Running at it is hopeless, and grenades bounce off it.

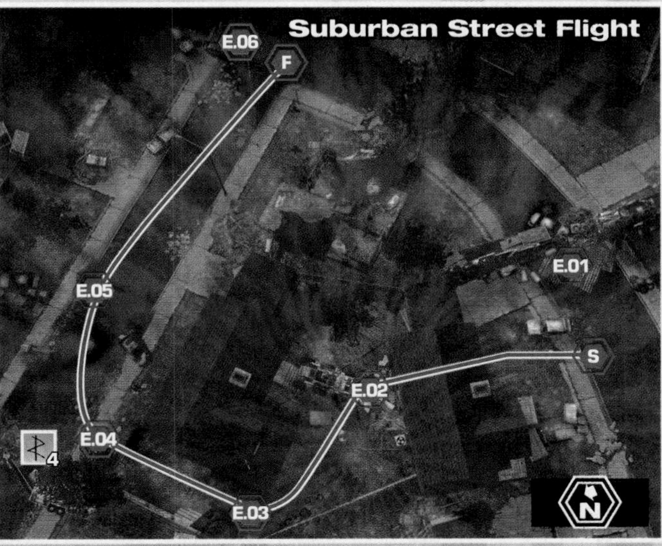

Objective: Follow Rianna

Connor and Hopper argue about taking the tank down, with a final plan being to flank the enemy vehicle and hit it from the rear. Run to where Rianna is standing, by a closed gate in a side yard of an adjacent property [E.03], and wait for her to kick the gate open. Then sprint out toward a nearby street.

The tank comes lumbering in from the right (south), and will fire on you constantly until you put Connor's plan into practice. You can't dodge those shells forever, so bring up the targeter. You can do this while hiding behind the wrecked vehicle to the right, or the tree to the left (north), with the tank in the distance. Or, you can bring the targeter up as soon as you reach the road **[E.04]**, sidestepping from south to north. Lock on, and activate Goliath!

The machine comes charging through the house you escaped around the side of, and launches a barrage of projectile strikes, engulfing the tank in fire **[E.05]**. The enemy machinery explodes, but not before returning fire and crippling Goliath in the process. As the smoke begins to clear, Hopper runs over and leaps aboard Goliath, arguing with Connor about mending his machine. Rianna joins Hopper, and soon brings Goliath back online **[E.06]**. This is just in time; Connor believes the team is going to need Goliath again. Be sure to check the barricaded area behind (northwest) of you for another news pick-up.

Objective: Follow Connor

HIDDEN HISTORY >> 4 (38/61)

Among the rusting appliances by a barricade, at the northwest end of the street where the tank was defeated.

TWO KOREAS UNITED IN LANDMARK VOTE

2/28/2015

Kim Jong-un, Nobel Laureate and son of former dictator Kim Jong-il was elected as president of a unified Korea in the first democratic elections held in the newly reunited country. More than seventy percent of the country's combined population turned out to give him an overwhelming majority in the popular vote.

Polls suggest that Jong-un's appeal is derived from his stance of unification, equality and an historical perspective of Korea as a great cultural power. While supporters have enthusiastically embraced his message, some critics have decried his viewpoints and messages as overly nationalist and jingoistic. The Korean president is also commander and chief of the military, and serves for a non-renewable 5 year term.

CHECKPOINT F: MISGIVINGS

Brooks

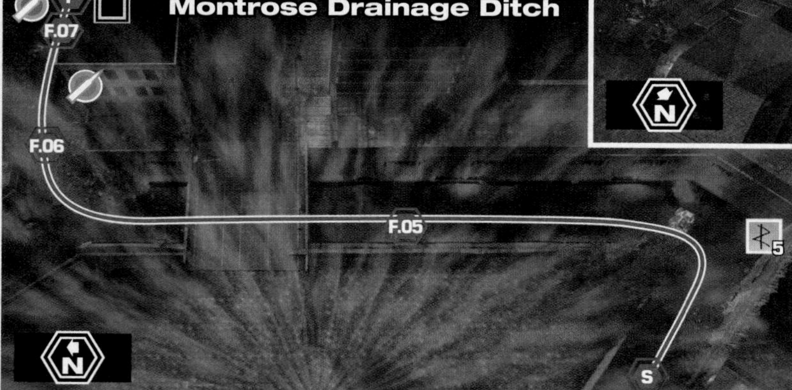

Disproportionate Response

Connor is in radio contact with Brooks, who's waiting near the Montrose wall, ready to punch a hole through that monstrosity. As Goliath trundles southeast down the street, follow Connor and the team around the shell of the burned-out tank **[F.01]** and over a fallen barricade near a green garbage truck **[F.02]**, where another Unique Weapon is nestled, by the front wheel of the truck itself. There's a considerable amount of smoke on the horizon, and as you reach a drainage ditch and the concrete pad that the Montrose water tower rests on, Rianna is the first to see what has happened.... Overkill. Literally.

Unique Weapons Detail: 11/17

WEAPONS >>
Woodland SCAR-H LMG [Mk1 Red Dot Sight]

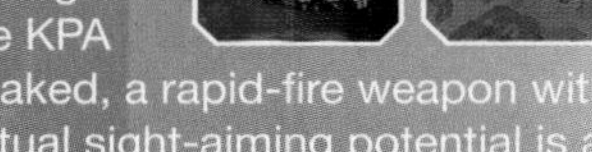

With your outrage at the KPA peaked, a rapid-fire weapon with actual sight-aiming potential is a devastating option; but watch those ammunition reserves!

Objective: Follow Connor

As you stand above the drainage ditch **[F.03]**, Montrose is ablaze, with the screams of the dying only marginally blocked by the deafening cluster bombs and heavy rocket barrages the KPA are inflicting on innocents. The team talks in stunned murmurs. Then Connor turns and heads down the steps, more determined than ever to see Boone's plan to completion. Follow him, heading over the partially crushed fence that Goliath drove over **[F.04]**. Check the drainage ditch to the south, in the corner by the graffiti, for more news.

HIDDEN HISTORY >> 5 (39/61)

On the small mound of weeds by the graffitied drainage walls, in the southern corner, just after entering the ditch.

THE CHARISMATIC AUTHORITY OF KIM JONG-UN

4/12/2016

He seems to be blessed with all of his father's charisma and none of his madness. The 33 year-old president of unified Korea has tapped into something that lies deep within the souls of many Koreans: the idea that their culture is special, and has a significant place in guiding the future of the world.

In his frequent addresses to the nation, Jong-un refers to the 20th century as the "Lost Century," a time when Japan took the country by force and the country split in two and went to war with itself. Jong-un seems to speak to his people on a deeply cultural level, providing a guiding light to a nation stuck in an economic morass and entrenched in cultural shame. He frequently refers to the Chosun Kingdom in his speeches, a reminder of the apogee of Korean culture, literature, science, trade and technology. The Chosun Kingdom existed for approximately five hundred years, between 1400 and 1900, and occupied roughly the same geographical area as present-day Korea. Jong-un wants his people to remember the distant past, forget the 20th century, and look to the future, which Jong-un believes will be defined by the Korean way of life.

Babbling Brooks

Begin to sprint through the ankle-deep water of the massive drainage ditch, leaving the massacre behind you. Rianna believes the cause is doomed, but Connor isn't hearing any of it. Sprint northward along the channel **[F.05]**, under a bridge as Connor convinces the team of the just and worthy task to come. Turning right (east), Connor meets a guard at a gate, telling him the team is looking for Brooks **[F.06]**. The gate slowly rolls open. Be sure you claim the Unique Weapon by the mesh fence before you reach the gate.

Unique Weapons Detail: 12/17

WEAPONS >> Woodland M4 Rifle [Mk1 Holo Scope]

A trusted rifle, along with an impressive scope allows the best mixture of tactical and aggressive fighting in the streets to come. Be sure you grab this before entering the gate, as there's no way back!

Brooks turns from his map-reading to greet Connor, amid the walking wounded of his small camp in a parking lot behind the main road **[F.07]**. He explains that there are RPG teams backed up by KPA regulars between here and the wall. Brushing off a protest from Hopper, Connor wants Goliath as a "mule." While Hopper and Rianna pack it with as much C4 as they can stuff into the vehicle's chassis, you're pushing through with Connor, clearing a path to the wall, so Goliath can follow behind with minimal enemy retaliation. Check the Kodex to the right of the exit fence, and the news pick-up by the trash bin behind you, then reload, tool up, and follow Connor into the roadblock zone. You may be interested in an M110 Sniper Rifle by one of the corpses, too.

Objective: Follow Connor

WEAPONS >> M110 Sniper Rifle

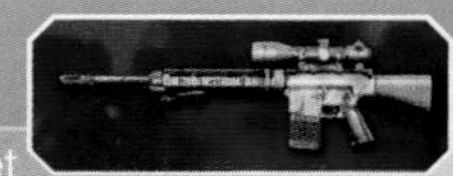

By one of the corpses with a sheet over it, close to Brooks and the exit gate.

KOREAN KODEX >> 1 (7/10)

On the white-washed wall near the refuse, behind Brooks' camp, near the exit gate and mesh fence.

HIDDEN HISTORY >> 6 (40/61)

In the corner by the wounded resistance fighter, in Boone's rendezvous area.

CANADA ENDS "OPEN BORDERS" POLICY WITH UNITED STATES *6/18/2016*

In a joint statement issued in Niagara Falls, representatives from the US Immigration and Naturalization Service, standing alongside their counterparts from Citizenship and Immigration Canada, announced an end to the longstanding "Open Borders" policy that has defined the relationship between the United States and its sister nation to the north.

Already required to present a passport at any border crossing, citizens of both nations will now have to apply for Visas at least a month in advance to travel across the border. Representatives stressed that special permits will continue to be issued for vehicles carrying critical supplies, including oil and building materials, as well as food and medicine.

CHECKPOINT G: ONCE MORE INTO THE BREACH

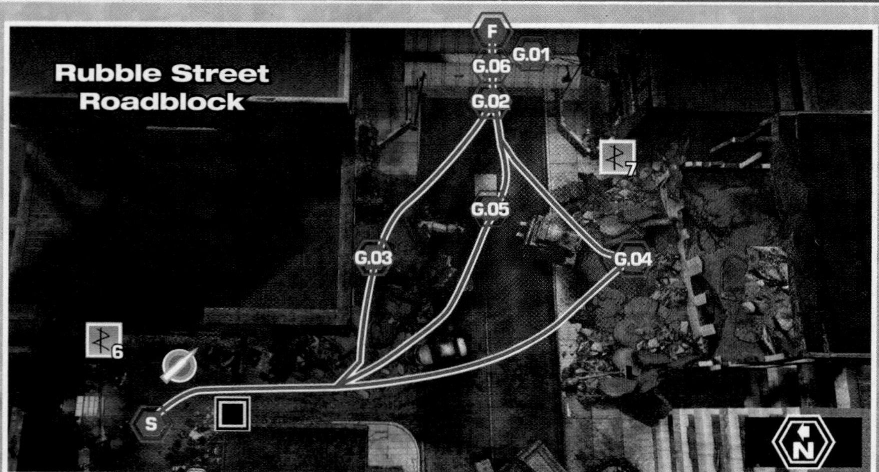

Friendlies

Connor

Fighters

Enemies

Soldier (Scout)

Soldier

Objective: Lower the Barricade for Goliath

"Get Out There and Bring That Roadblock Down!"

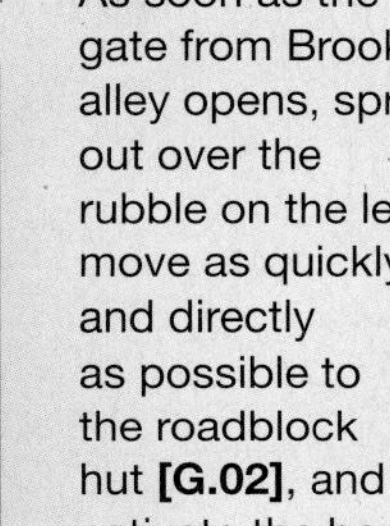

G.01

The plan is simple, but the execution requires a modicum of pre-planning and bravery. The first barricade to activate is on the main, rubble-filled street **[G.01]**, at a roadblock to the east. It is on ground level, and although the spiked metal barricade is to the left, the switch is in the hut in the middle of the roadblock itself. Reaching that involves one of the following executions:

Tactical Planning: Unblocking Barricades

Threat Assessment: KPA Forces

Checkpoints G and H feature at least 10 guards attempting to reach dug-in positions on the left (north) side of the scaffolding walkway, behind the roadblock, and along the right side where further scaffolding and concrete ground barriers serve as cover. Once the first metal barricade is activated, expect foes in a cluttered area of road filled with crates and concrete barriers, with a second roadblock to the east (foes appear from this location). Ignore that and concentrate on the White Castle and the foes appearing from inside.

TIP 영리한

Waiting around simply encourages more and more KPA reinforcements to arrive, so completing the objective becomes of paramount importance, unless you want a protracted battle and possible stalemate.

TIP 영리한

You should have picked up two Unique Weapons prior to this checkpoint. Using either or both of these is an excellent way to remove the remaining KPA between here and the wall.

Plan A: The Sprinter

G.02

As soon as the gate from Brooks' alley opens, sprint out over the rubble on the left, move as quickly and directly as possible to the roadblock hut **[G.02]**, and activate the barricade controls. If you try shrugging off fire as you go, you almost always die, so this Plan is only recommended on the easiest of difficulty settings. Cut down the two or three nearest foes, and then drop to a crouch or go prone once inside the hut as you lower the barricade. Then remain inside the hut, or pop out and return fire (or use grenades) to the foes immediately left and right of you. The enemy retreats once the barricade lowers.

Plan B: The Sniper

G.03

G.04

A more measured response is to rush up onto the rubble on the street's left side **[G.03]**. You can also rush across to the right side, and use the rubble there **[G.04]**, although that takes a bit longer to reach. You have a commanding view of the roadblock and the enemies milling about in the vicinity. Now take quick, exact, and preferably zoomed burst-fire shots at the enemies (using any rifle with a good scope, or the M110 Sniper Rifle found back at Brooks's hideout), starting with the foe behind the sandbags on the upper scaffold, lobbing a grenade into the area just behind the barricade (although you may want to save your grenades for the next checkpoint area), and tagging more foes to the right as you spot them. Don't elongate this battle because further foes appear (from around the corner, to the left, behind the roadblock). When only a few enemies remain and Connor yells "they're falling back!", sprint (Plan A) and lower the barricade, before further forces arrive.

TIP 영리한

Remember that going prone or crouching once you're holding down the activation switch helps you hide from incoming enemy fire.

Plan C: The Street Fighter

You don't need to use the rubble on either side of the street to repel the enemies; you can head down the middle of the street instead, using the concrete barricade as cover **[G.05]**, and quickly dropping foes who attempt to vault over. Your biggest threats are on the scaffold and either side of the street. Shoot anything that moves on the other side of the roadblock, until Connor gives you the order. Although you don't have as many places to remain hidden, or the height advantage, you can sprint to the barricade more quickly.

CAUTION 조심하다

You can't jump the concrete barriers, so don't waste time or risk being shot at attempting this.

When you've reached the "Activate" location **[G.06]** and lowered the barricade, the next checkpoint begins. Don't head onward, however, until you've secured your next news pick-up!

HIDDEN HISTORY >> 7 (41/61)

Next to trash bin, on the outside corner of the brick wall, at the Votypka Foot Massage store.

MARTIAL LAW DECLARED AS US CITIES DESCEND INTO CHAOS *10/29/2017*

The president declared and put into effect Executive Order 12919 today, allowing him to prioritize the allocation of materials, services and facilities as deemed necessary to promote the national defense. In a statement released from the White House, the heads of the major agencies including Agriculture, Health, Energy, Commerce and Transportation would co-ordinate under the Dept. of Defense and the Department of Homeland Security to help quell civil unrest in major urban centers and distribute goods to the population.

The military will be deployed to New York, San Francisco, Los Angeles and other major urban centers to distribute aid and to help restore order. Travel into and out of cities will be heavily regulated until further notice, and FEMA will establish aid camps outside of urban centers to assist the poor and displaced. Citizens are expected to adhere to the restrictions announced by authorities and prepare to relocate, if instructed.

CHECKPOINT H: PUSH TO THE WALL

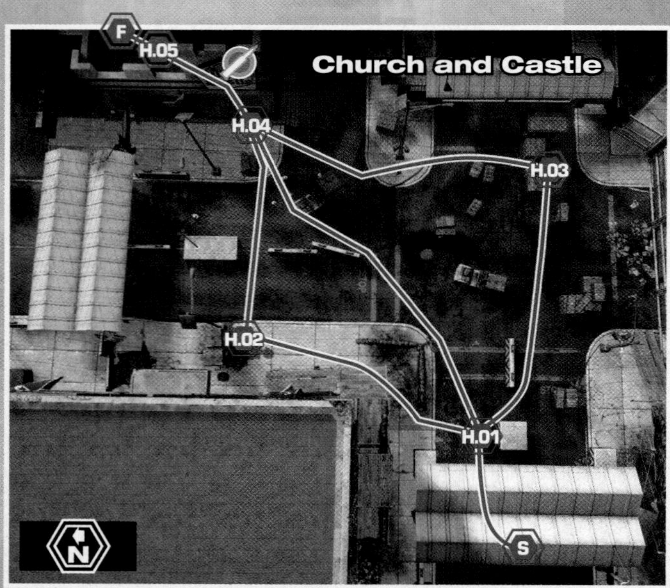

Enemies

Soldier (Scout)

Soldier

TIP 영리한

Using Frag Grenades is a great idea during these final checkpoints, because you can likely replenish your stock from the ground around fallen foes.

TIP 영리한

Remember! Your overall task here is to infiltrate, not kill everyone! You're likely to miss a straggler or two, so focus on the objective at hand.

Objective: Cover Connor

As soon as the barricade is down, you can push forward through the open roadblock **[H.01]**, and continue your charge. However, your objective states that you need to cover Connor. Keep him in front of you as you battle toward the White Castle to the northeast. This presents a few possible plans:

Battle for the Castle Plan A: Left Side Infiltration

With Connor in front or by your side, cut down foes on your right as you move and sidestep left, before lobbing a grenade at the enemies lurking around the entrance to the White Castle. Expect gunfire and more foes heading in from the road to the left (north); move behind the armored crates on the left sidewalk **[H.02]** so you can concentrate your fire to the east. Clear out the area, and then rush for the interior of the White Castle with Connor.

Battle for the Castle Plan B: Right Side Infiltration

While Connor rushes along the left side of the street, you may wish to repel enemies with a dash to the right, toward a parked truck, and sprint up into the flatbed, using the armored crates as cover **[H.03]**. This affords a height advantage, splits the enemies' targets (because Connor is across the street), and allows easy access into the White Castle, as well as providing obstacle-free shooting and grenade-lobbing opportunities. All these reasons make this the preferred plan. When most of the enemies are neutralized, make a break for the interior of the White Castle.

Battle for the Castle Plan C: Charge!

Waiting for your teammate is the advisable plan, but you don't have to. If you intend to rush the White Castle from the first barricade, simply shrug off any enemy fire, or lob a grenade to your left, and in the confusion charge directly through the front doors of the White Castle **[H.04]**, cutting down any enemies both outside and inside the premises. Because you're probably already wounded after using this lunatic tactic, use the counters as cover, or sidestep around into the storage corridor and use it as cover. Then wait for Connor to push through and greet you. This plan is dangerous but quick.

> **CAUTION 조심하다**
>
> **You can move to the second roadblock from the side of the road where the White Castle is, and peer through to the wall itself, as well as dropping the guards in this area. However, more will arrive, so you're simply wasting ammunition.**

Objective: Follow Connor into White Castle

White Castle Interior

Once inside the White Castle **[H.05]**, you may have a foe or two inside to deal with, so don't lower your guard. Clear the area, and check the counter to the right (southeast) as you enter. There's a shotgun here, which is an optional weapon to swap a current armament with. Choose this if you wish, then join Connor (or beat him to) the exit to the northeast. Quickly pass into an adjacent building and begin a final assault on the wall.

WEAPONS >>
870 Express Shotgun

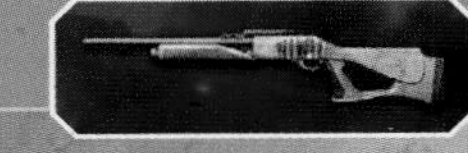

Near the counter, inside White Castle.

> **CAUTION 조심하다**
>
> **Although the shotgun may appear to be an excellent choice, your next checkpoint involves some long-range sniping. In addition, if you miss a foe with a blast at closer quarters, you're more likely to be cut down by their fire as you re-aim. Precise, one-shot takedowns are the order of the day if you choose this!**

CHECKPOINT I: THE GARAGE

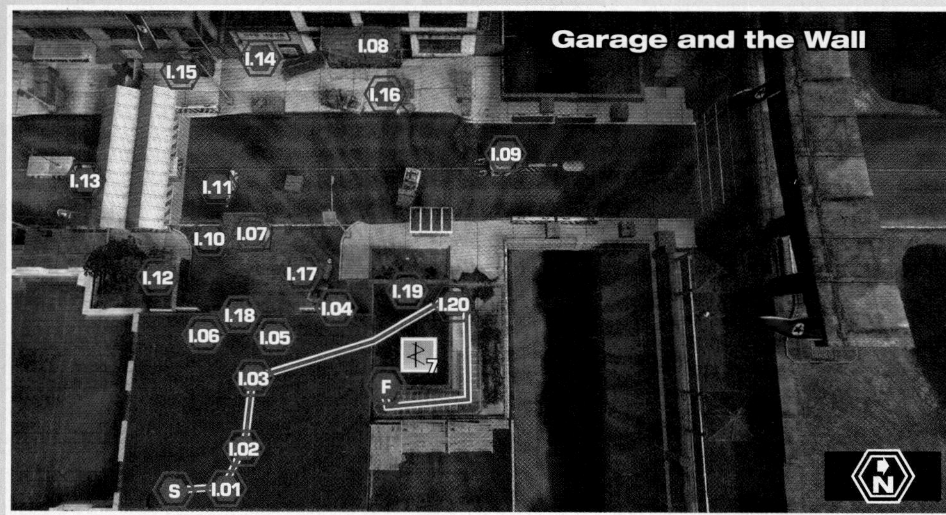

Friendlies

Hopper

Rianna

Enemies

Soldier (Scout)

Soldier

Soldier (RPGt)

Objective: Break Open the Door

Garage Clean Up

Connor is waiting at a metal door **[I.01]**, encouraging you to boot it open, so a side garage with access behind the last roadblock can fall to Resistance hands. Oblige him, and as the door bursts open, time slows for a moment. You have time for a single shotgun blast (or a burst of rifle fire), taking down three enemies to your right, left, and ahead of you (in that order, due to their proximity and threat to you) **[I.02]**. As time adjusts, make a final shot at the explosive barrel behind the fourth and fifth foes inside the garage, and eradicate all the foes with some adept blasting **[I.03]**.

TIP 영리한

You risk a melee attack if you forget or refuse to fire. However, each foe falls to only one bullet. This includes rifle fire, making the shotgun from the previous checkpoint an even worse choice.

Objective: Clear a Path to the Wall for Goliath

Tactical Planning: Activation and Elimination

Threat Assessment: KPA Wall Guards

The KPA is sending most of its remaining forces in the area to bolster the massive concrete fortified wall at the north end of the street. Expect six to eight foes by the numerous concrete barriers on the road, with more pouring over a wall on the west side to increase their numbers. These are augmented by three RPG foes who must be eliminated. One (easily overlooked) sharpshooter is to the west, on the upper (but inaccessible) floor of the Montrose Center. The other two are flanked by machine-gunners on a balcony on either side of the wall.

As soon as normal time resumes, make sure the garage is secure. Bring down one or two enemy guards to the right of the almost-closed metal garage door **[I.04]**, near the doorway to the right that leads into a small office. Then concentrate on tackling the RPG foes.

RPG Enemy Takedown Plan: Weaponry

Rifles: A rifle is the weapon of choice to remove RPG threats **[I.05]**. Using the scope and a quick burst of fire (or more than one burst) until the distant enemy falls is quick, allows you to see and react to any foes in your peripheral vision, and permits quick targeting of the machine gun enemies. This is the recommended weapon.

Sniper Rifle: If you still have the M100 from the beginning of this mission, this is another choice. The obvious benefit is the one-shot kill, but the downside is the lack of additional zoom, making the two wall guards hard to hit. You can't easily react to closer, encroaching enemies either. With these caveats, the sniper rifle is a good alternative.

Other Ordnance: Frag Grenades are obviously out, as is the shotgun with its terrible range.

RPG Enemy Takedown Plan: Tactics (1)

RPG Enemy #1: At the earliest opportunity, stand in the garage—ideally to the right of the parked Humvee **[I.06]**—and tag this foe in the window. This is incredibly easy and straightforward, and the garage shelters you from enemies on the road.

Roadblock: Although you can attempt other plans, such as engaging foes or tackling the RPG enemies on the wall, your next priority should be to quickly step into the hut to the west and activate the switch, lowering the final barricade **[I.07]**. Completing this first enables Hopper and Rianna (as well as Goliath, although Hopper controls its firepower) to provide covering fire, easing your burden for removing the remaining two RPG threats.

TIP

Remember you can crouch or go prone as you're holding the switch and waiting for the barricades to recede.

RPG Enemy Takedown Plan: Tactics (2)

From this point on, your most pressing concern is to tackle the RPG threats on the wall. Don't dismiss the foes closer to you though, because they advance along the streets and can cause considerable trouble to Resistance forces. Before trying a major part of this task (such as lowering the roadblock, or tagging an RPG enemy), be sure the enemies are pushed back to the bridge itself, using swift takedowns of the foes on the west scaffold **[I.08]**, or behind concrete cover. Use your remaining grenades during this time, too **[I.09]**.

RPG Enemy Takedown Plan: Tactics (3)

RPG Enemies #2 and #3: You can shoot them from a number of locations in and around the garage and roadblock, such as:

[RECOMMENDED] Sidestepping out from the garage door near the Humvee, and then back into the garage if you're struck by enemy fire, optionally using the hut where you activate the barriers as cover **[I.10]**.

[RECOMMENDED] The concrete barrier to the left (west) of the hut with the switch inside it **[I.11]**.

The wall with the tree, behind and to the right (southeast), adjacent to the roadblock **[I.12]**.

Behind the roadblock itself, close to the White Castle (but only after the roadblock is lowered) **[I.13]**.

The entrance alcove at the foot of the scaffold ramp, on the west side of the street. Sidestep here during a lull in the fighting, or face heavy fire (Enemy #3 only) **[I.14]**.

[RECOMMENDED] The sandbag to the left (west) of the roadblock, on the west side of the street **[I.15]**.

Any of the cover opportunities (boxes or armored crates) on the west side of the street, although the ones closer to the bridge are much more dangerous **[I.16]**.

CAUTION 조심하다

Advancing on the bridge is pointless (more enemies will appear until the objective is met) and dangerous (you're much easier to hit by rockets or the machine-gunners).

[RECOMMENDED] The forklift truck and exterior corner wall of the garage office, on the near (east) side of the street, although expect massive retaliation because you're a little too close to the enemy **[I.17]**.

The gap near the barrel, under the half-open garage door inside the garage. You must be prone (Enemy #2 only) **[I.18]**.

[RECOMMENDED] The service center office attached to the garage, which offers excellent opportunities to strafe the foes on the bridge, too (Enemy #2 only) **[I.19]**.

Objective: Regroup in the Office

Once all three RPG enemies have been removed, and the last barrier has been lowered, sprint back to the garage and into the service office. Check behind the counter for your final news pick-up (for this mission). Rianna kicks open the door **[I.20]**. Follow her into a narrow backyard—if you haven't removed the right-side machine-gunner, use the cover at the doorway and easily take him down—and up the stairs to the garage roof.

Objective: Follow Rianna

HIDDEN HISTORY >> 8 (42/61)

Below the computer monitor, on the floor behind the service counter, in the garage office.

KOREA DECLARES WAR AGAINST JAPAN *4/1/2018*

In his weekly radio address to Koreans, Kim Jung Un declared that Korea had a "heavenly mandate" to protect ethnic Koreans being murdered in Japan. Of the nearly 1 million now living there, an estimated 12,000 have been killed in a series of violent attacks over the past year following news of an alleged assassination attempt on the Japanese royal family.

"In the past few months, Koreans in Japan have seen a significant escalation of racial crimes against their property and their persons," Kim said in his address. "We have lobbied the United Nations and the international community to take action, but no action has been taken. Therefore, it has fallen on me to declare that a state of war exists between the nation of Korea and the nation of Japan. Korea will not allow the systematic murder of tens of thousands of its citizens as the world sits idle."

"On my orders, Korean Special Forces have begun taking specific strategic targets with the goal of gaining leverage against the government of Japan. These are the opening stages of what will be a broad campaign to restore an environment of peace to East Asia. My fellow citizens, the dangers to our country and the world will be overcome. We will pass through this time of peril and carry on the work of peace. We will defend our freedom. We will bring freedom to others. And we will prevail."

CHECKPOINT J: SACRIFICE

Enemies

Soldier (Scout)

Soldier

Humvee

Objective: Pick up the RPG

Objective: Shoot Goliath with an RPG

WEAPONS >>

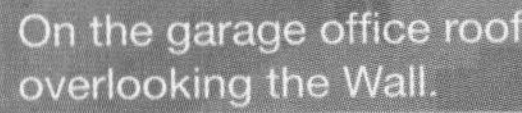

RPG Launcher

On the garage office roof overlooking the Wall.

Goodbye, Old Friend

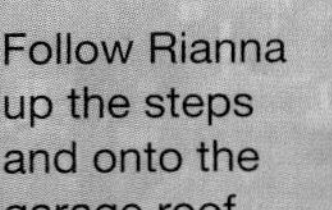

Follow Rianna up the steps and onto the garage roof itself. Propped against the roof lip in the opposite (northwest) corner is an RPG. Follow your team's advice, and pick it up. There are eight shots for this heavy weapon, but only one is needed. Although you might be tempted to aim a barrage at the enemies that have appeared on top of the wall, concentrate on Goliath, which has been moved forward to the base of the giant wall. You can optionally zoom in when targeting Goliath if you don't trust your regular aim. Then fire **[J.01]**.

If you hit successfully, Goliath explodes in a huge ball of fire, punching a massive hole and removing the metal gate that sealed the wall **[J.02]**. Escape time!

CAUTION 조심하다

There's no need to shoot any KPA infantry on the wall because your team helps out with that. However, the only foes you might wish to fire on are the machine-gunners if you left them in their wall nests during the previous checkpoint.

Objective: Get in the Humvee

West on 50 to Utah

Assuming you didn't shoot Goliath before it reached the gate, or used all the RPG shells and missed Goliath, or attempted to shoot Goliath without using the RPG, Hopper is waiting downstairs inside the garage, revving the Humvee **[J.03]**. Race downstairs through the office, and leap up the rear of the vehicle; you're manning the turret. Hopper quickly reverses out of the garage, and heads for the perimeter wall.

Now that you have 360-degree machine-gun fire, the enemies ahead of you stand little chance. Although you can shrug off their fire, it is always better to remove threats before you pass them, although you can ignore the ineffectual infantry, and instead target the KPA Humvees. You careen toward the smoking gap in the wall **[J.04]**.

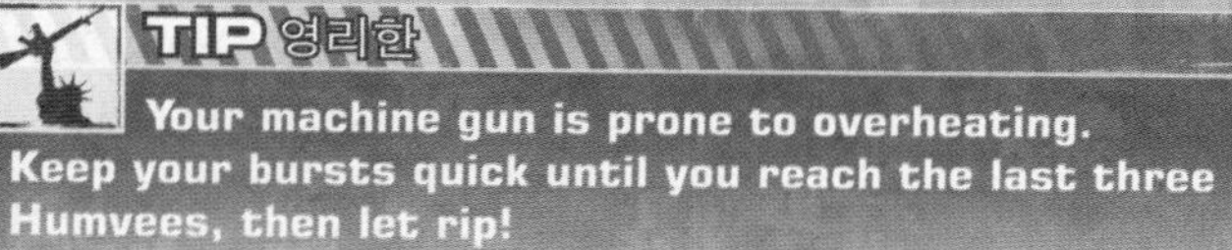

TIP 영리한

Your machine gun is prone to overheating. Keep your bursts quick until you reach the last three Humvees, then let rip!

The first Humvee to target **[J.05]** is on the right side just after you break out of the Montrose wall. There's a second **[J.06]** on the right side of the road, left of a school bus. Then strafe three more Humvees **[J.07]**, from right to left as you crash through a (much less secure) road barricade, swinging the turret round to finish the Humvees off as your team races off toward US 50. Next stop is the survivalists' camp, where Boone's old buddies are certain to help the cause....

Mettle of Honor

Award	Rating	Trophy
The Wall	10	Bronze

Completing this mission earns you this particular reward. Difficulty level, or how many times you restarted a checkpoint, do not matter.

Mettle of Honor

Award	Rating	Trophy
The Wall—Guerrilla	25	Bronze

Completing this mission earns you this individual reward. However, you must complete this on the hardest difficulty.

Mettle of Honor

Award	Rating	Trophy
Iron Man—The Wall	25	Bronze

Completing this mission without dying once or restarting a checkpoint earns you this reward. Lessen the difficulty if you're having problems completing this task.

MISSION SELECT >>05 >>HEARTLAND

After escaping Montrose, the squad finds itself in no man's land. They will have to bargain for the last piece of Boone's plan, a helicopter, with a gang of American survivalists. Their paranoia and savagery are the stuff of nightmares.

 **HIDDEN HISTORY** >> 13 (55/61 total)

 **KOREAN KODEX** >> 1 (8/10 total)

 **UNIQUE WEAPON** >> 2 (14/17 total)

CHECKPOINT A: THE DEAL

Friendlies

Connor

Hopper

Rianna

Enemies

Compound Veteran

Compound Guard

WEAPONS >>
M4 Rifle [Mk1 ACOG Scope]

WEAPONS >>
PWS Diablo SMG [Mk 1 Holo Scope]

You begin the mission with these weapons.

"I Guess the Deal's Off."

Connor motions for Hopper to hide behind one of the car wrecks **[A.01]**; the survivalists won't take kindly to his sort. Then he advances to meet a couple of neckerchief-wearing locals, and their leader. They recognize Connor, who asks for the chopper. The survivalists want to know where Boone is. Connor explains Boone is dead **[A.02]**. The tension ramps up considerably when Rianna strides forward to shout in the leader's face. She's grabbed in a chokehold as Connor attempts to calm the situation.

The leader demands Rianna and Hopper in exchange for the chopper **[A.03]**. Connor tells them they're getting the bad end of that deal, as Rianna grabs her captor's arm, breaks it, and pushes the crippled guard forward, knocking the other guard's gun away. Connor and Rianna pounce, killing the three survivalists **[A.04]**. It looks like the deal is off. Bursts of gunfire and yelling confirm this violent, but not altogether unexpected conclusion.

CHECKPOINT B: GONE SOUR

Objective: Eliminate the Survivalists

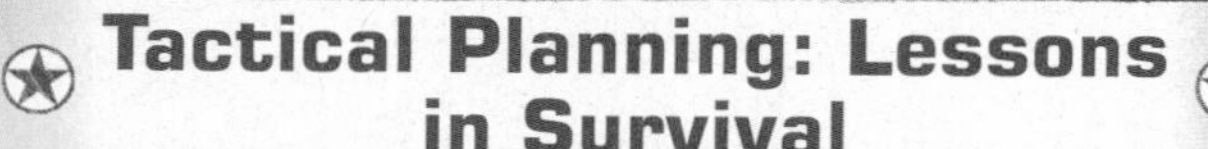

Tactical Planning: Lessons in Survival

Compound Guard

Threat Assessment: Survivalist Guards

You're facing around 10 dug-in survivalists, well armed with automatic weaponry, shotguns, and one RPG. You have a large expanse of clear ground to fire across, so patience becomes a recommended facet of your combat repertoire. Eliminate the foe in the watchtower, and (once Rianna and Connor push forward) the RPG-wielding goon up on the windmill to the right (north). But beware of foes at the windows of the dilapidated home on the right (north), too.

Rianna and Connor immediately rush to cover behind armored equipment crates on each side of the bridge you're on. You now have a choice of how to conduct yourself during this frantic battle:

Plan A: Massacre from Afar

While facing forward (north), you can retreat slightly, either to the vehicle Hopper is hiding behind **[B.01]**, or a small guard deck with a corrugated fence at the left corner of the start of the bridge **[B.02]**. From either of these locations, you can let your colleagues do some of the work, while you tackle any foes moving from right to left out of the house, or behind the parked big-rig or other cover. This isn't an optimal plan, but it keeps you safe.

Plan B: Encroach and Execute

Once your team is in cover, a better plan is to join either of them; Rianna is better positioned, and staying behind the adjacent armored crate and red pickup **[B.03]** allows you to fire on the foes coming out of the house to the right, or the rusting vehicles farther down the road. Connor's position **[B.04]** offers less-optimal line-of-sight opportunities to tag foes inside the house, but allows you to fire on enemies to the left (northwest), hiding behind the truck or a rusting AC unit.

Now whittle away at the foes using scoped bursts of rifle fire. As your other weapon is an SMG, stick to this longer-ranged rifle. Bring down foes racing from the house, or behind vehicular cover **[B.05]**. When prompted by your team, check the guard tower directly ahead (north) of you **[B.06]**, and shoot the foe sniping at you. This is important because he's dug in and much more difficult to aim at once you move forward.

You can stay at Rianna or Connor's position, and play a deadly game of hide and seek with the foes still behind cover on the road, or move forward to the armored crate at the far left (northwest) end of the bridge **[B.07]**. At this point, around six foes in the ruined house to your right pop up from windows, as well as a foe with an RPG firing down from the windmill to your right (northeast). Bring down the foe with the RPG first **[B.08]**.

TIP

Crouching behind cover helps minimize damage you receive from foes, although you can't instantly sprint.

The remaining foes inside the house sometimes edge out onto the cover behind the porch. You can defeat them from behind your initial cover **[B.09]**, or (if you've moved forward to the front crate) you can tag them from there, from one of the rusting vehicles, or from the large corrugated fence section close to the front yard of the house itself **[B.10]**. Keep the pressure on the foes until they're all dealt with; check all the windows until no more faces peer out.

Plan C: Close-Quarter Carnage

Your secondary weapon is an SMG, and if the red mist descends, you can (at any time during the previous two plans) charge forward and begin some systematic, close-quarter SMG takedowns. These are as spectacular as they are dangerous, because you can be shot when you sprint in toward your chosen foe. If you attempt this early, you can run around the parked vehicles **[B.11]**, cutting down a foe **[B.12]** and ducking behind cover, then repeating the plan. You can also attempt this using your primary weapon, or any of the Survivalists' weapons, as shown.

Or you can sprint for the house, and bring your chosen weapon to bear on the foes standing on or near the porch [B.13]. Then dive inside, blasting foes on the ground floor before sprinting up the stairs and finishing the foes above [B.14]. On the off-chance you're still alive, use your rifle to drop the foe on the windmill with the RPG, and the sniper in the guard tower. Then stand at a window or on the porch roof and blast any remaining foes on the ground. This is a difficult, reckless, and incredibly satisfying way to meet and beat the survivalists.

Objective: Rendezvous at the Gate

A Bit of Light Reading

With the enemies in the vicinity nullified, Connor wants you to regroup at the gate [B.15]. However, before you do, thoroughly inspect the initial area. There are three newspaper articles to find: one on the concrete side of the ruined house behind and right of the windmill, and two more past the truck of corpses, in each of the wooden barns the survivalists were using as a makeshift camp. There's little else to collect here, so return to Connor.

NOTE 알아두세요

The SMG uses bullets up quickly and then needs reloading. With this in mind, you can always switch to your rifle if you're in danger, or spray-and-pray with your SMG, and then back it up with a melee strike.

HIDDEN HISTORY >> 1 (43/61)

On the far right end of the alley between the ruined house and the windmill tower, near the compound entrance gate.

NORTH KOREAN SPECIAL FORCES AIM TO BE "BEST IN THE WORLD" *2/23/2017*

"I've never worked with soldiers as focused, committed, or relentless," Huh Kyung-Young related to me in accented English as we toured the newly constructed special operations training facility an hour south of Pyongyang in what was once North Korea. "These guys are the very model of a modern 'spec-ops' team—they never complain, they go for hours and they're total perfectionists."

After a lengthy tour of the facility, we sat down together to watch a series of demonstrations. The first was a specific type of fast rope insertion using a helicopter. The team would secure themselves on ropes hanging below the helicopter, which would move toward the insertion point—in this case the third story of a practice building. On approach, at a specific moment, the helicopter would pull up and hover as the team of six hanging from the helicopter would swing up to the roof and drop off at exactly the right moment. With literally no margin for error, it was one of the most spectacular things I have ever seen.

The day continued with demonstrations of elaborate tactics using high-tech gear from countries all over the world. One of the things that I noted was that they seemed to be training on American-made weapons and vehicles. When I asked Huh about this he said simply "Americans make the best weapons, and we want only the best." Huh went on to explain that his military wants to be prepared to take part in future coalitions of peacekeeping anywhere in the world. "Only then," Huh said, "will the world understand that Korea has arrived."

HIDDEN HISTORY >> 2 (44/61)

In the first barn to the left (west) of the entrance gate to the compound, on the plank table near the campfire.

AMERICAN MILITARY SEEN AS UNWANTED IN NEW ERA OF EAST ASIAN PEACE *5/4/2014*

One of the longest standing military alliances in the world came to an end on Tuesday as the United States and Japan broke off talks to extend America's presence on the Island of Okinawa. Initially planned as a continuation of a 2006 pact to re-organize the US Military presence in Japan, the talks stalemated in March as the two parties failed to come to a mutually satisfactory agreement.

As unification talks in Korea continue, the US military is seen as an increasingly redundant force in the area. Citizens in both Japan and the US see the massive economic costs resulting from the forces in the area as wasteful and not particularly valuable in an age of pronounced economic decline.

HIDDEN HISTORY >> 3 (45/61)

In the second barn to the left (west) of the entrance gate to the compound, on the concrete pad near the table box with candles on it.

NEW KOREAN PRESIDENT PLANS TO MODERNIZE THE KOREAN MILITARY

8/17/2015

It's a military that can be only described as patchwork. The newly unified, barely integrated Korean militaries have some of the latest, and oldest military technology working side by side. The North Korean soldiers that now form the backbone of the military have trained on nothing more advanced than upgrades of Soviet-era tanks and are expected to operate vehicles as advanced as the K1 MBT, a variant of the M1A1 Abrams Main Battle Tank.

In response to the obvious gaps in training of his soldiers, Korea's new president Kim Jong-un announced a plan to scrap most of the North Korean Army's ordnance and upgrade their training in an accelerated program to modernize the military. "The combined Korean military is now one of the largest standing armies in the world," said Geum Min, a spokesman for the Korean Defense Department. "We want not only the largest, but also the finest and most modern fighting force in history."

A Bit of Light Running

When you reach Connor, he hands you an M200 Sniper Rifle, and gives you the job of blowing away enemies from long distance, but only after he gives the word. He then kicks open the gate door, and runs up a grass path that winds up and to the right (northeast) past a red barn. Pause and check the ground to the left, near the hay bale, for another newspaper article.

WEAPONS >>

M200 Sniper [Silencer]

Given to you by Connor when you rendezvous with him.

HIDDEN HISTORY >> 4 (46/61)

On the top of the grassy gully by the barn fence and hay bale, once through the gate.

US PACIFIC FLEET CONSOLIDATED TO PEARL HARBOR

5/21/2016

Following a year-long study of the Defense Department's current budget, a bipartisan commission of senators known as the Sustainable Defense Task Force has recommended funding reductions totaling one trillion dollars. The new budget sees the canceling of the controversial missile shield project and the closing of nearly all bases still operating in East Asia.

As a result of these funding changes, the US naval fleet will be consolidated to Pearl Harbor for the first time since World War 2. The hardest-hit by this latest round of budget cuts, the Navy is expected to refocus its mission. The Navy will now focus on the rampart piracy and drug smuggling that plagues the west coast of North America.

CHECKPOINT C: BE VERY, VERY QUIET

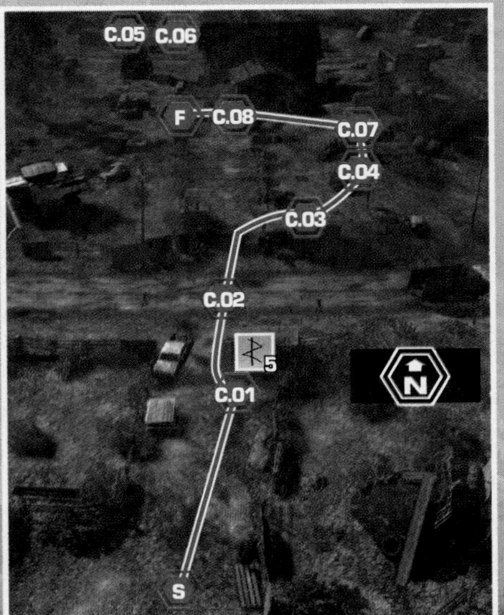

Enemies

Compound Guard

Objective: Remain Undetected

"Heavily Armed, and Out of Their Minds"

C.01

C.02

The only way to reach the chopper is to head through the sprawling survivalist compound. To avoid detection, Connor wants safeties on, and no one firing unless he gives the okay. Follow Connor as he carefully walks forward toward a crossroads in the path **[C.01]**. Ahead is a guard tower, but in front of you are two or three foes; keep out of their sight. Connor drops to his haunches at a small storage hut. Nestle in behind the nearby vehicle, or to the right of him. Pick up a newspaper article while you're here, and listen to the guards' conversations; they discuss the helicopter's location. Once they move away to the right (east), follow Connor's lead, and sprint across the dirt road **[C.02]**, stopping by the trespasser's sign on the other side.

CAUTION 조심하다

You can fire on the survivalists, head off the route that Connor is walking, or otherwise jeopardize the entire mission if you want. Just expect to fail instantly if you're spotted by anyone. Follow Connor's orders to the letter to avoid this.

HIDDEN HISTORY >> 5 (47/61)

Inside the small storage hut by the initial crossroads, after the grass gully, right of the rusting vehicle.

CARGO CARRIERS FIND NEW LIFE IN KOREAN MILITARY

6/9/2022

Just ten years ago, massive ships carrying enormous containers were an everyday sight at any large port in the world. The recent economic slide has turned the ships into an endangered species; many sit abandoned in ports across the world. The Korean military, however, may have found a new life for these relics of the Age of Oil. Its ranks newly swollen from the integration of soldiers from the member states of the Greater Korean Republic, the GKR Army has been on the hunt for a flexible means of transportation, and they think they've found it.

The first converted cargo carrier left from the Port of Busan in Korea today, carrying a contingent of troops to Japan to help quell the rebellious Northern Prefectures. The containers have been heavily modified for the purpose, and are constructed in such a way that they can be unloaded at port and be shipped to their destination, usually a military base. The containers house all of the amenities a unit needs to survive in the field, including personal effects. A modular system that has functional plumbing and air conditioning, many have been reinforced to give troops under fire additional protection in the case of an attack.

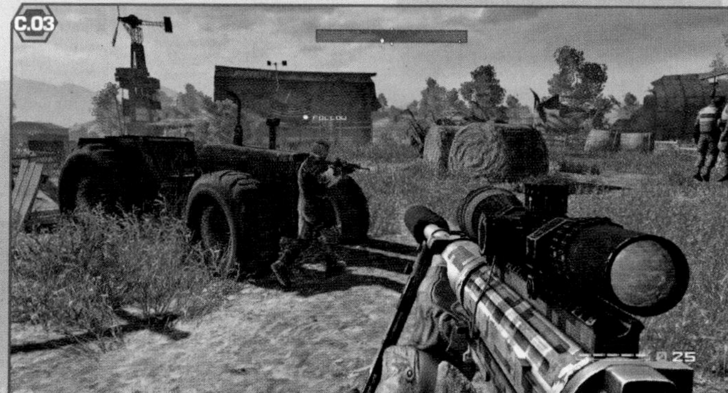

C.03

C.04

Wait for Connor to move, and then follow him as he sneaks around the tractor to the right **[C.03]**, away from the third patrolling guard. Pass the two hanging KPA soldiers, and ignore Rianna's advice to stay low; you don't need to crouch unless you wish to. Connor halts at a pile of farm machinery **[C.04]**.

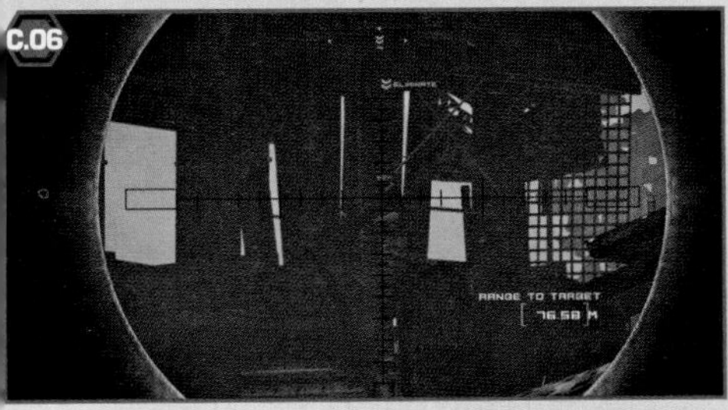

He warns you of a sniper standing on the windmill past the barn, to the northwest **[C.05]**. Level your sniper rifle at the foe, and use the scope. Then optionally use the zoom function to get even closer to the guard **[C.06]**. Now drop him.

CAUTION 조심하다

Pause until the tag on the guard changes from "Wait" to "Execute." If you fire before Connor's order, other enemies spot the takedown and the mission fails. Take too long with the execution, and guards in the compound spot you, also failing the mission.

NOTE 알아두세요

Did you drop the sniper rifle Connor gave you? This presents a problem, as the foes you're responsible for tagging are at extreme range. Try your best with a zoomed rifle shot, or try again.

Connor moves around the pile of machinery, and stops behind some low defensive cover. Two guards are shooting at the feet of a captured KPA soldier **[C.07]**. Wait for them to finish the Korean, then walk off to find another "dance partner." Hopper wonders how Boone hooked up with these psychotics.

Wait for the signal from Connor, and then follow him under some netting to the northwest as you close in on the barn and stop at the tractor **[C.08]**. When Connor moves again, so should you.

Connor skirts around to the north and west in a curving path past some stacked wood and a tree **[C.09]**. Follow him around, listening to a guard yelling at two enslaved KPA soldiers pushing some machinery. Head to the left of a section of wooden materials **[C.10]**, and look to the right (northeast). Rianna has spotted another foe with an RPG.

Connor orders Rianna to take out the guard blocking their exit. While she moves toward the foe near the trailer **[C.11]**, look up at the windmill (this is the same one you dropped a foe from earlier), and execute the foe when prompted **[C.12]**. Hit the head or the torso, and don't miss!

When the coast is clear, Connor moves forward, stepping over the guard whose neck Rianna just snapped. Run after them, toward the open doorway leading to a barn **[C.13]**. When you arrive, check the left (west) wall for two grenades, and another sniper rifle (which is useful if you discarded one previously, or need more ammo).

WEAPONS >>
M200 Sniper [Silencer]

WEAPONS >>
Fragmentation Grenade (2)

Against the left wall of the barn.

CHECKPOINT D: JUST FOR FUN

"We Gotta Stay off the Roads"

Your team listens as a KPA recon helicopter hovers into view from the hills to the north **[D.01]**. It swings around and follows the dirt road to the west, before it is blown out of the sky by an RPG. Because the same fate is likely to befall you if the shooters aren't dealt with, the clandestine romp through the Survivalists' stronghold continues. Step out, and follow Connor as he runs down the dirt road past some signs and a fallen silo **[D.02]**.

CAUTION 조심하다

The rapidly decomposing corpse of a KPA soldier lies near a small offroad vehicle near the barn you started this checkpoint in. Don't inspect it, or stray from the route, or you'll be discovered.

Your route is toward the farmhouse up ahead (west) of your current position, which should be close to the corrugated fencing at the crossroads **[D.03]**.

Enemies

Transport Helicopter

Compound Guard

Behind that fence a trio of guards play poker (you don't have to witness them playing, because this can give your position away) **[D.04]**. Take the sniper rifle on the ground nearby if you don't have one.

To the left (south) are the remains of a road blockade **[D.05]**. Follow Connor through the twisted metal; he notices a patrol truck heading away, along the road toward the entrance gate. Move up, heading west into the overgrown field, around a burned-out big-rig cab **[D.06]**.

WEAPONS >>
M200 Sniper [Silencer]

On the ground near the corrugated fencing, by the crossroads blockade.

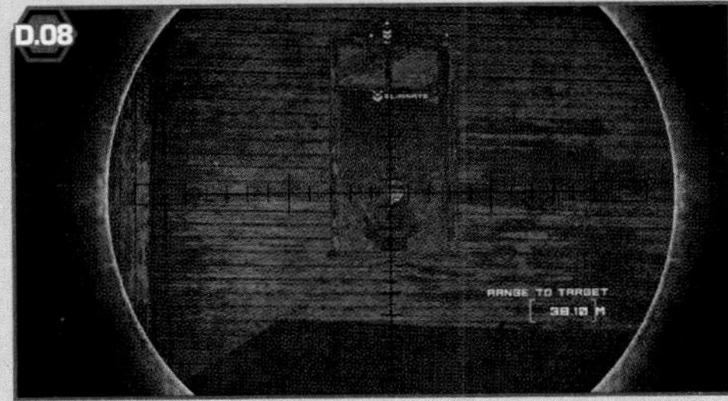

Your team halts behind a large, rusting AC unit. Connor spots movement on the second floor of the farmhouse building in front (west) of you **[D.07]**. Quick, accurate scope-zooming is called for as the foe walks from the middle window to the far left one. Blast his head off when he reaches the left window **[D.08]**, before he spots you and raises the alarm.

Rianna recommends hiding in the tall grass over in the field to the team's left. Connor is already jogging down a curved path, around a tree and some rocks **[D.09]**, and approaching some netting and a clearing.

You can stay and witness a KPA soldier digging his own grave **[D.10]**, complete with taunting from the yokels and an eventual, ignominious death for the Nork.

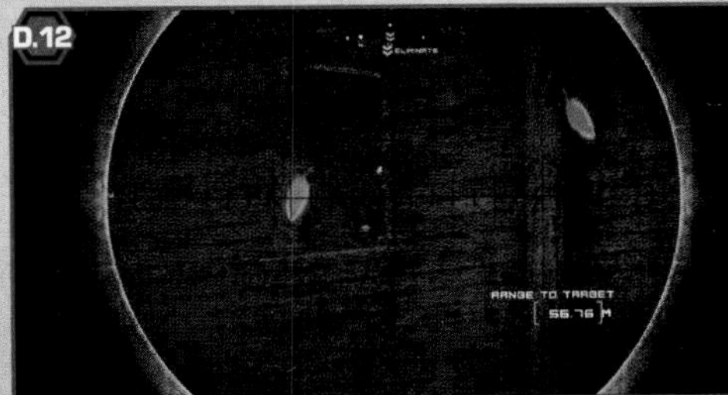

While the survivalists are preoccupied with their savagery, follow Connor and Rianna up and around toward the farmhouse, toward a metal skeleton of an old section of corral **[D.11]**. Watching the execution isn't wise; concentrate instead on the second floor middle window across (northwest) of you **[D.12]**. Execute the foe at the window with an unwavering aim. Then silently follow Connor toward the log pile on the outside wall of the farmhouse itself.

CHECKPOINT E: HOUSEBREAKING

Survivalist Compound: Farmhouse and Escape Route

Compound Guard

PRIMA OFFICIAL GAME GUIDE | PRIMAGAMES.COM

"Lights Out, Jacobs: Make it Quiet!"

Your continuous task of remaining undetected is still in effect. Connor realizes the team needs to cut through the house, and turns left (west), heading between the log pile and a tent to a ramp up to an open window **[E.01]**. Once inside, you have little time to investigate the sleeping bags, and collection of signs and bric-a-brac. Instead, turn left (west), slowly heading down into the garage area, and execute another guard **[E.02]**. This time, creep behind him and swiftly stab him with your knife in a melee strike.

TIP 영리한

A melee strike is the recommended way to tackle this foe at close range. However, a silenced sniper shot works just as well.

Creep down into the garage, remaining on the left side of the room so foes outside to the west don't spot you **[E.03]**. Ignore the cache of weapons, newspaper article, and wall code around you in this garage, and instead wait for the enemies to stop their chatter about cigarettes and stroll off to the left (south). Bring out your sniper rifle, and train it on the final RPG guard atop a windmill **[E.04]**. Bring him down; you're almost out of this initial compound area.

Now search the room (but remain quiet); you can swap out your weapons for any on the table (if you're finding the sniper rifle unwieldy). Then locate the newspaper pick-up, and the QR code on the wall where Rianna hid.

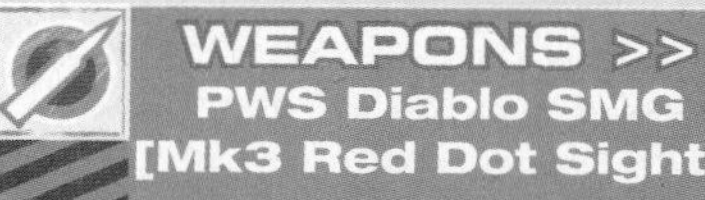

WEAPONS >>
PWS Diablo SMG
[Mk3 Red Dot Sight]

WEAPONS >>
M4 Rifle
[Mk1 ACOG Scope]

WEAPONS >>
T3AK Rifle
[Mk1 HOLO Scope]

WEAPONS >>
SCAR-H LMG
[Mk2 HOLO Scope]

WEAPONS >>
M200 Sniper
[Silencer]

WEAPONS >>
Fragmentation Grenade (2)

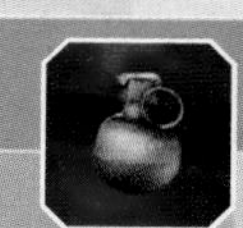

On the table by the left (south) wall of the farmhouse garage.

KOREAN KODEX >> 1 (8/10)

In a wooden picture frame on the west wall by the exit, where Rianna hid before the guards departed.

HIDDEN HISTORY >> 6 (48/61)

On the low shelf in the northwest corner of the farmhouse garage.

IRAN ACCUSES SAUDI ARABIA OF ESCALATING ARMS RACE IN MIDDLE EAST *4/24/2013*

Iran denounced Saudi Arabia's recent purchase of 91 M1A1 Abrams main battle tanks as a "hostile move" and an attempt to "thrust itself into the power vacuum left by the United States." Saudi Arabia and Iran—the two emerging superpowers of the Middle East region—have both announced plans to increase the size of their militaries, including the development and testing of ballistic missile systems on both sides.

Sean Johnston, an expert with the Gettysburg Strategic Policy Group warns that "it appears that we have the beginnings of an arms race here." His report goes on to say that the buildup on both sides could pave the way for a "significant international incident." The United States has all but left the region, and with the government of Iraq on shaky ground, the other major players in the area are scrambling for control.

You can now escape the compound, although silent running is still the plan. Follow Connor under the washing line, through the clumps of rocks and along the grassy verge next to the dirt road **[E.05]**. The road itself is blocked by a survivalist barricade, meaning you must follow Connor over a gap in the fence (next to a gruesome trio of Nork heads on poles), and drop down past a couple of rusting cars to a riverbed **[E.06]**. Don't forget the news pick-up on the way!

NOTE 알아두세요

You can see a church in the distance, to the northeast. This overlooks the final area where the helicopter is found, and you'll be heading there soon.

Objective: Follow Connor

HIDDEN HISTORY >> 7 (49/61)

Look left (east) by the rusting vehicles before dropping down into the river, and check the low bushes near a rock with a tire on it.

NORTH KOREAN DICTATOR REPORTED DEAD *1/2/2012*

It was announced by North Korea's primary news outlet today that Kim Jong-il, long serving supreme leader of North Korea died of a sudden stroke. Intelligence reports have suggested for years that the eccentric and reclusive dictator's health has been in a state of decline. His son and appointed replacement, Kim Jong-un, immediately issued a press statement praising the reign of his father and committing his government to a new era of peace and openness. The statement included an abandonment of North Korea's nuclear aspirations.

The passing of Kim Jong-il was met with cautious optimism in Seoul, the capital of South Korea. The two countries have technically been at war for more than 60 years and many in the region look forward to the day when the two countries are reunited.

CHECKPOINT F: THEY DON'T TAKE KINDLY TO OUR FOLK

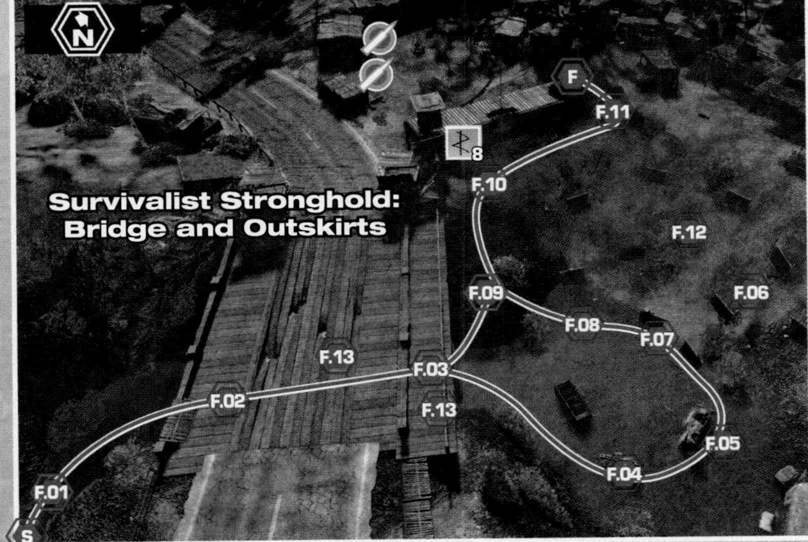

"The Only Way Through Is Up the Middle: Safeties Off!"

Enemies

Stronghold Guard

After grumbling about the way this mission is turning out, the team hears muffled gunfire as you follow Connor up the river **[F.01]**, toward and under a bridge **[F.02]**. You're greeted by the body of a KPA soldier dropped and hung from the bridge above. It appears that the time for subtleties is over; draw your preferred weapon, and ready yourself for combat. You can start shooting before or after Connor gives the signal and runs out to intercept the foes.

NOTE 알아두세요

The farmhouse garage had a choice selection of armaments for this fracas; you may wish to replay that checkpoint if you've arrived here with weapons you aren't happy with. Or take down the foes with what you have.

Objective: Eliminate the Survivalists

Tactical Planning: Death from Above

Threat Assessment: Survivalist Guards

These maniacs are just as competent and bloodthirsty as the ones you killed at the entrance gate. The only difference this time is the topography of the large pond you're wading through, which has a built-up area on two sides (north and west) where most of the 10 or so foes are attacking from. They have the advantage; the sun is in your eyes when you're looking west (meaning it's better not to attack with a looping route that leaves you squinting), they have cover, and they have a height advantage.

Rianna and Connor immediately rush to cover behind rusty scenery in the small lake ahead (northeast) of you. You now have a choice on how to help your brethren during this bloody combat:

Plan A: The Team Player

F.03

F.04

You can either take the lead or hang back at the bridge support (using it as cover) **[F.03]**, and shoot the foes you can spot, and then work your way eastward to the half-submerged AC unit, pallet **[F.04]**, and vehicle cover spots. All the time, train and fire your weapons to the east and north. The advantage here are your numbers; the foes have a choice of who to fire on, and you can shake off a few shots by crouching or going prone.

F.05

F.06

Work your way to the half-submerged vehicle in the lake **[F.05]**. Beware of foes on the hill or dug in behind the vehicle itself; expect combat at both close and long ranges. With around half the survivalists nullified, train your weapon on the fencing with foes behind it, on the hill above **[F.06]**. If two or more foes are behind cover, lob in a grenade. Then follow it up with your main weapons.

F.07

F.08

After some slow but methodical advancing to the north side of the water, use the other side of the fencing to remain in cover yourself, and dash to each section of fence **[F.07]**, watching and defeating any enemies that appear along the way. You may wish to circle around to the west, and climb up near the bridge to avoid squinting into the sun. This plan certainly deals with the enemy threats, but can lead to stragglers winging you, and the problem of firing into the sun needs to be overcome by circle-strafing **[F.08]**.

TIP 영리한

The enemies use the corrugated fencing dotted around the hill as cover, and move between these vantage points, sometimes looking out from them. Use these opportunities to wound them, or lob a grenade in to flush them out.

Plan B: The Team Flanker

Instead of following your teammates into the water, scoot around the bridge support, and flank the foes by heading directly up the earthen hill to the left of the bushes and decapitated heads **[F.09]**, hugging the bridge. Bring out a rapid-fire weapon, or one you're particularly adept with, and move to the highest ground close to the single-level home with the white plastic chairs **[F.10]**.

Expect foes coming around the end of the building ahead (north) of you **[F.11]**, as well as those now below you on the hill. Be quick and accurate as you massacre four or five of them. At this point, you're likely to have polished off most of the foes yourself (especially if you stood and fired at the initial enemies before leaving the cover of the bridge), and you can quickly find and pick off any stragglers **[F.12]**. This plan involves rapid movement and leaves you exposed, but it completely out-flanks the enemy and can end the combat in seconds.

Plan C: The Lone Wolf

If you've kept the sniper rifle and wish to utilize it to its fullest, remain at the cover below the bridge, and before Connor rushes out, drop the first foe you see in a small cluster with a few others on the opposite side of the lake, camping at this spot **[F.13]**. Then provide covering fire, remaining on your own at the bridge and dropping foes with single, well-aimed sniper shots **[F.14]**. The bridge allows for excellent cover, but there's one major problem with this plan; a foe usually sneaks in around the bridge defenses and shoots you, so be aware of foes coming around to attack at close quarters. Back up your team with headshots, then mop up using either of the routes in Plans A and B. Aside from the threat of close combat, this is another effective way to deal with the hillside yokels.

NOTE 알아두세요

After combat is completed, search the area for additional ammunition and reload your weapons to be ready for further intense firefights to come. Pick up a news report before reconvening with Connor and the crew.

Objective: Follow Connor

HIDDEN HISTORY >> 8 (50/61)

By the front step near a white plastic chair, at the foot of the long trailer home at the top of the hill.

MASSIVE BACKDOORS UNCOVERED IN KOREAN-SUPPLIED CIRCUITRY *5/28/2021*

It's no secret to anyone in the integrated circuitry community that Korea is the big kid on the block when it comes to the design, fabrication and supply of microchips. They have the most talented and innovative people and have made massive strides in the areas of fabrication and power consumption. In an age where every amp is at a premium, consumers flock toward the cheapest chips with the leanest power consumption profiles, and one surprising consumer is the US military.

Considering the massive popularity of the chips, why is it that every Korean-made microchip that we could get our hands on has a massive backdoor exploit just waiting to be activated? We found a simple system of 20 logic gates (out of more than a million) that allow any user to easily deactivate the system in the core processor. This system was present in a military two-way radio as well as a rack-mounted communications hub originally supplied to AT&T. The representative at Pyongyang Industrial Circuitry informed us that all chips are made to the specification of the client; every part of the chip comes from a requested design. Representatives from AT&T and the Defense Department were unavailable for comment. However, until we get confirmation that this highly unorthodox system was part of the submitted design, we remain both skeptical and cautious of Korean microchips.

CHECKPOINT G: DOG EAT DOG

Enemies

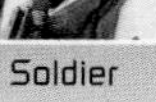

Soldier

Stronghold Guard

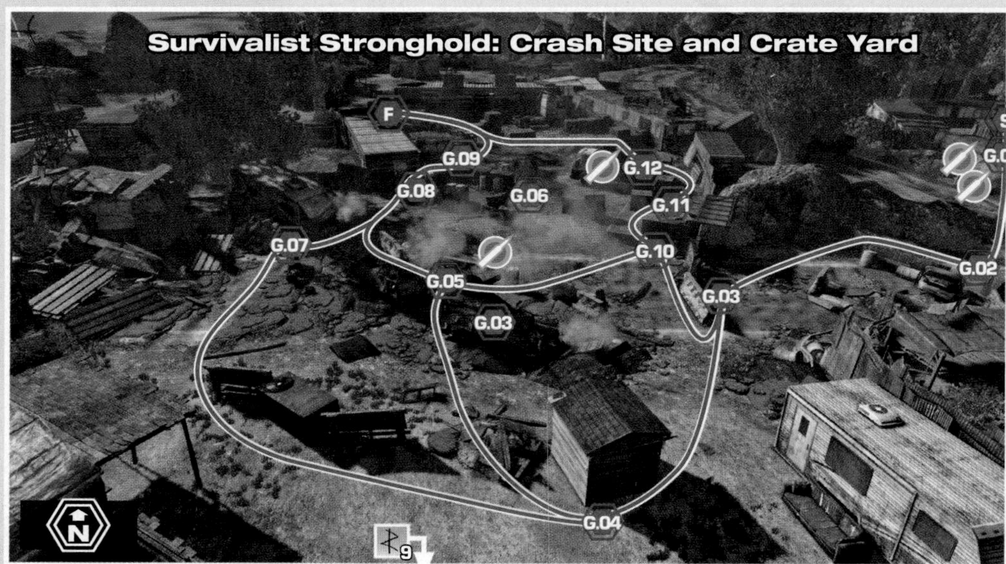

"Shoot Them All."

Once you meet up with the crew at a small pile of furniture they're hiding behind **[G.01]**, Connor sets off to the southwest. Follow the team by sprinting up the hill, past the washing lines, firepits, and shacks, and onto a tarmac road **[G.02]**. Before stepping onto the road, check the shack to the right for the following two weapons, which make the next gunfight a little more straight-forward.

WEAPONS >>
M4 Rifle
[Mk1 ACOG Scope]
[Silencer]

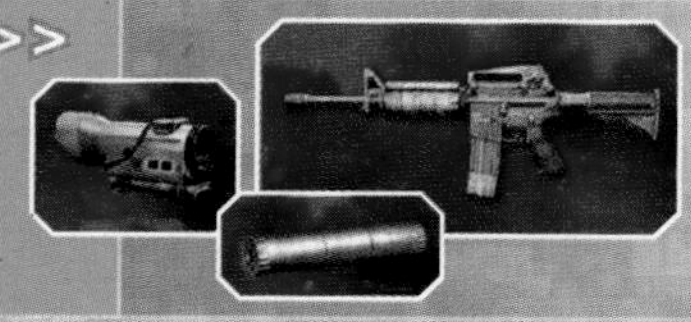

WEAPONS >>
PWS Diablo SMG
[Mk1 Red Dot Sight]

Propped against a corrugated metal fence just before you reach the tarmac road.

TIP 영리한

If you seek other weapons, keep a mental note of where you or your team dropped a foe, so you can efficiently run up and gather their weapon (or ammo) if you need to.

Sprint along the road to the right, following Connor around the barricades (don't take an alternate route because you'll reach an impasse). A plume of smoke up ahead and Rianna's startled comments reveal that the KPA chopper that was shot down earlier by an RPG has come down on the road **[G.03]**. Furthermore, the crew has survived! Tool up with your favored weapon (the M4 Rifle with a scope is a great choice), and begin a combat plan:

TIP 영리한

If you're ill-equipped to deal with the enemies here, search the bodies of the fallen helicopter crew you've killed for an M4 Rifle, which works well at blowing the heads off survivalists at distance.

Tactical Planning: Koreans First, Survivalists Second  

Threat Assessment: Dueling Factions

You're caught in a three-way fight between the Resistance team you're in, a quartet of KPA soldiers by their demolished helicopter, and a good 10 or so survivalists attacking from the right (north), as you watch from the concrete barriers. Although you can turn and attack the survivalists, you're shot at by the KPA while doing so, and getting caught between the two groups is very unwise. Bring the pain to the KPA first, or face a short and violent firefight that doesn't end well for you.

Plan A: Time to Pay, KPA 

G.04

To lessen your chance of being shot while swiftly taking down the KPA, sandwich them between your group and the survivalists. From the red-and-white concrete barriers, sprint southwest, not behind the husk of the helicopter but behind the small shed, and then stay behind the adjacent barricades while blasting the enemies into submission **[G.04]**. Grenades are available, but are best saved for future combat. KPA soldiers may be behind these outer barriers, which is another reason to flank them.

Plan B: Bloodshed at the Barrier  

G.05

A quicker way to end the lives of the KPA, but with possible fire coming in from both enemy locations, is to stay at the concrete barriers, and shoot at the heads of the KPA as they frantically scatter **[G.05]**. With most defeated, move behind the chopper, checking for stragglers, and then turn on the survivalists.

Objective: Eliminate the Survivalists

> **NOTE** 알아두세요
>
> **With only survivalists to shoot at, you have a choice of three further plans:**

Plan C: On Your Guard 

G.06

Dive behind the helicopter wreckage, and bring out a longer-range rifle (or even the sniper rifle) and begin to shoot the heads off anyone with a red plaid shirt **[G.06]**. Staying behind the chopper metal, or the red-and-white barrier a little farther forward (north) allows you to watch the entire crate yard for movement, and blast immediately. Lob a grenade if you spot two or more foes close to each other, or need to flush them out without moving forward. This plan takes a while to complete, and focuses all enemy fire in one area, but is relatively pain-free and means you won't be on your own.

> **NOTE** 알아두세요
>
> **There are foes on the ground, one in a truck, and a few running along the roof of a low, boarded-up trailer. All must be defeated.**

> **CAUTION** 조심하다
>
> **You can climb on top of the burnt helicopter to gain extra height and a good view of the crate yard but this makes you an extremely vulnerable target.**

Plan D: Crate Yard Left Flank: Blue Barrel Takedowns

G.07

With a little more courage, once the KPA are done for, sidestep to the left (west), around the concrete barrier near the flaming motor home **[G.07]**, and drop a couple of foes before sprinting for a stack of blue barrels. Foes are likely

on either side of this stack, so stay behind the (narrow but protective) cover it provides **[G.08]** and drop the enemies on the ground, and the one on the truck.

As combat progresses, you can edge farther along the left "wall" of the cargo yard, to a graffiti-daubed tanker trailer **[G.09]**, where you should stay to defeat the foes on the roof of the trailer home opposite, and the remaining enemies behind the crate pallets and parked big-rig cab at the far end of the yard. Stay nimble, stepping back into cover if you're shot at from the left or from a foe you haven't seen. Then keep tagging foes until Connor gives the all-clear. This plan enables you to outflank foes and draw their fire in different directions, and you don't need to put yourself in too much danger. Combat is over quicker, too.

Plan E: Crate Yard Right Flank: Keep on Truckin'

When the KPA are defeated, move around the initial concrete barricades, and drop to a crouch behind the (inaccessible) wooden boxes on a pallet. Turn left (northwest) and cut down all foes from the sides **[G.10]** while your friends do the same from behind the helicopter wreckage. Then move around to the armored Korean crates and use them as cover **[G.11]**. Expect heavy fire—this plan doesn't lack risks—but if you're a viciously adept shot you can drop the foes on the ground before turning your attention to the enemy on the truck.

Blast him through the gaps in the truck wall, then use it as cover, or jump on the flatbed and cab roof to attract more attention and locate the remaining threats **[G.12]**. Then quickly drop them before you're peppered with gunfire.

WEAPONS >>

M200 Sniper [Silencer]

On top of the flatbed truck.

TIP 영리한

Remember that you can use melee attacks if you surprise a foe as you round some cargo containers. Also don't underestimate the benefits of dropping to a crawl and locating foes by spotting their feet.

TIP 영리한

Out of Frag Grenades? Don't forget some of the guns you pick up have a secondary fire with instant-explosive grenades to use!

NOTE 알아두세요

Before you begin the next checkpoint, backtrack for a moment, and gather a news article.

HIDDEN HISTORY >> 9 (51/61)

On the ground near barrels on the left side of the mobile shack south of the helicopter wreckage, behind the small shed.

SUBURBAN FLIGHT GROWS AS MARTIAL LAW BEGINS TO RESTORE ORDER *11/18/2020*

There is a growing sense that order is being restored to America. Though it was met with outrage and shock when it was implemented by the Pentagon early last year, Operation Vital Archer has put the military in a lead role in the management of civilian authorities, completely supplanting the police and fire departments in many urban centers.

As energy costs continue to hold steady at sky-high rates, many Americans have come to depend on the military for basic needs like food and fresh water. The promise of basic goods as well as a semblance of order has caused many Americans to flee outlying suburban areas for the increasingly stable urban centers controlled by the military.

CHECKPOINT H: QUIET NEIGHBORHOOD

Enemies

Stronghold Guard

Compound Fracture

Your altercation with the survivalists doesn't end here. Another cluster of heavily armed thugs awaits in the hill compound itself. Bunch up with the rest of your crew as you round the corner **[H.01]**, and target the foe coming out of the first trailer you see, to the northwest **[H.02]**. This begins combat. Choose a plan, or use elements from any of them, and engage. Before you do, however, check the armored crates as you round the corner; a Unique Weapon is propped against one. Then, as the fight progresses, sprint across (north) to the opposite side of the compound arena, to a concrete pad with a propane tank shed and two sandbag crates on it, and secure your other Unique Weapon.

Unique Weapons Detail: 13/17

WEAPONS >>
Digital ACR Rifle [Mk2 ACOG Scope]

Offering the ultra-fast firing performance you'd expect from the ACR, this attractively painted unique variant also sports one of the best scopes, allowing you to easily target and drop foes from near to far. An essential pick-up.

Unique Weapons Detail: 14/17

WEAPONS >>
Urban SCAR-H [Mk3 ACOG Scope]

With an ammo barrel as big as your head, this ferocious weapon pops enemy craniums like balloons, but has the additional benefit of an incredible scope, making it the very best companion to the ACR Rifle for most of the rest of this mission.

Objective: Eliminate the Survivalists

Tactical Planning: Koreans First, Survivalists Second

Threat Assessment: Hilltop Hicks

The battle for the hilltop reaches its zenith here, with survivalists numbering around a dozen. Naturally, your team takes care of a few foes, but expect a ferocious firefight, with enemies on either side of a rather unpleasant central "wheel of death" with a dead KPA riveted to it. The white trailer to the right has foes running to and from cover. The central area is a deceptively small maze of crates and cover. The upper left side has a few foes dug in with commanding views of your team; don't underestimate them because they can devastate your team if they remain unchecked.

Plan A: Command and Control

As the team spreads out, Connor usually moves near the mobile home that the first enemy appeared from. Entering this structure is a good idea even if you intend to engage enemies from another location, as there's a cache of weapons on the table between the two doorways **[H.03]**. The weapons are of limited value (as you should be carrying both Unique Weapons), but there are four Frag Grenades, allowing you to expend all from your current inventory during this battle.

As your team ventures outside and bears the brunt of the enemy attacks, hole up inside the mobile home and begin to tackle enemies at long range. Start with the couple of foes on the white mobile home to the east **[H.04]**. Stay at the north end of the dwelling, because you can easily fire through the doorway and windows at additional enemies. Choose those who have spotted you, then those on the rooftop to the left, with the netting above them **[H.05]**. Venture outside only if there are no further threats you can blast, or you want to lob a grenade or two. This tactic lengthens combat, doesn't win you any medals for heroics, but maintains your safety at the expense of your teammates (who survive anyway).

WEAPONS >>
M9 Pistol

WEAPONS >>
M4 Rifle [Mk1 ACOG Scope) [Silencer] (2)

WEAPONS >>
M200 Sniper [Silencer]

WEAPONS >>
Fragmentation Grenade (4)

Inside the mobile trailer at the western end of the hilltop compound.

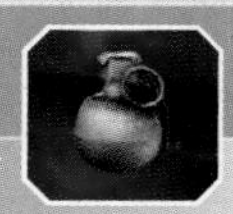

CAUTION 조심하다

You may be planning an attack by heading toward the KPA corpse tied to the spinning wheel on the side of the truck, and through the middle of this compound. This is such an unwise move that it hasn't even been given its own plan name, for good reason: You're attacked from both sides, and can't easily dispatch foes attacking from multiple directions. In fact, you're supposed to be trying this tactic on them!

Plan B: Hopper on the Right Flank

The journey along the right flank (with Hopper, although you can't rely on him to tackle every foe you miss) enables you to step around the armored crate where you found the Unique Weapon, and move forward with cover opportunities to your left (north), and trailer homes to your right (south). Stop at the first cover (crates, a board, and tires) **[H.06]** or second (a corrugated shed with a mattress inside) **[H.07]**. Systematically take down any foe that moves.

Remain behind he corrugated shed with the cement blocks veighing down he tarp roof, and ackle the foes on the trailer roof n front of you H.08]. Don't step out from behind this cover because you need o check to your eft on either side of the structure, vhere foes are argeting you or your team [H.09]. You've outflanked hem, so outgun them too.

Then look across (northward) toward the main sandbag defenses [H.10]. Lob in a couple of grenades and don't be shy; refill your inventory at the initial trailer house after combat. Gun down anyone still moving afterward, then move along the trailer porch between the tires, crouching if necessary to avoid gunfire, and arget the scattered but determined remaining foes [H.11]. This ncludes those nestled on the roof opposite, under the netting. Then quickly skirt the area, until Rianna spots the final RPG dweller on the windmill. This flanking tactic is more dangerous, out more thrilling, and completes combat much more quickly.

Plan C: Rianna on the Left Flank

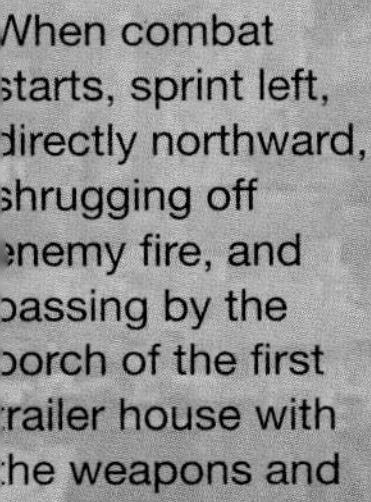

When combat starts, sprint left, directly northward, shrugging off enemy fire, and passing by the porch of the first railer house with he weapons and grenades inside. Remember to return here for grenades afterward. Rendezvous with Rianna at the concrete pad [H.12], and pick up the second Unique Weapon, and then step around to the left, moving to the marked Korean containers, and train your weapons on the rooftop foes ahead and above (east of) you [H.13].

From here, you can remain at the crates, because they offer good protection and a good view of the scurrying foes [H.14]. Lob in a few grenades to soften them up, and take down the foes on the far roof of the white mobile home, too. You're not likely to be attacked at close quarters here, and you can step back easily if a grenade lands close by. Move around this area, helping your team [H.15], and optionally advancing forward with the green-and-white wall of the trailer building on your left, but only if you need to. Helping Rianna enables you to use both Unique Weapons at the earliest possible time, and the scenery is particularly good for hiding behind.

> **TIP 영리한**
>
> **The sniper rifle is another option, and allows for single-hit takedowns during combat. This effectiveness is lessened due to the reload time, and your vulnerability if you miss. Try this out if you wish, but remain at range; Plan A is a good tactic to try with a sniper rifle.**

Objective: Eliminate the RPG Enemy

Last of the RPG Wielders

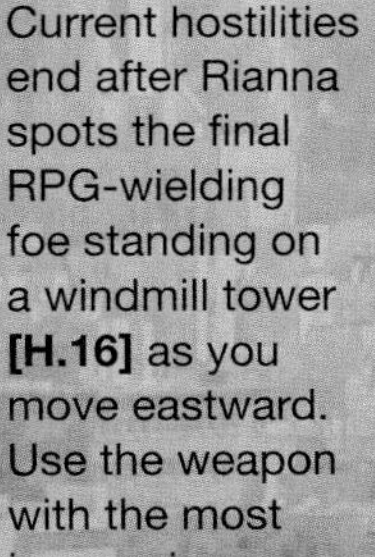

Current hostilities end after Rianna spots the final RPG-wielding foe standing on a windmill tower [H.16] as you move eastward. Use the weapon with the most impressive scope and eliminate him. Or fire with anything you have to hand. Or dive behind cover or keep your distance and watch the team take him out.

CHECKPOINT I: SOME ARE BETTER LEFT ALONE

Enemies

Stronghold Guard

Objective: Follow Connor

"These Guys are Animals."

When you've checked the dirt next to a gray trailer home for some news, oblige Connor and follow the team down the dirt track [I.01]. A helicopter is spotted, but this is a scout chopper, and not Koreans. It appears to land behind the hill with the church on it. As distant lightning flashes ominously, ignore the rusting vehicles along the road, cross the ford, and start up the hill itself.

HIDDEN HISTORY >> 10 (52/61)

On the dirt next to some sandbags near the entrance to a red-and-gray trailer home.

KOREA NOW LARGEST SUPPLIER OF AMERICAN PURCHASED MICROPROCESSORS *8/8/2020*

Though the consumer market is faltering, the government and military of the United States are still massive consumers of digital electronic parts. Korea has overtaken all other nations as the number one supplier of enterprise- and military-grade electronics, providing everything from rack mounted switching systems for cell phone networks to guidance systems for unmanned aerial vehicles.

"Korean microprocessor companies offer a suite of services at a one-stop shop," said Raytheon executive Tina Evola. "We subcontract everything from design to prototyping to fabrication. The cost is unbeatable." Many contractors are now acting only as middlemen in the process, taking their cut and passing on the real work to the Korean subcontractors.

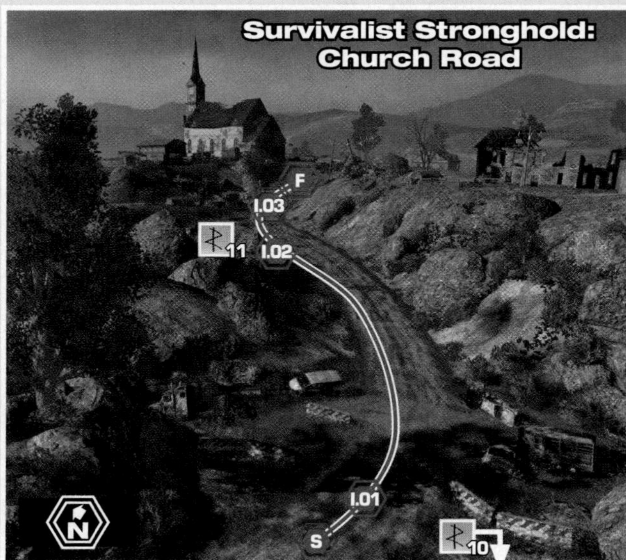

The team murmurs about the inhumanity of these survivalists as you all encounter a small cemetery down the hill from the church [I.02]. Inspect this gruesome scene if you wish, before you continue.

Afterward, check the immediate area for another newspaper article, and then follow Connor up the hillside to a fork in the road [I.03]. The team is scouting ahead, toward the west to a gate. You can't follow them; instead, you're tasked with removing all threats in the church and providing covering fire from the top of the steeple.

Objective: Enter the Church

HIDDEN HISTORY >> 11 (53/61)

At the edge of the hill cemetery, near the collection of KPA decapitated heads.

UN CONDEMNS NORTH KOREAN OCCUPATION OF JAPAN

10/5/2018

The United Nations today, led by the United States, passed a resolution condemning the recent destruction of a Japanese nuclear power plant by the Korean military as a human rights violation. Many of the countries that signed the resolution have already expressed concern over Korea's growing power in the region, and see this demonstration of power as a sign that Korea is willing to take extreme measures against perceived enemies. The UN adopted the non-binding text, proposed by the US on behalf of Japan, with a vote of 46 states in favor and 11 against.

The nations that voted against the resolution include Malaysia, Indonesia, the Philippines, Thailand, and Cambodia—all nations that have provided the Koreans with material support and are suspected of holding closed-door trade discussions with the East Asian power. Korea responded to the resolution by pulling its envoy to the UN from Brussels, completely disengaging from the body and fueling speculation that only the threat of force would bring the country in line.

CHECKPOINT J: SUNDAY MASS

Enemies

Stronghold Guard

There's nothing in the shacks by the ork in the road, so continue up the track toward some corrugated encing, a rusting pickup, and the church itself **[J.01]**. There are guards (four outside, three inside) standing near this dilapidated structure, and you can handle them in a variety of ways:

Tactical Planning: Going to the Chapel. Going to Get Harried

Threat Assessment: Churchyard Guards

Two guards stand at the foot of the steps to the church doors, which are initially shut. Once one of them spots you (or is shot), expect two more enemies to come running in on each side of the church. On the left (west) side, a foe races along the low scaffold, and drops into the yard you're in. On the right (east) side, another hick races along scaffolding, and drops to intercept you. When a second foe is killed, the front doors open, and three enemies head down the steps and seek cover.

Survivalist Stronghold: Church

Plan A: Reconnoiter, then Rampage

Adept marksmanship and one or two grenades (from the quartet you should have in your inventory) are keys to the optimal method of foe disposal. Creep around the initial fencing, and move right to left, around the front bumper of the pickup. At this point, you can:

Zoom in your scope and decapitate both guards in front of the steps in a second.

Or lob in a grenade just behind the right (east) guard, causing them confusion (as they can't run away, or toward you), catching them both in the explosion.

Or you can miss, and attempt a longer and more messy clean-up as the foes return fire and seek cover behind the numerous bits of scenery in this yard.

Assuming competence wins out, swing your weapon around to the north, and catch the left foe running down the scaffold. Bring him down before he reaches the edge of the planks he's running on, and drop to the ground **[J.04]**. Optionally circle around the left perimeter of the yard at the same time. The church doors fly open. At this point, quickly choose a target. You can:

Quickly aim at the foe on the opposite scaffold to the east, and drop him **[J.05]**. Then worry about the three foes heading down the steps from the church door.

Or, lob a grenade at the foot of the steps, or just above near the opening door, to waylay the foes, and then drop the enemy up on the right-side scaffold.

Now all you have left to defeat are the foes inside the church entrance, who may have descended the steps depending on your accuracy. Mow them down by standing to the side of the door, and killing them as they exit the church **[J.06]**.

Or take a less obtuse angle, allowing you a view through the doors, where you can zoom in and kill the remaining foes as they mill about **[J.07]**.

> **NOTE** 알아두세요
>
> **After the fight, and assuming every immediate enemy is dead, search the eastern corner of the yard for a newspaper article.**

Plan B: Same Plan, Around to the Right

A less satisfactory method of clearing the entrance yard and church door involves blasting the two guards at the front, and then sprinting for cover opportunities to the right (east). The initial threat is the foe coming at you from the scaffolding **[J.08]**. Bring him down first this time, and then remain behind cover, or move to the side against the church wall **[J.09]** and massacre the other enemies as they stream down the steps. You have farther to run, so this isn't quite as proficient as Plan A.

Plan C: Different Plan, an Unsubtle Fight

Or, if tactical planning makes your head hurt, simply rush the first two foes, mowing them down **[J.10]**.

Stand on the church entrance steps and look right and up (east), and bring down the hick on the upper scaffold. The doors swing open. Rush the steps, and rake the three foes inside the church entrance with gunfire (and perhaps a melee strike) until they (or you) are dead **[J.11]**. This is dangerous, but quick. Optionally nullify a straggler back in the yard so he doesn't follow you in.

TIP 영리한

Making a dash for the church entrance once the doors are open is a good plan if previous tactics have failed. Hold up inside and sidestep out to tag any outside foes before retreating.

HIDDEN HISTORY >> 12 (54/61)

In the corner of the churchyard, under the eastern scaffold, by the perimeter fence.

JAPANESE TOWNS, CITIES EVACUATED IN THE AFTERMATH OF NUCLEAR POWER PLANT DESTRUCTION

4/2/2018

Hundreds of thousands of Japanese citizens fled from cities and towns in southern Japan after Korean Special Operations teams destroyed the Chugoku nuclear power plant last week. A demolitions crew infiltrated the power plant and destroyed essential cooling systems, causing a chain of events that ended with the reactor's core melting down, resulting in a massive radiation leak. Concerns of exposure to radiation fueled a mass exodus from nearby cities and towns as well as surrounding rural areas.

The international community continues to condemn the incursion by Korea into Japan, calling the actions "a war crime" and "an act of terror"; however, many nations are unable to respond, citing domestic issues. Yesterday, Kim Jong-un appeared on Korean State Television in a broadcast that was immediately picked up by other major international news organizations. In his address he offered peaceful reconciliation provided a series of demands were met, including the surrender of the Japanese government. Kim strongly implied that other reactors would follow the same fate as Chugoku's if his demands weren't met.

Since the start of the war, the Korean army and Special Forces teams have captured 26 of Japan's nuclear power plants, many of them currently operational and located near major metropolitan areas.

Objective: Get to the Church Tower

CAUTION 조심하다

Although you may have stepped into the church, exercise caution as you ascend the tower; if you're defeated by guards, you begin outside, from the very start of this checkpoint.

Inside the church entrance hall, the doors in front are sealed, forcing you up the left (west) staircase. Amid the M4 Rifles the enemies have dropped, check a small stack of tires in the stairwell for a shotgun, and an M16 on the stairs themselves. Both are possible weapons if your Unique Weapons are close to empty, although you may find the 870 Express Shotgun a little too slow.

WEAPONS >>
870 Express Shotgun

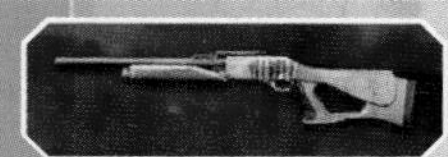

WEAPONS >>
M16 Rifle
[Grenade Launcher]

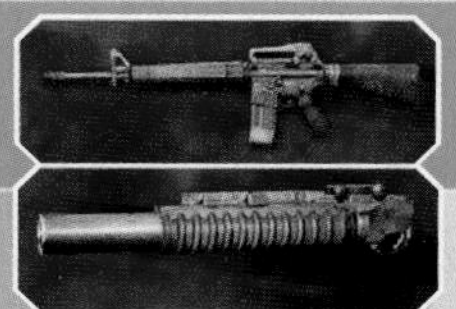

On the stairwell inside the church entrance.

Tactical Planning: Tower Ascension

Threat Assessment: Church Interior Guards

The biggest concern once inside the church is figuring out where the gunfire is coming from. Two easily missed foes are on the ground floor below your route. There are four more on the first balcony level, and two final enemies up in the tower walkway itself. To reach the tower, you need to access the ladder on the scaffolding-heavy second floor. The ladder is diagonally opposite (east) of the entrance.

CAUTION 조심하다

Be especially accurate with grenades because they tend to fall through the gaps in the planks you're walking on, missing enemies.

CAUTION 조심하다

When you're climbing to the tower, you can fall off the walkways. Plummeting from the upper floor kills you.

Plan D: Scaffold Savagery

Climb the stairs, ideally armed with a rapid-fire rifle with a full clip, and a couple of grenades. Be aware of six foes as you slowly peek through into the main gathering chamber. You can see the head of the first if you look slightly right of the doorway, behind cover on the far balcony **[J.12]**.

If you're quick, you can decapitate him before you even step into the room. Then drop in a grenade to soften up the two foes on the ground floor **[J.13]**. You can target them manually, or shoot the one you can see from the initial balcony before they are aware of your presence, but only if this is the first shot you fire.

If you're lucky, you'll have taken out one or two enemies. Proceed north along the left balcony, shrugging off fire from your right (east) side. Two foes on the opposite balcony guard the only ladder that leads to the tower. You can:

Drop behind the crates and look for them before returning fire.

Choose a better plan and keep a crate between you and them as you move forward, dropping the initial foe (if you didn't execute him earlier) **[J.14]**, and a second foe who runs in from behind a half-boarded doorway on the opposite side. Shoot him when he stands up **[J.15]**, or through the gaps in the boards (which is much more difficult).

Move around the balcony, keeping a section of barricade between you and any foes below. Stay on the left side of the balcony, so their shots don't hit you. Then quickly step out and cut down the two foes by the ladder **[J.16]**. If they aren't there, be careful of foes running in from the entrance to your left (north), behind the main church room. Once the enemies on this balcony level are dispatched, peer out between cover boards and cut down any foes below **[J.17]**, using muzzle flashes (or directional wounds that they inflict on you) to find them.

Other Options

Plan D is your mainstay path, but you may wish to try some variations. For a start, you can enter the room, and focus on the foes below you first, sidestepping right (east) and finding both enemies through the gaps in the scaffold floorboards **[J.18]**. The ladder upward can't be accessed from the southeast corner of this room, but there is a sniper rifle on an ammo crate. It isn't necessary to pick up though.

You can also drop down onto the main church floor, which is inadvisable unless you've cleared all foes from the scaffold walkway above (or you'll be shot at with difficulty retaliating, and catch gunfire when you attempt to ascend either of the ladders). This dead-end room contains a sniper rifle in the northeast alcove, but is otherwise simply a trap to fall into.

With an expertly thrown grenade, you can shatter the boarding on the opposite doorway, at the room's northwest end. Time your throw to dispatch the enemy behind the cover **[J.19]**. With this doorway open, you can step through into a set of stairs that links to the doorway opposite **[J.20]**, through which you can attack the remaining foes on this level (there are three if you simply focus on this tactic, one behind the other). This adds an element of surprise to your takedowns, and is worth attempting if you have the grenade handy.

Top of the Tower

Climb the only ladder that accesses a small mid-level section of scaffold on the eastern side of the church. There's another ladder to climb almost immediately, but vait a moment: Focus your attention on an upper doorway at the oof walkway to the southwest **[J.21]**. This is the precarious upper valkway atop the church.

Iead up the last adder, onto the valkway. Crouch mmediately if he foe to the northwest hasn't appeared. Then nvestigate the cubbyhole to he south for vet another sniper rifle. Keep your rifle (or shotgun) as your main veapon though; and head north toward the objective point **[J.22]**. You may need to rapidly down the last foe if he hasn't shown himself. Don't be shocked by his ambush on the right (east) side as you enter through the doorway; react with rapid fire or a melee strike. Once you're in the tower itself, the building shakes, and a roof section collapses behind you. In one corner is yet another sniper rifle. Take and use it from this point, but with a secondary weapon that has a fair amount of ammo as your reserve.

WEAPONS >>
M200 Sniper Rifle [Silencer] (4)

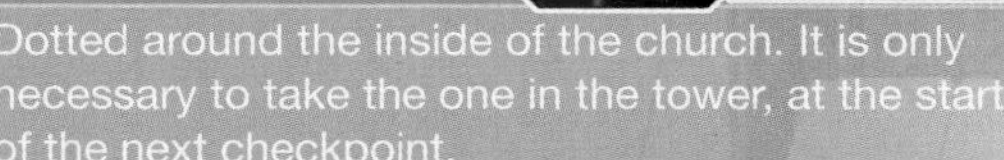

Dotted around the inside of the church. It is only necessary to take the one in the tower, at the start of the next checkpoint.

Mettle of Honor

Award	Stairway to Heaven	Rating	10	Trophy	Bronze

Rampaging from the front door of the church all the way to the crow's nest at the top of the tower within 240 seconds (four minutes) earns you this reward. With knowledge of the enemy locations, this challenge is relatively straightforward to complete; no dilly-dallying!

CHECKPOINT K: EYES ON THE PRIZE

Enemies

Stronghold Guard

Objective: Shoot Only Marked Targets

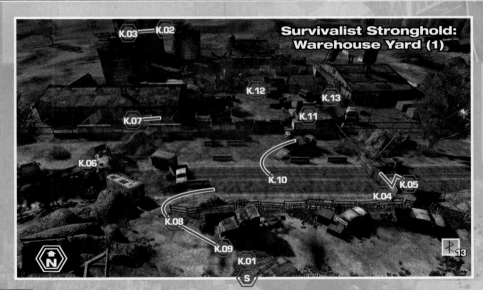

Survivalist Stronghold: Warehouse Yard (1)

K.01 K.02 K.03 K.04 K.05 K.06 K.07 K.08 K.09 K.10 K.11 K.12 K.13

Tagging From the Tower

Reload your sniper rifle—you must employ this weapon or the enemy takedowns become impossible to accurately complete—and drop to a crawl, peering out from the gap in the church tower's facade **[K.01]**. Your team is on the outskirts of a survivalist warehouse yard, fanning out and attempting to hatch a plan to reach the helicopter that landed at the far end of the yard. First though, Connor wants to thin out the enemy's ranks. He'll walk you onto your targets.

TIP 영리한

If you haven't already done so, familiarize yourself with the M200. Use the scope and zoom function for an even closer sight of the enemy.

CAUTION 조심하다

The following presents the required targets to shoot at, and their locations. Beware! The mission fails if:

- **You shoot anyone other than the intended targets.**
- **You shoot any of the explosive barrels.**
- **You shoot one of the intended targets before the "Execute" sign appears above their heads.**

Rianna tells you to sit tight; there's a truck coming. You can look down and right (northeast) and watch the security gates being opened. But it is better to ready your aim on the silo walkway to the left (northwest). A sniper patrols from right to left **[K.02]**. Train your rifle on the foe. Wait for it, then take the shot when Connor gives the order **[K.03]**.

Rianna pipes up again about a foe a little too close to her position, in the front-left warehouse. Ignore him for the moment, as Connor spots a new target: a gate guard heading directly for Connor's hiding spot **[K.04]**. The guard climbs a ladder in the lower-right (northeast) corner of your visual field. Wait until he stands on the platform **[K.05]**, and drop him.

There's no time to lose. Retract your sights and swing the rifle over to the left (northwest) side, and quickly zoom in on the guard walking along the warehouse balcony above Rianna's position **[K.06]**. Steady your aim so you don't hit the fencing in front of him, and drop the foe **[K.07]**. Rianna and Hopper move down into ground cover.

Another target walks toward Rianna and Hopper's position, then turns and moves up the grassy knoll **[K.08]**. Put him down when he's behind the red truck **[K.09]**, and not before. Do this quickly before he spots Connor and the mission fails.

The truck driver is next; focus on him as he wanders to the driver's side of the cab **[K.10]**, and then unload a single shot. Then shoot the enemy on the balcony just inside the yard gate **[K.11]**. Your sniping duties are officially over at this point.

ne team (except for you) dashes for the uck, and figures that the best plan to each the helicopter is to simply ram the ate and crash through the secondary efenses, into the helicopter landing ad. Somehow, this is successfully chieved **[K.12]**, although the dozen or o remaining foes are now alerted. One es an RPG at the tower **[K.13]**, setting e entire building ablaze. There's only ne thing for it...!

TIP 영리한

Before the church is struck, you can thin out the enemy using the remaining sniper rifle ammunition, dropping as many foes as you can; this helps during the next checkpoint. Fire on any explosive barrels with foes in close proximity, too.

CHECKPOINT L: THEY DON'T GIVE UP, DO THEY?

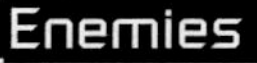

Stronghold Guard

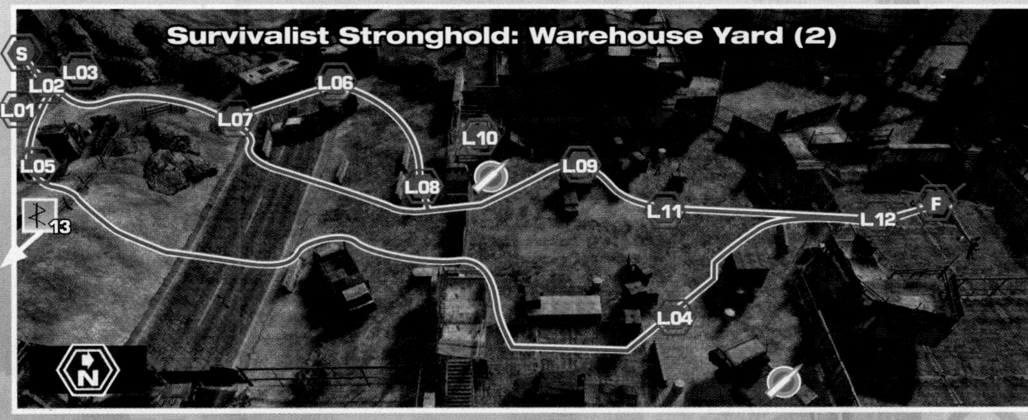

Towering Inferno

he church tower is now on fire. You can stay and burn to death, r smash your way from the tower **[L.01]**, and land on some ooden scaffolding from an earlier attempt to renovate the tructure. The latter is obviously recommended, after which you ave a few options.

Objective: Rendezvous at the Helicopter

Tactical Planning: Get to the Chopper

Threat Assessment: Warehouse Guards

Despite cutting down foes during their daring truck run, your compadres have left around a dozen pissed-off guards. Your friends aren't in any real danger, but you are. The enemies are scattered about behind the numerous vehicles, crates, and other cover. Expect at least four to six additional reinforcements to run in (from the west and east) as you remove these threats.

Plan A: Gunning, Then Running

You may be tempted to sidestep left, and drop to a lower platform and onto the grassy knoll overlooking the warehouse. This is an option (in fact, it's the start of Plan B), but a better bet is to remain on the upper platform and use up all your remaining sniper rifle ammunition, ideally on the guards milling about below **[L.02]**. The fire doesn't descend to your location, and although your teammates are yelling at you to get to them, you have as much time as you need to reach them. Why not use your scope **[L.03]**, and whittle down the numbers of foes before you engage any stragglers?

This allows you to practice the fine art of dropping foes at distance with a sniper rifle. Start at the lower-right corner of the warehouse, blasting the explosive barrels to take out two (or if you're lucky, three) foes at once **[L.04]**. Then decapitate (or shoot the torso of) each foe you can see. Expect reinforcements to run in; use up your entire sniper rifle ammunition, which should leave only around four or five foes to tackle at closer quarters. This plan makes the final dash to the rendezvous point significantly easier. Finally, if you've already fallen onto the grassy knoll with the red truck, keep to the right (east), optionally standing (then crouching or going prone) atop one of the rusting vehicles, and tag foes from this location instead **[L.05]**. Afterward, grab the easily missed news pick-up close by.

NOTE 알아두세요

Once you're done, begin Plan B, but with significantly fewer enemies to worry about.

HIDDEN HISTORY >> 13 (55/61)

On the far right (eastern) end of the grassy knoll below the burning church, on the grass near a rusting vehicle.

RACIAL CONFLICTS TURN BLOODY IN JAPAN *7/7/2017*

Thousands of Japanese are protesting for a second day in Shinjuku, Tokyo following an alleged assassination attempt by Korean agents on the Japanese royal family. Although a statement from Naicho (Japan's main intelligence agency) indicates that the prime suspects are reactionary nationals, the general public blames the so-called "North" Korean secret agents.

Several shops owned by ethnic Koreans were broken into and in some cases lit on fire by protesters. In one instance, a local store owner and his son were dragged onto the street and beaten by demonstrators. The Japanese government has condemned these attacks, pledging the support of police and military units to maintain order.

Plan B: Running, Then Gunning

If you want to play a more dangerous game, drop to the rough path leading down the grassy knoll, between the red truck and some wooden barricades. While you're still on relatively high ground, bring your sniper rifle (or your other favored weapon) out, and look to the left (northwest). Three guards run along the upper part of a barricade, then drop down and rush behind cover. Stand with an unobstructed view, and execute them as each one drops to the ground **[L.06]**. Otherwise, you face them at closer quarters **[L.07]**, so use the rocks and vehicles as cover.

ou can, of ourse, leap down om where the ews pick-up vas, over the arbed wire fence nd maneuver p along the ght side of the varehouse yard. However, this is less safe than stepping behind the vehicles on the eft side of the road and moving up to the stop sign at the fallen nain gate **[L.08]**. Either way works, though. Remain at the striped oncrete gate foundations and begin to target foes in the yard. Shoot explosive barrels either when foes are nearby, or before you each one **[L.09]** so it doesn't explode near you. The good news s that the enemies are firing on Connor and your crew, so they von't all be targeting you.

CAUTION 조심하다

Explosive barrels have a warning on them for a reason. Stand too close to an exploding one, and you die. So don't.

TIP 영리한

Grenades are a hot commodity, and there's some directly to the left of the gate as you approach it, and there's more to the right of the gate, in the truck bed, as you make your final assault.

Container yard infiltration continues. Although you can run, you risk being gunned down before you reach Connor and the chopper. Therefore, a slower and more methodical approach s usually better. Continue to move (ideally forward) though, so you're closing in on your allies. Now is the time to use any grenades you have left. Then move up along the left side of the warehouse yard (or the right, although locating foes is slightly tougher and more dangerous). You can climb the steps of two raised guard towers **[L.10]** (or the back of a truck on the right side). All offer elevated positions for quickly scoping and shooting foes, although beware of enemies sneaking up behind you. An empty, open warehouse along the left (west) side is a possible (but not optimal) place to shoot from. Ideally, remove the forces as you progress up the yard **[L.11]**, until Connor and the team are reached.

Objective: Steal the Helicopter

Once you reach Connor, he indicates where your skill-set is to be utilized next. Simply clamber aboard the waiting helicopter (it doesn't matter if there are enemies still to kill) **[L.12]**. There's no time for a pre-flight check, but the chopper lifts off without incident, and the signal from the fuel trucks is coming in clear. It's time to hijack those tankers!

Mettle of Honor

Award Heartland | Rating 10 | Trophy Bronze

Completing this mission earns you this particular reward. Difficulty level, or how many times you restarted a checkpoint, do not matter.

Mettle of Honor

Award Heartland—Guerrilla | Rating 25 | Trophy Bronze

Completing this mission earns you this individual reward. However, you must complete this on the hardest difficulty.

Mettle of Honor

Award Iron Man—Heartland | Rating 25 | Trophy Bronze

Completing this mission without dying once or restarting a checkpoint earns you this reward. Lessen the difficulty if you're having problems completing this task.

MISSION SELECT »06 »OVERWATCH

The squad is in hot pursuit of the fuel tankers. You'll provide close-air support while the others hijack the trucks. A gauntlet of enemy SAM sites, RPG teams, and blockades stands between you and the California border.

 **HIDDEN HISTORY** » 0 (55/61 total)

 **KOREAN KODEX** » 1 (9/10 total)

 **UNIQUE WEAPON** » 0 (14/17 total)

CHECKPOINT A: CHASE

Friendlies

Connor

Hopper

Rianna

Enemies

Humvee

LAV Piranha

 **WEAPONS >>** ASM Rockets

 **WEAPONS >>** Twin Machine Guns

 **WEAPONS >>** Missile Defeat Flares

 You begin the mission with these weapons (attached to your helicopter).

 **Objective:** Catch Up to the Convoy

"A Five Mile Stretch to Pull This Off"

Your flying skills have paid off. Leaving the compound behind, you're within five miles of the California border and the trio of fuel tankers currently under KPA guard. Connor remarks that the chopper has entered a communications dead zone **[A.01]**; the perfect place to pull off the hijack. Pay close attention to the on-screen prompts, and learn the following commands:

Scout Chopper Flight Checks

Test out your rockets [i]. You have an infinite supply of them, and although lining up targets is more difficult, the damage they inflict is much more severe than your machine guns.

Test out your machine guns [ii]. You have an infinite supply of ammunition. Simply line up the target crosshairs with the enemy unit and rake the general area until something explodes or falls over. Although less powerful than a rocket barrage, this is your mainstay weapon, and worth using on almost every foe.

Of course, you can alternate between each weapon, or follow up a rocket salvo with machine-gun fire to ensure that nothing survives your onslaught.

The Thermal Vision view is a must-use attribute, because it flags enemies in a red sheen, making them stand out against the rest of the landscape. Keep this turned on throughout this mission; it makes infantry enemies much easier to spot, which is important if they are carrying RPGs. Note the difference between regular vision [iii], and Thermal Vision [iv].

Activate your Thermal Vision active so you can see the cluster of five enemy vehicles on the road ahead (east). Begin to fire your machine guns on the mechanized enemies **[A.02]** as you close, following up with barrages of rockets. Keep this up as the road bends to the right (south), destroying the final vehicle just as Hopper spots the tunnel ahead.

TIP 영리한

Remember: you can fire both rockets and guns as often as you want, but not continuously, so watch for overheating. A second, diagonal set of crosshairs appears when your guns are hitting an enemy target, so focus on lining up your shots and making them count.

Swing around and descend so you're almost scraping the freeway asphalt, and line up your guns with the vehicle at the tunnel entrance **[A.03]**. Destroy it, and then fly straight through the tunnel.

CHECKPOINT B: HIJACK

Enemies

Humvee

LAV Piranha

Fuel Tanker

Objective: Destroy the Escorts

"Put Some Fire on Them!" 

Exit the tunnel and immediately tackle the RPG-firing vehicle on the corner of the mountain road **[B.01]**.

Ascend quickly, and ensure that the missile misses you. Make a sharp right (north) turn, and target the two rear KPA vehicles in the convoy **[B.02]**, which is likely to still be out of sight around a bend to the left (west). An excellent plan is to immediately ascend over the mountain on the right side of the road as soon as you exit the tunnel, so you reach the convoy before they head around the bend.

TIP 영리한

If you're fired on by an enemy with an RPG (whether infantry or vehicle), the following factors help you survive:

Make evasive maneuvers. This means ascending or descending immediately, or sidling left or right, so the missile physically passes you.

Your Missile Defeat Flares are only necessary when the "missile warning" alarm goes off. These are activated when homing missiles are spotted; regular rockets have a straight trajectory.

A general rule for the rest of this mission is to fly as high as you can when tackling multiple foes. Although your guns and missiles take longer to hit, you are much harder to take down.

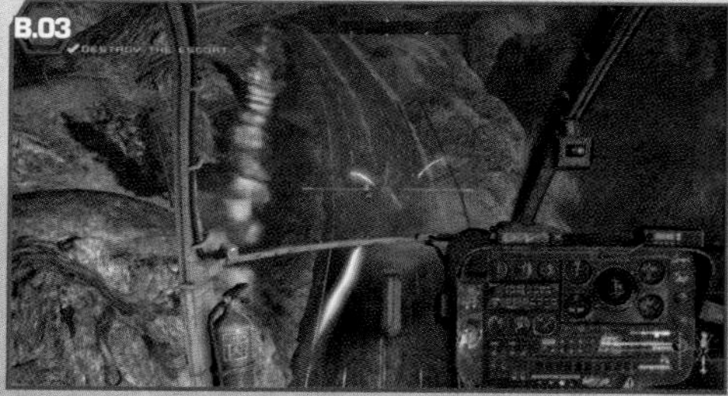

Swing around the corner, and begin to dismantle the rest of the convoy on your approach **[B.03]**, one troop-carrying guard vehicle at a time. There are three vehicles to destroy, and although the explosions are close to the fuel tankers, you're only likely to damage them (and fail the mission) if you actively target them. Primarily use your guns to precision-target these three vehicles. Your chopper's position can help or hinder the situation:

Low Bombing Run: You can follow the convoy low to the ground, sidling left and right and just avoiding the bumps in the road while strafing the enemy troop carriers with gunfire **[B.04]**. You can remove the threats quickly, but you have less time to react to their fire.

High Bombing Run: This is the safest plan because it allows you to fire on the convoy from a greater height, which takes more time (because you need to reach altitude and your weapons aren't as accurate), but you can avoid any enemy rockets much more easily **[B.05]**.

High Strafing Run: Or you can try some impressive piloting and pivot the craft so you're sidling right (west) while facing south, and then rake through the enemy vehicles **[B.06]**. This can remove threats in record time, but fire accurately or you'll hit the tankers.

CAUTION 조심하다

Notice that the fuel tankers are not color-coded as threats in your Thermal Vision. Don't target them because you need that fuel for Boone's final assault on San Francisco!

Objective: Hijack the Tankers

"Bring Us in, Jacobs!"

The fuel tankers haven't slowed down! While Hopper protests Connor's "Plan B," which obviously hasn't been thought through as thoroughly as Hopper might have liked, you should be targeting and removing the parked vehicle up ahead **[B.07]**. While your team chatters, slow down and position your chopper so you're trailing the rear fuel tanker, on the left side of it (because that's where the KPA driver is sitting) **[B.08]**.

Bring the helicopter to the front of the rear tanker's cabin, looking for the on-screen prompt, and watch as Hopper leaps and neutralizes the driver, and hijacks the vehicle **[B.09]**. Pull up alongside the middle tanker, and do the same **[B.10]**. You may maneuver in faster and glance off the ground or the tanker without ruining your chances, but don't make a habit of it! Rianna climbs aboard and defeats the driver, leaving Connor to complete the hijack on the lead tanker **[B.11]**. While Hopper protests this terror-inducing event, you progress toward your next checkpoint.

CAUTION 조심하다

Line up your hijacking relatively quickly, or you reach some SAM sites and the border checkpoint, failing this mission.

CHECKPOINT C: DOWNHILL

Enemies

Humvee

LAV Piranha

SAM Site

Soldier (RPG)

T-99 Main Battle Tank

Objective: Protect the Tankers

"Don't Stop Until We Reach San Francisco!"

Your role is to protect the three tankers for the rest of this escape. As you climb and follow the road around the right (south) bend **[C.01]**, a missile proximity sensor goes off. Immediately launch Missile Defeat Flares, or you'll be struck by a parked SAM site, on the road ahead to the left **[C.02]**. Destroy it quickly with gunfire.

TIP 영리한

Although you should always watch the proximity warnings, you don't need to actively stay above the road. Take shortcuts across the mountains to avoid winding corners, and so you can attack enemy installations well before the tankers are targeted.

There are two more SAM sites as you progress (westward) along a straight section of road with water to your left (south). Tackle the first on the left by the road's edge **[C.03]**, and the second perched halfway up the rugged promontory on your right, slightly farther along the road **[C.04]**. Once that second SAM site is neutralized, prepare to avoid further missiles.

Connor orders you to soften up the enemy at the road checkpoint ahead. While deploying your Missile Defeat, attack the vehicle immediately, as the ensuing explosion usually catches one of the four infantry troops, your other targets. Strafe both guard towers and the ground in front to take out all the enemies **[C.05]**. Although the troops may seem inconsequential, their RPGs can seriously damage your convoy.

Objective: Destroy the Blockade

"Ladies and Gentlemen, Welcome to California!"

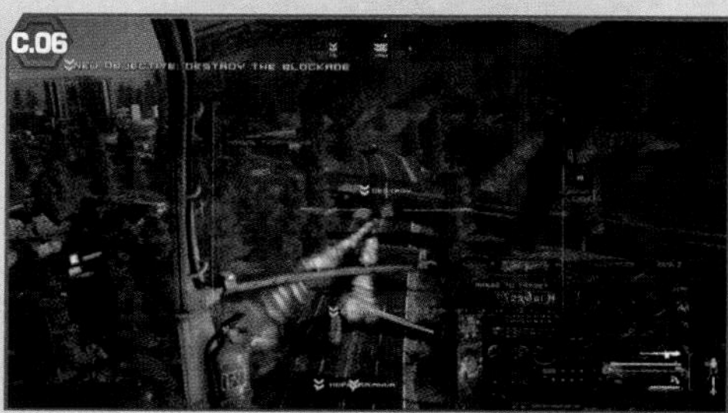
C.06

C.07

Now through the KPA checkpoint, the convoy continues to trundle down the main road, turning left (west) slightly. Without waiting for the on-screen objective prompt, immediately target the concentration of mechanized enemy units sitting on and below the freeway overpass [C.06]. Humvees race in to join the blockade. Concentrate all your firepower on the units clustered together, swinging left and right to avoid their missiles. Remember you're not governed by roads, so circle-strafe around to the side so you're facing south, keeping in motion so you aren't targeted. With a couple of rocket barrages and constant gunfire, the enemies—and the freeway section—explode and collapse [C.07]. This may have made a dent in the enemy armor, but it's cut off the main road out of here!

CHECKPOINT D: SUBURBS

Enemies

Humvee

LAV Piranha

SAM Site

Soldier (RPG)

T-99 Main Battle Tank

Objective: Protect the Tankers

Detour of Duty

D.01

Connor decides that the fallen freeway section isn't accessible (and he's correct), and instead drives off-road for a moment before doubling back through a small suburban neighborhood, with Rianna and Hopper following [D.01].

Hunting High or Low?

i

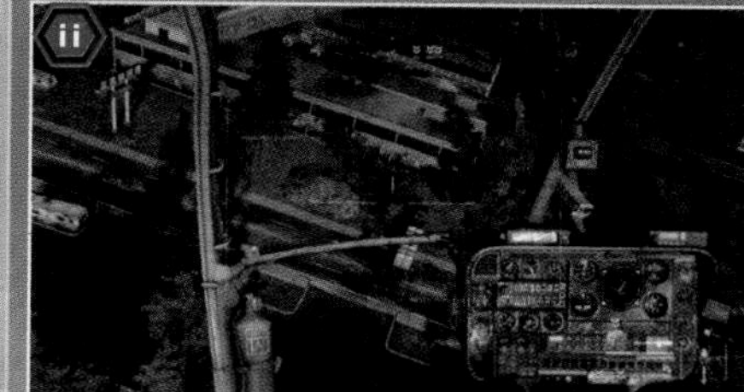
ii

You don't need to slavishly follow the convoy using the road or approaching from behind. Low altitude flying [i] may be impressive, but it keeps you from spotting enemies ahead. Therefore, you should fly ahead of the lead convoy truck, circling at a higher altitude [ii], with your Thermal Vision picking up heat signatures that would be otherwise difficult to spot. Clearing a path means removing threats as early as possible, before your teammates encounter them.

CAUTION 조심하다

Up until now, you didn't need to worry about your team's health, but now icons over each tanker indicate the damage they have suffered. Fortunately, the team members regenerate damage (just like you), but the change in color indicates that you should pay extra attention. Leaving your team to enemy fire will result in mission failure.

"KPA in the parking lot!" The cluster of buildings to the right of the convoy path has around 10 infantry foes milling about. A second later, an RPG enemy appears in the tower, while two enemy Humvees flank either side of the block. Cut down the Humvee closest to the convoy first, then rake the infantry in the lot **[D.02]**, but as soon as the RPG foe appears, blast him and the tower he's standing on **[D.03]**, because he inflicts the most damage to your crew. Humvees then block the intersection, so clear them out with more gunfire. Finally, optionally strafe any infantry you missed back in the parking lot.

"RPG team on the motel roof!" While Connor smashes through container trailers in a tanker that he's sure will survive the impact, swing your helicopter so it is facing the two-story motel to the south. Although your Thermal Vision is picking up a couple of vehicles nearby, don't go off and strafe them, as infantry soon stream out of the roof exit **[D.04]**. Lay them out with a rocket strike and constant gun barrages, or three of them will begin launching rockets at your team. The two Humvees now drive down the road and block it around the corner, to the south **[D.05]**. Hit them with your favored ordnance and clear the way for your team.

TIP 영리한

When dealing with infantry enemies streaming out of a doorway, simply launch rockets or fire your guns at the doorway, cutting them all down before they spread out. This focused death from above is thoroughly recommended!

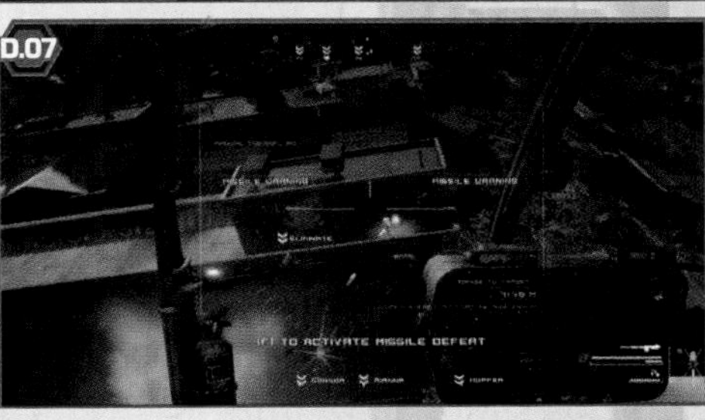

Cover the team (ideally from a good height) as they move around the road to the south, as it bends right (west). Cut down a few infantry stragglers at the corner, and running toward a guard tower. Sidle to avoid some rockets fired by a couple of vehicles and two enemies on a billboard, all to the west **[D.06]**. Make short work of them, using your Missile Defeat if prompted, as more infantry spread out along the north side of the motel roof your team just passed **[D.07]**. Situate yourself so you can swing to the right (north) and target them before they get into position. If you deal with the previous enemies first, you can remove the infantry threats before they get into position, because they appear only after the first two tankers in your convoy turn west.

Your convoy is approaching the next freeway on-ramp, which is located in the main conurbation of the port, between the two larger office buildings. On the overpass, and below on the same road as the convoy, the KPA have set up another blockade consisting of a tank, armored vehicle, and a few infantrymen **[D.08]**. Concentrate your fire on the tank first, and then demolish the remaining foes. The freeway superstructure remains intact.

NOTE 알아두세요

If you receive a missile warning, check the rooftops to the southwest. A SAM site may be on top of one of the roofs and on the shoreline road; deal with them right now, while your team makes its slow turn onto the freeway.

CHECKPOINT E: HIGHWAY

Enemies

SAM Site

Soldier (RPG)

Z-10 Chimera

To the Danger Zone

E.01

E.02

In the moments before Rianna yells about an incoming attack chopper, face southeast with a full view of your teammates, and check the skies behind the tall office building on the left side of the highway. Attack the KPA chopper **[E.01]** as soon as you can; ideally destroying it before it even flies between the two tall buildings. Launch countermeasures as soon as you see the warning.

A second or so later, while your team is driving up the highway on-ramp, strafe the hotel—the tallest building in town—with either two rocket barrages or gunfire (or both). There are RPG teams on the lower roof, and also on the upper balcony (which is still quite low to the ground) **[E.02]**. Cut them down immediately, optionally checking the Kodex on the building itself, before swinging around and hovering over the highway itself.

KOREAN KODEX >> 1 (9/10)

On the top left part of the concrete side of the tallest building in the port area, on the right side of the highway (when facing south).

E.03

E.04

Train your weapon sights on the doorway leading to the lower roof of the office building left of the highway, and rake the area with gunfire or a rocket volley to foil the KPA RPG team **[E.03]** before they fire on the convoy, which has started its highway drive. Then quickly switch to a side balcony on the hotel to the right **[E.04]**; more RPG teams need to be neutralized with your exceptional firepower.

> **NOTE** 알아두세요
>
> **You may have additional SAM sites around a half-sunken cargo ship to the southeast around the harbor. If any appear on your Thermal Vision, swiftly fly over and demolish them, before returning to your team.**

Mettle of Honor

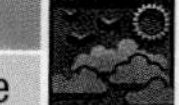

Award: Safer Skies | Rating: 10 | Trophy: Bronze

Destroying all of the SAM trucks in this level (which have been referenced throughout this mission) grants you this additional reward.

E.05

Your chaperoning continues as your team presses southward along the highway, and onto the bridge **[E.05]**. Next stop, 'Frisco! Of course, Connor's vehicle abuse comes back to haunt the team when they're halfway across the bridge; his tanker stalls, and the KPA are just behind!

CHECKPOINT F: BROKEN DOWN

Enemies

Humvee

LAV Piranha

T-99 Main Battle Tank

Bridge Control

Rianna spots the KPA heading from north to south, toward your stalled crew. Your task is to protect the team while Hopper rigs the bridge with C4 explosives, and Connor fixes his stalled tanker. Swing your helicopter to face north **[F.01]**, and ascend; you need maximum time to dodge any incoming rockets, as well as firing your countermeasure.

Enemy vehicles come up onto the highway on-ramp just before the bridge, and then weave around the wreckage, toward your team. You can stop them well before this happens, but it involves the cunning tactic of flying out of range of your convoy. The "Return to Convoy" warning and countdown begins, but you should be at the north end of the bridge, and able to lay down rockets **[F.02]** and gunfire **[F.03]** to cripple and explode all the enemies easily, and ideally before they reach the bridge.

CAUTION 조심하다

However, you don't want to fail the mission by abandoning your team; when the "Return to Convoy" counter reaches 5, quickly reverse southward toward your team, and then head north again when the timer resets.

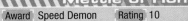

Continue your punishing barrage on the enemy vehicles, backing up if you need to. It is relatively easy to keep the foes from ever firing on the tankers. When Rianna asks "How much longer?!", there is a lull in the combat. Hopper detonates the bridge at Connors request and the bridge is destroyed.

Connor has fixed his vehicle, and the convoy begins to move off. Continue to assault the enemy at the north end of the bridge **[F.04]**, but slowly retreat to the flashing C4 beacons **[F.05]**, and wait for the convoy to move.

When Connor radios "We're on the move. Let 'em have it!", oblige and hit the bridge with a barrage or two. Usually your team helps with the blasting, and the bridge easily collapses **[F.06]**. Ignore the remaining KPA vehicles (who are cut off from your team now), and spin around, following the team south toward the tunnel **[F.07]**, and all the way to San Francisco!

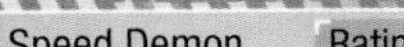

Mettle of Honor

Award	Speed Demon	Rating	10	Trophy	Bronze

Hijack the tankers in less than eight minutes in one life in Chapter 6: Overwatch. Learn the enemy locations, and fire as early and as accurately as possible!

Mettle of Honor

Award	Overwatch	Rating	10	Trophy	Bronze

Completing this mission earns you this particular reward. Difficulty level, or how many times you restarted a checkpoint, do not matter.

Mettle of Honor

Award	Overwatch—Guerrilla	Rating	25	Trophy	Silver

Completing this mission earns you this individual reward. However, you must complete this on the hardest difficulty.

Mettle of Honor

Award	Iron Man—Overwatch	Rating	25	Trophy	Silver

Completing this mission without dying once or restarting a checkpoint earns you this reward. Lessen the difficulty if you're having problems completing this task.

MISSION SELECT >> 07 >> GOLDEN GATE

The fuel has been delivered to the US military. Now join them in a major operation to retake the Golden Gate Bridge. An anti-aircraft emplacement is keeping the US from launching fighters, and the KPA is going to fight for every inch. Good luck.

HIDDEN HISTORY >> 6 (61/61 total)

KOREAN KODEX >> 1 (10/10 total)

UNIQUE WEAPON >> 3 (17/17 total)

CHECKPOINT A: FOB

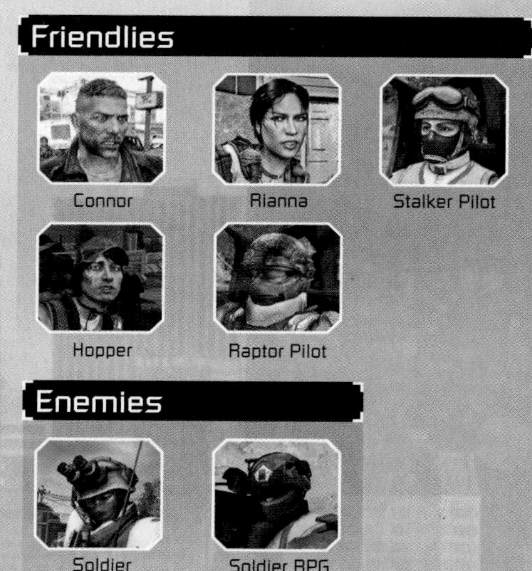

Objective: Board the Helicopter

WEAPONS >>
PWS Diablo SMG [Mk3 Red Dot Sight]

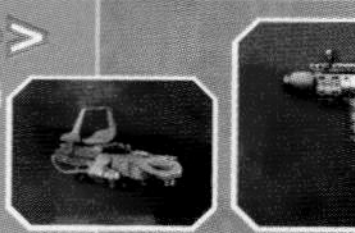

WEAPONS >>
ACR Rifle [Mk2 ACOG Scope], with [Grenade Launcher] (8)

WEAPONS >>
Fragmentation Grenade (4)

You begin the mission with these weapons.

"Throttle to 70 Percent. Avionics Are a Go."

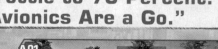

You begin with a rendezvous at a Forward Operating Base, part of Warpath command, the remnants of the US military in Marin County, just north of San Francisco **[A.01]**. The jet fuel allows military troops to get the air

support they so desperately need. But first of all, you're conscripted to aid in knocking out some AAs on the Golden Gate bridge. After a thorough inspection of the field command center (where another news pick-up is secured), board the scout helicopter Raptor 1-1, and take a seat next to Connor **[A.02]**. Warpath (central command for this op) clears you for take-off.

HIDDEN HISTORY >> 1 (56/61)

In the tarp-draped command tent north of your starting point, near a parked attack helicopter, on a table next to a laptop.

BLIX UNABLE TO FIND WMDS IN NORTH KOREA

3/18/2012

Hans Blix, called back from retirement by the UN Secretary General announced today that his team was unable to locate weapons of mass destruction anywhere in the country of North Korea. The inspections are a result of intense suspicion on the part of the US State Department, who believe that Kim Jong-il's government was actively attempting to develop a nuclear weapons program before his death. Kim Jong-un, the new Supreme Leader of North Korea has publicly stated on numerous occasions his intent to re-engage with the rest of the world and that a policy of openness and transparency is the first step on that road. This radical shift in policy was met with surprise in the international community, and has caused many to draw parallels between modern day Korea and Germany of the 90's.

As you leave the ground, Warpath radios that reinforcement choppers from the 160th are inbound. In the distance, the air is thick with smoke from AA ordnance explosions. The 160th Stalker airborne company joins as you leave the land and skim the water. As you approach the bridge, the Korean jets launch a fly-by strike, and Raptor 3 takes a critical hit **[A.03]**.

Raptor 2, with Rianna and Hopper aboard, was also struck, and the craft is losing hydraulic pressure. They won't be able to join you, and instead will land near the armored convoy. You pass a KPA submarine, veer off around away from Alcatraz, and as you close in on the Golden Gate, RPG teams fire, and Raptor 4 is struck, spinning down into the water **[A.04]**.

Raptor 1 flies under the bridge and toward the gigantic north support tower, where KPA infantry have taken up defensive postures on the scaffold. Some are armed with RPGs, which could make your flight a lot shorter. Be sure your ACR Rifle is cocked upward, with the grenade launcher attachment ready to fire as you swoop down, and begin a circle of the tower **[A.05]**.

Connor's advice—to use the grenade launcher—is the only way you're going to make an effective dent in the scurrying KPA manning the bridge girders. Immediately launch your first grenade, as Raptor 1 makes a counterclockwise circle of the structure. During this time, you have around 10 opportunities (between reloading) to target around a dozen foes that you see **[A.06]**. Fire, then quickly set up for the next foe and fire again, and don't worry about hitting every single enemy. Be sure to kill some of them though, just for the sake of your pride!

TIP 영리한

You have unlimited ammunition for the grenade launcher (but only while aboard the helicopter), so fire as often as possible. Try to fire your arcing shot when you're told there are enemies on the scaffold; begin as early as possible. Also, fire a little higher than your target reticle indicates, or your shots strike lower and may miss.

Mettle of Honor

Award	Wilhelm's Nightmare	Rating	10	Trophy	Bronze

If you succeed in launching ten enemies over the rail so they fall, you're given this reward. What a scream! Try to aim the GL so the explosion occurs behind the enemies, pushing them off the bridge and into a plummet; normal deaths do not count.

Warpath indicates your new landing zone is the Lime Point Lighthouse **[A.07]**, which must be secured before the heavy guns can roll in. The area is hot; there are five dismounted infantry and a T-99 at the base of the north tower. You'll encounter them once you clear the road, which has 15 infantry plus two RPG teams. Touchdown is in 10 seconds.

TIP

As you touch down, switch your ACR Rifle back to rifle fire, rather than the grenade launcher, because you immediately tackle RPG foes at the next checkpoint. You can also aim and arc grenades into the forthcoming area, but this won't diminish the number of foes to face in Checkpoint B.

CHECKPOINT B: ASSAULT THE MARINA

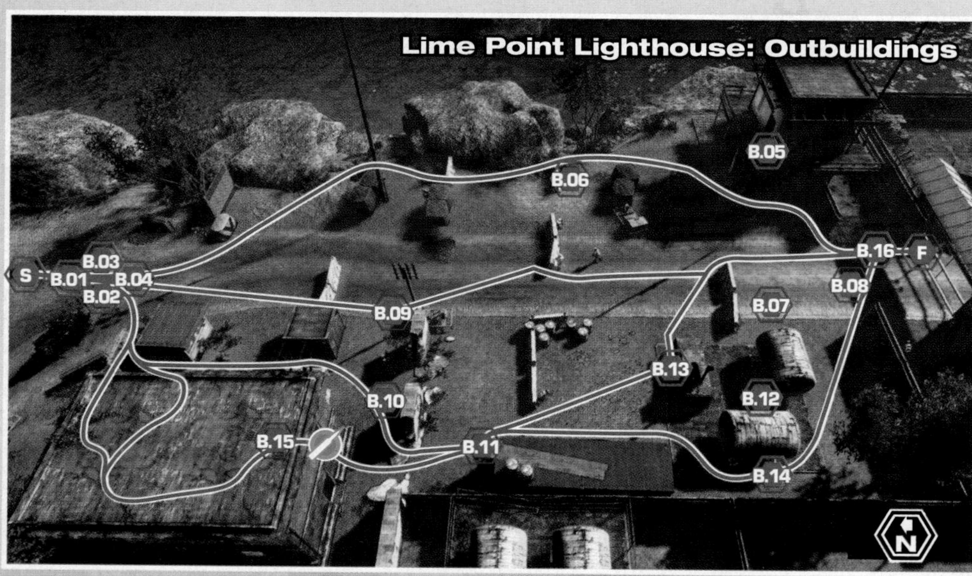

Friendlies

Private Hernandez

Sergeant Keyes

Enemies

Soldier (Scout)

Soldier

Soldier (RPG)

Objective: Fight to the Bridge Tower

"A Few More Yards and It's Ours!"

The moment you step out from the scout chopper **[B.01]**, a nearby helicopter is consumed by a direct RPG strike and explodes in a shower of twisted metal. The two RPG enemies are firing (one at a time; expect another to appear halfway through this fight) on the balcony of the command hut by the gates ahead (north) of you. Stay still, and you'll receive the next RPG shot and usually expire. Defensive actions are recommended, and now!

Tactical Planning: "Push Up! Push Up!"

Threat Assessment: KPA Marina Forces

Warpath's threat assessment is correct. There are around 15 infantry foes in this area; the first eight or so are already on the road and behind cover, while the remaining forces appear from behind the left and right metal walls. In addition, two RPG soldiers stand atop the balcony on the gate hut to the left (southeast) of you, across the sandbags and barriers. They randomly appear, one at a time, on the front-left or front-right corner of the structure. For best results, train your weapon on them as soon as you see them, because a direct hit by an RPG will kill you.

Weapon Choice

You have three possible weapons to employ during this fracas, and the first two are the ones you're currently carrying: the ACR Rifle **[B.02]** with the grenade launcher attachment **[B.03]**, and the PWS Diablo SMG with the red dot sight **[B.04]**. The former's grenade attachment is an ideal weapon for bringing down the clusters of enemies at the far (south) end of the road by the gate; simply punt grenades as they appear and drop them. You only need to worry because of the delay between reloads, so either make your shots count or immediately switch to your other weapon to tag a foe you missed (this is quicker than reloading the grenade launcher).

You can also target the RPG soldiers with your grenade launcher, but you need to be extremely accurate in arcing the projectile properly. If you can't manage this, switch to the ACR or SMG for these takedowns. You tend to run out of ammunition faster with the SMG, so watch your inventory. The ACR's scope is excellent, but the SMG's scope isn't that magnified, making it slightly more difficult to take down foes at range.

There's a weapon even more impressive than these two: the SCAR-H LMG hidden on the upper floor of the building to your right (west). The zoom of the scope, and the viciousness of this rapid-fire weapon allows you to cut down foes in seconds. Use this in conjunction with plans that involve the right flank.

Your fragmentation grenades are another excellent choice, although it is better to use up your ACR's grenades and then swap out the rifle for a new armament.

TIP 영리한

In this fast-firing and chaotic battle, it is sometimes quicker to switch weapons rather than wait for a reload, and this could save you from taking a terminal amount of damage.

Unique Weapons Detail: 15/17

WEAPONS >>
Dragon Fire SCAR-H LMG [Mk3 ACOG Scope]

With a special camo paint job, this SCAR-H allows you the flexibility to either spray and pray multiple foes from the hip, or line up a burst of fire using the excellent scope, with a range that betters both your current offerings. You may wish to swap your PWS SMG for this.

Plan A: Left Flank Rush (or Creep)

Utilizing the remaining grenades on your launcher attachment while risking a push up the left flank can yield a competent completion of this checkpoint. After exiting the chopper, drop the RPG foe on the balcony **[B.05]**, then sprint left, switching back to your grenade launcher. Melee strike the foe behind the low concrete barrier **[B.06]**, and shoot the second RPG foe just before you step underneath the balcony he was standing on.

An alternative is to creep up the left side of the road, focusing first on the RPG soldier, then at foes streaming out of the gate area. Use the cover judiciously, because you can easily be killed by enemy fire; in fact the slower you move, the easier time the enemies have hitting you. You can, of course, sidestep right and join the middle or right paths instead, but watch for a Chimera enemy helicopter to strafe the area to the right; only head there afterward.

If you're close or under the gate hut, punt two or three grenades into the cluster of assembling foes **[B.07]**, and remain under the balcony, optionally jumping on the two metal crates and taking up an ambush spot there. You can now rake foes where they spill out from behind the two walls on either side of the gate **[B.08]**, punting more grenades, or stepping out around the wall and delivering another grenade and stepping back before you're shot. The "rush" variant of plan is dangerous and requires precise aiming with your grenades but can end the fight in moments.

 Plan B: Up the Middle 

This option is usually the least safe of the three main routes (which can be interwoven at any time). The large sandbag crates and barriers are your only option to hide behind **[B.09]**, and you can't run up the road to the gate without stepping left or right or you'll be shot; hardly the best plan.

Plan C: Right Flank (Exterior)

With your marines moving up and backing you up, quickly shoot the RPG soldier, and sprint forward and right (southwest), toward a pair of concrete sections that used to be a wall, in front of the building on your right. This is the perfect spot to sidestep out or peer around a corner, zoom and cut down foes (or fire on them with your grenade launcher), and begin to whittle down the enemy numbers **[B.10]**.

You can survive the helicopter strafing the area, but not grenades that land close by, so move behind cover and then continue to cut down foes from various locations along the right wall. You can remain at these locations or continue to push forward, depending on your preference. The next location is the large metal container against the right wall **[B.11]**, which offers great cover and takedown spots as you can see behind the concrete barriers to your left.

The location after that is by two large cylindrical fuel containers in the southwest corner of the battle area. Be sure to punt a grenade (or lob a frag grenade) at both of them so they detonate **[B.12]**, ideally taking a few enemies in the explosion. If you don't, you may be caught by these containers exploding when another explosive device detonates near you. With the burnt-out shells of the containers coated in soot, patrol the area, using the concrete block between the containers **[B.13]**, or going prone by the right container itself **[B.14]**. This way you can cut down all the remaining foes that pour out from the sides of the gate. Be sure to use grenades if there are too many to cull at once, and remember you can fire under the footings of the burned-out containers, too.

Plan D (Variant): Right Flank (Interior)

If you desire a much more defensible position, and one you can provide covering fire from, then quickly head to the right (west), through either of the two doorways, into the stone building shell. Although you can fire on foes from the ground floor window and doorway openings, the optimal plan is to scale the crates and steel ramp to the upper floor, where the Unique SCAR-H is located. Take it, and begin to cut down foes from your vantage point **[B.15]**. This is particularly effective, because you can see over the tops of the barriers, allowing quick headshots and swift aiming between foes. Beware of rockets heading your way; take down the RPG soldiers, and crouch, or back up from the window so the enemy has less to aim at. You can remain here, blasting foes until the KPA is defeated in this area.

Remain in combat readiness until all of the foes at the gate have finished appearing, and your military brethren have reached the gate itself **[B.16]**. You may be at the tip of this spear or hanging back in the house; either way, when Sergeant Keyes yells to form up at the south gate, you should oblige him.

TIP 영리한

Before Hernandez opens the gate, or after the gate is open and the team waits for you to follow, take a moment to gather any weapons or ammo you wish, although a weapon resupply occurs after you complete Checkpoint C.

CHECKPOINT C: TANK

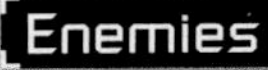

Enemies

Soldier (Scout)

Soldier (RPG)

Soldier

T-99 Main Battle Tank

Objective:
Follow Connor

Heavy Metal Thunder

Sergeant Keyes is the first through the gate, along with his men and Connor. Follow them to a section of low concrete barriers overlooking a courtyard and barracks. Keyes yells for you to hold the position, before his squad gets blown backward **[C.01]** as a Korean T-99 battle tank crashes through a wall ahead and left of the group **[C.02]**. As Connor yells at you to get into cover, it's time to formulate a tank-killing strategy....

Tactical Planning: Tanks, But No Tanks

Threat Assessment: KPA Tank and Infantry

The obvious threat here is the T-99, which has a massive main cannon (that can kill you with one shot), and a machine gun turret that is almost as potent. Without question, avoid direct line-of-sight with this killing machine; always have scenery between you and the tank. Otherwise, expect around eight KPA military in two barracks on the right (north) and far (west) sides of the courtyard you're about to run into. One has an RPG launcher, which must be "appropriated" for tank-killing.

Objective: Get to the Rocket Launcher

Plan A: Connor's Run

The optimal plan is to simply follow orders: Wait for the tank to appear, and then step back until Connor moves forward, running right (northwest) between two parked trucks, and follow him up the end steps of the first barracks **[C.03]**. Stop and you'll be shot by the tank, so keep sprinting! Once inside the barracks, you spot a trio of KPA at the far (west) end, although these are weakened severely (and usually killed) by the tank operator's injudicious cannon fire. With a hole in the left wall of the barracks, wait for Connor to move, covering him by cutting down any infantry still alive **[C.04]**, and race through the doorway opposite.

There's no time to wait as you run down the exterior steps, across a small section of yard **[C.05]**, where Connor is almost ripped apart by a cannon round hitting a parked Humvee, and up the steps to the second barracks. You can run the gauntlet with Connor, or dash to the right of a container, which is safer.

The second barracks contains four enemies **[C.06]**. Connor usually takes down the nearest one (if you let him run in first), leaving you to quickly drop the remaining three at the far end. Use the filing cabinet on your right if you need cover (because the left wall usually gets demolished by tank rounds if you wait around), and execute the foes with swift headshots, or soften them up with a grenade. Then rush in and grab the RPG.

> **NOTE** 알아두세요
>
> **It doesn't matter which weapon you drop to pick up the RPG, because you can swap out after the tank is destroyed.**

Plan B: Jacob's Run

A bit of a maverick? Then don't even wait for the tank to appear, and sprint around the parked trucks as the tank crashes through into the courtyard, and head up into the barracks **[C.07]**. Here, you're likely to face around five enemies, including two or three heading through the doorway opposite. Line up headshots one after the other, or lob a grenade in and then sprint across, keeping your fingers crossed the tank doesn't shoot you (it sometimes fires through the window).

Then sprint up into the second barracks, and quickly cut down the foe standing on the right before he shoots you **[C.08]**. Dive into cover, perhaps using a grenade on the three remaining enemies, and then salvage the RPG launcher before the tank shoots out more of the barracks left wall.

Plan C: Just a Bit of Fun

There are various (extremely foolish) ways to "lark" around this area. For example, you can run around the rear of the tank as it crashes through the wall **[C.09]**, and sprint behind a couple of containers along the courtyard's left (southern) perimeter wall. Sadly, although you can quickly peer out and tag some of the foes in the windows of the barracks (including the RPG soldier), you're always shot by the tank when you try to reach either barracks.

Running up the middle barracks steps is another lunatic idea that results in a quick death for you if you're not extremely careful. And firing at the RPG soldier from any barracks window usually results in you being struck by tank fire. Therefore, the only other safe location to tag the RPG soldier is by going prone near the parked truck, using it to absorb the tank's fire, and executing the RPG soldier using a line-of-sight from under the front of the truck **[C.10]**. This means you can quickly pick up the RPG when you finish either Plan A or B.

Objective: Destroy the Tank

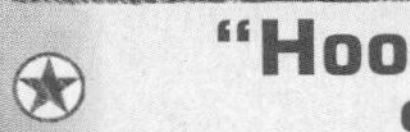

"Hoo-ah! Enemy T-99 Is Scrap Metal!"

There's one overriding plan here: line up the RPG launcher with the tank's structure and fire. However, this can take two to four shots depending on where you're standing. Zoom in if you want a more precise shot, although this takes a little longer to line up. Try to hit the front or rear of the tank, because it has much thinner armor there; attacking from the sides usually requires at least three shots.

Finally, you can fire from the window of the barracks **[C.11]** (although you're likely to be struck by a retaliatory tank shell), from

within the barracks (which is much safer), or outside the barracks, on the steps for the height advantage **[C.12]**. Running about isn't advisable; spend as little time as possible removing this threat. Sergeant Keyes informs Warpath, and they split to return to the quad, leaving you and Connor to scale the north bridge tower before you can rendezvous with Rianna and Hopper. Check the fallen walled area where the tank first rolled in from to secure an out-of-the-way news pick-up. Then follow Connor as he kicks open a gate and scales a ladder to the base of the tower itself.

Objective: Follow Connor

HIDDEN HISTORY >> 2 (57/61)

On a pile of debris close to a metal container in the walled area of the barracks courtyard, where the tank rolled in from.

US FORCES IN SOUTH KOREA HEAD HOME *8/27/2013*

Under pressure from Seoul, The United States Military will begin its withdrawal from South Korea starting this month, a Defense Department spokesman said to the press earlier today. "The United States and South Korea have a long standing commitment to maintaining a stable balance of power in their region," the official said, "and our commitment to that peace and to the strength of the North Korean government is not wavering." Although critics maintain that this is in response to the wave of nationalism that is sweeping the Korean peninsula following the groundbreaking peace talks initiated by Kim Jong-un, officials maintain that the withdrawal is part of a series of planned, gradual draw downs as the US military re-scopes its scale and focus. US forces are expected to be completely withdrawn from the area within five years.

CHECKPOINT D: BASE OF THE TOWER

Enemies

Soldier (Scout)

Elite 718

Soldier

Elite 718 (Heavy)

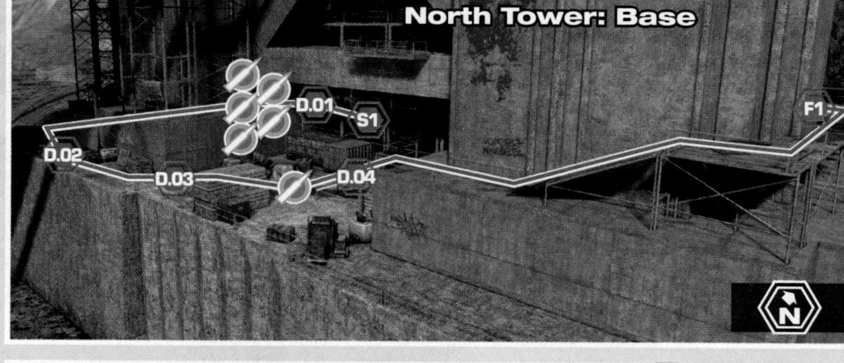

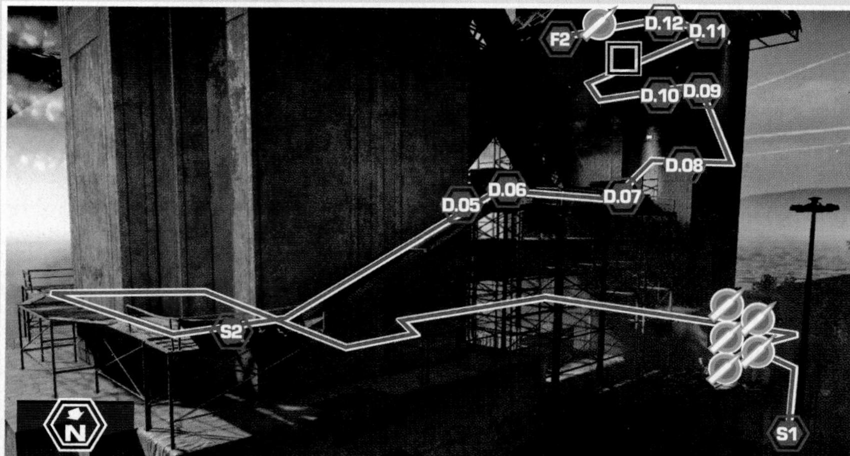

 **Objective:** Climb to the Deck of the Bridge

"Stock Up While You Can."

Once at the top of the ladder, follow Connor to the right, and pause at the collection of weaponry propped up against a couple of crates **[D.01]**. The selection is excellent; especially because you should have learned which armaments are your favorites. Of particular interest is the vicious M249 (with a handy scope), and the M16 which, although not fully automatic, is excellent for dropping the 718s with minimal ammo expenditure, and comes with a shotgun attachment for close-combat work. Definitely grab the C4, as it doesn't trade places with other items, and although it's of limited use, you want to be as tooled up as possible. Lose the RPG launcher; it isn't as proficient at taking out infantry foes as you'd think.

WEAPONS >>
PWS Diablo SMG [Mk2 Red Dot Sight]
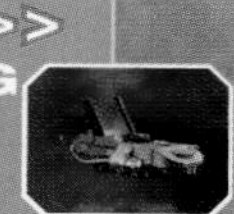

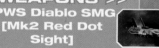

WEAPONS >>
M16 Rifle [Mk3 ACOG Scope] with [Shotgun] (25)

WEAPONS >>
M249 LMG [Mk1 Red Dot Sight]

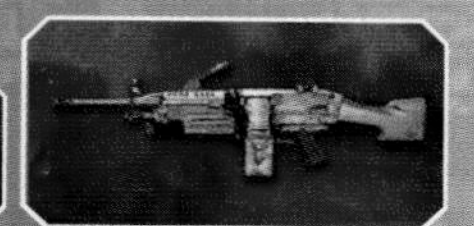

WEAPONS >>
ACR Rifle [Mk1 Holo Scope]

WEAPONS >>
C4 Explosives (4)
Located on a crate on the concrete ground area of the north tower footing.

The 411 on the 718

You're about to encounter a group of enemies among scaffolding, pallets, and an overhang. Here's the optimal plan: Run counter-clockwise around the base of the tower to meet up with Connor. As you arrive, he steps out, rushes a KPA clad in blue armor, and crushes the enemy's skull with the butt of his rifle **[D.02]**.

Don't fixate on this takedown; instead aim ahead (east) at a foe running around a stack of pallets **[D.03]**, and drop him before aiming through your scope at another foe on the walkway ahead and above. If you let Connor run past you at this point, and move forward only to the corner where you cut down your first enemy, he helps mop up the remaining foes. Start by hitting anyone on the wooden ramp. Quickly look left (north) and tag the two enemies among the containers, and then focus on quick, precise bursts to topple two regular soldiers, and two more rappelling from above. The M16 is an exceptional weapon for this.

The 911 on the 718

If you aren't interested in optimal tactics, there are many other ways to conquer this section of tower:

You can ignore Connor's yell and take out the initial foe by sprinting in and melee striking or cutting him down with weapon fire.

You can dash on ahead and tackle all of the enemies with Connor's help as an afterthought. Although shooting the rappelling foes as they descend is a testament to your aiming skill, do this only if no other foes are present, because this wastes time you could spend removing foes on the ground. Another excellent idea is to lob in a grenade toward the foot of the wooden walkway ramp so it explodes as the rappelling soldiers land, blowing up at least three foes altogether **[D.04]**. Then optionally swap out your fast-firing, spray-and-pray weapon with a Super V SMG; this is your first opportunity to try one.

WEAPONS >>
Super V SMG
[Mk1 Holo Scope]
Found near the corpses of some fallen 718 units.

CAUTION 조심하다
The 718 are the KPA's elite shock troops, and they're as hated as they are tough to tackle. They take a little more punishment before they yield, and their Super V SMG usually cuts you down after only a few shots, so out-draw them, and be ever-mindful that these aren't the conscripted fodder you've previously faced. Crouch behind cover to avoid their elite aim, and aim for their heads, because their torso armor is thick.

CAUTION 조심하다
Stepping off the scaffold results in a long and deadly fall, so watch where you're sidestepping!

Elite Ambush

Run up the ramp, following Connor around the precarious scaffold walkway as Seal Team One Lead announces that Alcatraz has been taken. When you reach Connor at the corner, he tells you to take the lead. Step around the corner, and slowly head up the wooden ramp. You hear a yell as a 718 trooper tries to pistol-whip you to death with a surprise melee ambush. Quickly execute him **[D.05]** with a melee strike, or cut him down as soon as he appears from your left. Then be extremely careful of two more foes ahead of you; their accurate firing can kill you in seconds.

TIP 영리한
You can prevent yourself from being shot at by ascending the ramp very slowly, coaxing the foe out and down into a run, giving you ample time to react offensively to him. You could always drop C4 and retreat, although that tactic is as dangerous as it is entertaining!

CAUTION 조심하다
Be very mindful of reloading your weapons. In-between clips, or the time you fire a shotgun blast, you can be cut down and killed by the enemy. Seek cover, and reload as often as possible.

You face four additional foes between the top of the wooden ramp and the doorway across the walkway. The first is peeking over a stack of walkway sections ahead of you; tag the bobbing head or face being massacred (use the top of the walkway you're on as cover, crouching or dropping prone if you need to). Then shoot the standing foe **[D.06]**

before advancing forward; two more enemies come out of the tower interior doorway **[D.07]**; wait for the first to hide behind an armored crate, then gun him down as he steps out again. Tackle the final foe by slowly creeping forward with your sights aimed at the walkway sections on the right; when he steps out, drop him.

Other options include lobbing a grenade in, rushing in and stepping behind the first stack on your left, or judicious use of a LMG.

Onward and Upward

At this point, wait for Connor to barge past you, stepping through the doorway, and watch as he shoots a foe who is standing on the metal walkway of the tower interior staircase **[D.08]**. Help him out if you want (you may have shot the foe already), or watch from the doorway. Then race to the top of the steps.

Alternately, drop the foe yourself and run up the metal steps without waiting for Connor; this is quicker.

At the top entrance, an armored 718 charges through the doorway you're at **[D.09]**. Connor can help if you waited for him, but your best bet is to strike the foe with a melee attack or drop him with a shot to the head. The shotgun attachment to the M16 is good here, but you need to have pre-loaded it, because the rush happens quickly.

Then you can watch from the doorway as Connor slowly tackles the two remaining foes in the interior storage room behind the doorway. This saves on ammunition, but there's a load lying around, so a better plan is to lob a grenade and remove both threats in seconds, or execute them with rapid headshots **[D.10]**. Then follow Connor up the steps; this is more tactical because you can create crossfire opportunities inside the top room. You may also wish to pause and view your final QR code.

KOREAN KODEX >> 1 (10/10)

On the wall to the left of the last set of stairs in the Checkpoint D interior area.

At the top of the steps, beware of (up to four) KPA foes on your right (east) side. If you barge into the room, you'll be the focus of their fire, and quick bursts while using the storage pallets as cover is your best plan. However, if you slowly creep up to the top of the steps, the foes close in on Connor, and you can shoot them from the side while Connor returns here, expertly dropping the first two or three of them **[D.11]**. Then clear the room **[D.12]**, ensuring you check the shelving opposite the exit doorway for a new SMG.

TIP 영리한

In any of these interior chambers, you may be able to drop C4 and retreat, waiting for the foes to step forward before detonating. However, this isn't an optimal plan.

Unique Weapons Detail: 16/17

WEAPONS >>
Dragon Fire Super V SMG [Mk3 Red Dot Sight]

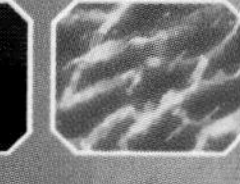

With the finest red dot sight around (move the weapon from side to side and you'll see the dot keeps the aim accurate), and a massive burst of fire, this kitted-out Super V uses ammunition extremely quickly, so check the corpses of some 718s to keep your supply plentiful. It's a perfect weapon for short- to mid-range combat.

CHECKPOINT E: TOWER INTERIOR 1

Enemies

Soldier (Scout)

Soldier

Elite 718

Elite 718 (Heavy)

Objective: Climb to the Deck of the Bridge

"Great. More Stairs. Let's Go!"

E.01

E.02

As you exit onto an outer walkway, you watch as a scout chopper takes on some KPA on the platform across and above you, before being blown out of the sky by enemy aircraft **[E.01]**. You can waste ammunition shooting the enemy, but it doesn't change the fate of the chopper. As the radio chatter continues (the friendlies are attempting to take out Angel Island's communications array), follow Connor clockwise and upward, to the northern edge of the platform that was just above you.

Two 718s are prowling this gantry, along with two regular soldiers who rappel down from above **[E.02]**. The best plan is to wait by the corner of the red steel bridge superstructure, close to where Connor has crouched, and use the corner as cover, tagging all four from this partial cover. Or, you can lob in a grenade (which can fall off the gantry and miss), or race in and cut the enemies down with quick blasts, a more dangerous option. Then continue across the platform, and ascend another ramped scaffold clamped to the bridge.

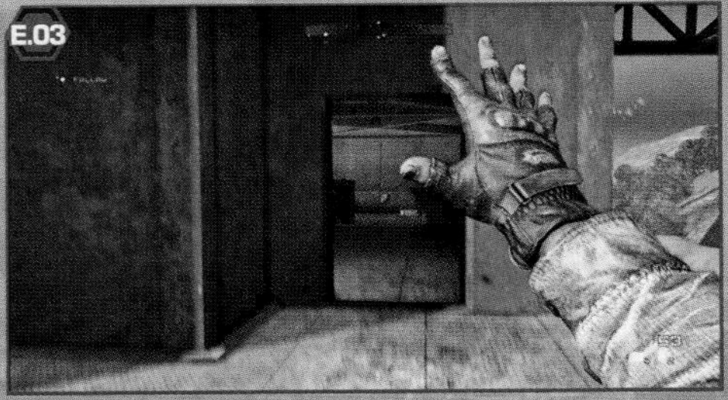
E.03

At the doorway, but before stepping through and announcing yourself to the enemy, Connor orders you to lob in a grenade. Oblige him, ideally bouncing it off the interior wall and killing two or three foes in the process, or forcing them to run out of the doorway and into your gunfire. Alternately, you can conserve your ammo and rush the interior room. There are two 718s and two regular soldiers to cull **[E.03]**; dive behind one of the metal crates and use that as cover while you whittle the enemies down.

E.04

Bound up another set of steps, across a landing where you'll find another news pick-up on a shelf and an LMG propped against a barrel, then up and around to a narrow room with steps leading up and outside. Two 718s appear at the doorway as you reach the opposite end of this exit chamber **[E.04]**; immediately cut them down with rapid fire before they enter the room (a scoped LMG is a good choice here). If you don't, use the cover to avoid their fire. Then escape back onto the upper walkway they came from.

TIP 영리한

Spin right to face south as you head up onto the upper exit room, so you can aim at the two foes at the earliest possible moment.

WEAPONS >> SCAR-H LMG [Mk 1 Holo Scope]

Propped against a barrel halfway up this interior section, under the stairs.

HIDDEN HISTORY >> 3 (58/61)

On the corner metal shelving unit in Checkpoint E's interior section, to the side of the stairs.

IRAQ: A NATION DIVIDED *8/18/2015*

Following Iran's incursion into the northern provinces of Iraq, Saudi Arabia moved into Iraq's southern provinces with the goal of protecting the Sunni Muslim refugees in the area. Iran moved into northern Iraq following the Iraqi government's collapse last month in an attempt to stave off growing ethnic unrest. Since the departure of the United States from the region, there have been a number of conflicts between Sunnis and Shiites in Iraq, but the presence of the two conflicting powers in Iraq sets a potentially dangerous stage for further conflict.

Iran has openly supported the formation of a Kurdish state in the north of Iraq, bringing it into direct conflict with its Turkish neighbor. Iran has directly allied itself with the Kurds, allowing them to manage the Kurdish regions of Northern Iraq, while Iran focuses on the majority Shiite regions. Although there have been no direct conflicts between Iranian and Saudi forces, there have been no peace overtures either.

CHECKPOINT F: TOWER INTERIOR 2

Enemies

Soldier (Scout)

Soldier

Elite 718

Elite 718 (Heavy)

Carnage on the Catwalks

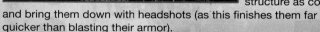

Back on the tower exterior, check the fires burning on Alcatraz to the east, then turn the corner, moving north toward a couple of sandbag pallets while Warpath radios in with some updates. There are two KPA 718s on the catwalk ahead and left (northwest) **[F.01]**. Optionally use the left corner of the bridge superstructure as cover, and bring them down with headshots (as this finishes them far quicker than blasting their armor).

Look up at two additional soldiers dropping down on ropes. They can descend faster than you can track them with a scoped weapon, so aim at the gantry and massacre them where they land. Then move around the sandbags and onto the catwalk itself. There are two more enemies to deal with; grenades can fall through the gaps, so drop them with rifle fire, using the pallets or cable reels as cover. Or bound up the metal ramp and step behind pallet cover at the top **[F.02]**.

CAUTION 조심하다

The ramped section of catwalk has no railings, so don't sidestep off into oblivion!

TIP 영리한

Check the catwalk where you dropped the previous foes for more grenades and ammo.

The remainder of the enemies—three more 718s—step around the opposite end of the catwalk. Bring them down while remaining in cover. You could sprint to the long section of walkway with numerous pallets to hide behind **[F.03]**, or step behind Connor and let him absorb the damage, but it is preferable to tag the heads of each foe with well-aimed, scoped bursts. Then cross to the ladder on the other (southwest) side.

CHECKPOINT G: CLIMB ONTO THE DECK

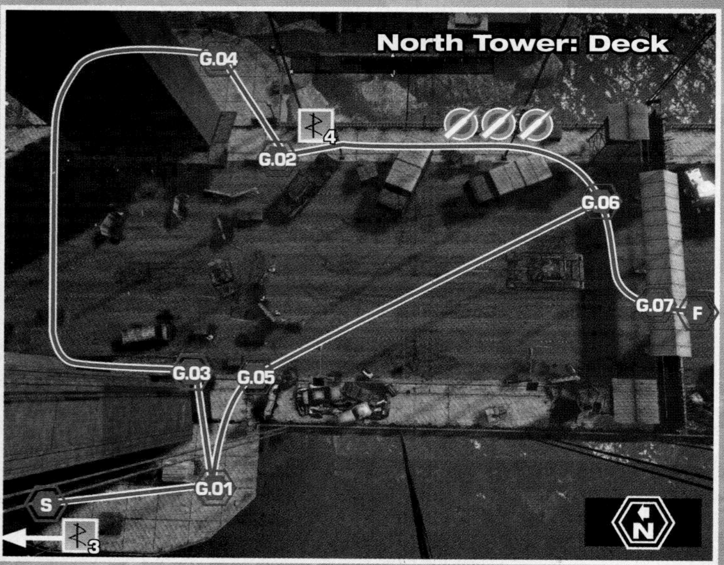

Friendlies

Hopper

Sergeant Keys

Abrams Main Battle Tank

Humvee

Rianna

Private Hernandez

Piranha LAV

Enemies

Elite 718

Elite 718 (Heavy)

T-99 Main Battle Tank

"We've Got 'em Flanked! Suppressive Fire!"

inally reaching the bridge span itself, Connor checks in with ianna, who is following an armored group of vehicles and about o smash through the northern gate. Just before this occurs, you ave the chance to cut down a group of four KPA who you've utflanked **[G.01]**, while they train their weapons on the convoy. ut down all four of them in quick succession. At this point, ou can:

Plan A: Stay n position and lrop more and nore foes as hey stream out f an entrance across the road. f you line up the ap between the rmored crate and ig-rig truck **[G.02]**, you can mow almost all of them down without ven changing your aim!

Plan B: Head p onto the antage point caffolding to our left, where Connor runs to G.03]. This offers good view of he enemies, but s a real problem ecause a KPA tank blocks the bridge, and if you're out in the pen for more than a couple of seconds, it will shell or machine un you to death. So remain on the ground, using the cover to our right (south).

Plan C: Dash eft (northward), round to where he friendly ehicles are rundling in from, nd follow them p with Rianna. Or, you can continue around n a clockwise loop, and cut foes down on the balcony where they ppear **[G.04]**; just watch for incoming tank rounds.

Plan D: Or, you can go slightly crazy and dash to the right (southward), running directly toward the tank and under its cannon and machine gun. Then sprint to the opposite (east) side and hide from its fire. This is simply hapless endangerment. A better plan is to bring the RPG launcher with you from Checkpoint C (where you defeated the previous T-99), and fire on it from your initial cover **[G.05]**. You can blow the tank up yourself, although this isn't necessary at all. C4 and grenades don't affect it.

> **TIP** 영리한
>
> **Line up your enemies one behind another, so your bullets strike the head of the first KPA and pass straight through into the second, killing them both with one burst.**

Objective: Regroup at the Checkpoint

With the enemies defeated, spend a few moments checking the area for ammunition: You can scavenge SCAR and Super V weapons from the fallen foes. Or locate the armored crates on the east side of the bridge, close to the regroup point, and swap your existing hardware for something new, depending on what you're happy using. A longer-range rifle and a close assault SMG or LMG is a good loadout. The eastern side of the bridge offers another news pick-up, too.

Once at the regroup spot **[G.06]**, there's just enough time for pleasantries before Sergeant Keyes orders the lead armor to begin clearing the bridge. The tank rams the gate and it topples over. A second later, it is struck by RPG fire and explodes **[G.07]**. Action stations!

WEAPONS >>
ACR Rifle
[Mk2 ACOG Scope] (2)

WEAPONS >>
SCAR-H LMG
[Mk1 Red Dot Sight]

WEAPONS >>
M16 Rifle
[Mk1 Red Dot Sight]

Located on the armored crate on the east side of the bridge, near the regroup area gate.

HIDDEN HISTORY >> 4 (59/61)

On a small crate behind the big-rig cab and transport truck, on the east side of the bridge, near the KPA spawn point.

AN ALREADY UNSTABLE IRAQ IMPLODES WITH VIOLENCE

6/8/2016

Iran declared its intent to defend Iraq from what it called "unacceptable Saudi intervention" today. Saudi Arabia, along with Syria, Jordan, Egypt and Turkey, declared a coalition to stabilize and guide the shaky nation of Iraq with support from the United States. Iran has stepped up its rhetoric on the issue, declaring that Saudi Arabia has turned Iraq into a "client state" and has stated that they won't allow colonization by a "corrupt group of thieves."

Iran launched its first incursions into Iraq, aided by the Kurds and the resurgent Afghani Taliban. They struck out at Kirkuk and Arbil, capturing both cities on the same day. Iranian bombers also struck key targets on Iraq's southern border, including a power station and a bridge.

CHECKPOINT H: ASSAULT DOWN THE BRIDGE 1

Enemies

Elite 718

Elite 718 (Heavy)

Elite 718 (RPG)

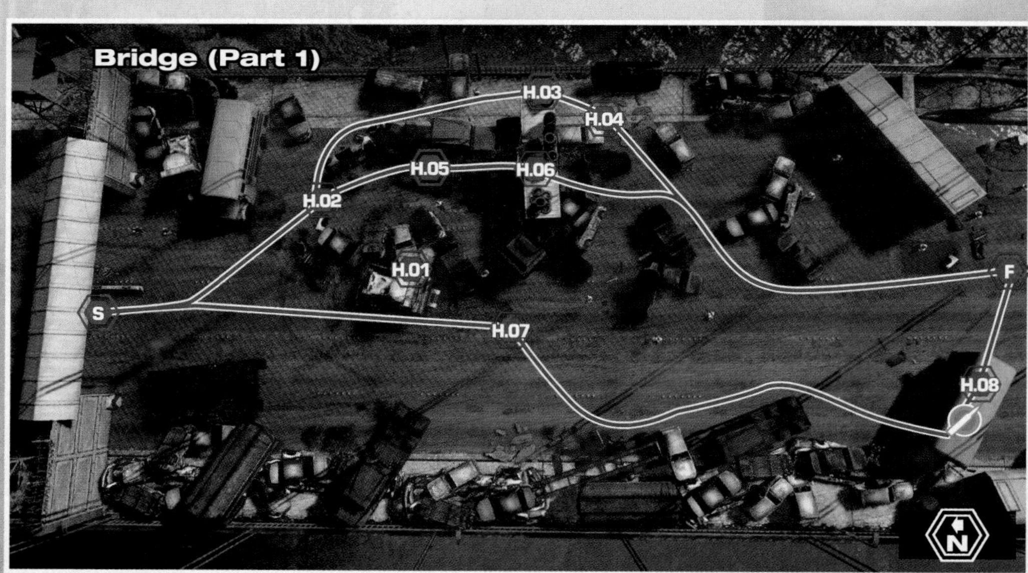

Objective: Eliminate the RPG Enemies

Racing forward with the school bus on your left, you, the US military, and your teammates begin to assault the collection of scrap metal and vehicles now used as a rough barricade **[H.01]**. You must balance your safety with the removal of both RPG soldiers. Your three immediate foes lurk within this collection of metal, and there are a few ways to tackle them. You can:

Hang back and let your allies remove all of the enemies on the near side of the big-rig and ramp.

Lob in a grenade to soften the foes, and then sprint in and dispatch them.

Dispatching them (with or without a grenade) can involve melee strikes, or quick bursts of rifle fire to the head **[H.02]**, although rushing in with more than one 718 firing at you usually results in your death.

Or you can run up the middle of the road, and then fire wildly
hile turning left (east) at the front of the big-rig, and cutting them
own from behind and sandwiching them with allied attacks.

Tactical Planning: Rocket Removals

Threat Assessment: 718 Bridge Forces

Two RPG soldiers are behind the first collection of vehicular junk, on the left (east) side of the bridge. These are vicious shots (don't expect to survive a single strike from their launchers unless you're prone), and they are backed up by around half a dozen 718 troopers who are extremely adept at emptying their clips into your hide. Your primary targets are the RPG soldiers, but you must cut through the other enemies to reach a safe place to tackle them.

TIP 영리한

If you restart this checkpoint, you may be able to see (and cut down) one of the RPG enemies before he finds cover. In addition, you can let your teammates deal with foes you pass, or stay behind them to let them absorb damage.

Plan A: Left Bridge Edge

n overlooked ath runs to the ft (east) of the amp to the top f the big-rig's ontainer section; ne or two nemies also tend o use it (so if ou're being shot om your left side hile attempting lan B, this is here to look). Rush forward nd along to the ft, and then be xtremely careful s you appear the junk area H.03] where the two RPG soldiers are visible; expect around four dditional foes patrolling.

Use the right edge of a vehicle as cover, and execute enemies vith headshots **[H.04]**; you can tag at least four, including one f the RPG soldiers this way, and usually without being hit. You nay need to crouch or go prone to avoid enemy fire and incoming ockets, especially as you advance into the second junk area.

Clear the foes that see you first, and then tackle the RPG soldiers; lobbing in a grenade first gains you some time between rocket blasts.

Plan B: Big-Rig Beatdown

Following Sergeant Keyes's advice to "get on top of that big-rig" sounds like a good idea, but don't stand and poke your head out from the tire pile when you reach the top of the ramp, or you get tagged by a rocket! Check the left flank for foes before you rush the ramp, then sidestep halfway up and clear the foes in the initial area first **[H.05]**. Once at the top, immediately crouch, and wait by the tires for the enemies to stop throwing grenades and launching rockets.

Don't target the RPG soldiers; instead look to the southwest and tag the reinforcements on the main road, working from right to left, and remaining behind the tire stack **[H.06]**. Watch for grenades and gunfire; back up behind the tires while prone if you're wounded. After tagging around six KPA (check the bus across the road; foes appear from it), quickly sidestep out, tag the RPG soldier, and sidestep back behind cover; ideally while crouched or prone. Continue to do this until you remove both threats. A grenade might help during this time, but standing up definitely doesn't!

Plan C: Right Flank Fury

Rushing up the middle of the road, or from the ruined vehicles along the right (west) side of the bridge is extremely dangerous and borderline suicidal. If you must attempt this plan, keep to the middle of the road and kill the initial enemies (before the big-rig to the left) by circling around behind them **[H.07]**. Then lob a grenade at the others, ideally using the front of the rig as cover and cut a few more down, then sprint for the parked school bus, which is your only source of protection on the right side. Here, you can go prone and shoot enemies running in, through the back doorway **[H.08]** (but watch for foes coming up into the bus behind you).

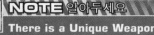

NOTE 알아두세요

There is a Unique Weapon inside the school bus on the right side of the bridge, but it is safer to grab once your LAVs come trundling in, at the start of the next checkpoint. You might also want to check the fallen foes for weapon ammo and grenades they dropped.

Unique Weapons Detail: 17/17

WEAPONS >>

Dragon Fire Super V SMG [Mk3 Red Dot Sight]

This Super V isn't as scoped as the previous model and uses ammunition extremely quickly, so check the corpses of some 718s to keep your supply plentiful. It's a perfect weapon for short- to mid-range combat.

Mettle of Honor

Award	Fatal and Tragic	Rating	10	Trophy	Bronze

From this point on, you can foolishly leap to your death on the left side of the bridge, or while you're under the bridge. Or, during the final Checkpoint, your Humvee can be pushed off the bridge; any of these plans nets you this reward.

CHECKPOINT I: ASSAULT DOWN THE BRIDGE 2

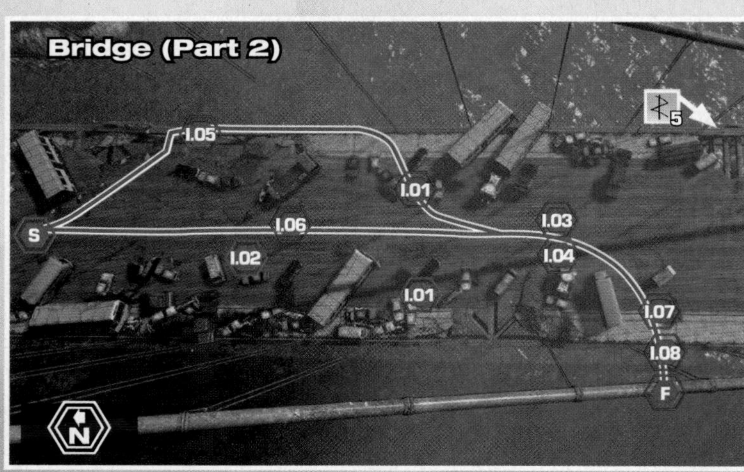

Enemies

Elite 718 | Elite 718 (Heavy) | Humvee | Z-10 Chimera | Sentry Tower

Objective: Assault Deck with the Convoy

"Form Up! Push Forward!"

With the immediate threats abated and RPG soldiers no longer firing, the LAVs come trundling down to meet you, and then continue southward to intercept more enemy defenses.

With such overwhelming firepower, you have a few moments of respite. The best way to take advantage of this is to follow Keyes's advice and stay just behind the lead LAV of the convoy, watching as it removes the 20 or so KPA 718 soldiers along both sides of the bridge **[I.01]**.

If a grenade lands close to you (which only really happens if you push too far forward from the group), simply back up. You can fire o the enemies **[I.02]**, but you're just wasting your ammo and putting yourself at risk; let the LAV's main cannon remove the threats instead As you advance, check the sides of the bridge in case the LAV or your team misses a foe, and remove him. The same is advisable if you're struck by enemy fire, because sometimes the LAV takes a little time to retaliate. Use the vehicle as cover, if you need to.

When two
›nemy Humvees
›creech to a
ıalt **[I.03]**, you
:an simply hide
›ehind any of the
'ehicles, or move
o a ramp resting
›n a parked
nilitary truck on

he left side, and watch the fireworks from this vantage point. You :an retaliate too, but lobbing grenades and shooting is wasteful; :onserve ammunition and let the vehicles kill on your behalf.)r, you can hide near the two orange plastic road markers and vrecked coach while the enemy Humvees are pummeled **[I.04]**.

Other Options

Of course, you could race ahead, become overwhelmed by the KPA, and get shot to death (or seek cover and wait for your reinforcements). You can also run ılong the extreme left (east) side of the bridge, where there's a ›recarious path with limited enemy engagement **[I.05]**. Or, you :an (from the big-rig or the military truck) leap and stand on op of one of the LAVs **[I.06]**, and watch the ongoing blasting ›f KPA forces from a new and improved (but certainly not safer) 'antage point.

Objective: Regroup with the Squad

After a half-dozen or so 718 troopers are nullified, you're ordered to regroup behind a military truck parked on the right. Up ahead are two Sentry Towers that have activated, and venturing any farther forward on your own gets you killed. The towers are also too far away to lob grenades or fire rockets at. Instead, huddle up and figure out your next move. Which, thanks to a bombing run from a KPA attack helicopter **[I.07]**, turns out to be an unavoidable and near deadly plummet off the side of the bridge **[I.08]**!

CHECKPOINT J: UNDERNEATH THE DECK

Enemies

Elite 718

Elite 718 (Heavy)

Z-10 Chimera

Objective: Get Back to the Deck

Sweeping the Underdeck

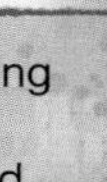

After watching a couple of vehicles (and soldiers) fall into the water below, and clambering back onto the underside of the bridge with grim determination, you face a frantic and precarious trek to rejoin your team back on the bridge road itself. Begin by running forward and taking cover behind a large cable reel **[J.01]**. You're peppered with gunfire from the attack helicopter (which can easily kill you if you don't

seek out this cover), and have three rappelling KPA to deal with. Carefully drop them one by one with precise rifle fire **[J.02]**, as the helicopter is firing, by peering out on the left or right sides and tagging the foes you can see. Finish the last one after the chopper flies away from your immediate vicinity.

TIP 영리한

This chopper is invulnerable to almost all your ordnance, with the exception of the RPG launcher you picked up during Checkpoint C. If you still have it, you can fire two shots at it from your starting position, wait for it to pass under and to the right (south) of you, and finish it with a well-aimed third shot as it flies away. Not that this makes any difference—a second chopper appears if you defeat the first!

Step through the support girders to the right, at the far (east) end of the initial gantry, and follow two enemies as they run across and around a raised platform ahead of you. You can tag them as soon as they appear (dashing from left to right), or wait for them to stop near a ramp, and tag them in the head. Or, if you're feeling rash, you can sprint up the ramp and attack them with close assault weapons **[J.03]** (a melee strike followed by SMG fire works well, too). Whatever the plan, don't miss the cunningly hidden news pick-up behind two plastic barrier sections.

HIDDEN HISTORY >> 5 (60/61)

Behind the two plastic barrier sections, at the lower end of the ramped gantry, under the bridge.

EAST COAST PARALYZED AS PANDEMIC STRIKES POPULATION

7/14/2021

The CDC issued a no-travel warning for Minnesota and Ohio today as cases of the highly pathogenic H5N1 strain of avian influenza were identified in St. Paul and Akron. With most of the Eastern United States under martial law, travel is already tightly restricted.

Dubbed the "Knoxville Cough" for its suspected origins in Tennessee, and regarded initially as simply a more virulent strain of the annual influenza, with nearly 100,000 deaths worldwide the disease has now officially been labeled a pandemic by the World Health Organization.

Citizens are ordered to remain in their homes if possible and travel only if necessitated by an emergency. Citizens in the affected area have also been instructed to listen to 1700 AM or 101.9 FM for ongoing emergency broadcasts.

Expect further confrontation from the enemy helicopter as it strafes you from the right (west). Continue along the platform until the railings disappear, and you're left with a drop down onto the bridge's under-girders, as the chopper makes another sweep below **[J.04]**. Careful footwork is needed, because falling from here results in a death dive into the bay. While the folks topside yell about the Sentry Towers, run across the girder and onto a raised platform. Drop two foes rappelling down across (southwest) from you **[J.05]**. Then nimbly cross to the western platform without falling, and use the ladder to return to the deck of the bridge.

CHECKPOINT K: FLANK THE SENTRIES

Enemies

Elite 718 | Elite 718 (Heavy)

Z-10 Chimera | Sentry Tower

Objective: Destroy the Sentry Towers

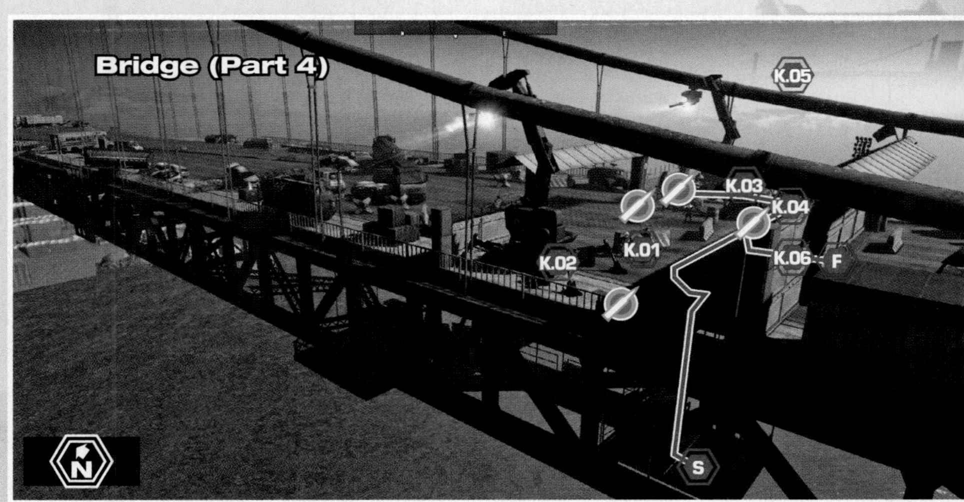

"We've Got to Get Up There With a Grenade!"

Your team is having trouble penetrating the Sentry Towers' defenses. Once at the top of the ladder, move right (southeast), and take cover behind the armored crates. There are five KPA 718 troopers to defeat **[K.01]**. The Sentry Towers can't strike you, so only worry about infantry. If you're quiet, you can drop to a crouch, and kill one or two before the enemies realize they're being outflanked. Then drop the remaining enemies with quick headshots when the foes stand up out of cover. Grenades are another option, but nothing beats a series of well-aimed decapitations. Now that all enemies except the Sentry Towers are defeated, you can simply lob in a grenade where indicated, behind each tower, and watch them crumple to the ground **[K.02]**.

CAUTION 조심하다

Racing to meet your team without dealing with the Sentry Towers is an obvious flaw in your gameplan, because you'll be cut down by the tower's fire. Instead, bomb the tower first.

"That's Suicide! There's Gotta Be Another Way!"

Once you've dealt with the enemies on foot, you don't have to rely on grenades to take down either Sentry Tower:

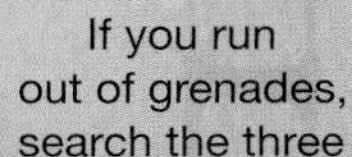

If you run out of grenades, search the three open grenade crates and gather additional supplies.

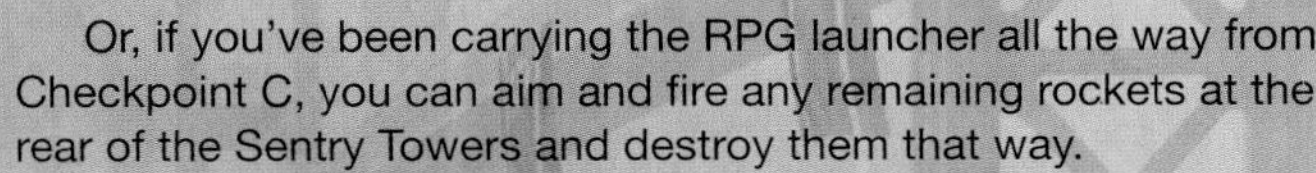

Or, if you've been carrying the RPG launcher all the way from Checkpoint C, you can aim and fire any remaining rockets at the rear of the Sentry Towers and destroy them that way.

Or, you can throw C4 on the back of each tower, and then detonate it **[K.03]**.

Or, you can move to the supply crate below the front of the far tower, and pick up the AAWS-M launcher (where you can also find extra grenades), and use that to blast the rear of each Sentry Tower.

TIP 영리한

You can also lob a grenade into the first Sentry Tower, blast the enemies, then take down the second. The order is unimportant, although you must defeat the infantry as a matter of urgency.

WEAPONS >>
AAWS-M Launcher

On the armored crate in front of the eastern Sentry Tower, between the gates.

Objective: Get the Javelin

"The Luckiest Son-of-a-Bitch I've Ever Met!"

Amid the incredulous welcome from your teammates, pick up the AAWS-M (Advanced Anti-tank Weapons System [Medium]) launcher and look through the sights, ideally as soon as the attack helicopter appears off the eastern side of the bridge. Use the crates as cover **[K.04]**, and then lock on and fire **[K.05]**—it's impossible to miss unless the rocket strikes scenery on the bridge, close to your location. The rocket, even if it is fired away from the helicopter, turns and homes in on the enemy craft. Shoot again; if you're quick, you can explode the chopper before it even makes its first pass across the bridge!

Alternately, you can manually destroy the chopper if you've brought (and then switch to, once you've picked up the AAWS) the RPG launcher. It takes three manually aimed shots to take the helicopter down. The best times to fire are before it passes over from east to west, and once it appears from behind the gate to the south, because it's flying more slowly.

Objective: Form Up On Connor

Search the ground for SCAR-Hs, ACRs Super Vs to add to your ammunition, or a better bet is to secure the M110 Sniper Rifle, and the M249 LMG, on the crates to the east, near the Sentry Tower. Connor explains, in no uncertain terms, the importance of succeeding in this next push **[K.06]**. This is the battle to remove the Anti-Air Guns.

WEAPONS >> M110 Sniper Rifle

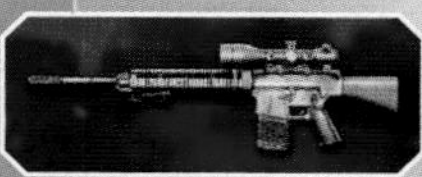

WEAPONS >> M249 LMG [Mk1 Holo Scope]

WEAPONS >> Fragmentation Grenades

On the armored crates to the sides of the Sentry Towers, between the gates.

CHECKPOINT L: ASSAULT THE AA GUNS

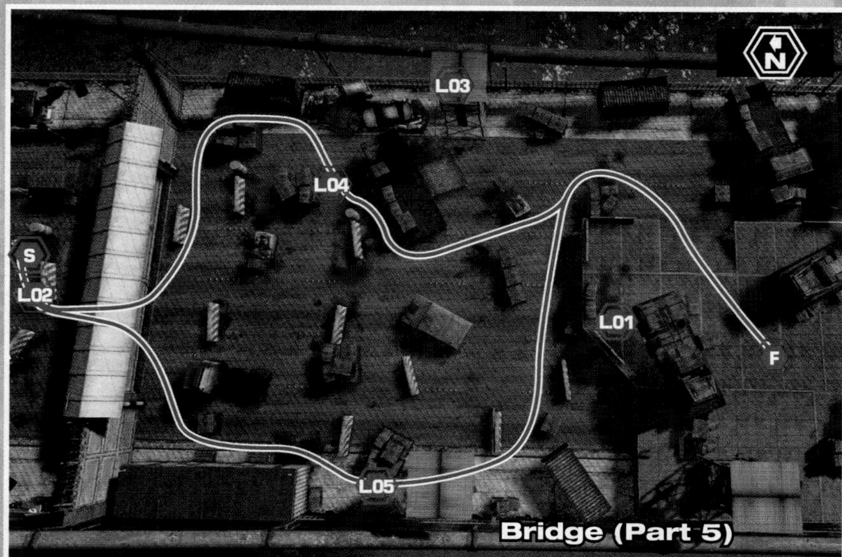

Enemies

Elite 718

Elite 718 (Heavy)

Elite 718 (RPG)

Objective: Take AA Platform

"We're Opening the Gates!"

After Connor's rallying cry, the gates open up, and your entire team is caught in a volley of shots by a very well-armed and dug-in enemy **[L.01]**. Expect grenades, RPG shots, and an instant death if you stand in the open area in the middle of the road when the gate opens. Take cover, and survey the hardened enemies you're facing.

Tactical Planning: The Last Line

Threat Assessment: KPA AA Gun Defenses

This checkpoint and the next has the highest concentration of KPA elite military personnel that you've ever encountered, and you should be prepared for extremely difficult combat. There are at least a dozen 718 troopers in between the scattered crates, parked vehicles, and AA defenses ahead (south) of you. Expect a foe in each of the four guard towers; two during your assault and two when defending the AA guns. Sprinting ahead simply gets you killed. Staying in the open gets you killed. A more clandestine plan is called for.

Plan A: Far Away Sniping

By far the safest plan is to arm yourself with the M110 Sniper Rifle, and hide behind one of the central concrete barriers. Crouch or go prone, and remain behind this cover **[L.02]**. Other sniping locations lack the radius of firing opportunities. Then work quickly from one side to the other, tagging the heads of the 718s in a competent series of sniping shots. Check the towers first and bring down any RPG soldiers as a priority (look for rockets from either guard tower, or the raised AA platform in the middle, ahead of you), and then focus on enemies on the ground. There's little need to move from this position until either Connor yells to move toward the AA guns or you can't see any more enemies to shoot.

TIP 영리한

If sniping is too much like hard work, but you're not brave enough for close assaults, sidestep to the grenade crates on either side of the gate, grab four of them, lob them into the KPA, and grab more when you run out. Vary your cooking and height for the throws, and keep going until no foes are left. Remember to replenish your grenades before you begin the next checkpoint too, no matter which plan you've chosen.

Plan B: Left Flank Battle

Stand to the left of the gate as it grinds open, and when the suicidally brave US troops rush into the fray, immediately sprint through the gate and around to the left. The firefight is so intense that if you don't sprint, or try to return fire, you're likely to die. Recover behind a large container, and then step forward around the crates and begin to attack the enemies as you see them (check the left guard tower for an RPG soldier first!) **[L.03]**. An LMG is a good choice here—you don't want to be constantly reloading your weapon or you'll be cut down during this time—and continue southward **[L.04]**. Don't run too far forward though; move with the rest of your team, or you'll be overrun.

Plan C: Right Flank Fracas

Scooting over to the right side of the gate before it opens allows you to try a similar flanking maneuver to Plan B, although this is less successful as the entrance to the AA platform is left (southeast) of you, and you can't easily dispatch the RPG soldier on the left guard tower. Move past the small command building on your right, and use the next stack of crates as cover for the rest of the fight **[L.05]**, pushing forward and eastward only after clearing the area. Watch for enemies on the steps of the far guard tower, too.

NOTE 알아두세요

The next checkpoint begins when you reach the area on the left (east) side of the bridge deck, close to the ramp leading up into the AA platform. Technically, you could sprint there (in-between cover stops to regain your health), and trigger the checkpoint just as you die.

CHECKPOINT M: DEFEND THE AA GUNS

Enemies

Elite 718

Elite 718 (Heavy)

Elite 718 (RPG)

Objective: Defend Hopper

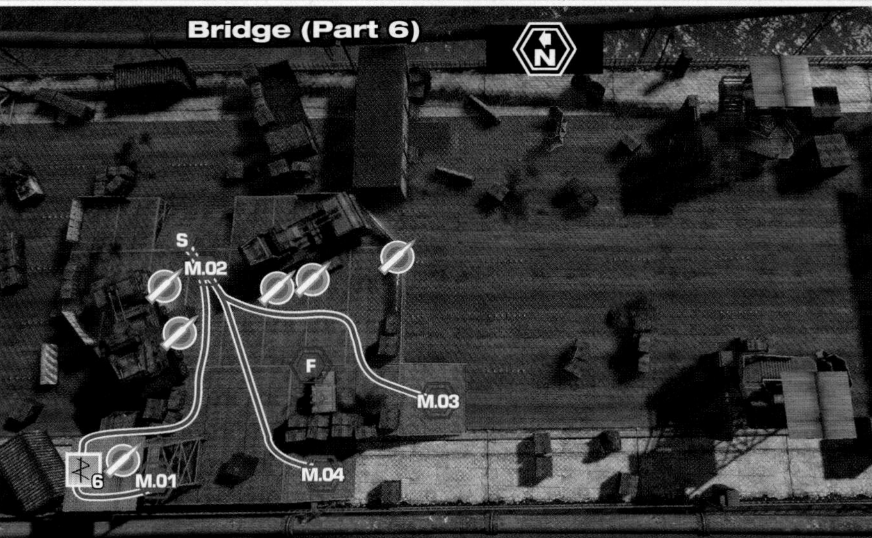

WEAPONS >> Fragmentation Grenades

On, propped up against, or inside crates around the AA platform.

Friend or Foe?

Connor does some more of his trademark yelling as you scramble onto the AA platform with the remaining military troops **[M.01]**. The KPA isn't letting up, so stay away from the southern edge of the AA platform, and concentrate on tagging any enemies with RPGs on the far guard towers. Hopper runs to the laptop linked to the AA guns, and reckons that instead of detonating them, he can rewire the automated IFF (Identification Friend or Foe) program so the guns "switch sides." He'll need some covering fire while he works his magic, though. Take stock of the large amount of weaponry, and choose what you need.

WEAPONS >> M110 Sniper Rifle (2)

WEAPONS >> M200 Sniper Rifle

WEAPONS >> SCAR-H LMG [Mk1 Holo Scope] (2)

WEAPONS >> Super V SMG [Mk1 Holo Scope]

WEAPONS >> ACR Rifle [Mk2 ACOG Scope] with [Grenade Launcher] (8)

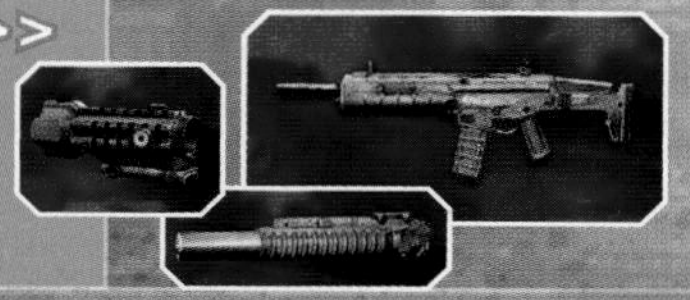

Plan A: Top of the Tower

Much in the same way that you may have utilized the sniper rifle during the previous checkpoint, use one this time around to defend the platform. Although the M110 is adequate, peering over the southern edge is dangerous. It is far better to sprint right (west) and up the guard tower steps, and use the M110, or the M200 propped against the guard tower's top platform, against the foes **[M.02]**. The combat is safer, simple, and ruthlessly efficient. Execute at least a dozen foes, and only stop when your objective updates (beginning the next checkpoint). This tower is also worth climbing for the final news pick-up.

HIDDEN HISTORY >> 6 (61/61)

By the M200 Sniper Rifle on top of the sniper tower on the AA platform.

9/18/2023

NORTH KOREAN MILITARY GROWS

Originally touted as a transformative economic alliance, the Greater Korean Republic has changed into something much different. Based out of Pyongyang in what was once North Korea, the KPA (Korean People's Army) has grown in size to 25 million strong, thanks largely to contributions from member states.

Now the largest standing military in the world, the KPA includes an Expeditionary Force of more than 5 million troops. Typically formed to achieve a specific goal in a foreign country, the EF has the stated mission of "helping countries torn by conflict create a lasting peace." In part due to this broad directive, the EF is a more dynamic, flexible fighting force than armies created solely for national defense.

While citizens of member nations of the Greater Korean Republic are guaranteed basic rights under the GKR Charter, joining the KPA is the only way to gain entrance into the people's party and secure special privileges, like unfettered travel among member states and additional fuel rations. Additionally, all family members are guaranteed employment while any one of them is serving in the Republic Military. Kim Jong-un, former president of Korea, is the Secretary General and Commander in Chief of the Greater Korean Republic, which includes Korea, Indonesia, the Philippines, Thailand, Malaysia, Cambodia, Vietnam and Korean-Occupied Japan.

Plan B: AA Platform Antics

If you didn't notice or ignored the guard tower, you need to fight the enemy in a highly dangerous shoot-out. The similarities are that enemies with RPGs on the guard towers ahead (south) of you are your primary targets. However, instead of pushing forward, you're to defend Hopper's position with anything short of your own life. This is achieved in a variety of ways, because the KPA can try to storm you from two entrances: the ramp ahead and right **[M.03]**, and the ramp behind and right of the laptop **[M.04]**. React accordingly:

M.03

M.04

Although sniping is the best plan by far, using an LMG with a copious ammunition clip and remaining in the southwest corner of the platform so you can see and react to foes coming up from either ramp is a possible plan. Then run to the edge, lobbing grenades, and backing them up with gunfire, focusing on any enemies rushing up the far guard towers. Replenish your grenades at either crate and use as many grenades as you can to blanket the barriers the foes are hiding behind.

TIP 영리한

There's C4 here too, but in the thick of battle, there aren't any real opportunities to drop C4 and detonate it effectively; just drop a grenade instead, and follow it up with LMG or rifle fire.

Combat continues until Connor lets Warpath know the AA guns are in the hands of the Resistance. But still the enemy comes! Fortunately, Warpath has a friendly UCAV (Unarmed Combat Air Vehicle) on site, and can patch you through to the laptop.

Mettle of Honor

RESISTANCE

Award Historian | Rating 30 | Trophy Gold

This is the first opportunity to have collected all 61 news pick-ups and read the complete Hidden History. Once done, this reward is yours. If you missed a pick-up, replay the mission because the reward is given once the last one is gathered, regardless of mission.

CHECKPOINT N: CALL UCAV

Enemies

Elite 718

Elite 718 (Heavy)

Elite 718 (RPG)

Humvee

Transport Truck

Objective: Call in a UCAV

Objective: Destroy the Enemy Convoy

Precision Bombardment

Run to the laptop that Hopper hacked **[N.01]**, and bring up the UCAV flight camera circling the action high above the bridge. After an optional strike against the enemies close to your position, concentrate on the enemy armor column incoming from the south.

There are three Humvees and five KPA transport trucks to destroy **[N.02]**. Each Humvee takes one shot to destroy. Each truck takes two hits to destroy.

N.02

Your shots can sometimes hit two vehicles if they are close together. Remember to use the zoom for a closer view of the enemy vehicles. You can ignore the infantry troops; they are not vital to strike. The target marker is also important to utilize **[N.03]**, because the rockets continue to home in on this target even after being fired, so keep it on the vehicle until the rocket hits home.

N.03

CAUTION 조심하다

Target as many vehicles as you can. If you ignore the vehicles, expect to fail this objective.

Mettle of Honor

Award	Soft Targets	Rating	10	Trophy	Bronze

Destroy all eight vehicles before the UCAV returns to refuel to receive this reward.

CHECKPOINT O: HUMVEE ESCAPE

Enemies

Soldier | Humvee | Goliath

Objective: Get in Humvee

One Wild Ride

O.01

Proceed through the burning wreckage your airstrikes just caused, optionally pausing to knife (or shoot) a burning KPA soldier or two **[O.01]**, before following Connor's orders and scrambling aboard the Humvee appropriated for your departure. You may have to fight a couple of soldiers if your bombing raid didn't extend to tagging all the infantry scurrying about.

O.02

Once aboard the Humvee, you're in a familiar position: manning the turret that has a 360-degree field of vision. As Connor peels out, tag the three infantry on the road, but pay most attention to the Humvee on the right (southwest) side **[O.02]**; focus your fire on that so it explodes. If you don't, it may fire back and damage the Humvee.

NOTE 알아두세요

The machine gun fires armor-piercing bullets, and is best fired for no longer than five seconds at a time; ideally in 3–4 second bursts at the most, so the barrel can cool down. If it overheats, you need to wait a couple of seconds, which can be problematic if you're facing a determined foe that needs constant shooting.

Objective: Destroy the Humvee

Continue down the road toward another fortified gate. Destroy two more Humvees as you go **[O.03]**, and any soldiers you can dispatch when you're not concentrating on the vehicle takedowns. Once you're at the gate, you receive a new objective; focus all your firepower on the parked Humvee blocking your path. Keep shooting until it explodes.

O.03

CAUTION 조심하다

Up until this point, you can ignore the enemies, although this can cause damage to your Humvee, which is detrimental to the next part of your escape.

Objective: Destroy Enemy Goliath

"Friendlies Danger Close!" 

The left gate opens and a Goliath enters the fray **[O.04]**. But this isn't controlled by Hopper; it is one of the KPA's, and must be destroyed! However, this is far less easy than rattling off rounds into an enemy Humvee. While Connor concentrates on the driving, you have two important duties:

Missile Countermeasures: Every time the warning to activate the Missile Defeat System appears on your screen, do so immediately **[O.05]**. If you don't, Goliath successfully launches its rockets, which can devastate the integrity of your vehicle. Three successful salvos from the enemy Goliath result in your death.

Goliath Destruction: Keep your swinging turret focused on the body of Goliath as much as possible **[O.06]**, and fire as often as you can, pausing when the enemy moves out of your sights, or between cool-down periods for your machine gun.

CAUTION 조심하다

Simply watching Goliath and not shooting at it results in a fiery end to you and your crew.

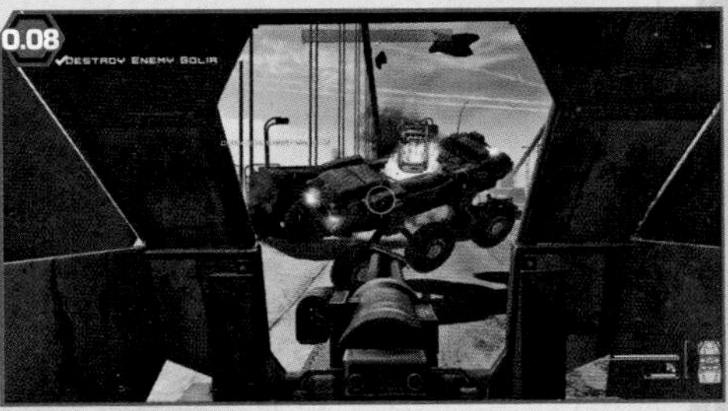

With some hazardous driving, Connor weaves through the piles of rusting vehicles and other debris, while you rattle off rounds into the Goliath. Continue with the countermeasures too, and Connor eventually careens through the last KPA gate with the Goliath on your tail. You narrowly miss plunging off into the bay and totalling the Humvee against a bus **[O.07]**, before the Goliath shunts into a fuel truck. Take Connor's yelling as a clue, and blast the fuel truck behind Goliath **[O.08]**; both explode in a massive gout of fire.

When you come to, you're sprawled on the bridge deck **[O.09]**, listening to Connor requesting an airstrike from Warpath, as the remaining KPA armored divisions are rolling up toward you. Warpath replies that allied troops are too close and they need more accurate pinpointing. Connor Morgan—never a man to shirk his responsibilities to the Resistance—provides that location in the only way he knows how. The first blow has been struck for freedom!

Mettle of Honor

RESISTANCE — Award: Golden Gate — Rating: 10 — Trophy: Silver

Completing this mission earns you this particular reward. Difficulty level, or how many times you restarted a checkpoint, do not matter.

Mettle of Honor

RESISTANCE — Award: Golden Gate—Guerrilla — Rating: 25 — Trophy: Silver

Completing this mission earns you this individual reward. However, you must complete this on the hardest difficulty.

Mettle of Honor

RESISTANCE — Award: Iron Man—Golden Gate — Rating: 25 — Trophy: Silver

Completing this mission without dying once or restarting a checkpoint earns you this reward. Lessen the difficulty if you're having problems completing this task.

MULTIPLAYER >> TRAINING

WELCOME TO MULTIPLAYER

This chapter introduces you to the world of online combat in *Homefront*. Expect combat basics, and information on the different game modes, and how to develop and gain experience for your online soldier.

Multiplayer >> Control Schemes

This chapter presupposes some degree of knowledge about starting an online game. To begin a Multiplayer match, consult your game's instruction manual, or on-screen information for the match type, and other choices. The following tables give you a quick reference for the available keyboard (PC) and controller (Xbox 360/PlayStation 3) commands.

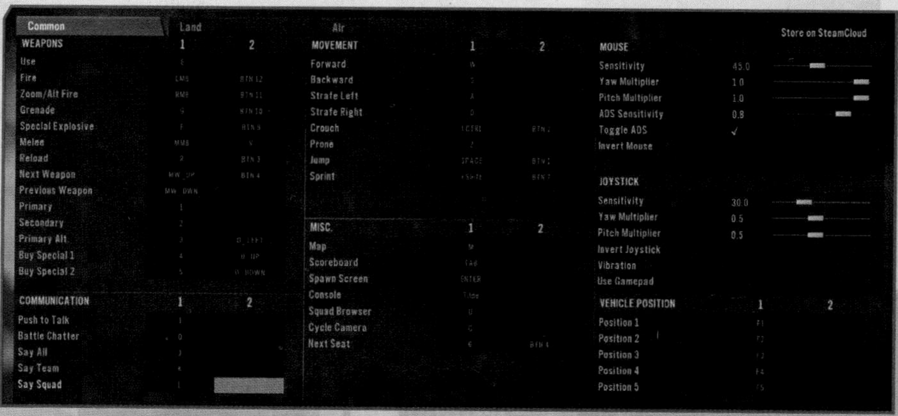

PC Control Schemes >> Common

These are the default schemes for controlling you as an infantryman, a drone, and for air vehicles during single player. You have complete freedom to change keys and commands. The "2" refers to an alternate key you can press, which is also completely customizable.

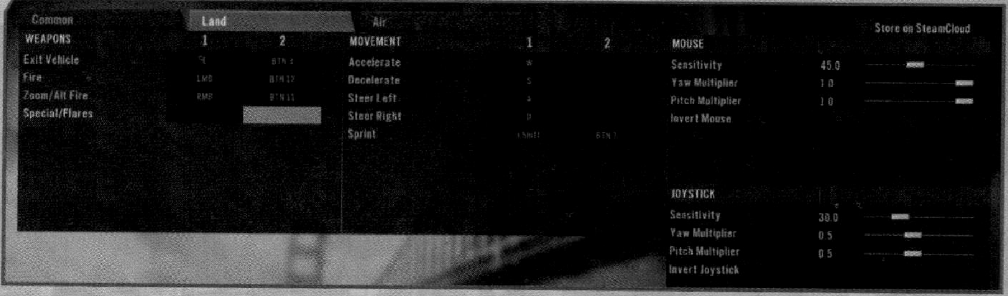

PC Control Schemes >> Land

These show the various gun and steering controls for any land vehicle; the Humvee, LAV, and Heavy Tank. As always, you can change any of them, as well as the sensitivity of the more incremental controls (such as yaw and pitch).

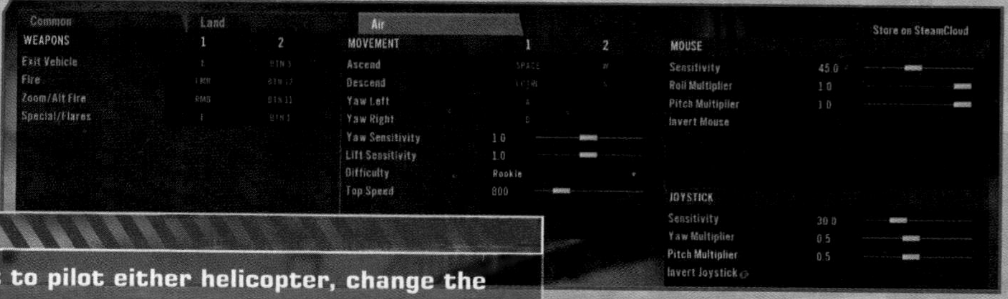

PC Control Schemes >> Air

These inform you of the various joystick and armament controls for either of the air vehicles; the Scout Helicopter and Attack Helicopter. As ever, meticulous tweaking is available.

CAUTION 조심하다

PC Only: If you're finding it difficult to pilot either helicopter, change the controls to one of the following:

Ace: Allows for the best maneuverability, but takes the most practice to master.

Veteran: Balanced difficulty and maneuverability.

Rookie: Pick-up-and-play level of difficulty, but the least maneuverable. This is the default setting.

Console Control Schemes >> Settings

This menu allows you to change the stick controls, how your button layout works, and how the tank controls. Also available is the ability to increase or decrease your "look" sensitivity (how quickly you move your "head"), as well as whether you want to invert your up/down view when controlling infantry, land vehicles, or air vehicles. Your controller's vibration function is also switchable (to on or off), and you can use "aim assist", which helps pinpoint an enemy when you aim (Xbox 360 shown).

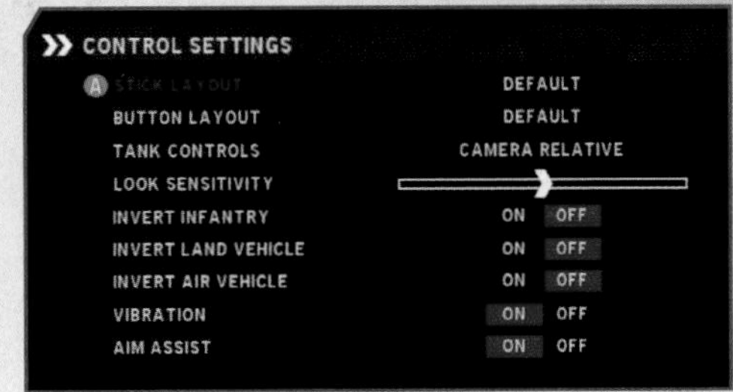

Console Control Schemes >> Button Layout

These are the settings to choose from regarding the button controls. Pick from Default or Southpaw, depending on how you access different button commands.

XBOX 360 CONTROLS

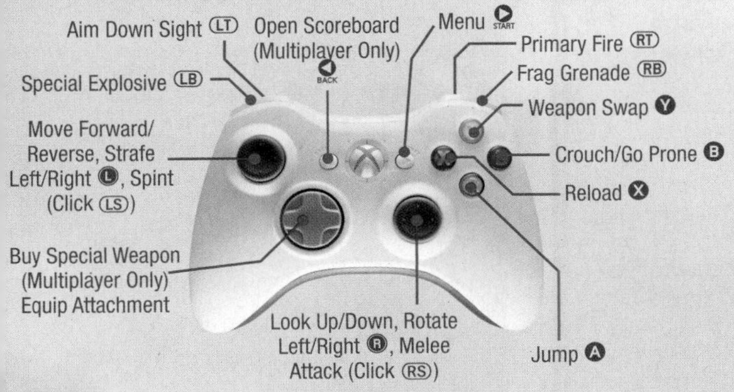

INFANTRY CONTROLS

Move Forward/Reverse, Strafe Left/Right	L
Sprint	Click LS
Look Up/Down, Rotate Left/Right	R
Melee Attack	Click RS
Jump	A
Crouch/Go Prone	B
Pick Up Weapon/Use/Enter or Exit Vehicle	X (hold)
Reload	X
Weapon Swap	Y
Aim Down Sight	LT
Primary Fire	RT
Special Explosive	LB
Frag Grenade	RB
Buy Special Weapon 1/2 (Multiplayer Only)	D-pad Up/D-pad Down
Equip Attachment	D-pad Left
Open Scoreboard (Multiplayer Only)	BACK
Menu	START

Ground Vehicles

Move Forward/Reverse, Strafe Left/Right	L
Turbo Boost	Click LS
Look Up/Down, Steer Left/Right	R
Activate Countermeasures	A
Enter or Exit Vehicle	X (hold)
Change Seat	Y
Zoom (Weapon)	LT
Primary Fire	RT

Aircraft

Move Forward/Reverse, Strafe Left/Right	L
Turbo Boost	Click LS
Look Up/Down, Steer Left/Right	R
Activate Countermeasures	A
Enter or Exit Vehicle	X (hold)
Change Seat	Y
Zoom (Weapon)	LT
Primary Fire	RT
Control Elevation – Down	LB
Control Elevation – Up	RB

PLAYSTATION 3 CONTROLS

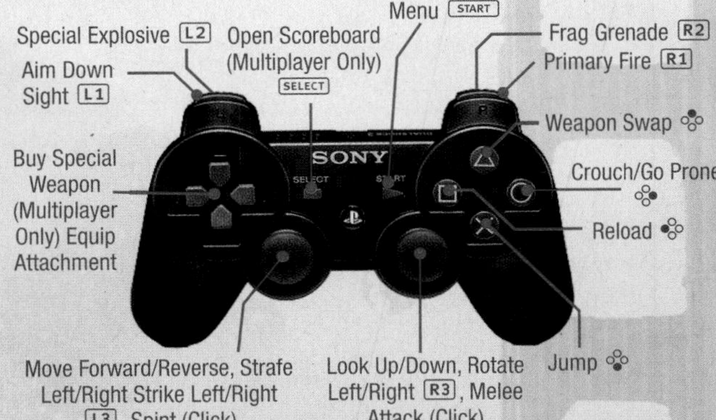

INFANTRY CONTROLS

Move Forward/Reverse, Strafe Left/Right	L3
Sprint	click L3
Look Up/Down, Rotate Left/Right	R3
Melee Attack	click R3
Jump	[button]
Crouch/Go Prone	[button]
Pick Up Weapon/Use/Enter or Exit Vehicle	[button] (hold)
Reload	[button]
Weapon Swap	[button]
Aim Down Sight	L1
Primary Fire	R1
Special Explosive	L2
Frag Grenade	R2
Buy Special Weapon (Multiplayer Only)	↑/↓
Equip Attachment	←
Open Scoreboard (Multiplayer Only)	SELECT
Menu	START

Ground Vehicles

Move Forward/Reverse, Strafe Left/Right	L3
Turbo Boost	Click L3
Look Up/Down, Steer Left/Right	R3
Activate Countermeasures	[button]
Enter or Exit Vehicle	[button] (hold)
Change Seat	[button]
Zoom (Weapon)	L1
Primary Fire	R1

Aircraft

Move Forward/Reverse, Strafe Left/Right	L3
Turbo Boost	Click L3
Look Up/Down, Steer Left/Right	R3
Activate Countermeasures	[button]
Enter or Exit Vehicle	[button] (hold)
Change Seat	[button]
Zoom (Weapon)	L1
Primary Fire	R1
Control Elevation – Down	L2
Control Elevation – Up	R2

Combat » Basic Training

An Overview

Are you looking for information on aiming (through crosshairs or scope, or from the hip); spray-and-pray or fluttering techniques, or headshots; standing, crouching, or going prone; jumping, sprinting, or sprint-jumps; strafing and sidestepping; outflanking; how damage occurs; enemy grenades; and cover opportunities **[01]**? Then consult the Basic Campaign >> Training Chapter at the front of this guide, as the information is just as relevant to Multiplayer.

Vehicles

Vehicles are available from the spawn menu once a Multiplayer match starts **[02]**, and you are able to drive or pilot during most (but not all) Multiplayer matches **[03]**. The type of vehicle that you can operate is determined by the number of Battle Points it costs to purchase. Buy the vehicle you wish, or join a vehicle already in battle in a secondary (and usually weapon-related) seat, and engage the enemy. Enter a friendly vehicle (or an abandoned enemy one before it explodes) by stepping near it and following the on-screen instructions.

Drones and Airstrikes

Small, unmanned vehicles **[04]** can be part of your soldier's loadout. They are remote-controlled (take cover in an unoccupied area of the map because you can't defend yourself and pilot a drone at the same time), and provide a variety of functions, from tagging troublesome foes to launching salvos against infantry and vehicles.

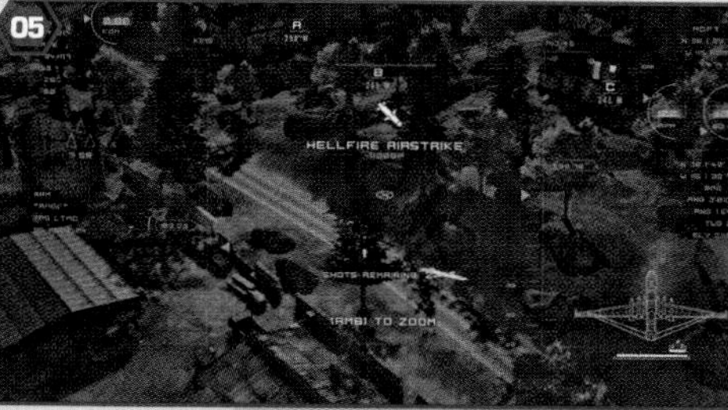

When you're ready to rain down hot death on a group of dug-in foes, employ an airstrike **[05]**. These barrage attacks are fired remotely, so remain out of sight while you target the enemy and watch the fireworks.

Just like vehicles, these are both purchased, but only after you add them to your chosen loadout, and purchase them during a match.

Check the Armory for complete vehicle and drone tactics (including how to best take each of them out), as well as information on airstrikes.

Clan Tag

Unlocked at Level 7, this allows you and your fellow clan mates or team members the option to add a four-letter prefix to your name to underline your loyalty.

NOTE 알아두세요

Steam clan tags are open by default.

MULTIPLAYER » BATTLE POINTS AND SCORING

Battle Points

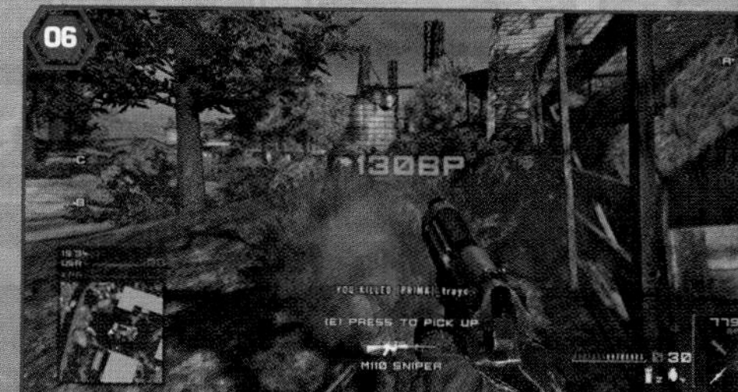

Homefront's currency takes the form of Battle Points. You earn Battle Points (BPs) **[06]** in all Multiplayer game types by killing enemies or completing objectives. As your BPs increase, you use them at any time to purchase equipment you've chosen and placed in your "Purchase Slots" in your character's loadout. These special items include Flak Jackets, drones, airstrikes, or RPG Launchers. Or, you can keep increasing your BPs with more kills or objective completions, and purchase a vehicle to spawn in after your next death.

Battle Point Purchases

There are two main types of Battle Point Purchases. The first are those that occur in-game; the two "Special" Equipment items you've chosen in your Loadout. These are selected from the following:

In-Game Purchases

Infantry Equipment (Thermal Goggles shown).

Drones (RQ-10 Parrot shown).

Air Strikes (Hellfire shown).

Rocket Launchers (RPG Launcher shown).

The second Purchase type are Spawn Menu Purchases, bought before you first spawn, or after you die but before a match has concluded. The equipment types you can pick from are listed below:

Spawn Menu Purchases

Land Vehicles (Humvee shown)

Air Vehicles (Scout Helicopter shown)

Battle Points Action Chart

The following information lists the different ways you can earn Battle Points, and the points that are available:

Action	BP Earned
Killing an Enemy	130
Revenge Kill	30
Avenge Kill	30
Co-pilot Assist (in a vehicle)	30
Vehicle Destruction Assist (using EMP)	30
Destroying a Drone	130
Kill assist	50
Marking a Target with a Drone	30
Death streak	20–100
Drone Kill Assist	30
Headshot	30
Spawn Camp Killing	0
BC: Killing a Spawn Camper	500

Action	BP Earned
BC: Assisting the Killing of a Spawn Camper	50
GC: Winning the Round	100
GC (without BC active): Capturing a Control Point	250
GC (with BC active): Capturing a Control Point	200
GC: Defending a Control Point	70
TDM & GC: Infantry Kill	130
TDM & GC: Infantry Kill (from Vehicle)	70
TDM & GC: Infantry Kill (Assist)	50
TDM & GC: Infantry Kill	130
Destroying Hummvee	150
Destroying LAV	250
Destroying Tank	400
Destroying Helicopter	400

NOTE 알아두세요

The cost of every piece of special equipment is listed in the Armory chapter of this guide. The BP bounties for killing Instigators in Battle Commander is listed later in this chapter.

TIP 영리한

Maximum Battle Points you can carry at any one time: 7,000

TIP 영리한

You can't take Battle Points with you after the match, so spend them as early as possible, but only when it benefits you and your team the most.

MULTIPLAYER » RANKS, EXPERIENCE, AND UNLOCKS

Wins

The number of times your team is victorious during matches is listed in the Leaderboards. You are encouraged to be on the winning side for the prestige and trash-talking you can inflict. Winning matches also completes a few Challenges.

Kills and Deaths

Killing a foe **[07]**, and being killed affects your Leaderboard standing, and every time you die, or drop a foe, this information is recorded. You also receive Experience Points (XP) for killing foes, and many challenges involve killing enemies in a variety of ways with every weapon in your arsenal.

Kill Streaks

Kill streaks are simply periods of time when you take down enemies consecutively, without being killed yourself. During Battle Commander matches, this makes you an Instigator, and assigned foes receive an additional bounty of Battle Points for killing you. Kill streaks not only instill a feeling of confidence in you and your team, but are also critical in obtaining some rather attractive camo schemes **[08]** you can add to your weaponry.

Ranks, XP, and Unlocks

You are encouraged to continue to play countless additional Multiplayer matches in order to improve your Rank. Think of your Rank, which starts at 1: Private, as your online level. This is displayed during matches, and can reach Rank 75: Supreme Leader (although that is likely to take the average player approximately hundreds of hours of constant play!).

You gain levels **[09]** by obtaining Experience Points, or XP. The Battle Points you earn during a match translate to XP when the match is over. Racking up kills, assisting teammates, capturing control points in Ground Control, and earning stars in Battle Commander all net you Battle Points. The total amount of XP awarded is determined by subtracting your starting Battle Points (500 BP) from your final total. You also receive XP for completing weapons, vehicles, and equipment challenges. Finally, you can earn bonus XP by equipping the Grizzled infantry ability that increases your XP by a whopping 50 percent!

Almost every new Rank gains you a reward. This could be a new weapon, drone, or piece of equipment; an ability (such as being able to carry additional special grenades, or a steadier aim down the sight of your weapon); or a new loadout you can tweak. At the highest levels, additional camo schemes are awarded.

NOTE 알아두세요

If a weapon or other item is unlocked at a certain level, this is noted in the Armory chapter. For a complete run-down of how many Experience Points you need to reach all 75 levels, consult this guide's Appendix.

NOTE 알아두세요

XP is not earned in Private Matches.

GAME TYPES

You play the part of a KPA (Korean) or USA soldier in all of the Multiplayer game types. There are two main types to choose from: Ground Control and Team Deathmatch. These are further augmented by Battle Commander, which adds additional threats during either a GC or TDM match. The following chart shows which game type is available on the Multiplayer maps (Battle Commander is accessible in either mode):

Map Name	Availability: GC	Availability: TDM
Angel Island	✓	—
Borderlands	—	✓
Crossroads	✓	✓
Cul-de-sac	✓	✓
Farm	✓	✓
Green Zone	✓	✓
Lowlands	✓	✓
Suburb*	✓	✓
(*only available on Xbox 360)		

Ground Control (GC)

Each side is split into two teams, starting on opposite sides of a map. In-between the two forces is a so-called "neutral zone," consisting of three (or sometimes, two) main locations **[10]** flagged as "control points." The objective here is to capture and hold these objectives to increase your team's score.

Every control point has a perimeter around its central marker where you can stand to capture it. The first trick is to learn where the perimeter is, so you can capture it more easily; for example, the perimeter may extend to a vehicle you lie prone behind and remain unseen.

During the capture of a control point, the opposing team may enter and "contest" the location; they must be defeated until the control point becomes yours (marked in green). Once this occurs, your team's score increases, and the first team to fill their meter (on the bottom-left of your HUD) wins the first round. For this to occur, you need to have captured two of the three control points at the very least. Combat continues as the points are continuously contested.

If you win the first round, you can advance into the enemy's third of the map, where three (or two) more control points appear. Claim these, and the battle is yours. If you're routed from these and the other team wins, you are pushed back to the middle of the map. The first team to win two rounds wins the battle itself.

TIP 영리한

The vast majority of the remainder of this guide is devoted to tactics in and around all of the Ground Control maps; consult each map individually for winning strategies. Default information throughout the map sections of the Multiplayer chapter assumes a Ground Control game.

Team Deathmatch (TDM)

You may be familiar with this mode of play. Each side is split into two teams, starting on opposite sides of a map; usually a section the third of the size compared to the area of the map used in Ground Control. The objective is stunningly simple: kill as many of the opposing force as possible [11]. You receive 100 points per kill. The first team to reach the score limit wins.

TIP 영리한

Specific tactics for each Team Deathmatch map are shown throughout the rest of this guide. Look for tactics with the TDM icon (shown above) that are relevant to this gameplay mode.

BC Battle Commander (BC)

This dynamic system layers on top of existing game modes to analyze and react to events as they unfold. During a match, your team's AI Battle Commander points out Priority Threats (AKA "Instigators") **[12]** for you to track down and remove.

Perform well enough at taking out enemies, and you'll be deemed a threat by the enemy's AI Commander, who places a bounty on your head. Keep your kill streak going and your Commander rewards you with Battle Points and ability boosts to help you stay alive, while an increasing number of enemies are assigned to hunt you.

The Battle Commander AI

Each team has a Commander. These Commanders data mine the MP match to acquire real-time information on each player. The following stats are collected:

- **Kills**
- **Deaths**
- **Spawns**
- **Equipment**
- **Battle Points**
- **Player Location**
- **Player Groupings**

Each Commander uses these stats to generate dynamic missions on the field. These missions protect their best players, and place bounties on the enemy's best players. As a result, direct conflict events are frequently occurring on top of the existing game mode. Each mission event will not only never play the same way twice, but will also increase in intensity and reward value for both sides as the target becomes higher Rank and more powerful.

Missions

Each mission is based on player performance. When a player does well enough in one life, they receive a mission as a reward. These missions come with perks to help the player perform even better, and to stay alive longer. On the other hand, these missions also catch the eye of the enemy Commander who sends troops to hunt that player down.

Escalation

Almost every Battle Commander mission starts with a base level of 1 Star and works its way up to 5 Stars. This escalation is built into the system to continually reward good performance with more ability boosts. The more Stars the player receives, the more bonuses they get.

For Example: A player gets three kills in one life. He instantly starts a 1-Star Kill Streak mission with a bonus Flak Jacket (additional armor). After another three kills without dying he receives the 2-Star Kill Streak mission with Flak Jacket and a UAV Sweep.

NOTE 알아두세요

The bonuses are always additive and stay around as long as the mission is in existence. On the other end of the spectrum, the more Stars a player has, the more enemies are looking for him.

Mission List

A. Individual Kill Streak

Instigator: Once a soldier gets three kills without dying, they will be put on a Kill Streak mission. This mission lasts until the player dies.

Hunter: Hunters are given the area of their prey on the mini-map and an in-world icon for that area. They are never told the exact location of their target. Once they kill the Instigator, they receive their Bounty reward.

Star Level	Kills	Reward	Hunters	BP Bounty Reward
1	3 Kills	Flak Jacket Boost	2 Hunters	100
2	5 Kills	UAV Sweep	4 Hunters	250
3	8 Kills	Faster Movement	6 Hunters	500
4	11 Kills	Increased Primary Weapon DMG	8 Hunters	750
5	15 Kills	All Enemies Marked	12 Hunters	1,000

B. Vehicle Streak

Instigator: Once a vehicle gets three kills without being destroyed, it will be put on a Vehicle Streak mission. Both primary and secondary vehicle seats count toward this kill total. The mission lasts until the vehicle is destroyed.

Hunter: Hunters are given the area of their prey on the mini-map and an in-world icon for that area. They are never told the exact location of their target. Once they destroy the vehicle, they receive their Bounty reward.

Star Level	Kills	Reward	Hunters	BP Bounty Reward
1	3 Kills	EMP Resistance	2 Hunters	100
2	7 Kills	UAV Sweep	4 Hunters	250
3	11 Kills	Increased WeaponDMG	6 Hunters	500
4	15 Kills	Auto-Repair	8 Hunters	750
5	20 Kills	All Enemies Marked	12 Hunters	1,000

C. Assault Drone Streak

Instigator: Once a drone gets five kills without being destroyed, it will be put on a Drone Streak mission. This mission lasts until the drone is destroyed.

Hunter: Hunters are given the area of their prey on the mini-map and an in-world icon for that area. They are never told the exact location of their target. Once they destroy the drone, they receive their Bounty reward.

Star Level	Kills	Reward	Hunters	BP Bounty Reward
1	3 Kills	UAV Sweep	2 Hunters	100
2	4 Kills	More Drone Health	4 Hunters	200
3	7 Kills	Infinite Drone-Battery	6 Hunters	300
4	10 Kills	Faster Drone Speed	8 Hunters	500
5	13 Kills	All Enemies Marked	12 Hunters	750

D. Recon Drone Streak

Instigator: Once a recon drone gets five marks without dying, it will be put on a Recon Streak mission. This mission lasts until the drone is destroyed.

Hunter: Hunters are given the area of their prey on the mini-map and an in-world icon for that area. They are never told the exact location of their target. Once they destroy the drone, they receive their Bounty reward.

Star Level	Marks	Reward	Hunters	BP Bounty Reward
1	5 Marks	UAV Sweep	2 Hunters	100
2	15 Marks	More Drone Health	4 Hunters	200
3	25 Marks	Faster Drone Speed	6 Hunters	300
4	35 Marks	Infinite Drone Battery	8 Hunters	500
5	45 Marks	All Enemies Marked	12 Hunters	750

E. Nemesis

Instigator: There is no Instigator for this mission.

Hunter: Once a player is killed by the same enemy four times in one match, they will be awarded an opportunity to Hunt that enemy. The Hunter is given the area of their prey on the mini-map and an in-world icon for that area. He is never told the exact location of his target. This mission ends if the Hunter kills his target or if the target kills the Hunter.

BP Bounty Reward
300

CHALLENGES

Part of the *Homefront* Multiplayer experience is becoming proficient with every piece of military equipment and hardware. For this to occur, you need to complete a wealth of challenges, where both experience (XP) and unlockable hardware are given, depending on your killing, kill streak, or match-winning prowess. Here's how the information breaks down:

CAUTION 조심하다

Remember that new items (such as scopes) that are unlocked after you complete a certain challenge are only available for the weapon you used, and not for every weapon. To unlock everything, you need to become proficient in every weapon, vehicle, game mode, or equipment!

Weapon Challenges

Weapon challenges are accomplished by getting a certain number of kills with the weapon. For each weapon, there are various challenges, each associated with a higher kill count.

Counting Your Kills

For a kill to count toward leveling a weapon, the player must dispatch the enemy with that particular weapon. For example, if an enemy is low on health, and you cut them down with an M4, the kill is obviously counted for the M4. But if you stop short of killing the enemy with the M4, and finish them off with a grenade, the kill counts for the grenade.

If you're in a vehicle, you earn the kill if you're operating the vehicle weapon that kills the enemy, or if you're driving a vehicle that runs over a foe.

If you're particularly adept with one weapon, but not another, you can complete challenges by using your favored killing equipment, and then finish the foe off with the one you're completing the challenge with, although that isn't possible with some weapon combinations (you can't carry two primary weapons, for example; but you can almost kill a foe with a SCAR-L, and then finish them with a pistol if you're having problems completing the Pistol Weapon Challenge).

Weapon Kills >> Challenge Tables

For each weapon, a particular kill count is assigned; when you reach that count you gain a reward. Each challenge is made up of the following information:

The number of kills required to complete the challenge.

An associated attachment that gets unlocked when the challenge is completed.

The amount of XP you gain for completing the challenge.

The follow tables show the weapons used, the challenge name you're rewarded, how many kills it takes to earn that challenge name, what each requirement unlocks (in terms of new equipment), and experience points rewarded.

Assault Rifles (M4, M16, T3AK, ACR, SCAR-L, XM10)

Challenge	Certified	Novice	Adept	Specialist	Marksman	Veteran	Sharpshooter	Expert
Kill Count	5 kills	15 kills	25 kills	50 kills	75 kills	100 kills	150 kills	200 kills
Unlock	Holo Scopes	Shotgun	Silencer	Red Dot Sights	Grenade Launcher	ACOG Scopes	Airburst Launcher	EMP GL Launcher
XP Reward	250 XP	300 XP	500 XP	1,000 XP	1,500 XP	2,000 XP	3,000 XP	5,000 XP

Light Machine Guns and Submachine Guns (M249, SCAR-H, Diablo, Super-V)

Challenge	Certified	Adept	Specialist	Veteran	Expert
Kill Count	5 kills	25 kills	50 kills	100 kills	200 kills
Unlock	Holo Scopes	Silencer	Red Dot Sights	ACOG Scopes	N/A
XP Reward	250 XP	800 XP	1,000 XP	3,500 XP	8,000 XP

Sniper Rifles and Pistol

Challenge	Certified	Adept	Specialist	Veteran	Expert
Kill Count	5 kills	25 kills	50 kills	100 kills	200 kills
Unlock	N/A	N/A	N/A	N/A	N/A
XP Reward	250 XP	800 XP	1,000 XP	3,500 XP	8,000 XP

Explosives and Melee (Frag Grenade, C4, Melee, WP Grenade)

Challenge	Certified	Adept	Specialist	Veteran	Expert
Kill Count	5 kills	25 kills	50 kills	100 kills	200 kills
Unlock	No attachments	No attachments	No attachments	No attachments	No attachments
XP Reward	250 XP	500 XP	1,000 XP	2,000 XP	5,000 XP

Weapon Kill Streaks >> Challenge Information

NOTE 알아두세요

For each weapon, a particular kill streak count is assigned where you earn Camo Unlocks. Each challenge is made up of the following information:

The number of kill streak kills required to complete the challenge. Kills while in a vehicle are not counted toward this kill streak.

An associated camo that gets unlocked when the challenge is completed.

The amount of XP you gain for completing the challenge.

You can unlock multiple camo patterns per weapon lifespan.

Weapon Kill Streaks only count kills made with that particular weapon.

All Primary Weapons

Challenge	Recruit	Soldier	Commando	Elite	Ghost
Kill Streak Count	2 kills	4 kills	6 kills	8 kills	10 kills
Unlock	Woodland & Desert	Urban & Digital	Digital C & Swamp	Shattered & Digital A	Dragon Fire & Ice
XP Reward	250 XP	500 XP	1,000 XP	2,000 XP	5,000 XP

Attack Drone Kills >> Challenge Information

NOTE 알아두세요

For each of the attack drones (Ground Assault: MQ50 MG Wolverine, Ground Anti-tank: MQ60 AT Rhino, Air Assault: AQ-11 Buzzard), a particular kill count is assigned, after which you earn a reward. The challenges are made up of the following information:

The number of kills required to complete the challenge.

The amount of XP you gain for completing the challenge.

Attack Drones (Ground Assault, Ground Anti-tank, Air Assault)

Challenge	Certified	Adept	Specialist	Veteran	Expert
Kill Count	5 kills	25 kills	50 kills	100 kills	200 kills
XP Reward	250 XP	500 XP	1,000 XP	2,000 XP	5,000 XP

Recon Drone Mark >> Challenge Information

NOTE 알아두세요

For the recon drone (RQ-10 Parrot), a particular mark count (the number of enemies you mark with the recon drone) is assigned where you earn a reward. The challenges are made up of the following information:

The number of marks required to complete the challenge.

The amount of XP you gain for completing the challenge.

Recon Drone

Challenge	Certified	Adept	Specialist	Veteran	Expert
Mark Count	5 marks	25 marks	50 marks	100 marks	200 marks
XP Reward	250 XP	500 XP	1,000 XP	2,000 XP	5,000 XP

Vehicle Kill >> Challenge Information

NOTE 알아두세요

For each vehicle, a particular kill count is assigned where you earn a reward. You earn a kill if you are in either position in the vehicle and you cause the kill to occur. The challenges are made up of the following information:

The number of kills required to complete the challenge.

The amount of XP you gain for completing the challenge.

Vehicles (Humvee, LAV, Tank, Scout Heli, Attack Heli)

Challenge	Certified	Adept	Specialist	Veteran	Expert
Kill Count	5 kills	25 kills	50 kills	100 kills	200 kills
XP Reward	250 XP	500 XP	1,000 XP	2,000 XP	5,000 XP

Mode Win >> Challenge Information

NOTE 알아두세요

For each mode, a win count is assigned where you earn a reward. You earn a win if you are on the winning team of a match. The challenges are made up of the following information:

The number of wins required to complete the challenge.

The amount of XP you gain for completing the challenge.

Modes (Ground Control, TDM, Battle Commander)

Challenge	Certified	Adept	Specialist	Veteran	Expert
Win Count	1 win	5 wins	25 wins	50 wins	100 wins
XP Reward	250 XP	500 XP	1,000 XP	2,000 XP	5,000 XP

METTLE OF HONOR

Ten Achievements or Trophies can be gained strictly from Multiplayer matches. Here's a list of them, along with any necessary advice.

Mettle of Honor

Award Weapon Expert | Rating 25 | Trophy Bronze

Complete an expert challenge for any weapon in Multiplayer. Consult the Challenge section of this chapter for further information, and choose a weapon you're most comfortable with.

Mettle of Honor

Award Vehicle Expert | Rating 25 | Trophy Bronze

Complete an expert challenge for any vehicle in Multiplayer. Consult the Challenge section; there are five vehicles, and the Humvee is cheapest, but the choice is yours.

Mettle of Honor

Award Drone Expert | Rating 25 | Trophy Bronze

Complete an expert challenge for any drone in Multiplayer. Consult the Challenge section for more information, and pick a drone you can easily use.

Mettle of Honor

Award Expert of War | Rating 100 | Trophy Gold

Complete all challenges for weapons, drones, vehicles, and modes in Multiplayer. As you'd expect, this is going to take a huge amount of your time; just be patient and check the in-game menu as you progress.

Mettle of Honor

Award Over the Hill | Rating 50 | Trophy Silver

Reach experience level 50 in Multiplayer. Once again, this is a reward you'll receive only after a large amount of Ranking up and experience. Check the Ranking chart in the Appendix for a play time estimate.

Mettle of Honor

Award Squad Commander | Rating 20 | Trophy Bronze

Enter a public match as the Party Leader of a 4-player Minimum Party in Multiplayer. This involves finding three friends, and creating a match for them. You have three friends, right?

Mettle of Honor

Award Medal of Honor | Rating 20 | Trophy Bronze

Win a public match as the Party Leader of a Party in Multiplayer. Combine this with the previous reward, and try not to lose when facing your enemies.

Mettle of Honor

Award Full Boat | Rating 30 | Trophy Silver

Enter a public match in a Party with 16 players in Multiplayer. This involves becoming more gregarious with your friendships; find 15 friends before starting a party match.

Mettle of Honor

Award 3-Star Threat | Rating 30 | Trophy Silver

Become a 3-Star threat in a Battle Commander public match. Check the section earlier in this chapter, and choose a mission that you can pull off with the most ease. This is a tricky one!

Mettle of Honor

Award 5-Star Threat | Rating 75 | Trophy Gold

Become a 5-Star threat in a Battle Commander public match. Once again, pick a Battle Commander mission you know you're good at, and keep those kills up!

GENERAL TACTICS

Read through this list of cunning tactics and tips before embarking on an online career!

- Follow bullet trails to spot snipers.
- Pay attention to enemy locations when spawning (Red Names).
- Use side armor on Tanks or LAVs to player's advantage (Rotate to face attackers).
- When attacking vehicles, aim for the front and rear where there's no armor.
- Use Thermal Goggles in levels with foliage.
- Proximity Launchers are effective against air vehicles (helis and drones), while the RPG Launcher is effective against ground vehicles.
- Recon Drones can be extremely effective, especially in close-quarter maps.
- Use tanks in open areas, though stay on the move to avoid getting hit by RPGs.
- Go for the high ground.
- Middle objectives are usually the center of attention and fluctuate the most. Attempt to control side objectives.
- C4 is a great way to defend objectives.
- Use EMPs (Grenades or the Launcher attachment) against ground vehicles. While EMPs render vehicles immobile, remember they can still attack.
- Drop out of a helicopter and land on a rooftop, then use it as a sniping position.
- Infantry and vehicles have slightly different outer perimeters, on the edges of MP maps. Vehicle perimeters are a little larger (especially if you're in a helicopter), and the additional space can be used to your advantage (executing turns, fleeing enemy fire, etc).
- Equip perks to your Infantry and Vehicle Loadouts to compliment your playstyle and maximize your effectiveness on the battlefield.
- Assisting the driver of a vehicle is not only recommended, but it gains you Battle Points and makes your vehicle more difficult to take down.
- Always cook grenades before you throw them, spam grenades at doorways or the interiors of control points before entering, to soften up the enemy.
- Helicopters aren't the best choice for claiming control points in GC, as the zone doesn't extend upward very far.
- The more teammates within the capture zone of a control point in Ground Control, the more quickly you take the objective.
- Each vehicle comes with a short boost. Use it to speed out of a deteriorating battle.
- When lying prone, your legs can clip into objects. Use this to your advantage to squeeze yourself in small spaces.

MULTIPLAYER >>ARMORY

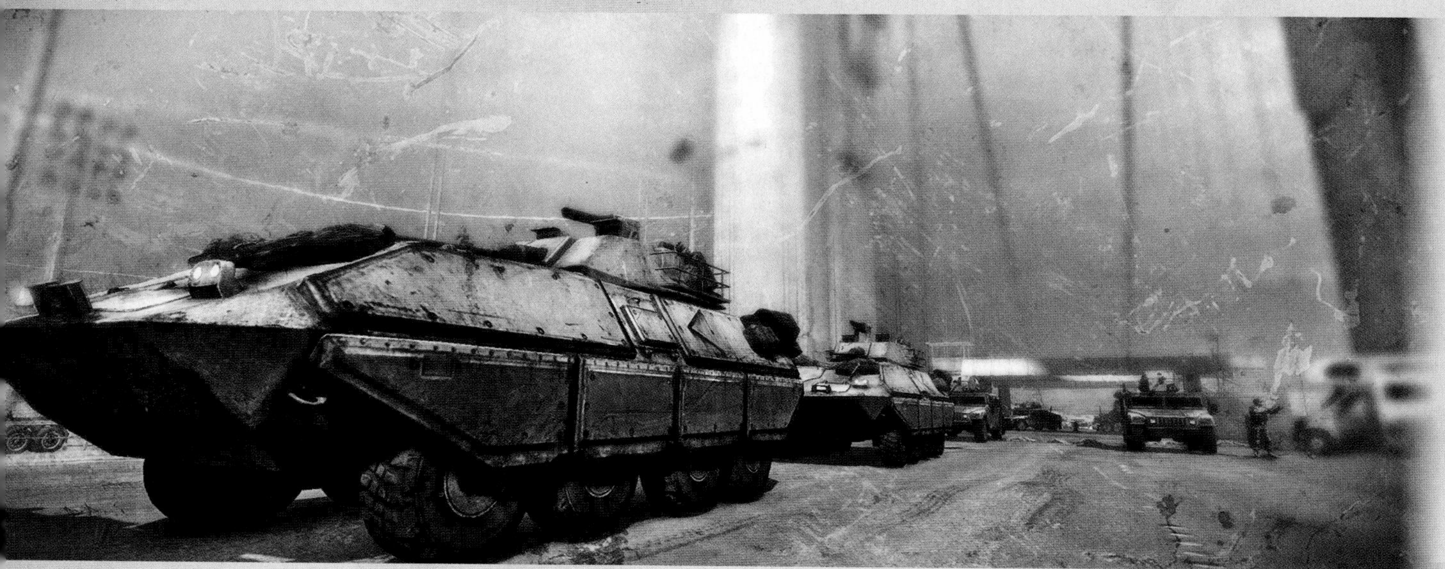

WELCOME TO THE ARMORY

This chapter copiously details loadouts, all of the available weapons and vehicles and their preferred tactical usage, and abilities you can choose to further enhance your player.

LOADOUTS

General Notes: Six Standard Loadouts appear in your Multiplayer menu. These are infinitely customizable once you unlock additional hardware, or come to prefer a particular set of offensive armaments. Optimal Loadouts (created for this guide) serve a particular purpose in the combat zone. You can use these, then tweak them, or build your own. More loadout slots are awarded as you level up.

TIP 영리한

Tweak a loadout if you're consistently not using an item during matches or simply don't like using the item. Swap in an item if you need to use it to complete a challenge. Tweak a loadout once you've leveled up and unlocked a more powerful weapon.

NOTE 알아두세요

Vehicle loadouts: Vehicle loadouts must be unlocked separately from the vehicles themselves; loadouts are accessible once you reach a certain Rank, while vehicles themselves are available in the Spawn Menu after you accrue enough Battle Points to purchase one. The five vehicle loadouts aren't nearly as customizable because vehicles can't have their weapons swapped. The only aspects you can change (and these are important) are the vehicle abilities, which are listed in the Abilities section of this chapter. Follow the advice there, and pick the ones that suit your style of play.

Standard Loadouts

LOADOUT >> ASSAULT

PRIMARY WEAPON >> M4 Rifle

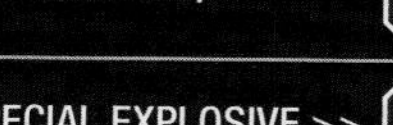

ATTACHMENT >> Mk1 Holo Scope

SPECIAL EXPLOSIVE >> EMP Grenade

PURCHASE SLOT 1 >> 300 BP >> Flak Jacket

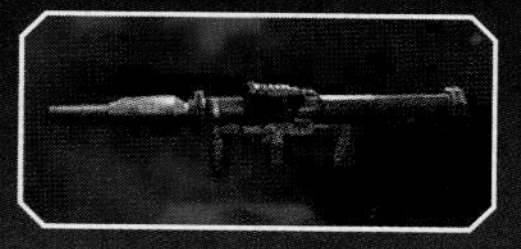

PURCHASE SLOT 2 >> 200 BP >> RPG Launcher

INFANTRY ABILITIES >>  Quickdraw  Fist Full

This is a great loadout for the majority of Multiplayer games. This is utilized both by newcomers and veterans alike who haven't graduated to setting up their own unique loadout choices, or want to quickly "dip into" a match without figuring out the various incremental differences between weaponry.

LOADOUT >> SMG
PRIMARY WEAPON >> PWS Diablo SMG
ATTACHMENT >> Mk1 Red Dot Sight
SPECIAL EXPLOSIVE >> Flashbang
PURCHASE SLOT 1 >> 300 BP >> Flak Jacket
PURCHASE SLOT 2 >> 500 BP >> MQ50 MG Wolverine
INFANTRY ABILITIES >> Tactical Reload, Straight from the Hip

This loadout is designed for indoor assaults, and flushing out enemies dug in behind cover. The PWS Diablo SMG, grouped with Straight from the Hip (better accuracy when you're not sight aiming) and Tactical Reload (reload speed is twice as fast) infantry abilities, improves your house-to-house takedown prowess.

Even the Red Dot Sight is an informed decision; it offers a thinner casing to the targeting crosshairs, and allows you to see more of the environment than the "clunkier" ACOG or Holo scopes. This allows for better peripheral vision, and therefore quicker reactions when enemies stray into your field of vision. Flashbangs disorient foes inside a structure, and the Flak Jacket absorbs a few more bullet strikes as you conquer the area, making this the main choice in urban warfare where adjacent structures need constant enemy flushing.

LOADOUT >> HEAVY
PRIMARY WEAPON >> M249 LMG
ATTACHMENT >> N/A
SPECIAL EXPLOSIVE >> EMP Grenade
PURCHASE SLOT 1 >> 1,300 BP >> Hellfire
PURCHASE SLOT 2 >> 250 BP >> RPG Launcher
INFANTRY ABILITIES >> Tactical Reload, Fist Full

This loadout is designed to provide back-up to your more agile teammates, and is great for holding a location, or storming one, backing up the SMG loadout teammates. The M249 takes a while to change magazines, so the Tactical Reload (which quickens this process) is an excellent related infantry ability. Heavy works well for tackling vehicles; the LMG's clip size lets you attempt to take down helicopter pilots or drones, while the EMP Grenade and RPG Launcher are obvious ground vehicle takedown weapons.

LOADOUT >> SNIPER
PRIMARY WEAPON >> M110 Sniper Rifle
ATTACHMENT >> N/A
SPECIAL EXPLOSIVE >> EMP Grenade
PURCHASE SLOT 1 >> 500 BP >> MQ50 MG Wolverine
PURCHASE SLOT 2 >> 1,300 BP >> Hellfire
INFANTRY ABILITIES >> Quickdraw, Drone Be Gone

This is for the long-range camper who is happy to locate an immediate hiding place, and offer cover to their teammates, as well as a constant source of annoyance and pressure to the enemy team. The hiding place can double as a location where you launch an Airstrike or Drone from, too.

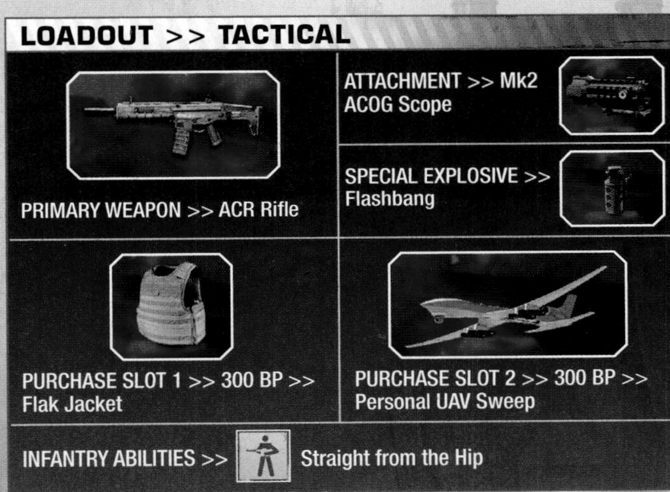

LOADOUT >> TACTICAL
PRIMARY WEAPON >> ACR Rifle
ATTACHMENT >> Mk2 ACOG Scope
SPECIAL EXPLOSIVE >> Flashbang
PURCHASE SLOT 1 >> 300 BP >> Flak Jacket
PURCHASE SLOT 2 >> 300 BP >> Personal UAV Sweep
INFANTRY ABILITIES >> Straight from the Hip

This is the thinking soldier's loadout, with weapons and items designed to help specific situations. Battle Point purchases are less expensive, with the UAV Sweep, Flak Jacket, and Flashbangs all benefitting a more subtle, almost stealthy mode of play. The ability is there in case you run into a problem and don't have time to employ the ACOG scope. While other loadouts focus on a primary weapon, this allows you to choose multiple items and use them in conjunction with each other.

LOADOUT >> EXPLOSIVE
PRIMARY WEAPON >> SCAR-H LMG
ATTACHMENT >> Mk3 Holo Scope
SPECIAL EXPLOSIVE >> C4
PURCHASE SLOT 1 >> 800 BP >> AQ-11 Buzzard
PURCHASE SLOT 2 >> 250 BP >> Proximity Launcher
INFANTRY ABILITIES >>
Tactical Reload
Boomer

This offers a variety of ways to destroy enemies by using weapons other than your primary one, although none are too focused (the Optimal Loadouts are more specific). Useful as an anti-vehicle loadout, this gives you both C4 and a Flak Jacket for daring raids against armor, or staying at a control point to defend it, while the drone helps your team pinpoint enemies for termination.

Optimal Loadouts

General Notes: The following loadouts are designed to give you a good archetype to copy, depending on how you play your games, and the tactics you like or your team needs. Feel free to change them to your preferred play style, although these loadouts have proved their worth in countless combat situations.

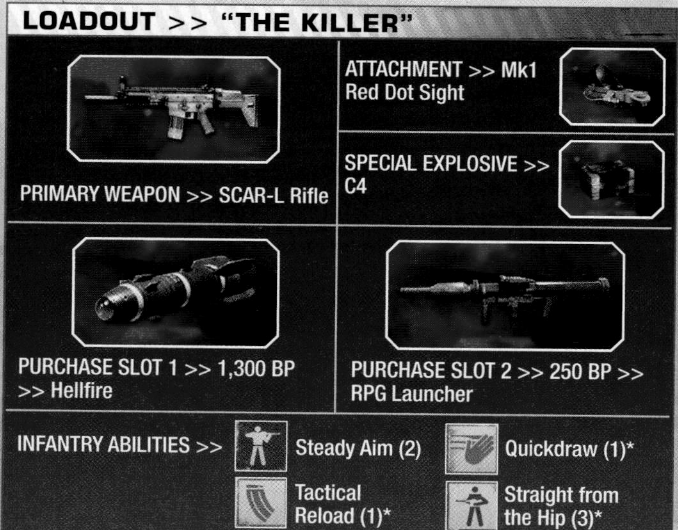

(*Choose one or more of these.)

This is arguably the best loadout for mid-range battles, with the option to easily snipe at enemies in the far distance. When choosing the abilities, definitely pick Steady Aim, and then choose the others with your remaining points. The Steady Aim ability combined with the Red Dot Sight makes the SCAR-L extremely deadly. An enemy can be killed in one or two semi-automatic bursts.

This assault alternative is useful when fighting at both mid-range and up close. The M4 Rifle is excellent at both ranges, while Ammo Resupply and Fist Full combined enable you to constantly throw cooked grenades in the direction you're moving, to clear out foes from buildings or covered locations, as well as making it easier to mop up wounded enemies.

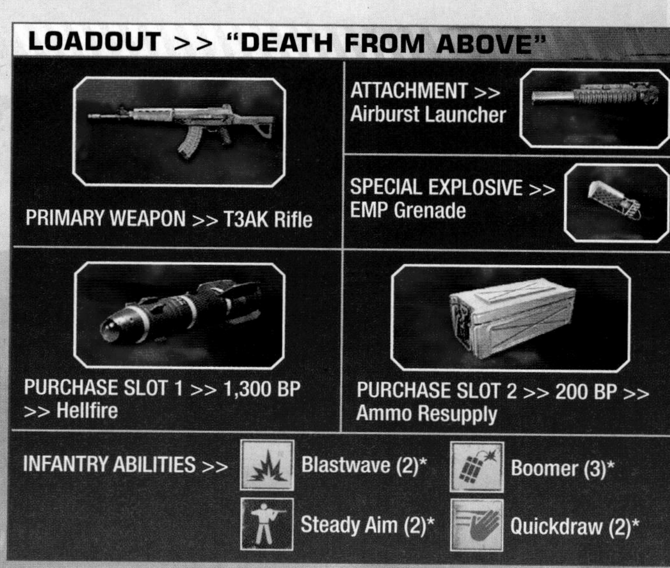

LOADOUT >> "DEATH FROM ABOVE"
PRIMARY WEAPON >> T3AK Rifle
ATTACHMENT >> Airburst Launcher
SPECIAL EXPLOSIVE >> EMP Grenade
PURCHASE SLOT 1 >> 1,300 BP >> Hellfire
PURCHASE SLOT 2 >> 200 BP >> Ammo Resupply
INFANTRY ABILITIES >>
Blastwave (2)*
Boomer (3)*
Steady Aim (2)*
Quickdraw (2)*

(*Use any combination of these abilities.)

Some might say this derivation from the assault class is "overpowered" or "cheap." These people are tasting the explosive end of your Airburst Launcher! The T3AK is a reasonable assault rifle, but has a good standard iron sight in comparison to the other assault rifles. But the rifle is a back-up to the Airburst Launcher attachment. Use this constantly, accessing additional ordnance via the Ammo Resupply.

LOADOUT >> "UP CLOSE AND PERSONAL"

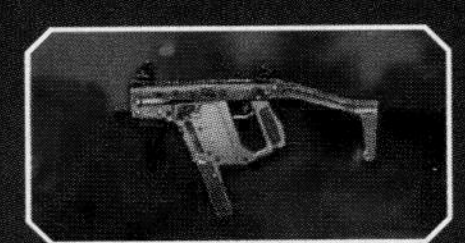

PRIMARY WEAPON >> PWS Diablo SMG*

ATTACHMENT >> Mk3 Red Dot Sight**

ATTACHMENT >> N/A

PRIMARY WEAPON >> Super-V SMG*

SPECIAL EXPLOSIVE >> WP Grenade†

SPECIAL EXPLOSIVE >> Flashbang Grenade†

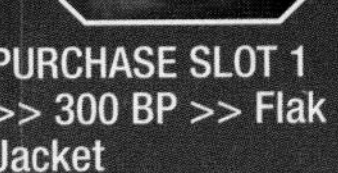

PURCHASE SLOT 1 >> 300 BP >> Flak Jacket

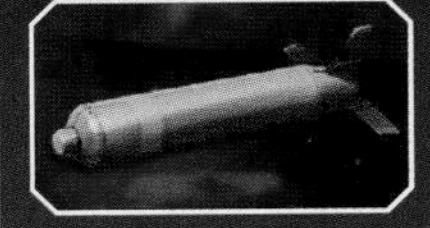

PURCHASE SLOT 2 >> 1,600 BP >> Cluster Bomb‡

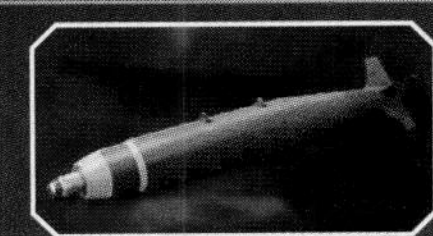

PURCHASE SLOT 2 >> 1,300 BP >> White Phosphorous‡

INFANTRY ABILITIES >>

Straight from the Hip (3)†‡

Blast Wave (2)†‡

Tactical Reload (1)†‡

Utility Belt (2)†‡

(* Either SMG is worth using, consult the SMG section for more details.)

(† Either of these grenades are worth considering; try them both out and decide on a favorite.)

(‡ Either of these are worth considering.)

(†‡ Take Straight from the Hip, and then choose from the rest.)

This variation on the SMG class is designed to wreak as much havoc at close quarters as possible; use this on smaller maps like Cul-de-sac and Suburbs. Either SMG is a must-have primary weapon on closer maps without vehicles. Because you aren't spending Battle Points on vehicles, the Flak Jacket is more handy; wear it before you lob in a Flashbang, then burst into a house, and spray and pray with your SMG and a steady aim with Straight from the Hip ability.

LOADOUT >> "THE CAMPER"

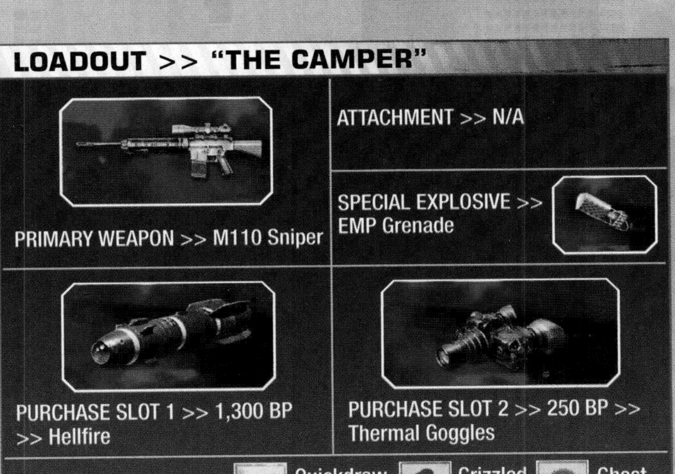

PRIMARY WEAPON >> M110 Sniper

ATTACHMENT >> N/A

SPECIAL EXPLOSIVE >> EMP Grenade

PURCHASE SLOT 1 >> 1,300 BP >> Hellfire

PURCHASE SLOT 2 >> 250 BP >> Thermal Goggles

INFANTRY ABILITIES >> Quickdraw (1), Grizzled (3), Ghost (1)

This loadout is built for an ace sniper, with long-range combat abilities. The M110 is chosen over the (longer ranged) M200 because of its faster fire-rate; the bolt action of the M200 can't keep up. Although the M110 doesn't come with built-in Thermal Vision (as does the M200), donning Thermal Goggles negates this problem; which is particularly helpful on maps with a large amount of foliage.

LOADOUT >> "THE DRONE RANGER"

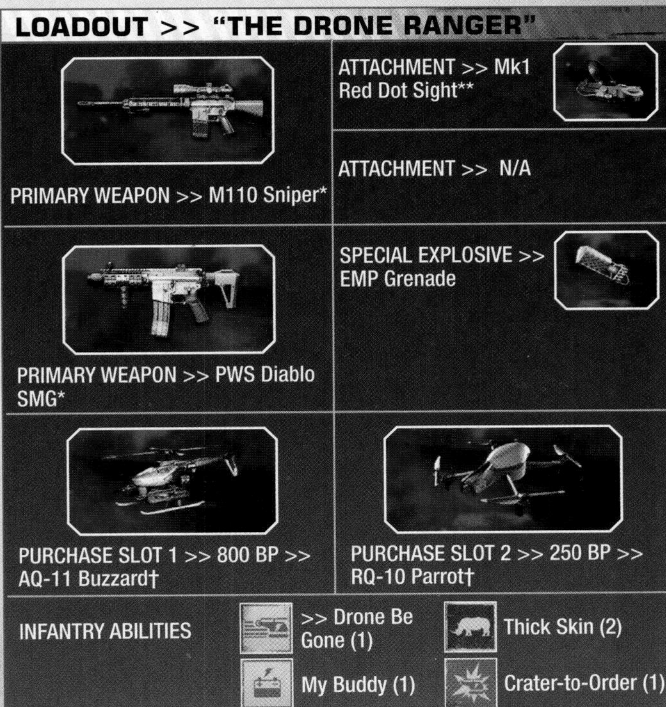

PRIMARY WEAPON >> M110 Sniper*

ATTACHMENT >> Mk1 Red Dot Sight**

ATTACHMENT >> N/A

PRIMARY WEAPON >> PWS Diablo SMG*

SPECIAL EXPLOSIVE >> EMP Grenade

PURCHASE SLOT 1 >> 800 BP >> AQ-11 Buzzard†

PURCHASE SLOT 2 >> 250 BP >> RQ-10 Parrot†

INFANTRY ABILITIES >> Drone Be Gone (1), Thick Skin (2), My Buddy (1), Crater-to-Order (1)

(* Choose the SMG for smaller maps.)

(** The sight is used with the SMG; ignore the attachment if you're using the sniper rifle.)

(† Either Air Drone is recommended; choose the one you're most comfortable with.)

If you enjoy crouching behind cover, remotely controlling a favorite drone, this is the loadout for you. Stay away from actual fighting and choose a drone. Air drones are arguably recommended because they can become an annoying distraction much more easily, and are more difficult to take out. Utilize the EMP Grenade if an enemy drone comes close to pointing out your hiding position. Be sure your team is the one patrolling the battlefield.

LOADOUT >> "SCRAP METAL MERCHANT"

PRIMARY WEAPON >> T3AK Rifle

ATTACHMENT >> EMP Launcher

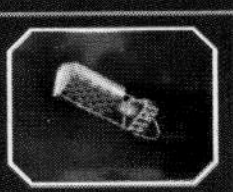

SPECIAL EXPLOSIVE >> EMP Grenade

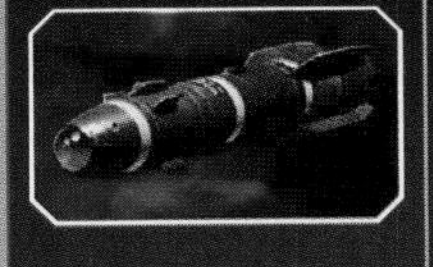

PURCHASE SLOT 1 >> 1,300 BP >> Hellfire

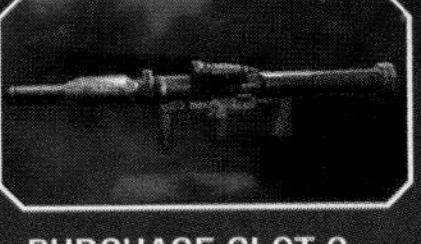

PURCHASE SLOT 2 >> 250 BP >> RPG Launcher*

PURCHASE SLOT 2 >> 400 BP >> MQ60 AT Rhino*

INFANTRY ABILITIES >>

Boomer (3)**

Blastwave (2)**

Utility Belt (2)**

(* Choose either depending on your preference and play style.)

(** Use any combination of these abilities.)

This loadout has been specifically designed to cater to the anti-vehicle infantryman, who is sent out on larger maps (making this loadout less useful in Cul-de-sac and Suburb) to thwart enemy mechanized units. The T3AK isn't actually your main weapon (it was chosen for its iron sight, and is employed when facing infantry). Using EMP devices and the RPG Launcher (plus either a Hellfire or drone from cover) are your main battle tactics.

PRIMARY WEAPONS

This section details the different guns you can bring to the battle.

Assault Rifles

Strengths: Well-rounded, excellent at medium range, and with scoped options, can be used to snipe too.

Weaknesses: Less effective at close range or tight, infantry-only maps, where an SMG can out-gun you.

General Notes: Assault rifles are usually used with most proficiency at medium range, both shot from the hip or via a sight or scope. They can also be used to snipe if employed correctly. For example if you "flutter" (burst fire), and tap the trigger while expending only a few bullets at a time, you can dispatch a foe from a distance almost rivalling a sniper rifle; a technique used to great effect in the combat zone, and something that just isn't possible with SMG-class weapons.

ARs are the perfect choice for a map with a mixture of long- and medium-range combat, such as Farm, which has large open areas (where regular fire and sniping using a scoped AR is possible), as well as buildings that still provide reasonable space to move and aim (such as the church). These are usually favored around 70 percent of the time over SMGs, simply because of their range and versatility, although map choice is another point to consider; smaller maps with cramped interior spaces such as Cul-de-sac are more often fought using SMGs.

Don't consider the sights that are initially attached to each AR as the ones to use; they are incredibly inferior compared to the ACOG, Holo, and (to a greater extent) the Red Dot Sight, the latter of which is recommended for veteran players. The only partial exception to this is the T3AK.

NOTE 알아두세요

None of the rifles have different firing modes. For example, the M4 Rifle is fully automatic, so you can't fire it in semi-automatic mode.

M4 Rifle

Unlocked at: Level 1

Fully Automatic: Yes

Notes: The main assault rifle for the US Armed Forces. High rate-of-fire and low recoil make it a balanced choice for outdoor and close-quarter combat.

A military standard, the M4 rifle is your all-purpose firearm suitable for an impressive range of combat scenarios. While the M4 excels at mid-range, it holds its own in close-quarters combat and can be surprisingly accurate across long distances when crouching or lying prone. The high rate of fire and solid accuracy make it a great choice for large, dense maps such as Green Zone and Suburb, where neither sniper rifles nor close-range SMGs quite fit the bill.

M16 Rifle

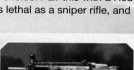

Unlocked at: Level 27

Fully Automatic: No

Notes: The primary infantry rifle during the Vietnam War. Limited to semi-automatic operation but has greater accuracy, range, and damage than the M4.

This fires one shot per trigger pull. This is advantageous over the other fully automatic weapons because the shots are more powerful and a lot more accurate. For maps with a long distance between choke points (such as Farm), and if you favor accurate firing over spraying-and-praying, this is an optimal choice. Pair this with a Red Dot or ACOG, and it becomes almost as lethal as a sniper rifle, and can certainly fire faster.

SCAR-L Rifle

Unlocked at: Level 14

Fully Automatic: No

Notes: A lightweight, modular rifle developed to meet the needs of SOCOM. It features a burst fire mode that delivers three rounds for each trigger pull.

As with the M16, this gun's burst fire mode is highly beneficial. Veteran players gravitate toward the SCAR-L because of its inherent power and bullet management. This already-impressive weapon becomes the premier assault rifle when paired with the Steady Aim Infantry ability (providing less recoil when aiming down the sight), as the rifle's three-round burst—which usually recoils, meaning the second or third bullet may miss a target at range— is focused in a much smaller area. This an incredibly powerful combination lets you take down enemy infantry with one or two bursts—even at extremely long distances.

Because of the bullet management, this also lasts a long while before needing to be reloaded. In fact, the only less-than-impressive aspect of this weapon is the default sight; replace it with the ACOG for firing at extremely long distances, or the Red Dot Sight for general use.

T3AK Rifle

Unlocked at: Level 40

Fully Automatic: Yes

Notes: A Chinese-manufactured assault rifle based on the AK-47. This is slower firing than the M4 or ACR, but deals considerably more damage at medium range.

This weapon has the best default scope (except for sniper rifles). The scope (which isn't an attachment, but comes with the T3AK) is extremely minimal. You can see around your weapon very well, which helps spot enemies.

Without a scope or sight necessary, you can attach a Grenade .auncher (a potent combination), Airburst Launcher, or Silencer to this veapon; a particularly potent combination is the Airburst attachment; vhich essentially turns the T3AK into an explosive sniping armament, is well as an adept medium-range assault rifle.

ACR Rifle

Unlocked at: Level 3

Fully Automatic: Yes

Notes: Incorporates several features rom other modern rifles into one platform. Leads the M4 in sheer damage, but has greater recoil.

The ACR is an extremely powerful assault rifle. Even though he damage rating looks quite low, this can pulverize an enemy; hink of it as a slightly slower-firing M4, which trades off speed for stopping power. Use the ACR when defending objectives during a Ground Control match to quickly kill enemies at close range. It's more accurate than a shotgun and deadlier at a much farther distance, which makes it ideal for defense.

XM10 Rifle

Unlocked at: Level 46

Fully Automatic: Yes

Notes: Under development until he project lost its funding in the economic collapse of 2018. A number of prototypes have found their way onto the field.

This assault rifle's strength is its extremely fast firing mechanism, and despite the statistical data to the contrary, users have experienced bullets leaving the chamber at almost the speed of an SMG. Unsurprisingly, this increased rate of fire means greater recoil. As such, it's best suited for close-range combat, but given the accessibility of the Diablo SMG, the XM10 Rifle's increased power makes it only marginally more useful.

Light Machine Guns

Strengths: Huge ammunition reserves, perfect for battling multiple infantry at once, or attacking helicopters.

Weaknesses: Not very accurate.

General Notes: The benefits of the M249 and SCAR-H over other guns types are the huge ammo count or clip size, which allows you to fire for longer at foes before a reload. This in turn allows you to battle one or multiple enemies without worrying about running out of ammunition or stopping to reload. This helps to offset the inherent shortfalls of both weapons; they are less accurate than SMGs, and far less accurate than rifles. But the larger bullet size means that of all the guns, LMGs are the ones most favored when taking down the scout or attack helicopters.

M249 LMG

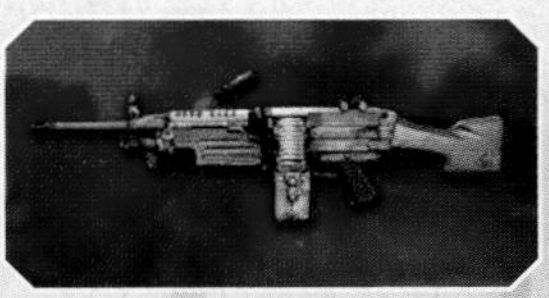

Unlocked at: Level 1

Notes: Primary LMG of the US Armed Forces. The box magazine holds 100 rounds of linked ammunition. Difficult to control due to high recoil.

Of the two LMGs, the M249 is usually preferred due to its greater power; which is the main point of a light machine gun. The standard scope on an M249 is also preferable to the one on the SCAR-H. Furthermore, this military standard has a more powerful shot that makes it more effective bullet for bullet compared to the SCAR-H. Recoil is an issue, and while it's less than the SCAR-H, it's enough to make it a poor choice for anything but close-range combat.

SCAR-H LMG

Unlocked at: Level 32

Notes: The MG variant of the SCAR comes equipped with a high-capacity 75-round twin drum magazine and a vertical foregrip with integrated bipod.

The SCAR-H shoots faster than the M249, but sacrifices strength of damage compared to its LMG rival. A higher rate of fire translates to more recoil, which makes it less desirable than the default M249. Still, it's effective at mowing down infantry squads and useful in dealing with drones, particularly the Wolverine and Rhino. Be careful when employing the SCAR-H against helicopters, because the recoil complicates firing on a moving aerial target.

Sub Machine Guns

Strengths: Fast-firing, designed to remove enemy threats from close range. The perfect "spray-and-pray" weapon.

Weaknesses: Extremely fast ammo expenditure, no subtlety to the attacks. Not designed for long range or scoped use.

General Notes: These are used up-close and personal, and are favored in maps such as Cul-de-sac or Suburb. It is more difficult to "flutter" an SMG; this technique is usually ditched in favor of the tried and tested "spray and pray," where as many bullets as possible are fired, usually from the hip. As long as you're at close range (within 20 feet of a foe, and the closer the better), the high rate of fire wins the day, with your foes overwhelmed by bullet strikes. However, if your enemy survives the 10 seconds or so of continuous fire that it takes to empty a clip, he's likely to shoot back and drop you, meaning ammunition expenditure is your biggest concern.

Although adding an ACOG scope to this weapon can tweak the accuracy and range slightly, this isn't how the weapon was designed to function. Both weapons are a blast to use, both figuratively and literally; rushing to a door of a suburban house and spraying bullets from the hip is what these guns were designed to do.

PWS Diablo SMG

Unlocked at: Level 1

Notes: Has similar ergonomics to the M4, but is lighter and shorter. Its vertical foregrip makes it the perfect tool for close-quarters combat.

Both the PWS Diablo and the Super-V offer impressive damage—better even than the LMGs—but go through a clip in around five to seven seconds. This isn't a problem if an enemy falls to the hail of bullets, but if he doesn't, expect to come off second-best during the reload time. Although close, the PWS Diablo is usually favored over the Super-V due to its overall balance. With the larger clip size, you can kill two enemies without worrying about a reload, which the Super-V can't usually achieve.

Super-V SMG

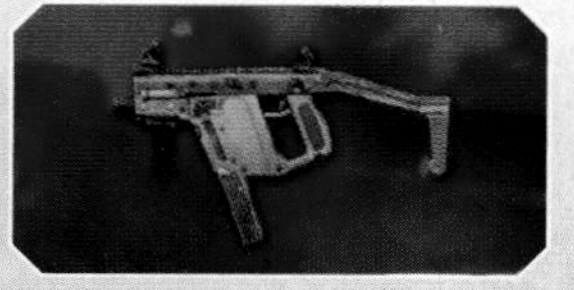

Unlocked at: Level 9

Notes: Uses an asymmetrical system to reduce recoil. Allows operators to put more rounds on-target at close range. Extended magazine comes standard.

This has a slight advantage over the PWS Diablo, because it fires even faster, but both weapons are comparable. The Super-V is lacking a little in accuracy and has less ammunition, meaning you'll run out of it even faster. Avoid using either weapon in large maps such as Farm, because you're usually too far from a foe. The Super-V may cut down an enemy at top speed, but there are usually no bullets left to finish a second foe without a (usually deadly) reload period.

Sniper Rifles

Strengths: Ruthless at long range. Usually a one-hit kill. M200 has built-in Thermal Vision.

Weaknesses: Useless at close quarters. Almost impossible to aim when fired from the hip.

General Notes: For larger maps with a variety of topographical features to hide behind, and where enemies won't be charging your location, the sniper rifle is your weapon of choice. Designed to provide covering fire to your teammates, and extreme annoyance to your rivals, the two sniper rifles are fired via the built-in scope (because firing from the hip and hitting anything is almost impossible), which means you can't affix an attachment to them.

M110 Sniper

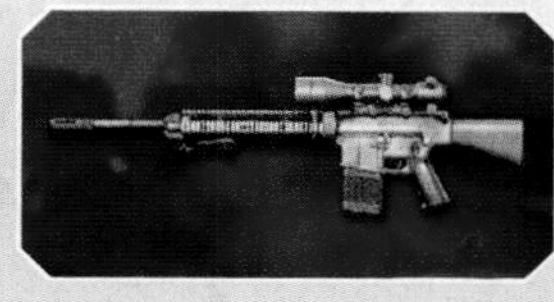

Unlocked at: Level 1

Notes: Semi-automatic sniper rifle that features a 3x scope and detachable 10-round magazine. Chambered for 7. 62mm. Effective at long range.

While offering a slightly less devastating shot, the M110's rate of fire (or more specifically, time between shots) is significantly higher than the M200 Sniper, making it the usual choice for those favoring a camping spot. The M110 is extremely powerful; it can be used almost like a semi-automatic assault rifle, and burst-fired manually, making it the choice for most long-range takedowns. Choose the M110 in about seven of ten matches due to these favorable features.

M200 Sniper

Unlocked at: Level 19

Notes: Bolt-action sniper rifle. Magazine holds five custom-tooled cartridges. Effective at extreme range. Has 4x thermal optics and a laser rangefinder.

The M200 offers the most devastating single-shot damage of any gun, and although has a very slow rate of fire (which impedes it when compared to the much quicker M110), it comes into its own under certain map-specific conditions. For example, on Angel Island, it lets you peer through foliage, because its scope has the thermal optics built in, allowing you to see enemies through greenery or behind rocks. The additional magnification (4x compared to the M110's 3x) is perfect for the larger maps, too.

Downloadable Guns

870 Express Shotgun

Unlocked at: Special

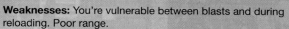

Strengths: Extremely damaging at close quarters, it can be easily backed up with a melee strike. An SMG alternative.

Weaknesses: You're vulnerable between blasts and during reloading. Poor range.

Notes: Pump-action shotgun widely used by civilians and law enforcement. Devastating at close range. Top-mounted tactical rail accepts a variety of optics.

This is a stand-alone shotgun, with a reasonable number of shots before a (lengthy) reload. As expected, its power at close range is incredible—it can drop a foe with one or two blasts at close or melee range. Of course, the rate of fire is similar to a sniper rifle, leaving you open to attack between blasts or during reloading. It also has a very short range, making it a poor choice for larger maps (unless you're catching a ride in a vehicle, and then defending a control point). Otherwise, this should be seen as an alternative to an SMG, and employed on smaller maps. Add scopes to improve accuracy.

For a different (and some might say, a more well-rounded) option, try fitting an under-barrel shotgun attachment to your assault rifle, which offers far more versatility. You won't be able to use a sight or scope attachment though.

 Primary Weapons Table

The following chart compares the various aspects of each weapon, so you can figure out which is better for certain tasks, or find the one that suits your style of play.

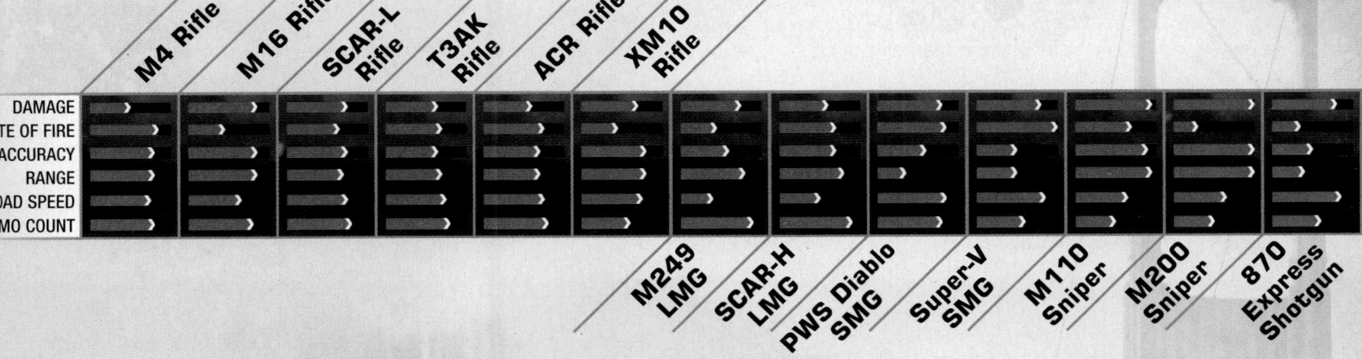

 Weapons: Already Equipped

Although these weapons (such as the Knife, shown), don't fit into a class, and aren't employed as regularly as an assault rifle or SMG, these are still worth toying with. You'll need to perfect each of them to complete weapon challenges. You come to the battle with these items, no matter which loadout you choose.

M9 Pistol

Unlocked at: Level 1

Cost: 0 BP

Strengths: Quite powerful, with a good lack of recoil, distance, and ammunition supply. Fast-firing, if you're adept.

Weaknesses: Manual firing, only iron sights are available, and lacks attachments.

Notes: Don't underestimate the M9; it is incredibly useful for picking off foes with precise and damaging shots. The pistol can be fired as quickly as you can pull the trigger, effectively making it the fastest firing weapon (if you're quick and adept enough!). Aside from the two LMGs, the M9 holds the most ammunition, so it remains effective for a long time.

Frag Grenade

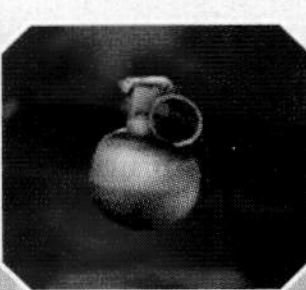

Unlocked at: Level 1

Cost: 0 BP

Strengths: Cooked grenades are instant and lethal. With trajectory prowess, these are deadly.

Weaknesses: The explosion can kill you as well as foes. Uncooked grenades are easily dodged.

Notes: This isn't strictly counted as an explosive, because you begin with two of these (or four; various abilities augment this weapon). Use Frag Grenades to flush enemies out of cover, wound them, or ambush them with your primary weapon backing up your attack. Be sure to "cook" a grenade (holding it for 2–3 seconds before lobbing it) or the enemy can easily dodge it when it lands. A cooked grenade explodes immediately, making it far more effective. Don't forget to use grenades indirectly: ricochet them off walls or objects so you can kill foes around corners.

Knife

Unlocked at: Level 1

Cost: 0 BP

Strengths: An instant kill when the melee strike hits successfully.

Weaknesses: You're extremely vulnerable if it doesn't hit; it has very limited range, even at close quarters.

Notes: This knife is usually a last resort, or a quick ambush strike you can inflict on a foe who hasn't seen you or is reloading and close enough to charge. Beware that you're vulnerable after you swipe the knife (although an ability called Now That's a Knife lessens this time considerably), so use this in closed-in areas. Ground drones are particularly susceptible to knife attacks, which are a great way to take them down.

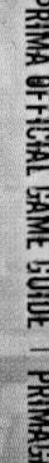

ATTACHMENTS

These slot onto your primary weapon and come in two main types. Sights and scopes sit on top of your weapon and improve aiming. Under-barrel attachments offer an additional weapon, usually one with projectile grenade attacks. Choose only one type of attachment, either a sight/scope, or an under-barrel attachment, not both.

Attachments: Scopes and Sights

General Notes: Three different types of attachments help pinpoint your shots more accurately. These are ACOG Scopes **[01]**, Holo Scopes **[02]**, and Red Dot Sights **[03]**. In general terms, the ACOG scopes provide accuracy at a longer distance. Although the Holo Scope offers a degree of magnification (which the Red Dot Sights do not), the Red Dot is significantly less bulky, which is a bonus.

ACOG scopes are useful on assault rifles, and to a lesser extent, LMGs. Do this when playing on larger maps, where the additional zoom function is useful. Otherwise, employ Red Dot Sights on every weapon (including SMGs); definitely choose this on tighter maps (such as Cul-de-sac), or larger maps if you don't need the additional range (due to infantry abilities, weapon, or play style). Holo scopes are a personal preference, but they are bulky and offer no more help than a Red Dot Sight.

TIP 영리한

Holo Scopes work almost exactly the same as the Red Dot Sights, but are more bulky. Many tactical fighters prefer a Red Dot Sight because it takes up less of your view. Compare the nearby pictures [02], [03] to see how much more of your view the Holo Scope covers. Because peripheral vision is extremely important during fraught battles, many choose the Red Dot Sight every time.

NOTE 알아두세요

Each scope has three variants: Mk1, 2, or 3. Although you may initially think that a "Mk3" is better than a "Mk1," the differences are mostly cosmetic; it is more important to pick the appropriate type of attachment (ACOG, Holo, or Red Dot Sight) than the variant of each. The only "non-cosmetic" point to remember is that some variants are bulkier and take up more screen real-estate. Solve this by choosing the scopes made of thinner metal compounds.

CAUTION 조심하다

When you unlock scopes (via a number of enemy kills), you don't unlock the scope for every weapon, just the one you've killed with. Practice with every gun if you want a particular scope or sight choice for each one.

ACOG Scopes

Strengths: These offer the longest scopes of the three types.

Weaknesses: They are bulky.

Mk1 ACOG Scope

Unlocked by Kills: 100

Notes: 1.5x telescopic sight with non-illuminated mil-dot crosshairs.

Mk2 ACOG Scope

Unlocked by Kills: 100

Notes: 1.5x telescopic sight with non-illuminated mil-dot crosshairs.

Mk3 ACOG Scope

Unlocked by Kills: 100

Notes: 1.5x telescopic sight with non-illuminated mil-dot crosshairs.

Holo Scopes

Strengths: These offer a reasonable scoped view.

Weaknesses: They are bulky.

Mk1 Holo Scope

Unlocked by Kills: 5

Notes: Projects a holographic reticle onto the sight picture for easier target acquisition.

Mk2 Holo Scope

Unlocked by Kills: 5

Notes: Projects a holographic reticle onto the sight picture for easier target acquisition.

Mk3 Holo Scope

Unlocked by Kills: 5

Notes: Projects a holographic reticle onto the sight picture for easier target acquisition.

Red Dot Sights

Strengths: These offer excellent accuracy and peripheral vision around the gun.

Weaknesses: They don't offer the magnification of an ACOG.

Mk1 Red Dot Sight

Unlocked by Kills: 50

Notes: Projects a red dot onto the sight picture for easier target acquisition.

Mk2 Red Dot Sight

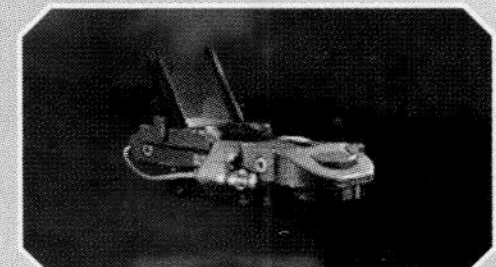

Unlocked by Kills: 50

Notes: Projects a red dot onto the sight picture for easier target acquisition.

Mk3 Red Dot Sight

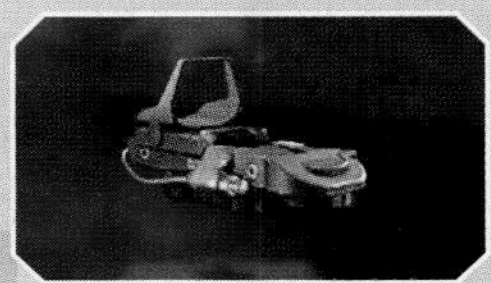

Unlocked by Kills: 50

Notes: Projects a red dot onto the sight picture for easier target acquisition.

Attachments: Launchers and Silencer

04

05

General Notes: Often overlooked by players focused on scopes and sights, launcher attachments **[04]** add another weapon to your arsenal, usually an explosive one. Launchers are ideally employed on any rifle, although the T3AK is a great choice because it has a reasonably good default iron sight. You cannot have a scope or sight and a launcher or silencer **[05]** attachment in Multiplayer matches.

Airburst Launcher

Unlocked by Kills: 150

Strengths: Very damaging, highly accurate when used properly. Removes the guesswork from trajectory aiming.

Weaknesses: Limited ammunition.

Notes: Single shot 40mm underbarrel grenade launcher with laser rangefinder and airburst grenades. Set desired distance by holding the trigger, and release to launch.

> **NOTE 알아두세요**
>
> **An excellent weapon, this shoots out a similar projectile to the Grenade Launcher but has much more impressive aiming system. Aim this attachment's laser at a target (such as a vehicle) and a readout informs you of the distance. Then hold (not tap) the trigger to "lock" the distance, and the grenade fires that far.**
>
> **This is useful in situations where you face a dug-in foe; for example, on top of a silo or the church steeple in Farm. A Grenade Launcher won't reach that location, but a distance-targeted airburst (ideally at the foe's feet, after perhaps stepping up a couple of feet to ensure the grenade doesn't explode in front of the enemy) most certainly will. This removes the problems of trajectory angles inherent in other launcher types. Those who argue that this is overpowered are likely to be on the receiving end. Due to the long distance you can accurately fire this, think of the Airburst Launcher as a sniper rifle with an explosive attack.**

> **TIP 영리한**
>
> **Combine this with the Ammo Resupply to really ruin your foes' day. Combine this with a T3AK for all the benefits of aiming down a decent default sight with the long range grenade-sniping of the Airburst—a lethal combination!**

EMP Launcher

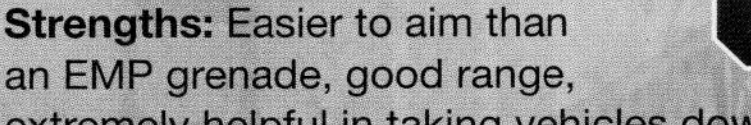

Unlocked by Kills: 200

Strengths: Easier to aim than an EMP grenade, good range, extremely helpful in taking vehicles down.

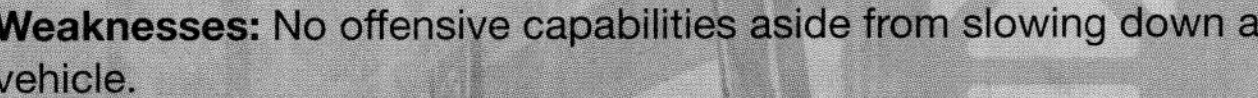

Weaknesses: No offensive capabilities aside from slowing down a vehicle.

Notes: Single shot 40mm underbarrel grenade launcher with experimental EMP rounds. Proximity detonation. Affects vehicles and drones.

This defensive launcher is useful for taking down tanks and other vehicles, and is an essential part of your arsenal if you expect to encounter a mechanized enemy. The longer range (compared to the EMP Grenade) makes this a slightly safer, if often overlooked, option. Because this doesn't provide immediate gratification (it is usually used in conjunction with teammates who use RPG Launchers to finish the enemy vehicle) it may not be used as often as it should.

Grenade Launcher

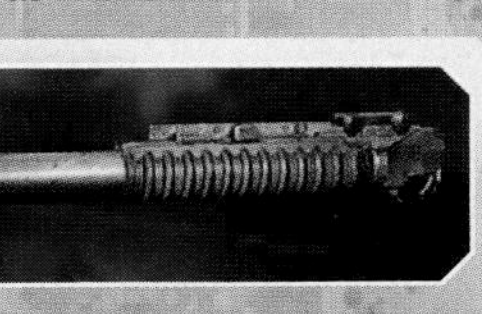

Unlocked by Kills: 75

Strengths: Lethal takedowns and one-shot kills from range.

Weaknesses: You may find Frag Grenades easier (and quicker) to use, and they don't replace your scope.

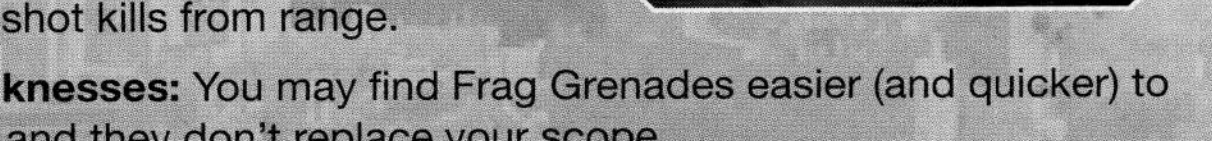

Notes: Single shot 40mm underbarrel grenade launcher that fires high-explosive rounds. Contact detonation requires minimum arming distance.

This is a standard grenade launcher, which lobs (or punts) a grenade a specific distance before it reaches a solid object (usually the ground or a foe) and then explodes. Although the target reticle changes, it is still difficult to judge the distance, so play a few practice matches to ensure that you can accurately hit a target. The practice is worthwhile, because the damage inflicted is severe (similar to a Frag Grenade), and can drop an infantry foe with a single hit.

Shotgun

Unlocked by Kills: 15

Strengths: Very damaging at close quarters; easily backed up with a melee strike or your primary weapon.

Weaknesses: Limited ammunition and range.

Notes: Underbarrel 12 gauge pump-action shotgun with an internal magazine.

Take this attachment if you can cope without a scope or sight on your primary weapon, and want a shotgun for close-assault takedowns. Although grenade launcher attachments are a little more flexible, slotting this in under your main weapon's barrel allows you to use it on smaller maps, or to back up or augment an assault rifle attack. If you're planning to fight at both range and closer quarters, or want more firepower during room-to-room takedowns or defending, this is an option.

Silencer

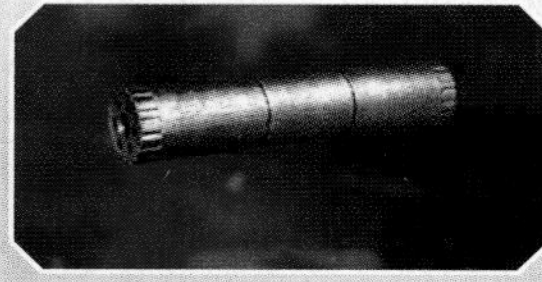

Unlocked at: Level 25

Strengths: Quiet weaponry, lack of appearance on the in-game map. Can be attached to any gun.

Weaknesses: Scope cannot be mounted as well. Only useful if you're playing with stealth in mind.

Notes: Reduces the amount of noise and flash produced by a weapon when fired. Users do not appear on the mini-map when firing a suppressed weapon.

There are two different ways you show up on the mini-map. The first is when you shoot a gun without a silencer attached to it. Appearing on the mini-map isn't a huge problem, because you disappear after a couple of seconds, and most of the time, players aren't actively scrutinizing their radar, making this attachment less than necessary (and the silencer adds to the space your weapon takes up on your screen).

The second way you appear is when an opposing player purchases a UAV Sweep, which isn't that often due to the wealth of more "instantly gratifying" and violent options to spend BPs on. You appear on the UAV Sweep whether you have a silencer attached or not.

The biggest problem with the silencer is that you must choose either a scope/sight or a silencer, and the former attachments are much more useful in a variety of situations. If you're constantly moving, firing, and outflanking the enemy, the silencer isn't for you. However, if you enjoy locating a less-trafficked spot and quietly picking off enemies with a rifle, this is an essential pick.

Weapon Camo

General Notes: This purely optional choice is a paint job for your primary weapon **[06], [07], [08]**, unlocked via reaching a level, or completing a kill streak. Camo patterns marked "Special" are a pre-order bonus. This can match the map you are playing (for example, "Woodland" or "Urban") or a more noticeable design ("I <3 My Gun") that simply invites enemies to shoot, or annoys them if they're on the receiving end of a shot from a gun that garish. Mainly though, this is a personal preference choice.

06

07

08

Chrome

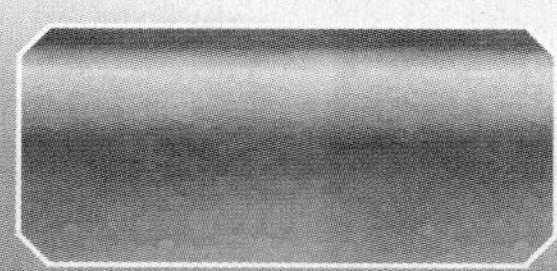

Unlocked by: Reaching Level 55

Notes: Nothing comes closer to that classic hot rod look like this clean, chrome finish.

Cracks

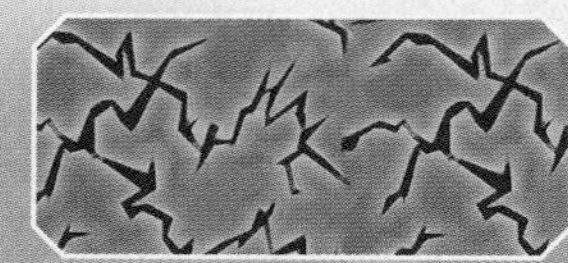

Unlocked by: Special

Notes: Though structurally sound, subtle stress fractures lace this exclusive finish.

Desert

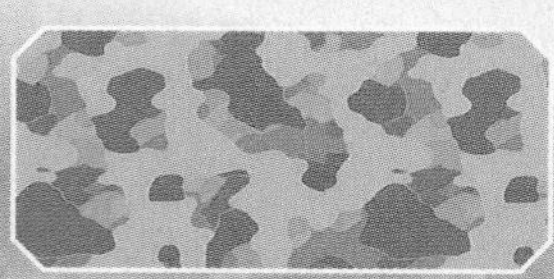

Unlocked by Kill Streak: 2

Notes: This desert pattern packs so much heat, your enemies think you're a mirage.

Digital

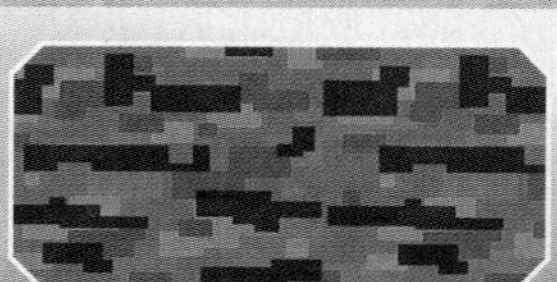

Unlocked by Kill Streak: 4

Notes: Your gun may look digital, but your bullets are still analogue.

Digital Advanced

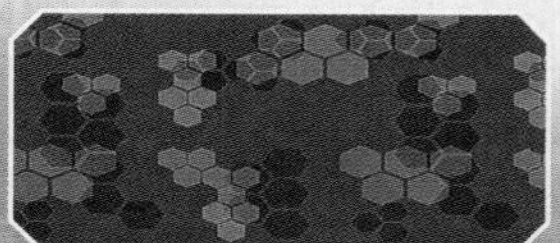

Unlocked by Kill Streak: 8

Notes: Bee all that you can be with this futuristic honeycomb pattern.

Digital Circuit

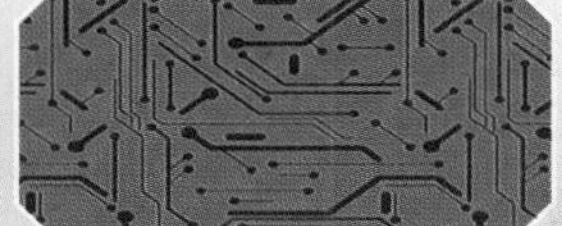

Unlocked by Kill Streak: 6

Notes: You used to be captain of the A/V squad; now you're squad captain. Show your nerd pride.

Dragon Fire

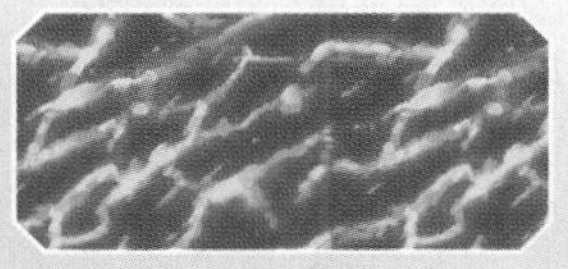

Unlocked by Kill Streak: 10

Notes: "Some say the world will end in fire, Some say in ice." You've chosen to end it with fire.

Dragon Ice

Unlocked by Kill Streak: 10

Notes: No ice dragons were harmed during the manufacture of this dragon scale camo pattern.

Frost

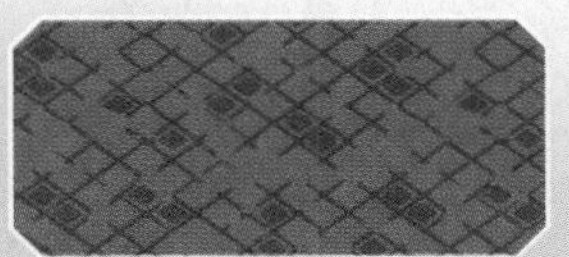

Unlocked by: Special

Notes: You're as cold as ice and so is your weapon with this exclusive camo.

Golden

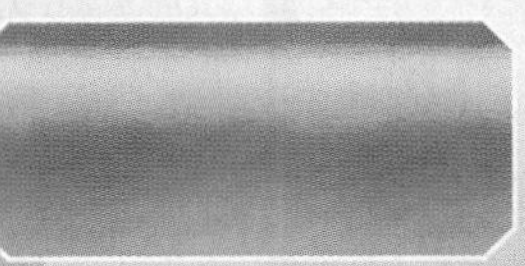

Unlocked by: Reaching Level 60

Notes: Your enemies will fear the flash of your bling as much as the flash and the bang that come with it.

Jigsaw

Unlocked by: Special

Notes: Your enemies will go to pieces when they see you wielding this exclusive finish.

Perses

Unlocked by: Reaching Level 70

Notes: Perses was the Greek Titan god of destruction. Honor him by using this aggressive pattern.

I <3 My Gun

Unlocked by: Reaching Level 75

Notes: You love your gun. Now show the rest of the world with this final, fabulous camo scheme.

Shattered

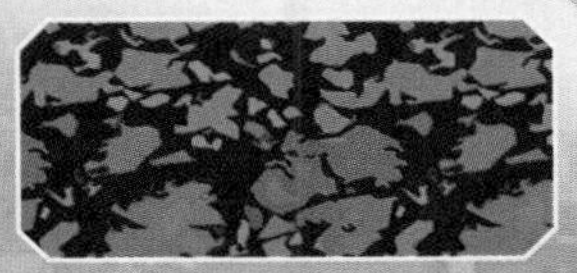

Unlocked by Kill Streak: 8

Notes: Break your opponents' spirits and shatter their confidence with this finish.

Swamp

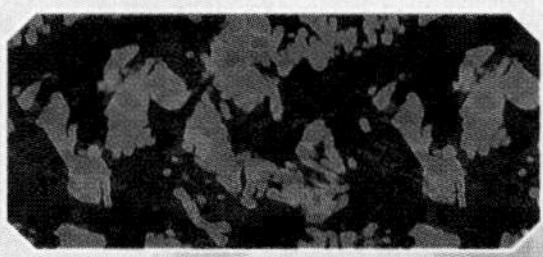

Unlocked by Kill Streak: 6

Notes: You may not have been born on the bayou, but your weapon will look the part with this pattern.

Urban

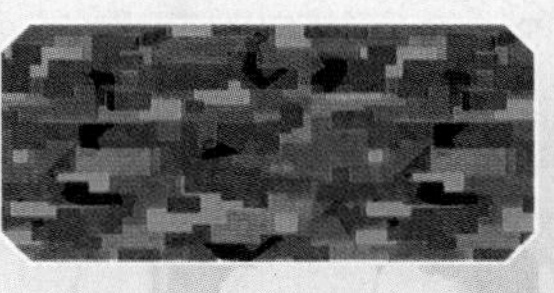

Unlocked by Kill Streak: 4

Notes: You'll blend in like a chameleon in a concrete jungle with this urban camo.

Viper

Unlocked by: Reaching Level 65

Notes: The viper is feared the world over for its quick strikes and deadly venom. Make the world fear you as well.

Woodland

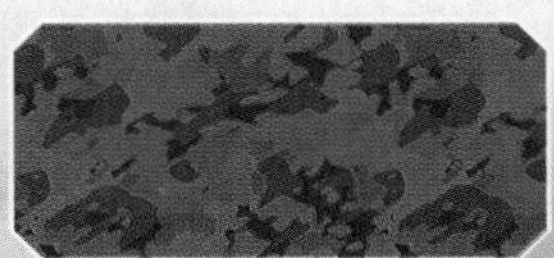

Unlocked by Kill Streak: 2

Notes: This traditional forest pattern is best used when hunting deer, elk, and enemy patrols.

Explosives

General Notes: Aside from the Frag Grenades that you always carry, you can employ other grenade types. All grenades are lobbed in the same way, and are the same general weight, so throwing an EMP, Flashbang, Frag, or WP Grenade **[09]** is the same maneuver. In objective-based games, such as Ground Control, tactical use of the Flashbang, C4, and WP Grenades are more prevalent and recommended. Matches involving simple kills allow you to employ the EMP to tackle vehicles, although this all depends on your play style.

You must learn the fine art of "cooking" your grenades; this removes the grenade icon that appears when a grenade lands nearby, and instantly kills (or wounds) the foe when the grenade hits the ground instead. If you aren't cooking your grenades, you might as well not use them because you're simply announcing your arrival, and enemies have ample time to step away as the timer ticks down.

C4

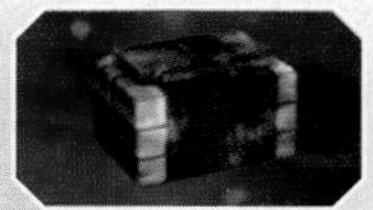

Unlocked at: Level 24

Strengths: It can be shot with guns, or exploded by a trigger device. Great for ambushes and vehicle takedowns.

Weaknesses: The C4 has a red flashing light making it visible. It can be shot and exploded.

Notes: Composition 4 plastic explosive with remote detonation trigger. Multiple bricks can be placed and detonated simultaneously.

Mainly a defensive weapon, but an extremely potent and useful one, C4 can be laid one at a time, or in a group, and then detonated with a single trigger press. The blast radius of the ensuing explosion is very large, and its primary function is to defend an area (such as a control point) once you've claimed it. Placing C4 at the entrances or choke points prevents foes from rushing in; back this up with teammates firing their primary weapon for an impenetrable location. Place C4 around corners so it isn't immediately spotted.

C4 has another highly important function: taking out enemy vehicles. Two will dispatch an LAV, so be ever-mindful of this tactic, too, but remember that you can't throw it as far as a grenade. You can shoot the C4, too, enabling you to switch to a more offensive posture if you can aim at the C4 to detonate it. Remove C4 by firing at it (look for the pulsing red light it gives off), or lobbing a grenade in to clear an area.

EMP Grenade

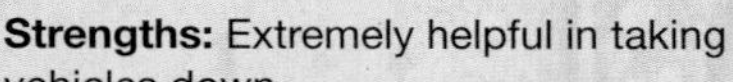

Unlocked at: Level 1

Strengths: Extremely helpful in taking vehicles down.

Weaknesses: No offensive capabilities, aside from slowing a vehicle down.

Notes: Experimental electromagnetic pulse grenade developed by the US Military in 2017. Temporarily disables vehicles and drones.

The temporary and partial shutdown of any enemy vehicle or drone for around 10 seconds is extremely useful when playing maps (such as Farm) where vehicles are often employed. The mechanized target isn't completely prone though. For example, a tank can slowly turn its turret but is otherwise crippled. This allows you to dodge the vehicle's attacks more easily. Produce an RPG Launcher to take the enemy vehicle out with. This makes it thoroughly recommended as a mid-range thrown projectile. No vehicles on your map? Then be sure to choose another explosive!

Flashbang

Unlocked at: Level 1

Strengths: Effectively stalls an enemy in their tracks, forcing them to fight blind.

Weaknesses: The blinding flash doesn't affect the enemy 100 percent of the time.

Notes: Non-lethal stun grenade that disorients targets with a bright flash and loud noise.

Lob a Flashbang into a building before you run in and spray the enemies inside with (ideally) SMG bullets. The white flash blinds and disorients the foes, who usually crouch in corners or become confused, so step in and check hiding places for adversaries waiting out the blindness. And don't expect an incapacitated foe every time.

Lobbing Flashbangs into the church in Farm, for example, is an excellent plan because the interior is enclosed enough that foes get blinded but don't have many corners or stairs to step behind. However, you may find a cooked Frag Grenade is more beneficial, so practice with both.

WP Grenade

Unlocked at: Level 43

Strengths: Great for killing enemies and blocking off thoroughfares or choke points.

Weaknesses: A relatively small area of effect.

Notes: Produces a cloud of burning smoke that is lethal when inhaled

After the WP Grenade bounces or ricochets once or twice, the intended area is engulfed in fire. Usually, enemies react to grenades by dodging them, and then sprinting over the explosion area a second or so afterward. Not so with the WP Grenade because the white phosphorous keeps burning, and coats the foes in fire, killing them. This is also extremely useful tactically to block off entrances from opposing forces. For example, as you enter the church in Farm, lob a WP Grenade at the opposite entrance, which becomes a wall of fire for five or six seconds, giving you the upper hand. After this, you can continue to block the area with WP, or try another tactic (C4, or aiming at the entrance). Essentially, this grenade gives you additional time to take or hold an area.

Equipment

General Notes: Purchasing equipment is vital to augment your battles but requires Battle Points, so spend wisely on items that help your cause. Each of the following pieces of equipment has a specific function, from resupplying your weapons to enhancing your vision **[10]**.

Flak Jacket

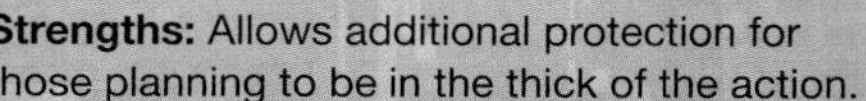

Unlocked at: Level 1

Cost: 300 BP

Strengths: Allows additional protection for those planning to be in the thick of the action.

Weaknesses: Only available once per life. Not as rewarding as more offensive items to buy.

Notes: Body armor consisting of hard ceramic plates in a synthetic fiber vest. Can be purchased once per life.

This allows you to absorb a few more enemy hits, at a slightly inflated cost. The Flak Jacket is extremely useful, but only under certain conditions, such as assaulting an infantry-only map like Cul-de-sac. At lower experience levels, you can't purchase certain airstrikes and you shouldn't hold on to Battle Points, meaning the Flak Jacket becomes one of only a few choices.

However, at higher levels, Flak Jackets are discarded in favor of more "rewarding" items, such as airstrikes or a helicopter (which can give you multiple kills and a large number of Battle Points, instead of slight protection to you, and no Battle Points). There are more effective items to spend your BPs on.

ersonal UAV Sweep

Unlocked at: Level 4

Cost: 400 BP

Strengths: Locates foes, which can be relayed to the rest of your team.

Weaknesses: Doesn't offer instant gratification; isn't helpful if your team isn't playing well together.

otes: Calls in an unmanned aerial drone that highlights enemies on ne mini-map for a limited time.

Although it's often overlooked by players due to its defensive ather than offensive) capabilities, don't underestimate the UAV weep's usefulness. Many players prefer to purchase a drone, vehicle, r airstrike to increase their kill to death ratio, and deem this to be an xpensive map enhancement.

This is equipment for the team player who is happy to reduce ossible offensive attacks for the overall good of the team by showing ne rest of the squad where foes are located. Obviously, good team ommunication is essential. The player using the UAV Sweep should nform teammates of enemy locations, possibly while remaining in defensive posture, either as a sniper or while hiding and utilizing a rone.

UAV Sweeps aren't purchased as often as you'd think. Usually player wants "more bang for the buck," and is content to wait for higher-priced item to spend their Battle Points on. Furthermore, ecause there isn't an "instant" and violent result from the UAV weep, it isn't seen as a viable choice, especially if your team doesn't ommunicate constantly.

Ammo Resupply

Unlocked at: Level 36

Cost: 200 BP

Strengths: Incredibly useful for the power player who can stay alive. Offers multiple types of ammunition replenishing.

Weaknesses: Less useful if you're less competent.

otes: Emergency restock of ammunition, grenades, and special xplosives.

Arguably one of the most useful purchases, the Ammo Resupply as a low Battle Point cost, but fully loads all your offensive weaponry. his includes your guns, grenades, and even attachments to weapons. you have infantry abilities that enhance your ammo count, such s the Fist Full ability (doubling your grenades from two to four), this ecomes an even better purchase.

So why wouldn't you get this? Well, if you're less competent, and ie before you use up your ammunition, this isn't going to be much se. This also doesn't reload your Rocket Launchers, so you'll need to urchase an additional launcher to finish off a tank. But for the dug-in niper (for example), who can continuously rack up BPs, then reload ne sniper rifle, this is extremely helpful.

Thermal Goggles

Unlocked at: Level 49

Cost: 250 BP

Strengths: Excellent for spotting enemies through greenery.

Weaknesses: Not useful in more urban environments. Useless with the M200, which already has this capability.

Notes: Head-mounted low-light and thermal goggles. Toggle on/off after purchase. Can be purchased once per life.

Thermal Goggles are inexpensive and exceptionally useful when battling on maps with lots of plant life, such as Angel Island. They mark every enemy in a hue that aids in taking them down, especially if you're using a longer-ranged assault or sniper rifle. The M200's scope has this function too (making goggles unnecessary if you're predominantly employing that rifle). Thermal Goggles are less useful in urban environments (such as Green Zone).

Drones

General Notes: Choose from four different drones: two ground drones, and two air drones. Ground drones **[11]** are obviously more vulnerable to attacks, but EMP strikes, LMG fire, and even melee strikes from a knife all destroy these small automated devices. Air drones **[12]** are more susceptible to attacks from helicopters, but are more troublesome to your opponents.

MQ50 MG Wolverine

Unlocked at: Level 1

Cost: 500 BP

Strengths: High-powered machine gun ideal for taking on infantry.

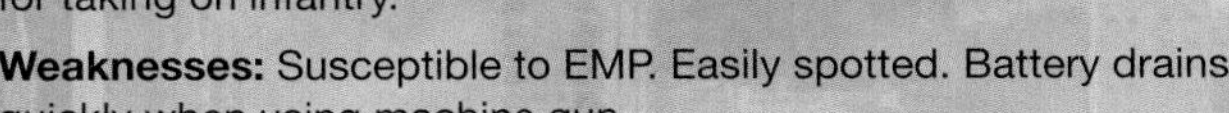

Weaknesses: Susceptible to EMP. Easily spotted. Battery drains quickly when using machine gun.

Notes: A battery-powered, multi-terrain tracked drone. The assault variant is equipped with a machine gun. Vulnerable to EMP and melee damage.

This is the ground drone alternative to the MQ60 AT Rhino. Unlike its rocket-equipped counterpart, the Wolverine is built precisely for combat against infantry. The drone's powerful machine gun can cut through swaths of enemy soldiers, although at a dramatic loss of battery power. Overheating the machine gun is a concern, so avoid extended continuous fire and opt for short, accurate bursts. Given the Wolverine's conspicuousness and weakness to EMP, grenades, and other explosives, avoid exposed areas in favor of interior spaces when deploying.

AQ-11 Buzzard

Unlocked at: Level 28

Cost: 800 BP

Strengths: Agile and airborne.
Unguided rockets effective against vehicles, particularly Humvees and LAVs.

Weaknesses: Limited rocket supply. Weak armor.

Notes: A battery-powered, remote-control helicopter. Armed with two unguided rocket pods. Vulnerable to EMP, small arms fire, and anti-air rockets.

This is the air drone alternative to the RQ-10 Parrot. Cheap, easy to control, and powerful, the Buzzard is your go-to gadget when you want to attack from the air, but don't have enough Battle Points to spend on an Attack Helicopter. While it's easily taken out by an EMP blast or RPG, the drone's small size and maneuverability make it a hard target to hit. Furthermore, its pair of unguided rockets pack a punch that can seriously weaken a vehicle. While the Buzzard isn't tailored as an anti-infantry drone, its rockets can be effective in dispersing enemies guarding tightly enclosed interior locations.

RQ-10 Parrot

Unlocked at: Level 6

Cost: 250 BP

Strengths: Can paint a target for your entire team to see. Useful when working well with a team.

Weaknesses: No offensive capabilities, weak armor, and very susceptible to EMP.

Notes: A battery-powered, remote-control quadricopter. Cameras relay targeting info to teammates. Vulnerable to EMP, small arms fire, and anti-air rockets.

This is the air drone alternative to the AQ-11 Buzzard. This has no offensive capabilities, but can "tag" specific enemies for the rest of your team to intercept and kill. Once the Parrot finds a foe and targets them with a large red marker, the enemy's location is transferred to every teammate. The location is visible even through buildings, and is extremely annoying for the targeted foe, but isn't permanent. This allows you to find your opposing team's more troublesome players, or those sniping from a particular area, or at a particularly advantageous choke point, and nullify them (or alternately, avoid the area).

MQ60 AT Rhino

Unlocked at: Level 21

Cost: 400 BP

Strengths: Excellent at taking down enemy vehicles, especially tanks. Lock-on attacks are great for helicopter take-downs.

Weaknesses: Very poor against infantry units, so not advisable on maps without vehicles.

Notes: A battery-powered, multi-terrain tracked drone. The anti-tank variant has two modes of fire: unguided and lock-on. Vulnerable to EMP and melee damage.

This is the ground drone alternative to the MQ50 MG Wolverine. The "AT" in this drone's title should give away its primary (and recommended) function: to destroy tanks and other vehicles. Do not employ this against enemy infantry units (except as a last resort), because the accuracy against human targets is extremely inconsistent. Instead, use its lock-on target to defeat helicopters and ground vehicles. Rhinos are extremely effective at removing airborne threats, and should definitely be part of an anti-vehicle loadout.

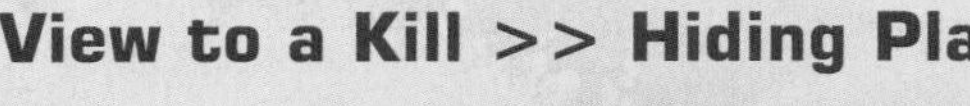

View to a Kill >> Hiding Places

When using drones or airstrikes, you should be crouching or proned. It isn't worth keeping a teammate around to guard your back—they are more valuable in the combat zone—so you need to be as hidden as possible. Whether that's hanging out under a bridge **[13]**, or pushing yourself into the corner of a wall in an area on the edge of the map where nobody goes **[14]**, seek out a low-trafficked area to control your vehicles from.

Airstrikes

General Notes: Whenever you call for air support to provide a large offensive missile, you access a UCAV over the battlefield, which brings up a targeting map **[15]**. Then you can point to a location and launch a massive retaliatory strike **[16]**.

Hellfire

Unlocked at: Level 1

Cost: 1,300 BP

Strengths: Complete control over the rocket all the way to the ground. Two attacks; almost always results in a kill each time.

Weaknesses: The explosion radius isn't as wide as the other airstrikes.

Notes: Two UCAV-launched air-to-surface precision guided missiles. Fly-by-wire allows post-launch guidance correction. Highly effective against vehicles.

Many players favor this airstrike over the other two. It's available at a lower level, costs less, and gives you the most control over where the missiles land.

It comes with two rockets. You constantly guide each missile (one at a time) down to the ground. With this ability to continuously change lirection all the way to ground contact, this missile's only drawback s its relatively small explosive blast radius (compared to the other airstrikes). With competent aiming though, you're usually guaranteed kill for each missile; concentrate on removing one enemy per missile strike. This attack is more useful on larger maps (such as Farm), where enemies tend not to bunch up; allowing you to fire your second missile n a completely different location.

Cluster Bomb

Unlocked at: Level 44

Cost: 1,600 BP

Strengths: Devastating when used on grouped enemies. Extremely powerful. Good to use in maps without vehicles.

Weaknesses: Expensive. Unguided.

Notes: A single-use, UCAV-launched guided cluster bomb. High-altitude dispersal creates large area of effect. Effective against nfantry and vehicles.

This airstrike features only one bomb and costs a lot of Battle Points, so reserve it for removing a large number of enemy threats. The detonation occurs above the target area, and the blast radius is ar bigger than the other two airstrikes.

Some players deem the cost of this weapon to be too high for ts effect. You can purchase the Hellfire much earlier, or have points eft over for other advantageous purchases. This is best used where wo or three enemies are bunched, in tighter maps like Cul-de-sac or Suburb. If the foes are closer together, this attack makes even more sense. It's something to purchase when playing maps that don't allow vehicles.

White Phosphorous

Unlocked at: Level 17

Cost: 1,300 BP

Strengths: Great for taking out groups of foes. Good to use in maps without vehicles.

Weaknesses: Expensive to purchase. Unguided.

Notes: A single-use, UCAV-launched white phosphorous guided missile. Large area of effect. Tissue burns and smoke inhalation cause nstant death.

When you've picked a point on the battlefield for this missile to explode, the detonation occurs above the area, and not at ground evel. A reasonably large (but not as big as a Cluster Bomb) sized area s coated in fire. Like the Cluster Bomb, this is best used where at east two or three enemies are bunched together, in tighter maps like Cul-de-sac or Suburb. You may find it easier to save up for this when playing maps that don't allow vehicle purchases.

Rocket Launchers

General Notes: Rocket launchers are not designed to be fired at infantry, and will most likely miss them. They're specifically designed for ground vehicle and aircraft takedowns, so target vehicles **[17]**.

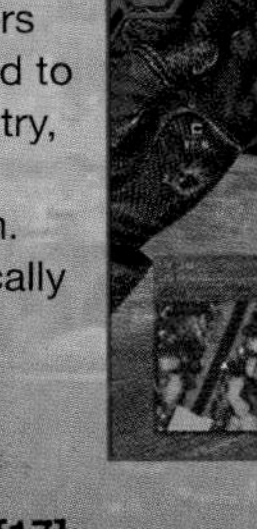

17

RPG Launcher

Unlocked at: Level 1

Cost: 250 BP

Strengths: Excellent for vehicle takedowns; especially tanks, LAVs, Humvees, and ground drones.

Weaknesses: Difficult to strike airborne enemies or infantry.

Notes: Disposable dumbfire rocket-propelled grenade launcher. Comes equipped with high-explosive warheads.

This is an extremely potent weapon when employed against enemy vehicles, and especially the ground vehicles (tanks, LAVs, Humvees). Although you may wish to use it against enemy infantry (especially clusters of them, or when attempting a one-shot kill), the RPG Launcher is much less effective, and usually misses. Ignore infantry targets unless you have no other offensive option.

The RPG Launcher rocket fires at a slightly slower rate than the Proximity Launcher, but is more powerful and can demolish a mechanized enemy in fewer shots. However, it can be avoided easily by air vehicles.

Proximity Launcher

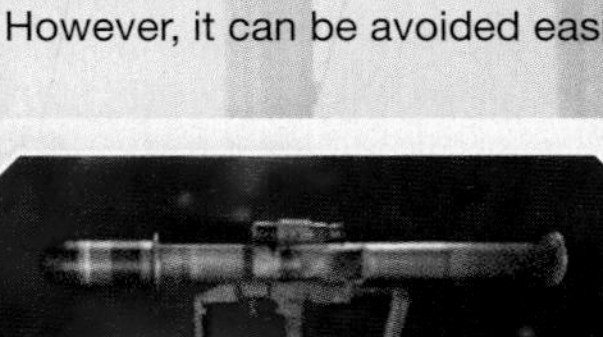

Unlocked at: Level 31

Cost: 250 BP

Strengths: Excellent for ground or airborne vehicle takedowns, especially air drones and helicopters.

Weaknesses: Difficult to strike infantry. Less damaging than an RPG Launcher.

Notes: Dumbfire rocket launcher that uses a sophisticated distance sensor to trigger detonation when in close proximity to an enemy vehicle.

Remember that the rockets fired from this launcher are intelligent enough to know when they are close to an enemy vehicle, and will explode immediately afterward. The Proximity Launcher projectile is much faster than the RPG Launcher, and is therefore favored when tackling helicopters. However, the attack strength isn't as powerful as the RPG Launcher.

Proximity Launchers are ideal for taking down enemy air drones, and offer a solution for removing these often annoying threats.

Vehicles

General Notes: Available on most (but not all) maps, vehicles offer faster movement, toughened armor, and enhanced weapons systems, and can turn the tide of a battle when used effectively. You can purchase three ground vehicles **[18]**, and two airborne helicopters **[19]**, or join in a passenger seat, usually with a weapon to use. Vehicles are slowed and crippled by EMP weapons. There is no difference, aside from coloration and slight visual differences, between the USA and KPA vehicles. Damage Humvee and LAV ground vehicles with the RPG Launcher, grenades, C4, and LMGs and to a lesser extent, the Proximity Launcher and assault

18

rifles. You can also damage a tank using explosives; guns don't penetrate the thicker armor. Cripple a vehicle using EMP Grenades or the EMP Launcher; this slows any turrets as well, allowing your teammates more time to finish their job.

Another excellent choice for removing enemy vehicles is the Hellfire missile, which can be launched from a hiding spot, without the usual hassle of moving to get a clear shot. This is well worth the BP expenditure, especially due to the BPs you accrue for this takedown. The Hellfire's controllability (so you can keep targeting the enemy vehicle) wins out over the other "dumbfire" airstrikes.

Vehicles are also useful the moment you or your rivals capture and hold the control points and the match moves up to the next set of points. Instead of sprinting there on foot, some players like to hitch a lift, or kill themselves (with a grenade), and respawn in a vehicle to quickly drive and hold a new control point.

Be sure to try and run over an enemy you can't quite shoot at; striking one usually results in an instant kill. Also try using the LAV and tanks as defensive vehicles; when you've captured a control point, have your ground vehicles roll in and keep enemies at bay (and this works very well, as long as you have enough space).

TIP 영리한

Every ground vehicle has a boost; press it for a burst of acceleration, which is useful for reaching control points, heading uphill with more speed, or hitting enemies. The more mobile the vehicle, the more effective this boost is.

TIP 영리한

Some vehicles already come equipped with one or two abilities, although these can be swapped out just like infantry abilities: A very useful vehicular ability is the Monkey Wrench, which allows the vehicle to self-repair. This is usually recommended over most (if not all) of the other abilities, for obvious reasons.

TIP 영리한

Taking down vehicles is very lucrative, because you receive Battle Points for the vehicle destruction, and each enemy killed inside the vehicle. Sometimes it is worth the expenditure for (for example) a Hellfire missile, because this can almost pay for itself.

Humvee

Cost: 300 BP

Strengths: Fast and cheap to purchase. Run over enemies for an instant kill.

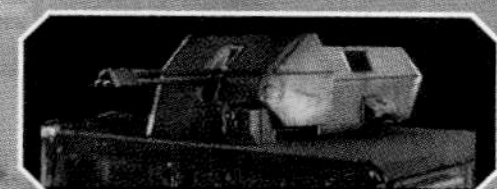

Weaknesses: Light armor and lack of offensive weapon for the driver.

Abilities: Full Tank (1)

Notes: During console matches, up to two persons can be inside the Humvee. During PC matches, up to four persons can be inside the Humvee. The first (driver) position does not feature a weapon (aside from the vehicle itself, which you can ram into opponents). The second (gunner) position offers a 360-degree view, but is vulnerable to enemy shots (usually sniper fire). Constant movement by the (trusted) driver is of paramount importance. The Humvee is the fastest of the three land vehicles, and the cheapest to purchase.

Humvees are most useful during the initial spawn in for a Ground Control match because they can be sued to quickly advance to objectives and are readily available with the default Battle Points allotment.

A well-placed rocket (or Proximity Launcher, although that is usually for air vehicles) will destroy a Humvee in one or two shots. This makes making it extremely vulnerable to enemy fire, -- so keep moving. This isn't to say the Humvee can't be a considerable offensive force; with a nimble driver and an accurate gunner, these can be very troublesome.

Light Armor Vehicle

Cost: 1,000 BP

Strengths: Extremely effective with two adept gunners. More agile than a tank, and better armored than a Humvee.

Weaknesses: Medium-strength armor suffers when bombarded by a tank or rockets.

Abilities: Big Stick (3)

Notes: During console matches, up to two persons can be inside the LAV. During PC matches, up to four persons can be inside the LAV. The first (driver) position has access to the vehicle's primary weapon: a powerful cannon that is mainly used to defeat enemy infantry. The LAV is also effective at taking down aerial vehicles, enemy Humvees, and to a lesser extent, tanks.

The second fire position allows the user to fire from a protected position inside the turret with either dumbfire missiles or ground-to-air lock on missiles. In fact, two adept players working in tandem in an LAV and firing both weapons can take out a tank with speed and ease. Naturally, you'll need to do this quickly, because two shots from a tank can sometimes take out an LAV if hit in the correct spot.

The LAV has a maneuverability (and slight speed) advantage over the Heavy Tank, because it can trundle to a corner, peek out and fire a few rounds, and reverse into cover far more adeptly than the tank. It can skirt a map to reach a control point or remove snipers, or simply zoom up a road to take and hold a middle control point. The LAV's turret spins more quickly than a tank's, too -- making it a preference for some players.

The LAV is excellent for taking down Scout Helicopters -- both the primary and secondary weapons are ideal for this role. If you're being buzzed by one of these enemies, spawn an LAV, and fire on it. The Scout Helicopter's machine guns cause only minor damage to the LAV armor, giving you an advantage in this instance.

Heavy Tank

Cost: 1,200 BP

Strengths: Exceptional armor and devastating offensive capabilities. Great for hunting other vehicles.

Weaknesses: The least agile vehicle, the tank is more difficult to maneuver in tight areas, and slower to turn.The focus of enemy fire. A slow turret.

Abilities: Faster Reload (2)

Notes: During both console and PC matches, up to two persons can be inside the Heavy Tank. The first (driver) position allows you to fire the vehicle's main cannon, which is incredibly powerful. Whether you're striking an infantryman or another tank, this usually removes the threat in one or two shots. The second position wields a machine gun from the turret, an extremely effective weapon (except against other armor). The rotation speed of the machine gun is much faster than that of the main cannon -- so use this machine gun to keep foes at mid to close range at bay. This may include infantry who are attempting to EMP or hit the tank with rockets or C4.

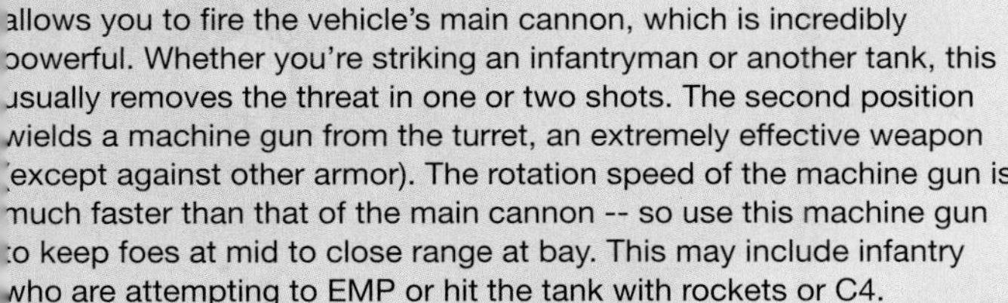

The tank offers the heaviest armor of all ground vehicles, but at a cost of speed thus making it easier to hit and the focus of many attacks. Some players use a tank to lure enemies away from other locations: the foes focus on the tank rather than quicker vehicles or infantry attempting to reach a tactically important area.

Tanks are excellent for hunting LAVs and Humvees. The increased protection that a tank has compared to the LAV or Humvee can allow infantry to use it as a shield from enemy attacks. Be sure to use your side armor, switching sides when the first armor is damaged.

TIP 영리한

When you're attacking either an LAV or Heavy Tank, aim for the front or back of the vehicle, where the armor is almost nonexistent!

If you're being attacked while inside a vehicle, turn your machine to the side that has the most armor left, especially if one side has already been weakened. Look at the damage reading on your screen to judge this.

If you've been attacked with an EMP blast, and your turrets have slowed, make sure you choose the Coated or Gyro Vehicle ability next time, which lessens this problem considerably.

Whether you're respawning or not, accompanying a teammate in a vehicle is an excellent plan. Two teammates in a vehicle are a far more potent threat and very difficult to destroy. Remember that you can run and leap into a friendly vehicle (or out of one) at any time, too.

Scout Helicopter

Cost: 1,500 BP

Strengths: Extremely agile, able to hide behind large scenic cover, powerful weapons, and small size.

Weaknesses: Susceptible to most weapons. Not as powerful as an Attack Heli.

Abilities: Big Stick (3)

Notes: During console matches, one person pilots this airborne vehicle. During PC matches, there is a second position in the cockpit used to help spot enemies using a very similar functionality to the Recon Drone (the RQ-10 Parrot).

Although many players are initially attracted to the armaments of the Attack Helicopter, the Scout Heli offers a whole host of advantages. It is arguably the most proficient killing machine available. Its combination of speed and small size means that once you've mastered the controls, you can hide behind almost any large object -- whether that's a billboard, water tower, clump of trees, or building.

Making use of cover is imperative because the Scout Helicopter is easy to take down (compared to tanks or the Attack Heli). Be constantly on the move, diving down behind cover opportunities while laying waste to the opposition. The only weapons are dual machine-guns, one on each side of the craft. Use these against infantry less versus vehicles because these weapons aren't strong enough to heavily damage the armor.

This craft, like all other vehicles, has a boost and is another great choice for racing to capture a control point, although you're much more vulnerable at lower altitudes.

CAUTION 조심하다

You can receive damage from most weapons (not just LMGs), so keep at a distance, and high up to avoid being taken out of the sky.

TIP 영리한

The Proximity Launcher is a good choice for removing this foe, as are Hellfire missiles and the Rhino drone. RPG Launchers are not recommended, because the pilot can easily avoid them. You can also take down either helicopter using EMP Grenades, although a much better option is to employ an EMP Launcher attachment, which is much easier to aim. The helicopter falls out of the sky, but doesn't explode. However it will once your team attacks! Are you in the helicopter? Then gain altitude so the EMP Launcher shot explodes under you and misses.

Attack Helicopter

Cost: 2,200 BP

Strengths: Devastating rocket salvo attacks; a great tank killer. Rockets affect infantry. Long-range machine guns.

Weaknesses: Not as mobile as a Scout Heli. Expensive.

Abilities: Faster Reload (2)

Abilities: Missile Defense (2)

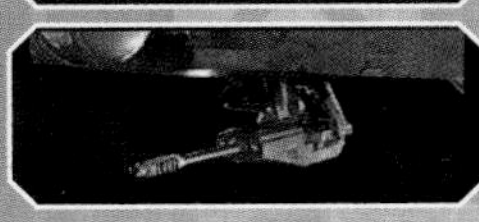

Notes: During console and PC matches, one person pilots this airborne vehicle. There is also a second position.

The pilot controls the craft, and can launch a burst of rockets, which must recharge before another salvo can be launched. These are remarkably powerful and one of the easiest ways to take down a tank (or other ground vehicle). While most projectiles aren't that effective against infantry, this isn't the case with the Attack Helicopter's weapons -- they dominates all ground firepower and can kill multiple foes. The number of vehicles and ground troops you can demolish makes up for this vehicle's high cost.

The secondary position offers a machine gun option, making this arguably the most useful vehicle available. The machine gun can drop foes a great distance away as well as viciously taking infantry out in one or two bursts.

To lengthen your lifespan inside an Attack Helicopter, keep moving and hover behind cover. Think of this as a flying Heavy Tank, and the Scout Heli as an airborne LAV, with a trade off of mobility instead of power.

 Damage Table 

The following information shows the severity of each type of damage a specific weapon inflicts on an enemy, or portion of an enemy. With this information, you can gauge which weapons do the most damage, and to what.

Weapon	Infantry	Infantry (Head)	Ground Drones	Ground Drones Weak Spot (back)	Recon & Air Assault Drones
M4 Rifle	★★★☆☆ †	★★★★★ †	★★☆☆☆	★☆☆☆☆	★★☆☆☆
M16 Rifle	★★★★☆ †	★★★★★ †	★★☆☆☆	★☆☆☆☆	★★☆☆☆
SCAR-L Rifle	★★★★☆ †	★★★★★ †	★★☆☆☆	★★☆☆☆	★★☆☆☆
T3AK Rifle	★★★★☆ †	★★★★★ †	★★☆☆☆	★☆☆☆☆	★★☆☆☆
ACR Rifle	★★★☆☆ †	★★★★★ †	★★☆☆☆	★☆☆☆☆	★★☆☆☆
XM10 Rifle	★★★☆☆ †	★★★★★ †	★★☆☆☆	★☆☆☆☆	★★☆☆☆
M249 LMG	★★★★☆ †	★★★★★ †	★★☆☆☆	★★☆☆☆	★★★☆☆
SCAR-H LMG	★★★☆☆ †	★★★★★ †	★★☆☆☆	★★☆☆☆	★★★☆☆
PWS Diablo SMG	★★★☆☆ †	★★★★☆ †	★☆☆☆☆	★☆☆☆☆	★☆☆☆☆
Super-V SMG	★★★☆☆ †	★★★★☆ †	★☆☆☆☆	★☆☆☆☆	★☆☆☆☆
M110 Sniper	★★★★★💀	★★★★★💀	★★★★☆	★★★☆☆	★★★★★
M200 Sniper	★★★★★💀	★★★★★💀	★★★★☆	★★★☆☆	★★★★★💀
870 Express Shotgun	★★★★★💀 †	★★★★★💀 †	★☆☆☆☆	★☆☆☆☆	★★☆☆☆
M9 Pistol	★★★☆☆ †	★★★★★ †	★★☆☆☆	★☆☆☆☆	★★☆☆☆
Frag Grenade	★★★★★💀	★★★★★💀	★★★★★	★★★★★	★★★★★
Airburst Launcher	★★★★★💀	★★★★★💀	★★★★☆	★★★★☆	★★★★★
Grenade Launcher	★★★★★	★★★★★	★★★☆☆	★★★☆☆	★★★☆☆
Shotgun Attachment	★☆☆☆☆ †	★★☆☆☆ †	★☆☆☆☆ †	★☆☆☆☆ †	★★☆☆☆ †
C4	★★★★★	★★★★★	★★★★★💀	★★★★★💀	★★★★★💀
WP Grenade	★★★★★💀	★★★★★💀	☆☆☆☆☆	☆☆☆☆☆	☆☆☆☆☆
MQ50 MG Wolverine Machine Gun	★★★★☆	★★★★☆	★★☆☆☆	★★☆☆☆	★★☆☆☆
MQ60 AT Rhino Anti-Armor Missiles	★★★★★	★★★★★	★★★☆☆	★★★★★💀	★★★☆☆
MQ60 AT Rhino Rockets	★★★★☆	★★★★☆	★★★☆☆	★★★☆☆	★★★☆☆
Hellfire	★★★★★💀	★★★★★💀	★★★★★	★★★★★	★★★★★
Cluster Bomb	★★★★★💀	★★★★★💀	★★★★★	★★★★★	★★★★★
White Phosphorous	★★★★★💀	★★★★★💀	☆☆☆☆☆	☆☆☆☆☆	☆☆☆☆☆
RPG Launcher	★★★★★	★★★★★	★★★★☆	★★★★★	★★★★★💀
Proximity Launcher	★★★★★	★★★★★	★★★☆☆	★★★★★	★★★★★💀
GAU-19 .50 Cal Gatling gun	★★☆☆☆	★★☆☆☆	★☆☆☆☆	★★★★☆	★★☆☆☆
LAV Anti-Armor Missiles	★★★☆☆	★★★☆☆	★★★★★	★★★★★	★★★★★
LAV M242 Autocannon	★★★★★	★★★★★	★★★★★	★★★★★💀	★★★☆☆
LAV Rockets	★★★★★	★★★★★	★★★★☆	★★★★☆	★★★★★
Heavy Tank Shell	★★★★★💀	★★★★★💀	★★★★★💀	★★★★★	★★★★★
Heavy Tank M2 .50 Cal Machine gun	★★☆☆☆	★★☆☆☆	★☆☆☆☆	★★★★☆	★★☆☆☆
Scout Heli 30mm Chaingun	★★★☆☆	★★★☆☆	★★☆☆☆	★★★★☆	★★★☆☆
Attack Heli 30mm Chaingun	★★★☆☆	★★★☆☆	★★☆☆☆	★★★★☆	★★★☆☆
Attack Heli FFAR barrage	★★★★★	★★★★★	★★★★★	★★★★★	★★★★★

(† This indicates that the weapon's damage varies by range; this is the median value. More damage is inflicted at closer range.)

This chart shows the damage caused per bullet or explosion; fast-firing weapons may inflict the rated damage much faster than single-firing ones

Humvee	LAV	Heavy Tank	Heavy Tank Front	Scout Heli	Attack Heli	UAV Drone
★☆☆☆☆	☆☆☆☆☆	☆☆☆☆☆	☆☆☆☆☆	★☆☆☆☆	★☆☆☆☆	☆☆☆☆☆
★☆☆☆☆	☆☆☆☆☆	☆☆☆☆☆	☆☆☆☆☆	★☆☆☆☆	★☆☆☆☆	☆☆☆☆☆
★☆☆☆☆	☆☆☆☆☆	☆☆☆☆☆	☆☆☆☆☆	★☆☆☆☆	★☆☆☆☆	☆☆☆☆☆
★☆☆☆☆	☆☆☆☆☆	☆☆☆☆☆	☆☆☆☆☆	★☆☆☆☆	★☆☆☆☆	☆☆☆☆☆
★☆☆☆☆	☆☆☆☆☆	☆☆☆☆☆	☆☆☆☆☆	★☆☆☆☆	★☆☆☆☆	☆☆☆☆☆
★☆☆☆☆	☆☆☆☆☆	☆☆☆☆☆	☆☆☆☆☆	★☆☆☆☆	★☆☆☆☆	☆☆☆☆☆
★☆☆☆☆	☆☆☆☆☆	☆☆☆☆☆	☆☆☆☆☆	★☆☆☆☆	★☆☆☆☆	★☆☆☆☆
★☆☆☆☆	☆☆☆☆☆	☆☆☆☆☆	☆☆☆☆☆	★☆☆☆☆	★☆☆☆☆	★☆☆☆☆
☆☆☆☆☆	☆☆☆☆☆	☆☆☆☆☆	☆☆☆☆☆	★☆☆☆☆	☆☆☆☆☆	☆☆☆☆☆
☆☆☆☆☆	☆☆☆☆☆	☆☆☆☆☆	☆☆☆☆☆	★☆☆☆☆	☆☆☆☆☆	☆☆☆☆☆
★☆☆☆☆	☆☆☆☆☆	☆☆☆☆☆	☆☆☆☆☆	★☆☆☆☆	★☆☆☆☆	★★☆☆☆
★★☆☆☆	☆☆☆☆☆	☆☆☆☆☆	☆☆☆☆☆	★☆☆☆☆	★☆☆☆☆	★★☆☆☆
★☆☆☆☆	☆☆☆☆☆	☆☆☆☆☆	☆☆☆☆☆	★☆☆☆☆	☆☆☆☆☆	☆☆☆☆☆
☆☆☆☆☆	☆☆☆☆☆	☆☆☆☆☆	☆☆☆☆☆	★☆☆☆☆	☆☆☆☆☆	☆☆☆☆☆
★★★☆☆	★★☆☆☆	★★☆☆☆	☆☆☆☆☆	★★★☆☆	★★☆☆☆	★★☆☆☆
★★★☆☆	★★☆☆☆	☆☆☆☆☆	☆☆☆☆☆	★★★☆☆	★★☆☆☆	★★★☆☆
★☆☆☆☆	★☆☆☆☆	☆☆☆☆☆	☆☆☆☆☆	★★★☆☆	★☆☆☆☆	★★★☆☆
☆☆☆☆☆	☆☆☆☆☆	☆☆☆☆☆	☆☆☆☆☆	★★☆☆☆ †	☆☆☆☆☆	☆☆☆☆☆
★★★★★	★★★☆☆	★★☆☆☆	★☆☆☆☆	★★★★★	★★★★☆	★★★★☆
☆☆☆☆☆	☆☆☆☆☆	☆☆☆☆☆	☆☆☆☆☆	☆☆☆☆☆	☆☆☆☆☆	☆☆☆☆☆
★☆☆☆☆	☆☆☆☆☆	☆☆☆☆☆	☆☆☆☆☆	★☆☆☆☆	★☆☆☆☆	☆☆☆☆☆
★★☆☆☆	★☆☆☆☆	★☆☆☆☆	★☆☆☆☆	★☆☆☆☆	★☆☆☆☆	★★☆☆☆
★☆☆☆☆	★☆☆☆☆	☆☆☆☆☆	☆☆☆☆☆	★☆☆☆☆	★☆☆☆☆	★★★★★
★★★★★	★★★★☆	★★★☆☆	★★★☆☆	★★★★★	★★★☆☆	★★★★☆
★★★★☆	★★★☆☆	★★★☆☆	★★★☆☆	★★★☆☆	★★★☆☆	★★★★☆
☆☆☆☆☆	☆☆☆☆☆	☆☆☆☆☆	☆☆☆☆☆	☆☆☆☆☆	☆☆☆☆☆	☆☆☆☆☆
★★★★☆	★★★☆☆	★★★☆☆	★★☆☆☆	★★★★★	★★★★★	★★★★★
★★☆☆☆	★★★☆☆	★★☆☆☆	★★☆☆☆	★★★☆☆	★★☆☆☆	★★★☆☆
★☆☆☆☆	☆☆☆☆☆	☆☆☆☆☆	☆☆☆☆☆	★☆☆☆☆	★☆☆☆☆	★☆☆☆☆
★★★☆☆	★★★☆☆	★★☆☆☆	★★☆☆☆	★★★☆☆	★★★☆☆	★★★☆☆
★★☆☆☆	★☆☆☆☆	★☆☆☆☆	★☆☆☆☆	★☆☆☆☆	★☆☆☆☆	★★★☆☆
★★★☆☆	★☆☆☆☆	★☆☆☆☆	★☆☆☆☆	★★★☆☆	★★★☆☆	★★★☆☆
★★★★★	★★★☆☆	★★☆☆☆	★★☆☆☆	★★★★★	★★★★★	★★★★★
★☆☆☆☆	☆☆☆☆☆	☆☆☆☆☆	☆☆☆☆☆	★☆☆☆☆	★☆☆☆☆	★☆☆☆☆
★☆☆☆☆	☆☆☆☆☆	☆☆☆☆☆	☆☆☆☆☆	★☆☆☆☆	★☆☆☆☆	★☆☆☆☆
★☆☆☆☆	☆☆☆☆☆	☆☆☆☆☆	☆☆☆☆☆	★☆☆☆☆	★☆☆☆☆	★☆☆☆☆
★★★☆☆	★☆☆☆☆	★☆☆☆☆	★☆☆☆☆	★☆☆☆☆	★☆☆☆☆	★★★☆☆

LEGEND

★★★★★ ☠

Devastating

Usually an instant kill

★★★★★

Very Strong

Incredible damage

★★★★☆

Strong

Impressive damage

★★★☆☆

Effective

Moderate damage

★★☆☆☆

Light

Low impact damage

★☆☆☆☆

Weak

Very minor damage

☆☆☆☆☆

Ineffective

Absolutely no effect

ABILITIES

General Notes: Internal skills that you've chosen for yourself or a vehicle you're driving are known as abilities. You have five points to spend on abilities, which cost 1, 2, or 3 points. Choose two or three abilities to reach five points, and then test out the abilities during matches to see which you find most beneficial. The following lists give some tips on whether an ability may be right for you.

Infantry Abilities

Crater-to-Order

Unlocked at: Level 34

Cost (Ability Points): 1

Notes: Large drone explosion on death

If you're purposely focusing on drones to help you in battle, purchase this ability. A lot of drone abilities are cheap, so use them! Although beneficial to both drone types, this turns an aerial drone into a real instrument of destruction; fly straight at the enemy when your battery is dying, and attempt the extra kills.

Drone Be Gone!

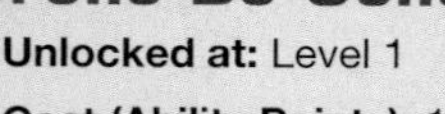

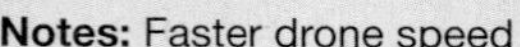

Unlocked at: Level 1

Cost (Ability Points): 1

Notes: Faster drone speed

If you're purposely focusing on drones to help you in battle, purchase this ability. This is particularly excellent for aerial drones, because it makes them more difficult to hit, or easier for them to hide behind cover, and helps prevent them from getting shot down.

Ghost

Unlocked at: Level 1

Cost (Ability Points): 1

Notes: Hidden from UAV sweeps

This relies on the fact that UAV Sweeps are being used by your enemy, which may not happen as often as you'd think. Many players prefer combat-based abilities, although this can help if you're focusing on a stealth-based loadout (a sniper, or hiding while sending out drones).

My Buddy

Unlocked at: Level 8

Cost (Ability Points): 1

Notes: Longer drone battery duration

If you're purposely focusing on drones to help you in battle, purchase this ability. This allows your drone to last longer before it becomes inoperable, allowing for a large kill streak, or at the very least, enabling you to reach an enemy and attack them for longer.

Quickdraw

Unlocked at: Level 1

Cost (Ability Points): 1

Notes: Quicker speed into aiming down sight

This is extremely useful when you need to "outdraw" an enemy; targeting them more accurately using sight aiming (not firing from the hip), or once you chance upon an opponent and need to dispatch them through a scope, as fast as possible. The larger the weapon, the longer it takes to aim down, making this perfect for sniper rifles.

Tactical Reload

Unlocked at: Level 1

Cost (Ability Points): 1

Notes: Faster reload speed

This is ideal for an SMG (for example) because you lessen the chances of dying during the SMG's numerous reloads. LMGs, which take longer than assault rifles to reload, are another weapon to use with this. It even benefits sniper rifles, allowing faster shooting.

Blastwave

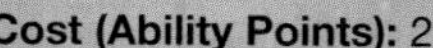

Unlocked at: Level 42

Cost (Ability Points): 2

Notes: Larger blast radius for explosives

This doubles the radius of any grenade, RPG, or C4 explosion (but not vehicle explosives such as the Attack Heli's rockets). As with Utility Belt, if you're a practitioner of explosives use, this is a must-have ability. Note this doesn't increase the damage (choose Boomer for that), just how wide the explosion is.

Grave Robber

Unlocked at: Level 18

Cost (Ability Points): 2

Notes: Pickup ammo dropped by dead soldiers

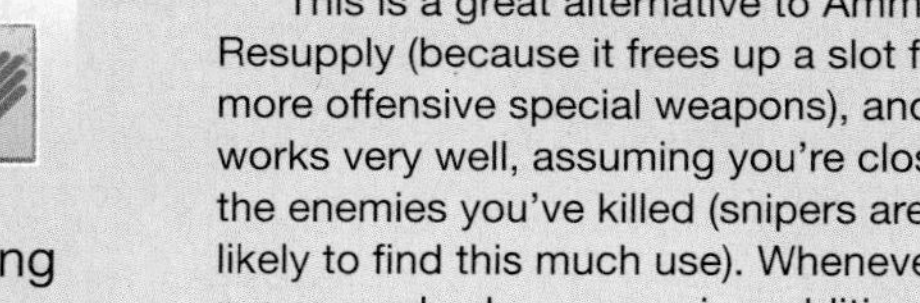

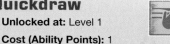

> **NOTE 알아두세요**
>
> When the notes mention an ability allows you to accomplish something "quicker," think around half the normal time. Ability costs are color-coded: 1 Point = Gray. 2 Points = Blue. 3 Points = Red

This is a great alternative to Ammo Resupply (because it frees up a slot for more offensive special weapons), and works very well, assuming you're close to the enemies you've killed (snipers aren't likely to find this much use). Whenever you run over a body, you receive additional ammo related to your weapons, no matter what you or your foe was carrying.

Now That's a Knife

Unlocked at: Level 1

Cost (Ability Points): 2

Notes: Increased melee range with quicker recovery

When you attempt a melee strike, you lunge at an enemy (once your reticle turns red), and go in for a stab. This doubles the distance at which the strike is effective, and quickens the time in-between strikes. Combine this with a pistol, because putting the pistol away takes less time compared with other weapons. A great choice in close-quarter fighting against infantry or drones.

Penny Pincher

Unlocked at: Level 5

Cost (Ability Points): 2

Notes: Equipped special weapons cost less

If you're thinking of purchasing an RPG Launcher or airstrike, this ability lessens the purchase price. Because it removes only a modicum of Battle Points from an item's cost, and your choice of other abilities is now more limited, this isn't usually the first choice for many players.

Quick Healer

Unlocked at: Level 47

Cost (Ability Points): 2

Notes: Faster health regeneration

When you get shot, your vision becomes redder. This fades to normal if you hide, and fades to black if you're continuously shot. This ability returns you to normal health twice as quickly. Because

you rarely manage to hide after being shot (usually the enemy finishes you with glee), this a less-used ability, ditched in favor of offensive abilities (such as Steady Aim). Combine this with the Flak Jacket and become a toughened shock trooper!

Steady Aim

Unlocked at: Level 26

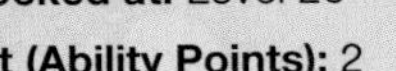

Cost (Ability Points): 2

Notes: Less recoil when aiming down sight

Many players prefer using the SCAR-L simply because of this ability; typically the SCAR recoils into the air, but with this, all shots usually land where you aim. This is great even at extremely long ranges; the most vicious of recoils is tamed. This is also useful for any other primary weapon except the shotgun.

Thick Skin

Unlocked at: Level 1

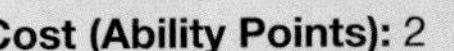

Cost (Ability Points): 2

Notes: Increased drone health

If you're purposely focusing on drones to help you in battle, purchase this ability. This ability makes your drone more difficult to destroy. Effective for both types of drone, this is especially useful for ground drones because they are more easily shot at compared to aerial drones.

Utility Belt

Unlocked at: Level 38

Cost (Ability Points): 2

Notes: Extra special grenades

This gives you four WP, Flashbang, EMP, or C4 "special" explosives or grenades instead of two. This allows you to spam grenades into a target or location, and not worry too much about running out. If you use these grenades all the time, pick this!

Boomer

Unlocked at: Level 30

Cost (Ability Points): 3

Notes: Increased explosive damage

Blastwave increases an explosive's radius of damage. Boomer increases the actual damage of any special grenade, RPG, or C4 explosion (but not vehicle explosives). As with Utility Belt, if you're a practitioner of explosives, this is a must-have ability, but be wary of some limited effectiveness. An Airburst Launcher (for example) usually kills a foe anyway, and your foe can't be "even more dead."

Fist Full

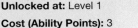

Unlocked at: Level 1

Cost (Ability Points): 3

Notes: Extra grenades

Bumping your total starting Frag Grenade (and only your Frag Grenades) count from two to four, this is an excellent ability if you employ them. Learn when it is most beneficial to use grenades, and if this suits your style of play, pick this ability. Spamming grenades and cleaning up a wounded enemy with an AR is a great tactic that is helped by this. Remember to cook your grenades!

Grizzled

Unlocked at: Level 13

Cost (Ability Points): 3

Notes: Increased experience gains

This doesn't affect your Battle Points, only the experience you are awarded in battle. It is reasonably fast to level up at lower levels, making this less helpful than a more potent combat ability. If you're constantly worried about increasing your level, then pick this. It's one for bragging rights.

Straight from the Hip

Unlocked at: Level 1

Cost (Ability Points): 3

Notes: Reduced weapon deviation when shooting from the hip

When you're rushing a house, you're not likely to be aiming down your sights; so pick this to keep your regular (hip) aiming steadier. The bullet fire won't spread out as much, making it excellent for SMGs, AR, and LMG loadouts. Use with a SCAR-L for a lethal three-round burst that hits home almost every time. Extremely effective.

Vehicle Abilities

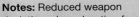

Full Tank

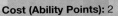

Unlocked at: Level 1

Cost (Ability Points): 1

Notes: Longer vehicle sprint times

Boosting the vehicle farther lets you get just that bit closer to a control point or area of cover, which has numerous benefits. Cheap to purchase, either this or the Speed Boost are usually chosen.

Gyro

Unlocked at: Level 1

Cost (Ability Points): 1

Notes: Faster turret turn speed

If your vehicle doesn't have a turret (such as the Scout Heli), then refrain from wasting your time with this. However, for the ground vehicles this is an excellent choice, especially for vehicles (like the tank) that have slow turrets to begin with. For the Humvee, with a turret that's already quick, this may not be as vital.

Speed Boost

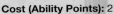

Unlocked at: Level 33

Cost (Ability Points): 1

Notes: Faster top speed

Figure out whether you're the sort of driver who hits the top speed of the vehicles you're driving. You may need a longer sprint (Full Tank ability) instead, although a quicker tank or a more nimble helicopter is even more dangerous!

Coated

Unlocked at: Level 11

Cost (Ability Points): 2

Notes: Shorter EMP durations

Coated is beneficial to ground vehicles more than airborne ones, and handy only if the enemies are ruthless in their use of EMP weapons. Choose this to shake off an EMP attack at a faster rate than normal. The Gyro ability may negate (or augment) some of the help this gives, because a faster turret (even when the vehicle is crippled) is always handy when every other function has failed!

Faster Reload

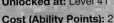

Unlocked at: Level 1

Cost (Ability Points): 2

Notes: Faster reload and cooldown for weapons

More offensive capabilities? Making your vehicle that much more devastating is always a good idea. However, if you're dominating already, or the enemy is taking you down despite your firepower, think about a different ability, such as Coated.

Missile Defense

Unlocked at: Level 41

Cost (Ability Points): 2

Notes: Faster cooldown for Missile Defeat

With vehicles that allow you to send out flares to defeat missiles, this can be

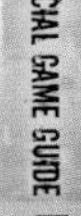

extremely helpful. Helicopters benefit greatly from this, because it makes them even more difficult to hit. If you don't use this function, or find other ways to avoid missiles (such as flying at higher altitudes or hiding behind cover), ignore this.

Big Stick

Unlocked at: Level 1

Cost (Ability Points): 3

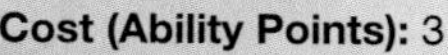

Notes: Increased vehicle damage

A vehicle is troublesome enough to take down at the best of times, but with additional damage, they become increasingly difficult to stop. This means you can try entering areas of higher enemy concentration, and is great if you plan to spend most of your time in a vehicle.

Ejection Seat

Unlocked at: Level 20

Cost (Ability Points): 3

Notes: Auto-Eject on vehicle destruction

This obviously important ability allows you to make more daring maneuvers, knowing that you're safe until the bitter end, and that the enemy won't receive Battle Points for killing you inside your metal tomb. Guaranteed additional life? Only ignore this if you've already learned the precise moment when a vehicle is about to become a fireball, and can trust yourself (and your passengers) to manually eject in time.

Monkey Wrench

Unlocked at: Level 48

Cost (Ability Points): 3

Notes: Passive vehicle repair

This can turn an annoying Scout Heli into a harbinger of doom. With this regenerative ability, any driver or pilot adept enough to find cover can keep a vehicle working for as long as is necessary. This is usually more effective if you're constantly moving, or providing supporting fire, rather in the thick of it.

WELCOME TO THE MULTIPLAYER MAPS

Seize America or save her—whether you take on the mantle of the expansionist KPA or fight for freedom as a US soldier, knowing how to read maps is essential to claiming victory on the multiplayer battlefield. Learn the fundamentals to navigate the maps in the chapters that follow:

Game Modes

Each map supports a specific set of modes. Reference these five icons at the top-right corner of the main map to identify which modes are offered.

Ground Control

Battle Commander Ground Control

Team Deathmatch

Battle Commander Team Deathmatch

Xbox 360 Only

Map Legend and Icons

Each maps is divided into three zones: Neutral, KPA, and US. Icons appearing on the map show points of interest in each of these zones. Many of these points are tagged to pictures in the Tactics section that follows each map. Use the following icons to help shape your tactics on the battlefield:

Control Point Objective

Zone Boundary

Vantage Point

Key Locations

Tactical Icons

Tagged to every tactic are a set of handy icons that let you know the type of action described. All tactics outlined are for Ground Control, although many are applicable to Team Deathmatch as indicated by the handy icon shown below. Because not all zones are available for Team Deathmatch, only those maps supporting the mode feature the icon. Use the following icons to quickly identify tactics pertinent to your situation:

Team Deathmatch-specific tactic

Offensive tactic

Defensive tactic

Good hiding spot

US-specific tactic

KPA-specific tactic

YOUR INTRODUCTION TO THE MULTIPLAYER MAPS BEGINS NOW!

ANGEL ISLAND

The forested hills of Angel Island are anything but heavenly—KPA forces have made this once-tranquil island into a hellish battlefield dominated by snipers, attack helicopters, and armored vehicles. This expansive Ground Control map features three zones partitioned by large wooded hills and dirt roads.

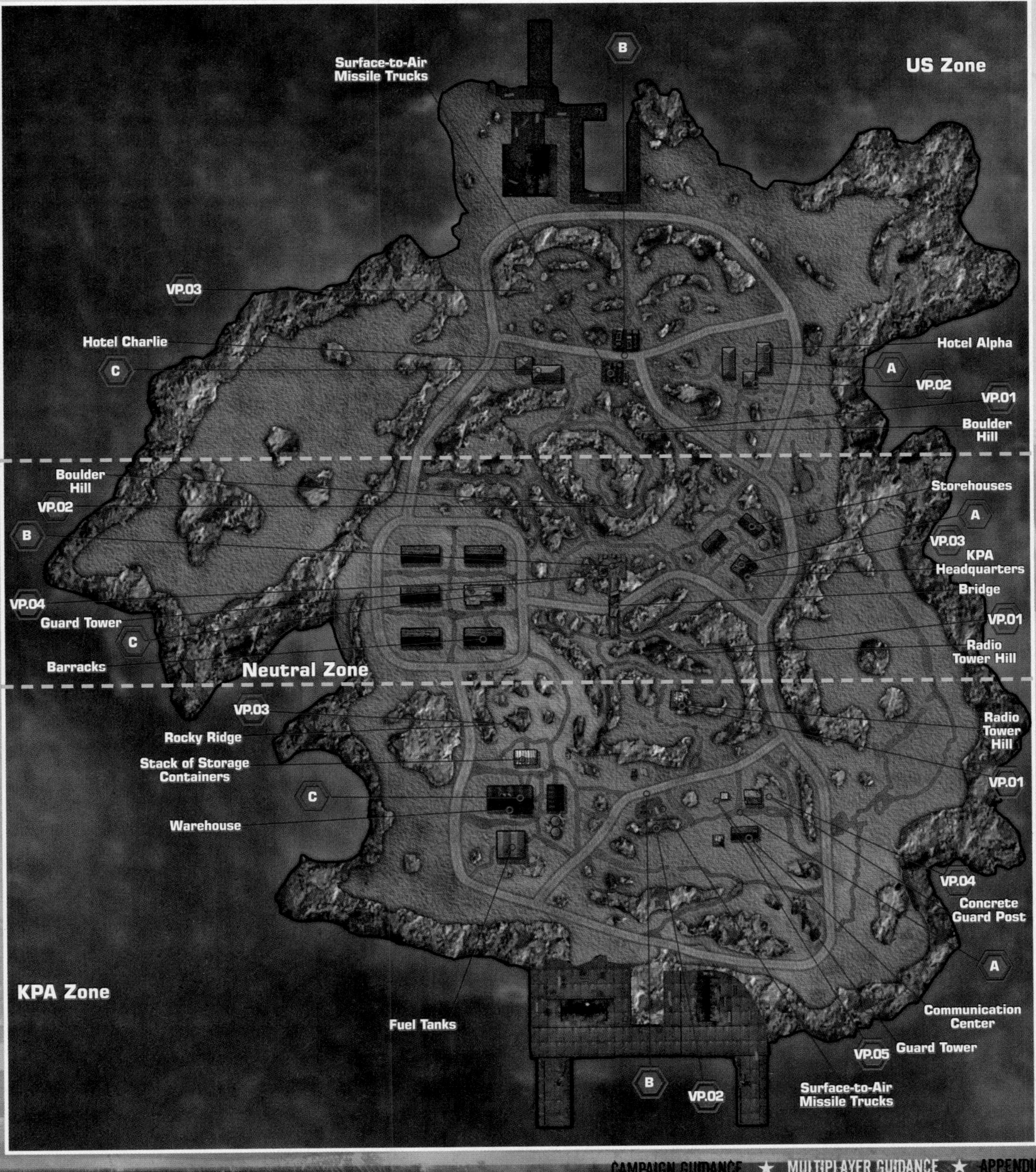

US Zone
B
Surface-to-Air Missile Trucks
VP.03
Hotel Charlie
C
Hotel Alpha
A
VP.02
VP.01
Boulder Hill

Neutral Zone
Boulder Hill
VP.02
B
VP.04
Guard Tower
C
Barracks
Storehouses
A
VP.03
KPA Headquarters
Bridge
VP.01
Radio Tower Hill

KPA Zone
VP.03
Rocky Ridge
Stack of Storage Containers
C
Warehouse
Radio Tower Hill
VP.01
VP.04
Concrete Guard Post
A
Communication Center
Guard Tower
VP.05
Fuel Tanks
B
VP.02
Surface-to-Air Missile Trucks

NEUTRAL ZONE

Spanning the central part of Angel Island, the neutral zone encompasses a residential area requisitioned by KPA forces and turned into barracks, KPA Headquarters on the island, and a lookout station with bridge access to Radio Tower Hill.

Resting within the valley created by three hills—Radio Tower Hill on the KPA side, and Boulder Hill and Rocky Ridge toward the US side—the neutral zone is a sniper's paradise with a slew of fantastic vantage points at your disposal. The team that dominates the sniping battle in the hills is likely to win the game.

Key Locations

- Radio Tower Hill
- Boulder Hill
- Barracks
- Bridge
- Guard Tower, Control Point Bravo
- KPA Headquarters
- Storehouses

Make capturing Control Point Alpha top priority when playing as US given its close proximity to your spawn point. Similarly, it's easiest to go for Control Point Charlie when playing as the KPA. The battle for Bravo is predictably tougher because it sits between the Alpha and Charlie.

Attacks from helicopters and drones, not to mention regular air strikes, make cover imperative. Minimize time spent out in the open and always stay on the move when traveling between points. While not tactically important for capturing areas, the buildings surrounding each control point are good havens from such attacks.

Tactics

Control Point Alpha

CAPTURE DIFFICULTY: ★★★★★

KPA forces have seized the two-story house next to Control Point Alpha and set up a field headquarters **[A]**. As a KPA operative, it's your job to hold it against US soldiers eager to reclaim it. Surprisingly little fighting occurs in the surrounding storehouses. Instead, prolific use of vehicles makes them necessary as cover rather than combat spaces.

Capturing Alpha Out in the Open

While inadvisable given its exposure to aircraft and snipers on the hillsides, capturing Control Point Alpha on foot is tough, but possible. Your best shot at taking it by foot is at the start of the battle when snipers have yet to settle into place and helicopters haven't taken to the skies. Grab the control point quickly, then dart into KPA Headquarters or either of the two storage shelters to defend your new territory. Use the crates and vehicle parked in front of the two storehouses for cover when defending your newly captured territory.

Vehicular Tactics

Pile teammates into a Humvee for a quick capture or save Battle Points to purchase a more powerful Battle Tank and hold Alpha with the threat of cannon fire. Be on the lookout for RPGs and Apaches that can bust up your vehicle. Equip C4 charges and an RPG to defend against vehicles, crouching behind the crates in front of the storehouses or taking aim from the second floor of the KPA Headquarters. An Apache is highly effective in eliminating tanks, but only if you can afford the stiff price.

Seeking Shelter in the Storehouses

Best used as cover from air strikes and helicopter fire, the two storehouses that box in Control Point Alpha can be used for defense. Remain out of sight in either structure and emerge to contest Alpha when an enemy tries taking it. This works particularly well against vehicles, because you can fire rockets or detonate C4 from a safe distance. When playing as the US and seeking to seize Alpha from the KPA, first clear the area by attacking from the storehouses, then push toward the KPA Headquarters.

Defending from KPA Headquarters

Head up to the second floor and peek out the windows overlooking Control Point Alpha for an effective defensive vantage point. The windows facing the control point offer the best attack position against opponents actively contesting Alpha. With the immediate area clear, use the window facing Control Point Bravo to put down enemies as they approach. As the KPA, you can make great use of the headquarters building and fire at US soldiers spawning in the distance behind the storehouses.

Control Point Bravo

CAPTURE DIFFICULTY: 

Elevated above the valley in which Control Points Alpha and Charlie rest, Bravo offers a variety of tactical opportunities [B]. The bridge connecting Radio Tower and Boulder Hills is a high traffic route, enabling you to flank snipers on both hills. The guard tower can be used to capture and hold Bravo, as well as to fire on Control Point Charlie down the road. Lastly, navigating the steep dirt road up Boulder Hill is worth the advantage of capturing Bravo from the protection of an armored vehicle.

Hiking in on Foot

Hiking up the hill isn't advisable because snipers monitor the slopes leading to Control Point Bravo, though you can pull it off with a little skill and a lot of luck. Supply crates offer minimal cover, leaving you with no choice but to capture the point while exposed from all angles. Once you succeed, plant C4 at the center of the control point and take up a defensive position in the guard tower.

Drive-in

Thank goodness for four-wheel drive—spawning a Humvee or LAV to reach Control Point Bravo is a smart tactic that affords speed and protective armor. Taking a tank up the hill is harder, though it can withstand more explosives attacks. Another, needlessly expensive, option involves parachuting out of a helicopter to capture Bravo. But why bother when you can rack up kills and clear the area for your teammates to capture?

Bridge to Bravo

For the KPA, the bridge offers the most direct access to Control Point Bravo; however, expect considerable resistance from US forces holding the control point. Use the burned out cars and assorted debris crowding the bridge for cover as you cross. Coordinate an aerial strike with teammates to create a distraction that can draw attention away from the bridge, freeing the route to Bravo. To defend against such an approach, lay C4 charges on the bridge to discourage crossings.

Guard Tower at Bravo

If you approached Bravo on foot, take a position at the top of the guard tower next to the bridge. While it's not the safest point—snipers have a clear line of sight from all angles and you can bet drones and helicopters will take aim too—the guard tower delivers one of the best views of Control Points Bravo and Charlie. Even better, you can actively capture Bravo from the top of the tower.

Control Point Charlie

CAPTURE DIFFICULTY:

Cozy island homes transformed into dirty barracks set the scene for the battle over Control Point Charlie [C], located in the family room of one such house. Close-quarters combat rules the roost. Vehicles can be helpful, but not critical in winning control. Focus on sniping from Boulder Hill and the neighboring barracks, as well as storming the control point on foot.

Merciless Direct Assault

The fastest, no-frills plan for taking Control Point Charlie is to walk in with guns blazing. Chuck cooked grenades into the living room before stepping inside, then unload on anyone who remains. Opt for a weapon with a high rate of fire such as the Diablo SMG, or go for bombast with an M4 equipped with the shotgun attachment.

Sniping the Neighbors

For a more cautious approach, head into the barracks on either side of Control Point Charlie and aim at enemies occupying the family room. Deploy a Rhino or Buzzard drone to get at hard-to-reach enemies hiding behind the pile of broken furniture at the control point.

Lying Prone on the Furniture

Drop C4 charges at the front door and in the doorway to the adjoining living room to halt would-be invaders before tucking behind the jumble of furniture inside Control Point Charlie. It's a great spot for capturing Charlie and a viable defensive position; just pop up and cap enemies, then sink back behind the furniture. Lie prone and enemies won't be able to see you when sniping from the neighboring barracks, although be prepared to flee from lobbed grenades and disable any nosy drones.

Killer Spot in the Living Room

Sneak into the barracks via the back door and you can peek through the front-facing living room window into Control Point Charlie. Gift a grenade to anyone hiding within Charlie; just angle your throw so that it goes through both windows. Even if you don't manage to kill your opponent, they're likely to pop up and escape, giving you the opportunity to shoot at them through the window.

Second Floor Defense

Guard possession of Control Point Charlie from the front windows on the second floor. Using a mid-range rifle, you can dispatch opponents as distant as the bridge. However, because half the roof is missing, enemies have no trouble calling in air strikes, sending in drones, or firing at you directly from a helicopter.

Vantage Points

Radio Tower Hill

For the best view of the neutral zone, Radio Tower Hill can't be beat **[VP.01]**. KPA forces have the advantage when it comes to sniping from here, given the nearby spawn point, although you can sneak to the hill when playing as the US if you're crafty enough. Sniper wars between Radio Tower Hill and Boulder Hill across the island are common. Equip thermal goggles to identify enemies hiding underneath the foliage.

Boulder Hill

The counterpart to Radio Tower Hill located across the valley, Boulder Hill offers a phenomenal view of the neutral zone **[VP.02]**. Depending on which side of the hill you stand, you can look down at all three control points. Focus on Control Points Alpha and Charlie, as well as taking out snipers situated on Radio Tower Hill. Keep thermal goggles handy to see the heat signatures of enemies hidden beneath the trees.

KPA Headquarters

This defensive vantage point on the second floor of KPA Headquarters allows you to protect Control Point Alpha from capture **[VP.03]**. Take aim from the second floor window facing Control Point Bravo for maximum effect when playing as the US; there's no worry about surprises from the other angle because of the US spawn point down the road. Playing as the KPA is more challenging because you need to monitor the valley near Bravo and the area around Alpha for encroaching US forces.

Guard Tower

Although the Control Point Bravo guard tower lies within multiple lines of sight—Radio Tower Hill and Boulder Hill have a clear view of it—there's still reason to consider using it **[VP.04]**. The risk of death from another sniper's bullet is worth a short stint attacking from atop the guard tower while you capture Bravo below. Once you've seized control, move to a better defensive position on Boulder Hill.

KPA ZONE

KPA facilities along the perimeter of Angel Island come under fire in the battle for this zone. Snipers have fewer vantage points in this coastal area, though the immense Radio Tower Hill still provides an excellent vista and other lower spots can be used to great effect.

Vehicles continue to be relevant on this side of the island, where both Control Points Alpha and Bravo can be taken from inside a ride. Helicopters are even more useful, letting you rain down rockets and machine gun fire on opponents scrambling between control points. As such, cover is vital when hiking between control points on foot.

Key Locations

- Communication center
- Concrete guard post
- Guard tower
- Surface-to-air missile trucks
- Fuel tanks
- Warehouse, Control Point Charlie
- Stack of storage containers
- Radio Tower Hill

A battle plan similar to those used in the other two zones of Angel Island works well here: focus on capturing and holding Control Points Alpha and Charlie, while bickering for the ephemeral Bravo. Avoid attacking Bravo on foot; instead, rush in with a vehicle, then hurry out to avoid getting obliterated by explosive weapons fire.

The uncovered, exterior Control Point Alpha is harder to nab than Charlie, though working with snipers stationed on Radio Tower Hill can help you secure the area. Air strikes and helicopters help too. Control Point Charlie is a tad less chaotic as a result of being located within a warehouse, yet you can expect plenty of indoor shootouts.

Tactics

Control Point Alpha

CAPTURE DIFFICULTY: ★★★★★

The KPA made full use of US communication facilities built on Angel Island prior to the start of the war, though now their control of the communication center is in question. Surrounded by a radio tower, concrete guard post, guard tower, and communication outpost, the wide-open Control Point Alpha is crucial in winning the battle for the KPA zone **[A]**.

Marching on Alpha

With little cover from air strikes and no way to shield yourself from enemy gunfire, marching to Alpha on foot isn't the wisest battle plan. If you must, hurriedly take the control point and head into the communication center or inside the concrete guard post for a secure defensive position.

Cruising into Alpha

The best tactic for taking Control Point Alpha is to rev up a Humvee, LAV, or Battle Tank and roll right in. Considering the Humvee's startling lack of fortitude when facing rocket fire, either opt for the sturdier LAV or Battle Tank, or cram a bunch of teammates into the back in hopes of quickly seizing Alpha. Predictably, the Battle Tank is the premium option with its high price tag and extraordinary power. Still, stay on the alert for RPG fire coming from the structures surrounding the control point.

Aerial Assault on Alpha

Helicopters won't help you capture a control point, but they can clear the way for your teammates to do the job. Take off in a Scout or Apache to mop up resistance at Control Point Alpha. Pay attention to the communication center and concrete guard post, because enemies love to fire from inside.

Concrete Guard Post

Climb the ladder inside the concrete guard post for a secure view of Control Point Alpha. The concrete walls are thick enough to shield you from incoming fire, while three windows enable you to watch for approaching enemies. Plus, because it's only accessible by ladder, you can easily kill anyone who tries to climb up and attack. Better still, drop a C4 charge at the base of the ladder for some explosive insurance.

Guard Tower at Alpha

While not as safe as the nearby concrete guard post, the guard tower provides a better view of the area. You're more vulnerable to helicopter attacks, which means you should be prepared to counter with the proximity launcher. The guard tower is also great for firing RPGs against tanks eager to steal Alpha.

Communication Outpost

Remain out of sight inside the communication outpost and the moment an enemy tries taking Control Point Alpha, rush outside to finish them. While it's not as good a strategy for defending Alpha as preventing members of the opposing faction from ever reaching Alpha in the first place, it's a decent backup plan.

Control Point Bravo

CAPTURE DIFFICULTY: ★★★★★

Several surface-to-air missile trucks wait for orders at the hotly contested Control Point Bravo **[B]**. Like other outdoor control points, vehicles—particularly the LAV and Battle Tank—are the best way to capture and hold. Limited cover in the form of empty storage containers makes capture on foot possible, although it's wise to avoid loitering long after.

Container Capture

A rarity among outdoor control points: this one has cover! Crouch inside the empty storage containers sitting within Control Point Bravo to capture it, protecting yourself from air strikes and helicopter fire. You're still exposed to enemy gunfire and grenades, though. Once you've captured Bravo, take a defensive position across the road or on the butte overhead after priming C4 charges to ward off control point takers.

Rolling in to Bravo

As with all outdoor control points, seizing Bravo is best done from the driver's seat. Either load up a Humvee with teammates to quickly capture the control point or use an LAV or Battle Tank to protect yourself from explosives attacks as you grab Bravo on your own. Having a teammate join you in the machine gunner's seat is extraordinarily helpful, especially when dealing with snipers on the butte overlooking the control point and helicopters patrolling the skies.

Flying over Bravo

Destroying the vehicles that roll into Control Point Bravo is admittedly difficult on foot given the sparse cover and thick armor of LAVs and Battle Tanks; as such, mount an attack from above using a helicopter. An Apache will clear Bravo of any pesky enemy vehicles with its rockets, but you can just as well use a Scout to wipe up resistance and clear the area for teammates to run in and capture the point. Beware of proximity launcher fire coming from the butte overlooking the control point.

Roadside Assistance

With Control Point Bravo situated on one side of the dirt road, it's possible to stage a defense from the other side. Drop C4 in Bravo before hustling over to the enclosure across the road, taking cover behind the waist-high crates. Purchase an RPG in anticipation of vehicles rolling in to take Bravo and keep an eye out for air strikes and helicopters.

Control Point Charlie

CAPTURE DIFFICULTY:

A supply station consisting of a covered lot with fuel tanks, a silo, and two warehouses, Control Point Charlie is a prime target for aerial attacks **[C]**. Stick to the buildings and empty storage containers for cover. A number of hiding spots make defending Charlie a feasible strategy once you manage to wrest control for your faction.

Capture and Hold Hiding Spot

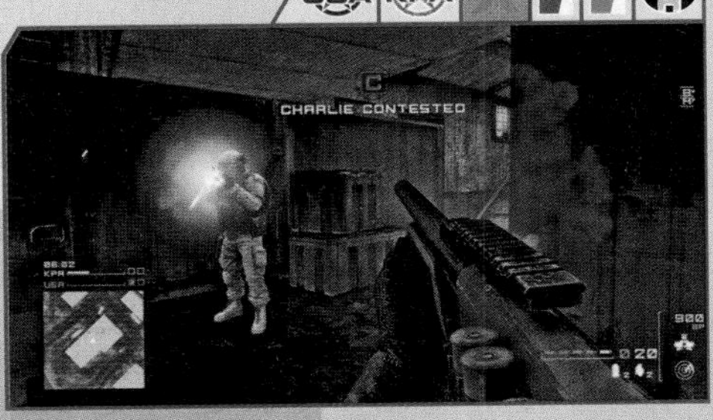

The best way to capture and hold Control Point Charlie is to hide among the storage containers stacked inside the warehouse. Withdraw into blue container parallel to the wall to effortlessly capture the point, although backing into this enclosed space puts you at high risk of being blown apart by grenades. You can even climb onto the blue container and conceal yourself in the gray container on top. Another option involves stationing yourself on top of the containers in the opposite corner. From here you can capture Charlie and defend it without being seen from any of the warehouse entrances. Throw out some C4 at the entrances for added defense.

Assault from the Adjacent Warehouse

Mainly used as cover against air strikes and helicopter fire, the warehouse adjacent to Control Point Charlie doesn't offer much tactically in an offensive push. Nevertheless, use it to stage an attack on the control point. Cook grenades while sprinting between the warehouses, throwing them in as you pass by Charlie. Then mop up any remaining resistance using an SMG or shotgun.

Fuel Tank Ambush

Playing as the KPA affords you the unique opportunity to approach Control Point Charlie from behind. Rather than attacking from the interior of Angel Island, you can push from the water's edge. Because the ground slopes down, your approach will be partially covered until you reach the collection of fuel tanks. Use them for cover, hurling grenades into the warehouse before making a final push with guns blazing into the warehouse. You face a mix of mid- and close-range combat, so load up on an all-purpose firearm like the M4 accompanied by the grenade launcher attachment or stock of extra grenades (apply the Fist Full infantry ability to double your supply).

Empty Storage Containers

Before reaching the warehouse containing Control Point Charlie, use the storage containers assembled underneath the shelter for cover. From here you can deploy drones to scout the situation inside the warehouse and prepare yourself for a push to take the control point. Be mindful that although the containers shield you from air strikes and helicopters, you're still visible to anyone who passes on foot.

Vantage Points

Radio Tower Hill

With the battle shifting from the center of the island to the coastal outskirts, sniping spots become harder to find. Fortunately, Radio Tower Hill retains the title of most spectacular vantage point, offering killer views of all three control points **[VP.01]**. Fewer trees on this side of the island also means you can skip thermal goggles in favor of another piece of equipment, such as ammo resupply that will refresh your stock and keep you firing.

Butte over Bravo

Your second option for sniping lies above Control Point Bravo. The small butte overlooking the control point allows you to gain just enough elevation to see all three control points; however, it's much lower than Radio Tower Hill and therefore constantly under threat of sniper fire **[VP.02]**. For quick sniping sessions or to clear Bravo before an assault, this is a great spot. Extended use should occur only after you eliminate snipers on Radio Tower Hill to ensure you won't be sniped yourself. Equip a pair of thermal goggles to peer through the thick foliage and get at the snipers hiding underneath.

Rocky Ridge

The low-lying Rocky Ridge looks out on Control Point Charlie **[VP.03]**. Hike up to the top of the ridge and aim at opponents seeking to nab Charlie. Rocky Ridge also has the benefit of largely being out of sight from snipers nested on Boulder Hill, meaning you can worry less about being sniped and more about nailing enemies. Yet, the view is limited to the buildings around Charlie, making it an average vantage point at most.

Concrete Guard Post

Although the concrete guard post forward from Control Point Alpha has a limited line of sight, it's recommended mainly for its safety **[VP.04]**. The concrete walls protect you while you fire at enemies approaching the control point. Better yet, it's a good vantage point from which to fire RPGs at ground vehicles without being exposed to their return fire.

Guard Tower at Alpha

More exposed than the superior concrete guard post, the guard tower at Control Point Alpha makes up for its lack of protection with a better view **[VP.05]**. Not only do you get a wider perspective on Alpha, but you can also get at part of Control Point Bravo down the road. It's also easier to fire at helicopters from the top of the guard tower, even if you are more vulnerable to their attacks.

CAUTION 조심하다

Unlike other maps where rooftops are wholeheartedly recommended as vantage points, on Angel Island the hills are taller than the buildings, making the rooftops an inferior vantage point. Specifically, avoid the temptation to climb onto the rooftops at Control Point Charlie. Snipers aiming down from the surrounding hills will take you down in an instant.

US ZONE

Boulder Hill and Rocky Ridge peer down at the sparse US zone, which consists of a missile launcher hub sandwiched by two courtyard hotel buildings. All three structures lean against the base of the hilly interior of the island, enabling deadly sniping at soldiers scurrying about below.

Vehicles dominate the strategy in the US zone. Not only do ground vehicles enable you to travel quickly, but they ease capture of exterior Control Points Alpha and Bravo. Drones and attack helicopters can help put immense pressure on all three control points, including the interior Charlie.

Key Locations

- Hotel Alpha
- Surface-to-air missile trucks
- Hotel Charlie
- Boulder Hill

Both factions should station snipers along Rocky Ridge overlooking Control Points Bravo and Charlie for cover fire. When playing as the US, go for Control Point Alpha first; it's close to the previous spawn point in the neutral zone, which provides a slight advantage when the zone switches. As with the other zones, concentrating on Alpha and Charlie is best. Leave Bravo to the vehicles.

Tactics

Control Point Alpha

CAPTURE DIFFICULTY: ★★★★★

This ain't the Holiday Inn—this hotel features trashed rooms, crumbling walls, and a courtyard that echoes with the sound of gunfire **[A]**. Rush in with a vehicle to capture this control point, but stay to defend it using the second floor walkway that surrounds the courtyard. There's also a third floor vantage point ideal for standing guard over Alpha.

Crazy Courtyard Capture

Taking Control Point Alpha on foot isn't as ludicrous a strategy as you might think. Despite air strikes, enemy gunfire from the balcony, and even helicopter strikes from above, you can nimbly maneuver around the edges of the courtyard to seize Alpha. Throw out some C4, then duck inside the hotel once you succeed in seizing the control point.

Free Parking at Alpha

Park your Humvee, LAV, or Battle Tank in the courtyard at Control Point Alpha for a quick capture. There might not be a meter maid waiting to issue a ticket, but defenders will be glad to pound your ride with explosive ordnance. Pay attention to the hotel balcony for RPGs, particularly the third floor vantage point. Additionally, be on guard for Apache rockets that can obliterate your vehicle. Once you capture Alpha, pull out of the courtyard and find a more defensible position—staying parked in the courtyard makes you a sitting duck for rocket fire.

Attacking Alpha from Above

Counter vehicular assaults on Control Point Alpha using a helicopter. The Apache is the preferred attack option with its six rocket barrage, though the Scout can whittle down an LAV with its rapid-fire gun. Approach the control point from the interior of the island to prevent defenders on the balcony from firing at you. Once Alpha has been taken by teammates on the ground, transition into a defensive patrol of the area.

Entering Alpha from the Sides

Approach the hotel from the side rather than the courtyard for a sneakier assault. Enter the building and run up the stairs to the second floor, where you can eliminate enemies defending the courtyard. Load up an SMG and spray bullets as you run the length of the balcony. Grenades can help too, although they may end up bouncing off the walls and down into the courtyard.

Second Floor Balcony Blitz

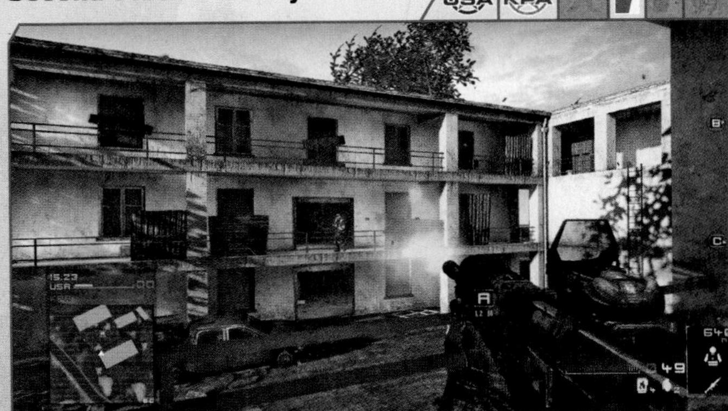

Your greatest advantage in holding Control Point Alpha relates to the balcony that encircles the courtyard. Exploit it fully. Purchase an RPG or equip the proximity launcher in anticipation of vehicles driving into the hotel courtyard eager for an easy capture.

Third Floor Defense

The best position from which to defend Control Point Alpha is the third floor balcony. Although most of it is inaccessible, you can reach a small area via a ladder in the courtyard. Place a C4 charge at the base before climbing up, then ready yourself with an RPG and mid-range rifle. You contend with drones and helicopters, though, so be prepared to flee should you come under heavy fire.

Control Point Bravo

CAPTURE DIFFICULTY: ★★★★★

Remnants of the KPA attack on San Francisco, surface-to-air missile trucks sit on both sides of Control Point Bravo **[B]**. Unfortunately, they're insufficient for cover, which means you have to rely on vehicles to hastily get in and out of the area to avoid being left out in the open.

Fools Rush In

With no available cover, attempting to seize Control Point Bravo on foot is practically suicide. If snipers don't get you from the hills, you're sure to be bombarded by air strikes, drones, or helicopters. There's also the risk of being run over or obliterated by tank fire. While it's possible to get lucky—squeezing into a corner can shield you from some gunfire, but you're still at risk of being blown up by grenades and air strikes—there's no viable tactic for capturing Bravo on foot, so you're better off mounting an offensive with a vehicle. As for defending Bravo on foot, consider it a foolish notion.

Speedy Vehicle Capture

Control Point Bravo favors vehicles: zoom in for the capture, speed out to escape attack from above. Parking yourself at Bravo inside a vehicle isn't a good idea because it makes you an easy target for air strikes and Apache rockets; make any vehicular battle plan a quick in-and-out operation. There's a small chance a defender may catch you with an RPG, but given the lack of cover it's unlikely that many will patrol the control point on foot.

Off-road Approach to Bravo

Instead of tackling Control Point Bravo from the road, keep a lower profile by approaching from the sides. As the US, climb up from the docks and enter the surface-to-air missile platform next to the control point. When playing the KPA, descend from Boulder Hill to access Bravo. While you still have to contend with the lack of cover, at least this side approach draws less attention.

Bravo Sky Patrol

There are two ways to clear Control Point Bravo from the air: hammer it with an air strike or rain down bullets and rockets from a helicopter or drone. The former can be highly effective, particularly if you opt for an area-effect strike such as white phosphorous that will drive defenders out of Bravo; however, you'll have to wait until the effect dissipates before heading in to capture the control point yourself. Hellfire strikes are a quicker, cheaper option. Spawning in a helicopter is the best option. Not only does it offer awesome firepower, but it also lets you pass over the other control points.

Control Point Charlie

CAPTURE DIFFICULTY: ★★★★★

Although Control Point Charlie shares similarities with its counterpart Alpha on the other side of the US zone, a different layout requires different tactics **[C]**. The indoor control point requires close-range tactics, including use of hiding spots to capture and hold, and ambushes that take advantage of sniper covering fire and multiple hotel access points.

Checking in at Ground Level

Holding the interior is critical to maintaining control. Hide behind the debris piled up near the door. Lying prone enables you to capture the point out of sight and away from the door. Bolster your defense by placing C4 at the front door and stairs descending from the second floor. Additionally, rely on an SMG to quickly put down opponents who waltz in to contest the control point.

Second Floor Assault

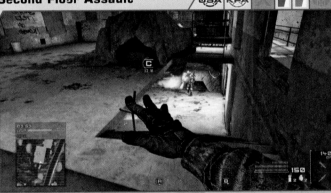

Rather than brazenly walking through the front entrance at ground level, it's wiser to enter from the second floor. Climb the ladder to the second story at the back of the building. Eliminate any defenders before dropping grenades down the stairwell to the control point below. Step down carefully, because your grenades may not have tagged defenders hiding behind the pile of rubbish on the far side of the room. An SMG is ideal for quick kills as you move between floors.

Second Floor Defense

Your first line of defense ought to be on the ground floor, but it's equally important to monitor the second floor to prevent enemies from sneaking in. Ladders grant access to the second floor in both the front and back of the building. Lay C4 at both ladders to discourage use. Station yourself in the room above the control point with an SMG or shotgun to guard the ladder from outside and the two staircases into Charlie.

Vantage Points

Boulder Hill

This towering mound offers the best sniping spots anywhere in the US zone. Overlooking Control Points Bravo and Charlie, Boulder Hill enables you to support teammates assaulting or to defend either point **[VP.01]**. When you see a vehicle pull into either control point, call forth an air strike. Because it faces the ocean, you needn't worry about sniper wars; however, because both factions want this premium vantage point, expect to tussle with other snipers eager to claim the best spots. Unfortunately, there's no line of sight into Control Point Charlie, which lies indoors. Still, you can offer cover fire for advancing teammates and help clear Bravo down the road.

Hotel Alpha, Third Floor

Purely for defense, the third floor of Hotel Alpha, accessible only via ladder, provides an excellent view of the control point below **[VP.02]**. Equip an RPG or proximity launcher to deal with vehicles. A sniper rifle can pick off US soldiers in the distance, but you're better off with a mid-range rifle like the M4, which can shoot a fair distance and hold its own at closer ranges.

Rocks Near Hotel Charlie

Sniping from the ground isn't usually the best tactic, but the rocks near Control Point Charlie can be leveraged when playing as the US **[VP.03]**. Lying prone on the larger rocks can provide a decent view of the action around Hotel Charlie. Of course, snipers on Boulder Hill behind the control point can identify you, so snipe with caution.

BORDERLANDS

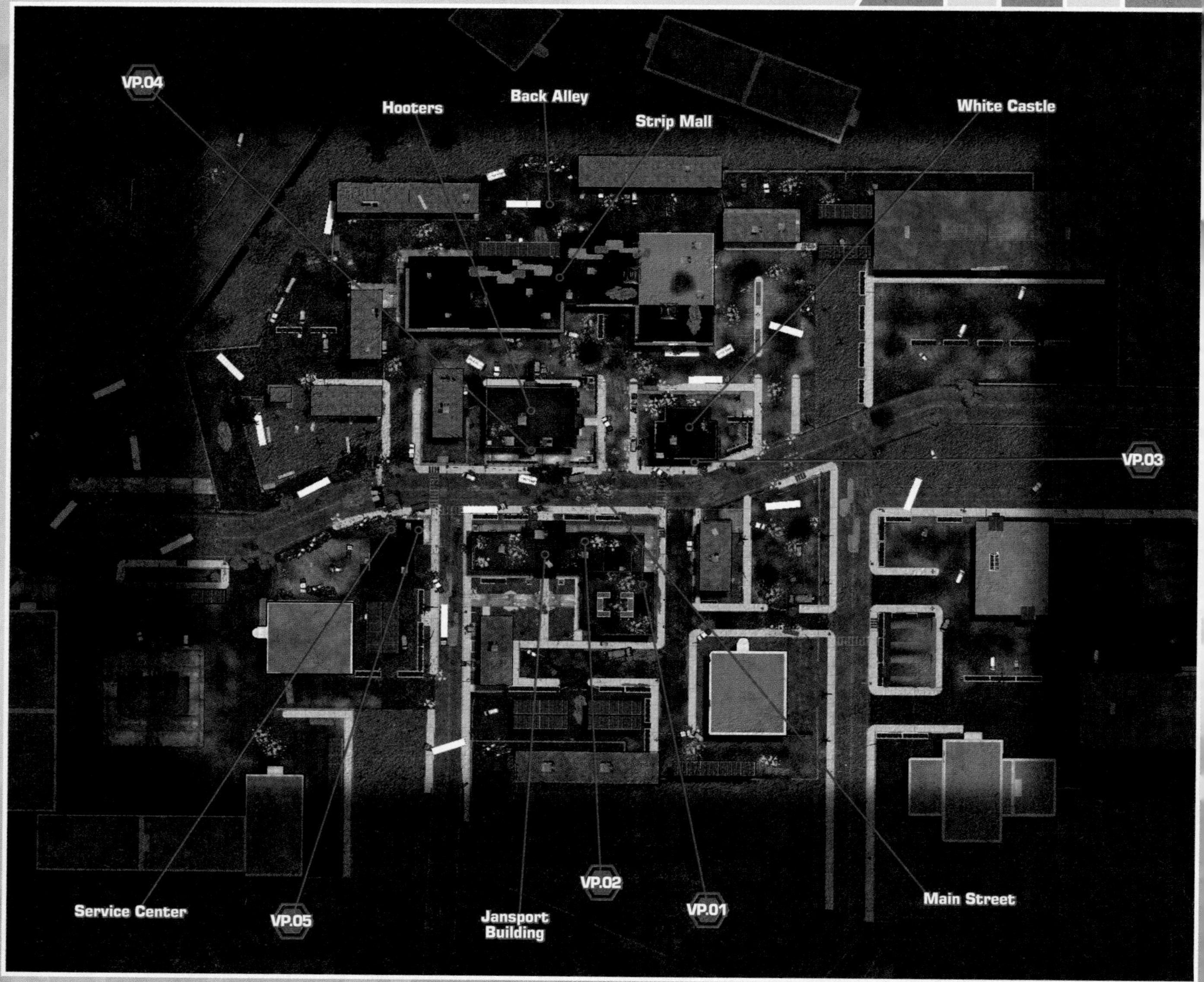

VP.04
Hooters
Back Alley
Strip Mall
White Castle
VP.03
Service Center
VP.05
Jansport Building
VP.02
VP.01
Main Street

Empty store shelves, closed restaurants, and abandoned office buildings tell a depressing story in Borderlands, the once vibrant commercial center that has transformed into an ugly battleground.

It's all-out war in this Team Deathmatch–only map where US and KPA forces fight not for land, but blood. Your sole aim is to eliminate as many of the opposition as possible, leveraging vantage points, hiding spots, and vehicles to get the job done.

Key Locations

- JanSport building
- White Castle
- Hooters
- Service Center
- Strip mall
- Back alley
- Main Street

This small map comes packed with streets and alleys, interior ambush spots and vantage points. Most are at the center of the map lining Main Street, where much of the action takes place. Concentrate on this area to rack up kills.

Vehicles, both ground and aerial, are crucial for winning this map. Work with teammates to fully staff spawned vehicles, increasing the attack power of helicopters and tanks by filling machine gunner seats.

DEATHMATCH ZONE

Tactics

t's All About the Wheels

'ehicles, vehicles, ehicles—the ıction that makes ıe most of ground ehicles wins the ay. Despite the onfines of the ıap, Borderlands ; won or lost ased on how ffectively you everage vehicles to put pressure on the opposition. The Battle Tank an do some serious damage, though given its high price tag, you eed to rack up some Battle Points before spawning it; a LAV is a ood, reasonably priced starting point. Avoid the Humvee, which von't last long against RPG attacks. Keep moving to avoid rocket re and peek down the side streets for potential kills. Additionally, aving a teammate join you in the machine gunner seat dramatically ıcreases your firepower; similarly, spawn directly into a team ıember's vehicle whenever the option is available.

Attacking from the Air

Dish out levastating ıttacks to enemies stationed on he rooftops by deploying ıerial drones ınd helicopters. Buzzard drones ıre an affordably priced option for aking out RPGs and snipers camped out atop Hooters, White Castle, ınd the JanSport building. Better yet, save up for a Chimera helicopter hat can send a rooftop-clearing barrage of rockets. As when using ground vehicles, buckle into an already spawned helicopter or have ı teammate join you in the machine gunner's seat when spawning he Chimera to maximize your firepower. Because it's harder to target ıircraft compared to ground vehicles, you're likely to earn more kills while in the skies.

JanSport Building Interior

Access the JanSport building second floor from a staircase that originates in the car park near the Service Center or directly from the patio. Use the second floor set of windows overlooking Main Street to rain bullets on the opposing faction, taking full advantage of the elevated view and waist-high windowsill for cover. Even when crouching for cover, this is a highly visible spot, and the drawback to such a good spot is that you're sure to come under heavy fire.

White Castle Front Window

While not as close to the heart of the action as Hooters or the JanSport, White Castle has the advantage of being a tad safer for street-level tactics. Because you're farther down Main Street, you're unlikely to be the target of as much gunfire, yet you can just as easily nail vehicles with an RPG or proximity launcher. Escape through the back door or crouch behind the counter in the middle of the restaurant if you come under heavy fire.

Hooters Prime Time View

Load up an RPG and fire at vehicles patrolling Main Street from a crouched position behind the Hooters windows facing Main Street. Along with prime access to the street itself, these front windows offer a clear view of the JanSport building all the way through to the car park in the rear where the US spawn. Sniping down this line is a bit harrowing given the frenzy of vehicles at street level, but it's worth the risk to exploit this choke point.

Hooters Interior

While there's more than enough action to keep you busy at the front of Hooters, you can make use of several other spots in the joint. Crouch behind the bar and pop up to surprise enemies passing through with a spritz from an SMG or quick blast from a shotgun attachment. Several booth partitions also make good ambush spots, along with the kitchen accessible from the side street.

Strip Mall Search

The strip mall and adjoining back alley are fairly removed from the action, though that doesn't mean you can't hunt in the abandoned stores and trashed alleys. Three stores are open for combat: Votypka Foot Massage and Montrose Liquors behind Hooters, and an unnamed store directly behind White Castle. Empty shelves make for decent cover, which you're sure to need if you're a US soldier traipsing so close to KPA turf. On the whole, there's not much to see or do and your time is better spent getting a piece of the action closer to Main Street.

Sneaky Spawn Point Access

USA KPA

If you're feeling cheeky and want to unload on the other faction as they spawn, skirt the map's edges to reach each side's spawn point. When playing as US, you need to reach the strip mall back alley; as KPA, you want to gain access to the car park located behind the JanSport. While difficult, staying out of sight along the sides of the map can get you there—surviving once you're there, however, is another story.

Vantage Points

JanSport Building Patio

USA KPA

Not offering quite as impressive a view, the JanSport building patio nonetheless qualifies as a worthy vantage point **[VP.01]**. Easy access is the biggest disadvantage with stairs running from the side street on which the EAT restaurant sits, another set from the car park in the back, and a flight open from the interior of the building accessible via the Service Center side street. Guarding all three access points can be tough, particularly when you consider the limited view of Main Street and White Castle; however, it's valuable as a choke point. Prevent enemies from taking out teammates sniping from the nearby rooftop by holding fast at the patio.

JanSport Building Rooftop

USA KPA

Without question the best vantage point in Borderlands, the top of the JanSport building grants full view of Main Street, Hooters, White Castle, and the two side streets **[VP.02]**. Access is only possible via the adjacent patio—there's no ladder access to the roof. This makes the JanSport building rooftop the most secure vantage point because you can easily monitor the single flight of stairs leading up to the area. Still, you have to deal with the threat of air strikes, drones, and helicopters. These are formidable dangers; enlist the help of teammates to keep them in check or flee to survive.

White Castle Rooftop

USA KPA

Up the road from Hooters and the JanSport building, White Castle doesn't offer as impressive a view, but it's useful nevertheless **[VP.03]**. The view from the side facing Hooters is preferable to that over the front of the restaurant. From this angle, line of sight stretches all the way down Main Street. Exploit this fully by sniping at enemies as they scurry across the street. Guard the two access ladders to avoid getting ambushed while you're sniping. Having teammates monitor the ladders and back of the restaurant helps. Additionally, flee at the sign of an air strike or threat of Z-10 Chimera rocket fire, otherwise you're toast.

Hooters Rooftop

USA KPA

Rivaled only by the top of the JanSport building, the Hooters rooftop looks over the center of Main Street. All the action is right here—a full view of the street below, a direct line of sight into the JanSport building, view of White Castle, and even access to the back alley **[VP.04]**. Such phenomenal access makes it great for sniping and hailing rockets on the tanks patrolling Main Street; however, two easily climbed ladders and a lack of cover make it a vulnerable vantage point. Work with teammates to protect ladder access. Additionally, maintain constant watch over the skies to avoid getting obliterated by air strikes, aerial drones, and helicopter fire. The proximity launcher is your friend while up on this rooftop.

Service Center Rooftop

USA KPA

Across the side street from the JanSport building, the Service Center offers a limited view of Main Street. Climb the ladder on the Main Street side to access the roof where you can view the area in front of JanSport and Hooters **[VP.05]**. While you won't catch the bulk of the action from this vantage point, you can pick off soldiers at the edge of the fray and those attempting to sneak around the map's border to the spawn points. The Service Center favors the US given its proximity to their side of the map, but if you're a gutsy KPA operative, it can be a lucrative vantage point.

ROSSROADS

.PA tanks roll along America's reat highway system, eager to vade the heartland one mile at time. Only fierce US resistance an force the KPA to exit the ighway and send them packing.

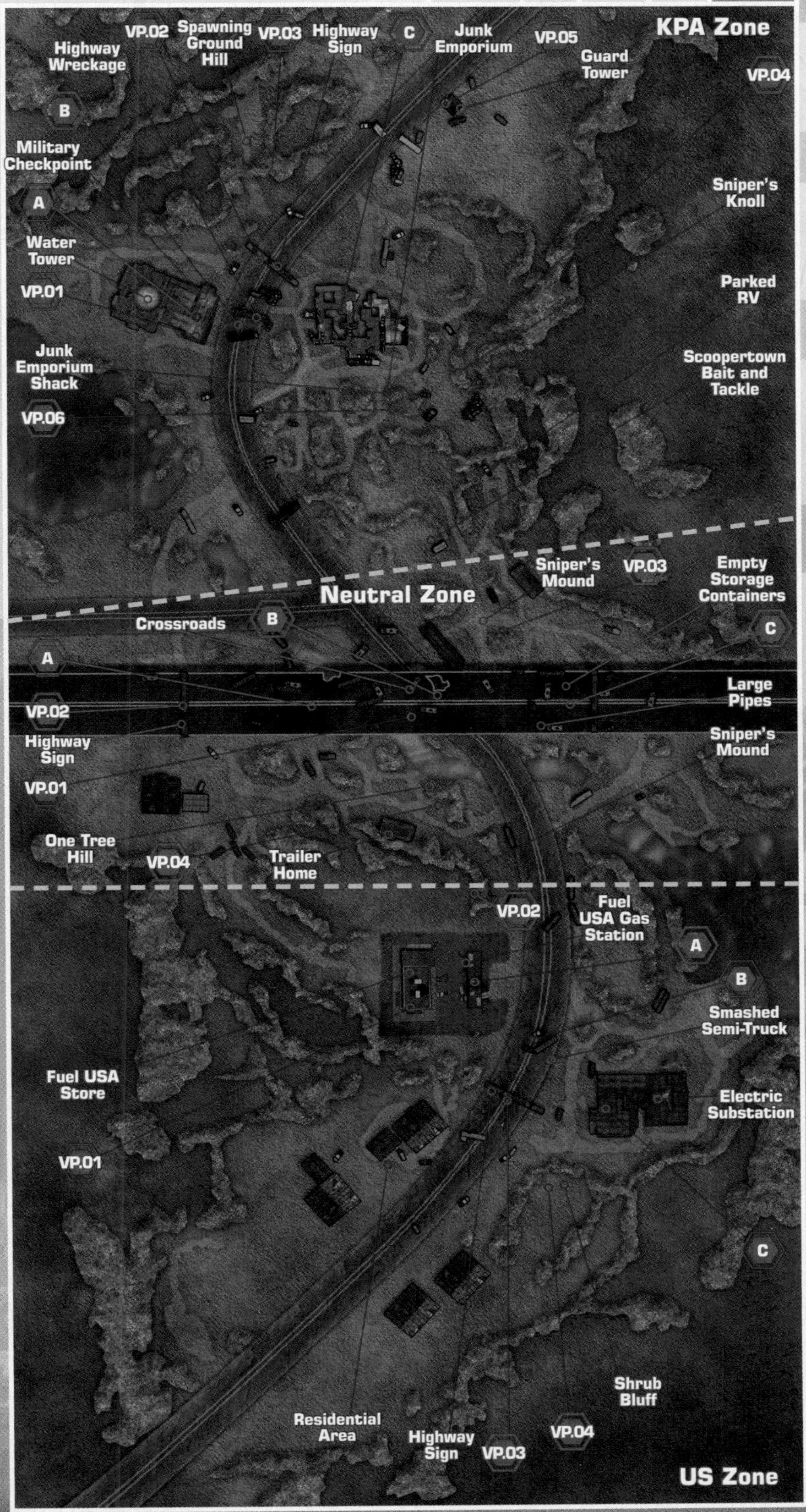

KPA Zone

Highway Wreckage
VP.02
Spawning Ground Hill
VP.03
Highway Sign
C
Junk Emporium
VP.05
Guard Tower
VP.04
B
Military Checkpoint
A
Sniper's Knoll
Water Tower
VP.01
Parked RV
Junk Emporium Shack
Scoopertown Bait and Tackle
VP.06

Neutral Zone

Sniper's Mound
VP.03
Empty Storage Containers
Crossroads
B
C
A
Large Pipes
VP.02
Highway Sign
Sniper's Mound
VP.01
One Tree Hill
VP.04
Trailer Home

US Zone

VP.02
Fuel USA Gas Station
A
B
Smashed Semi-Truck
Fuel USA Store
Electric Substation
VP.01
C
Shrub Bluff
Residential Area
Highway Sign
VP.03
VP.04

NEUTRAL ZONE

A crumbling highway overpass dominates this zone, covering each of the three control points situated in the paved ravine below. Long stretches of road and gently rolling hills give clearance to combat vehicles that complicate infantry tactics.

Still, much of the action is on foot and the faction with a better ground game ultimately owns the zone. While Control Points Alpha and Charlie can only be captured on foot, objective Bravo can be captured by both infantry and vehicles.

Key Locations

- Highway overpass
- Highway sign
- Empty storage containers, Control Point Alpha
- Large pipes
- Crossroads, Control Point Bravo
- Abandoned supply crates, Control Point Charlie
- One-Tree Hill
- Sniper's Mound

Use the overpass to stage attacks on the control points underneath, either approaching from the ramps at the sides of Alpha and Charlie or by circling around the overpass and flanking the opposing team. Additionally, the overpass is an ideal vantage point for both sides, enabling you to snipe enemies while removed from the fray.

Tactics

Control Point Alpha

CAPTURE DIFFICULTY: ★★★★★

With its multiple access points and few hiding spots, Control Point Alpha is one of those tough to capture, even tougher to hold objectives **[A]**. An aggressive defense with snipers on the overpass above and anti-infantry Wolverine drones below works well for holding this tricky spot.

Storage Container Capture

USA KPA

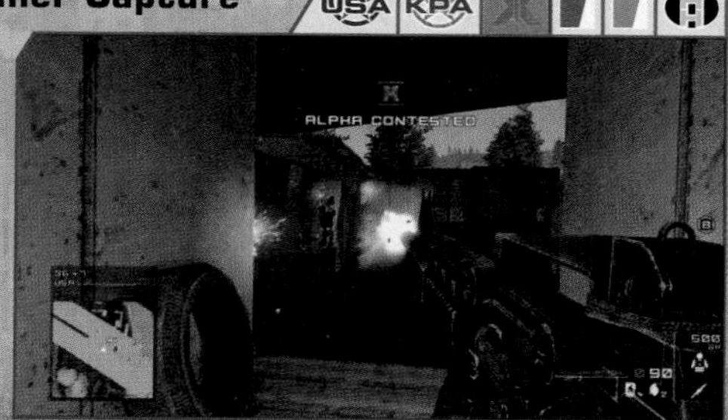

Stand inside the empty storage container at the base of the slope leading up to the overpass to capture Control Point Alpha out of sight. KPA have a slight advantage because approaching US soldiers can't fully see into the container, but it's not the most secure hiding spot. It's the most obvious place from which to nab the objective, and easily spammed with grenades.

Pipe Cleaning

USA KPA

Pipes angled down to the base of the ravine under the highway overpass make a great hiding spot when advancing toward Control Point Alpha or defending it. Station yourself inside the pipes when playing as the US to halt KPA efforts to sneak into Alpha from below. Augment your defense by placing a C4 charge at the base of the pipes. As KPA, the pipes are useful for defending the control point. Hide inside and reveal yourself when a US operative tries taking the objective.

Highway Ramp Assault

USA KPA

Instead of assaulting Control Point Alpha head-on, approach from the side using the overpass ramp. Roll grenades into the control point via the concrete slope, then load up a Diablo SMG or more powerful M249 LMG capable of putting down enemies with a few well-aimed shots. Coming in from the side is also a good tactic when piloting a Buzzard drone because most defenders won't expect an aerial attack from this direction.

Falling Through the Cracks

Drop grenades onto Control Point Alpha via tiny cracks in the highway overpass above. These minuscule rifts are hard to spot while standing so crouch and search for two breaks in the asphalt along the KPA side of the bridge. Aim carefully and throw cooked grenades through the narrow cracks to give your opponents a devious surprise.

Drone Patrol

The mobile home at the edge of the neutral zone on the US side makes a great drone deployment spot. Deploy a Wolverine anti-infantry drone and wheel it into Control Point Alpha to clear any KPA defenders. The powerful machine gun works well for stopping attackers, though you need to monitor the limited battery.

Control Point Bravo

CAPTURE DIFFICULTY:

As with so many centrally located objectives, Control Point Bravo hosts a back-and-forth contest between the KPA and US that focuses on vehicles **[B]**. While an on-foot approach is feasible, keep to cover to avoid a confrontation with a patrolling LAV or Battle Tank.

Vehicles at Bravo

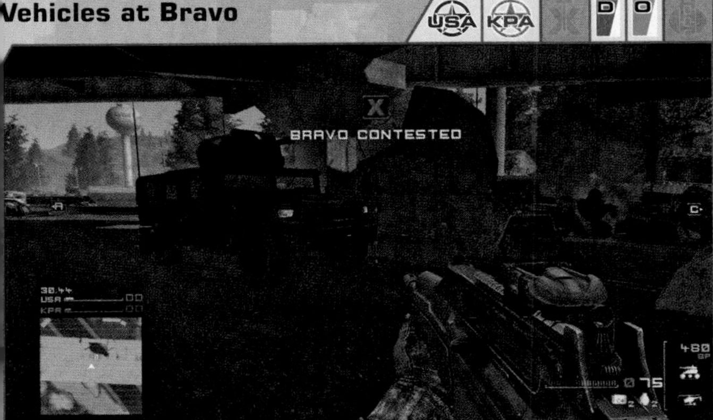

Start the battle by loading up a Humvee with teammates and rushing under the overpass to take Control Point Bravo. Because Battle Points are scarce at the beginning of a game, the Humvee is a great way to quickly grab the objective. Later, buckle up behind the wheel of an LAV or Battle Tank to hammer defenders and seize the control point. Helicopters aren't a great tactical option in the neutral zone because the overpass obstructs view of the control points, but if you're looking simply to rack up kills—spawn kills, anyone?—it's the way to go.

Concrete Capture

Cram yourself in the tight space created by two slabs of concrete near the overpass pylon to capture Control Point Bravo out of sight. Crouch to lower your profile, but don't go prone.

Rifling Through the Dumpster

Hop into the blue dumpster in Control Point Bravo when playing as the KPA to capture the objective away from the eyes of US onlookers. Unsurprisingly, grenades are a serious threat when hiding in this tight space, so discourage US forces from getting close enough to throw them by releasing a WP Grenade on the road leading into Bravo from the US side.

Gunfire Through the Cracks

Large rifts in the overpass enable you to attack Control Point Bravo, then defend it from above. Fully exploit these holes in the highway—drop grenades into Bravo to scramble defenders before jumping down, mowing down any remaining enemies, and capturing the control point. On the flip side, these gaps make great defensive overwatches. Station yourself above the control point and monitor enemy attempts to nab Bravo with the muzzle of your M4 rifle.

Guarding Bravo on the Steel Girder

From the highway overpass above, drop through a gap in the concrete to land on a steel girder directly on top of Control Point Bravo. Enemies definitely won't be expecting an attack from here, which makes it a fantastic, if not a little dangerous, defensive position.

Control Point Charlie

CAPTURE DIFFICULTY:

Like Control Point Alpha, Charlie is tucked under the highway overpass. Unfortunately, there are fewer hiding spots, which means winning the objective requires bold tactics such as flanking the opposition via the highway or sending in drones.

Direct Assault on Charlie

Speed into Control Point Charlie using a vehicle and hop out for a quick capture. The open layout makes it easy to zoom in with a Humvee or LAV (you can't capture the objective due to supply crates blocking access). Without a vehicle, bombard the control point with cooked grenades to eliminate opposition and capture it by crouching against supply crates. Take to the side opposite the other faction; as the KPA, for example, press against the gray container to protect yourself against attacking US soldiers. There aren't any hiding spots, so make the best of what little cover there is to seize control.

CAUTION 조심하다

Watch out for the fires that have broken out among the wrecked cars and piles of debris. You'll burn yourself if you venture too close to the flames, so keep a safe distance!

Flanking the Opposition

Rather than running right into Control Point Charlie, flank the opposing faction by going around the bridge. Not only does this surprise enemies who aren't expecting an attack from behind, but it also keeps them occupied and allows time for teammates to rush in and capture Charlie.

Up and Down the Highway Ramp

If you're not willing to risk trudging into KPA territory to flank Control Point Charlie, go halfway. Descend on Charlie via the ramp at the start of the overpass. Chuck a cooked grenade down the incline while firing at enemies defending the control point. An SMG is a good option for quickly taking out opponents. The ramp can also be used defensively. Crouch under the overpass on either side and shoot enemies who attempt to come down the ramp toward Charlie.

Drone Patrol

Send a Wolverine anti-infantry drone into Control Point Charlie to deny US occupation. Deploying this machine gun–equipped ground drone is best done from behind either the RV or mobile home at the edge of the neutral zone on the KPA side. This ensures you're out of sight from enemy snipers, but still fairly close to Charlie.

Vantage Points

Highway Overpass

Stand at the edge of the highway overpass to shoot enemies scrambling to reach the control points below **[VP.01]**. Largely ignored in favor of direct attacks on the objectives, the overpass is highly recommended whether you're playing as the KPA or US. Plus, cracks in the structure allow you to drop grenades on Control Point Alpha and shoot down at Bravo if the situation at either objective gets hairy.

Highway Sign

Climb the highway sign posted above the overpass for the best view of the neutral zone **[VP.02]**. You won't be able to snipe at any of the control points underneath the bridge, but you can aim at spawning soldiers on either side of the map. Support flanking maneuvers by sniping enemies from this overwatch as teammates move on foot.

One-Tree Hill

Across from Control Point Charlie on the KPA side of the neutral zone, the rock-strewn One-Tree Hill is a popular sniping spot **[VP.03]**. The reason: a clear line of sight into Charlie. Better still, turn to toward the edge of the map to monitor the highway for US soldiers attempting to flank your teammates at Charlie.

Sniper's Mound

The counterpoint to One-Tree Hill on the KPA side of the neutral zone, Sniper's Mound on the US half offers a line of sight onto the highway overpass, into Control Point Alpha, and a partially obstructed view of Bravo **[VP.04]**. Taking a position higher up the mound enables you to see farther across the map, though it becomes more difficult to tag enemies at the objectives below the overpass.

KPA ZONE

Away from the highway overpass, the battle for Crossroads takes a dangerous turn as vehicles come into play on the open lanes that run between Control Points Alpha and Bravo. Infantry maintain primacy, but the increased number of vehicles dramatically shifts the nature of combat in the KPA zone.

Tanks, LAVs, and helicopters play an aggressive role in hammering objectives with rockets and machine gun fire. Anti-tank weaponry—RPGs, Rhino drones, Proximity Launchers—are essential for stopping vehicles in their tracks.

Key Locations

- Military checkpoint, Control Point Alpha
- Highway sign
- Spawning Ground Hill
- Water tower
- Highway wreckage, Control Point Bravo
- Junk emporium, Control Point Charlie
- Junk emporium shack
- Scoopertown Bait and Tackle
- Sniper's Knoll
- Parked RV
- Guard tower

None of the objectives are easily taken. Control Points Alpha and Bravo are tough to hold given their position on the side of the highway. Combining use of vehicles with successful anti-vehicle measures to defeat enemy armor is key.

Charlie frequently changes hands as both factions pour into the junk emporium from every angle. The emporium's open layout makes defending Control Point Charlie difficult, although smart use of drones can put a stop to the revolving door.

Tactics

Control Point Alpha

CAPTURE DIFFICULTY: ★★★★★

Don't let the awning over Control Point Alpha fool you into thinking this military checkpoint is safe; on the contrary, this wide-open objective is constantly bombarded with tank and helicopter fire **[A]**. Despite the stacked crates and supply containers, there are few good defensive positions and no hiding spots of note.

Quick Capture by the Crates

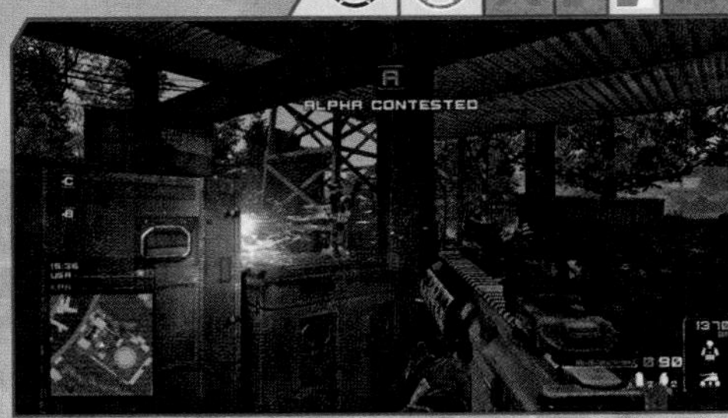

With Control Point Alpha situated on the upper tier of the military checkpoint at street level, options are limited when it comes to capturing the objective. Crates and supply containers provide a bit of cover, but don't stay in one spot for too long. Enemies constantly run through Alpha, and the presence of vehicles on the adjacent road makes an extended stay unwise.

Step-by-Step Capture

Crouch on the stairs leading up from the lakeshore for a semi-hidden capture position. Work with teammates to guard lakeshore access to Alpha, which in turn protects your flank and leaves you to worry about attackers approaching from the road. While it's possible to defend Alpha from the steps, drop a C4 charge on the concrete and take to a vantage point for a more reasonable defense.

Lakeshore Approach

You can bet on a military traffic jam on the highway that separates Control Points Alpha and Bravo, which makes an on-foot approach a dangerous and unrecommended option. Take to the lakeshore instead. Flank Control Point Alpha by walking along the water's edge—KPA have a shorter walk than the US on the far side of the map—and leap up the concrete steps to seize the objective. Prepare for vehicle fire coming from the road by equipping an RPG or calling in an airstrike to push enemy vehicles back long enough to capture the control point.

Roadside Assistance

You can't take Control Point Alpha from inside a vehicle, but you can lend firepower from behind the wheel that can help your team seize it. Commission a Battle Tank and bombard Alpha with cannon fire. Even if you don't kill enemies defending the objective, you'll spook them. That's precisely what you want; fleeing or cowering enemies are easy for your teammates to pick off. Once the area is clear, defend your mates as they capture the control point.

Water Tower Hide 'n' Seek

Helicopters can be used to great effect in the KPA zone. For instance, play hide and seek with enemies at Control Point Alpha from the cockpit of an Attack Helicopter. Hover around the water tower and fire rockets at the control point, then hide behind the tower to avoid getting shot out of the sky by an RPG or Proximity Launcher.

Similarly, use the highway sign near the KPA spawning ground to fire rockets on vehicles patrolling the road between Control Points Alpha and Bravo.

Control Point Bravo

CAPTURE DIFFICULTY: ★★★★★

Make no mistake, this is the most dangerous spot in the KPA zone. While there's some cover and a couple worthwhile hiding spots, the overbearing presence of tanks on the road makes this a hotly contested area **[B]**.

Seizing Bravo Behind the Wheel

Any serious attempt to seize Control Point Bravo centers around vehicles. Whether you use a Battle Tank to pound Bravo before storming on foot or you opt to roll into the control point via LAV and capture behind the wheel, vehicles are the way to go. There's simply too much action on the road to make an infantry approach safe—beyond the risk of getting run over, machine gun fire and tank cannon blasts will tear you to pieces. That said, vehicles aren't invincible and explosives attacks coming from the guard post at Control Point Alpha and around the junk emporium at Charlie must be taken seriously.

School Bus Hiding Spot

If you're crazy enough to approach Control Point Bravo on foot, take cover inside the wrecked school bus. Crouch or lie prone inside to shield yourself from vehicle attacks while capturing the control point. It's a decent defensive position because vehicles largely can't get at you if you lie prone.

Open Container on the Road

Hide inside the gray storage container on the asphalt to seize Control Point Bravo. Unfortunately, vehicles can fire on you as you crouch inside, which makes this an inferior hiding spot compared to the school bus. As such, use this for cover when running from Control Point Alpha over to Charlie or when trying to access the school bus.

Tight Spot

Cram yourself into the small space between the truck and gray container to capture Control Point Bravo. Sure, it might not be the most secure hiding spot, but in a bind you can crouch down and nab the objective before racing off to find a safer position.

Control Point Charlie

CAPTURE DIFFICULTY: 

Crates, containers, cars, and other assorted debris has been compiled into a big junk emporium housing Control Point Charlie **[C]**. Controlling this objective is a significant challenge due to the lightning-fast pace of close-quarters combat and lack of hiding places.

Coordinated Attack on Charlie

With so many access points and much of the area visible from the sky, Control Point Charlie is best attacked with teammates. Coordinate an assault that splits the attack squad into two teams: one that heads into the junk emporium to nab the objective and a second to patrol the perimeter and deny entry to enemies. Additionally, you can capture the objective more quickly with the help of teammates, making this the best available tactical option.

Capturing Charlie Solo

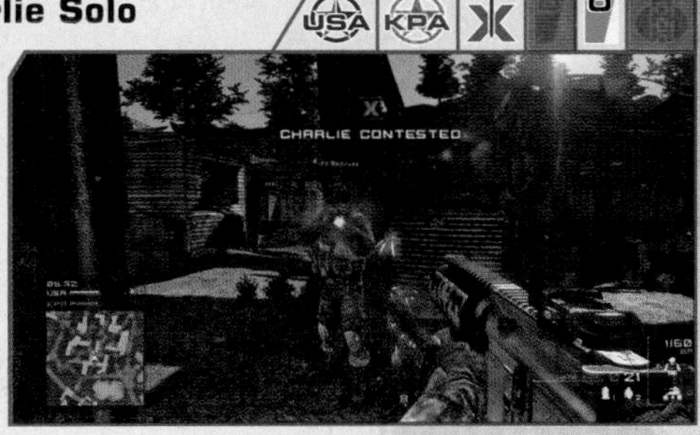

While a coordinated team assault is the best way to capture Control Point Charlie, the reality is that you probably need to take matters into your own hands. Lock and load an SMG or LMG—either suffice; you want something fast and powerful—and head into the junk emporium to seize Charlie. Immediately find a corner in the capture zone and keep your eyes peeled. Laying C4 charges at the two nearest access points provides a bit of insurance. Additionally, use a WP Grenade to cut off a path through the emporium.

Drones in the Junkyard

Wolverine drones are great for defending Control Point Charlie because they keep you safe while enabling you to gun down attackers from within the junk emporium. When rolling out a drone, station yourself behind the hills surrounding the KPA spawning ground, or behind Scoopertown Bait and Tackle or the parked RV trailer when playing as the US. Remember that Wolverines are susceptible to EMP blasts and can be taken out with a single melee hit, so fire quickly and stay on the move.

Aerial Assault on Charlie

Although sheet metal covers a few spots in the junk emporium, helicopters have a pretty solid view of the area. Use this to your advantage and clear the way for teammates to capture the point by firing from a helicopter or Buzzard drone. Even with Charlie in your team's possession, hailing rockets from above is a great way to deter enemies from trying to seize the control point.

Like Shooting Fish in a Barrel

Put your back to the wall of debris and blast enemies as they enter the junk emporium. Equip an SMG or shotgun to quickly fire on enemies as they enter. With several access points, you're best off sticking to the entrances closest to the KPA spawn point up the highway when playing as the US. The opposite is true when playing as

KPA: guard the entrances nearest the US side of the map, particularly the one facing Sniper's Knoll.

Flanking the Flotsam

The slew of access points make Control Point Charlie difficult to defend. Exploit this weakness when launching an assault. Flank the defending faction by going around the outside of the structure along the base of Sniper's Knoll. Enter from the KPA side when playing as the US, for example, and you're sure to catch the enemy by surprise. Give them fair warning by hurling a cooked grenade or flashbang before you step inside.

Vantage Points

Guard Post at the Military Checkpoint, Control Point Alpha

While not the safest vantage point in the KPA zone, the guard tower at Control Point Alpha does offer one of the better views of the area **[VP.01]**. Sniping isn't advisable, but anti-tank posturing is highly recommended. Equip an RPG or Proximity Launcher to take on LAVs, Battle Tanks, and even helicopters on the prowl.

Highway Sign

Favored by the KPA who spawn nearby on the back half of the map, the tall highway sign provides a great line of sight on Control Points Alpha and Bravo **[VP.02]**. The lack of cover is a concern, but because the sign is far back from the main battle at the objectives, you often can snipe without much hassle. Sneak onto the sign when playing as the US for devilish KPA spawn kills.

Spawning Ground Hill

Aim at US forces from the hill that rises from the lakeshore along the edge of the KPA zone **[VP.03]**. While it fails to grant a line of sight into any of the control points, sniping from the hill does enable targeting of enemy snipers on the other side of the highway, as well as soldiers running between the three objectives.

Sniper's Knoll

The counterpoint to Spawning Ground Hill on the KPA side of the map, Sniper's Knoll is a far superior vantage point that gives the US an upper hand when it comes to long-range combat **[VP.04]**. Not only does it provide an excellent line of sight to Spawning Ground Hill across the highway, but it also extends the length of the KPA zone. This enables you to see into Control Point Charlie in the junk emporium, identify enemies contesting Bravo, and even pop shots at Alpha.

Guard Tower on Highway 20

Set far down the highway past the KPA spawning ground, the guard tower offers a limited view of the action that rages near the control points **[VP.05]**. Still, there's plenty of value to be extracted from this distant vantage point. It's extremely safe because it's so far away, which also means US soldiers won't be expecting an attack from this location. Due to the extreme distance, use this spot only if you have confidence in your sharpshooting skills.

Shack Above the Junk Emporium

The small sheet metal shack on the small hill above the junk emporium makes a nice little vantage point when sniping on the US side **[VP.06]**. It provides just enough cover to keep you safe from KPA snipers on the other side of the map, and a clear line of sight into Control Point Charlie enables you to support an assault or protect the objective from afar.

US ZONE

One of many stops along the highway, the large gas station at the center of the US zone fuels the battle between factions with hard-fought control points featuring minimal cover and clear lines of sight for snipers and helicopter pilots.

Control Points Alpha and Bravo are both situated outdoors, making capture tough without vehicle support. Tanks run the ground game—there's no way to avoid confronting armor when attacking or defending either objective.

Key Locations

- Fuel USA gas station, Control Point Alpha
- Fuel USA store
- Sniper's Mound
- Trailer home
- Crashed semi-truck, Control Point Bravo
- Highway sign
- Electric substation, Control Point Charlie
- Shrub Bluff
- Residential area

Despite also being outdoors, Charlie differs because of its location within a fenced-off electric substation. Defending it is tough, nonetheless. US should focus on seizing Charlie, then fighting for nearby Bravo to win the zone. KPA have a built-in advantage on Control Points Alpha, but have to fight hard to get Bravo and Charlie.

Tactics

Control Point Alpha

CAPTURE DIFFICULTY: ★★★★★

Located among a group of burnt cars, Control Point Alpha can only be seized on foot in spite of the vehicles that swarm this outdoor objective **[A]**. Utilize helicopters and drones to clear the area for capture, then use the nearby hills and Fuel USA store to mount a defense.

Between a Truck and a Hard Place

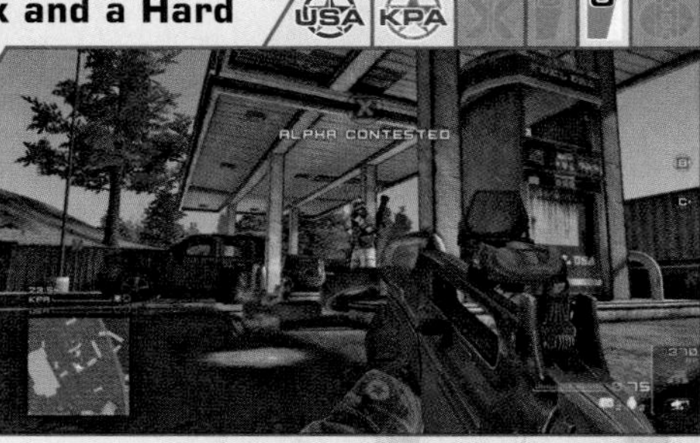

There aren't any hiding spots from which you can easily capture Control Point Alpha, but it's still possible to take some cover while nabbing it on foot. Crouch into the corner created by the trashed van and burnt truck. It's particularly useful when playing as the KPA because US gunfire coming from up the highway is blocked by the truck. Watch your back when playing as the US because KPA soldiers will sneak into the capture zone via the gas pumps.

Drone Deployments

When on the US side, deploy drones—Wolverines are great for attacking enemies at Control Point Alpha with its anti-infantry machine gun—from the protected residential area up the highway. It's immediately accessible after you spawn and KPA rarely if ever venture to this area. It's much easier to send a drone into the control point after your faction has seized it, at which point you can roll a Wolverine into the capture zone to guard the control point. The same is true when playing as the KPA, although the hiding spot differs. Situate yourself behind the trailer on the other side of the hill behind the Fuel USA store to remain out of sight, but within striking distance of the objective.

Helicopter Hideaway

An excellent way of halting a US push to Control Point Alpha is piloting an Attack Helicopter into the small airspace between the Fuel USA store and hillside separating it from the residential area. Hover and fire at US soldiers streaming toward the gas station via the highway. If a Proximity Launcher-equipped enemy arrives on the scene, retreat to safer airspace.

Gas Station Defense

Defend Control Point Alpha from atop the Fuel USA store, providing cover for teammates who can push back US forces on the ground. Because you spawn close to the building as KPA, holding it is essential to controlling Alpha and keeping the US away from your spawning ground. Alternately, lead an effort to seize the building when playing as the US. Approach the building along the hillside separating the building from the residential area, climbing up the ladder to the roof at the back of the building. Turn it into a defensive overwatch and snipe KPA soldiers attempting to capture Alpha. It's much more difficult on the US side to take the building, but if you succeed it bodes well for your chances of winning the round.

Control Point Bravo

CAPTURE DIFFICULTY:

Although Control Point Bravo appears to be yet another hazardous open-air objective, the ability to hide in the semi-truck cargo trailer makes an infantry approach legitimate **[B]**. Nevertheless, vehicles are the most effective way to capture and defend the control point.

Grabbing Bravo from the Back of the Truck

If you manage to make it to Control Point Bravo on foot (use a vehicle to speed onto the highway, then quickly hop out for a semi-safe arrival), climb into the cargo trailer to capture the objective away from vehicles. Move into the center of the trailer and crouch or lie prone among the crates to shield yourself from any gunfire that manages to find its way inside. Staying here after the control point has been captured isn't the best plan, so flee the scene and take up a defensive position elsewhere, such as the highway sign up the road.

Carside Capture

Take a ride on the wild side by brazenly capturing Control Point Bravo crouched against the car next to the semi-truck on the highway. Have an RPG handy for blasting vehicles. Sure you might get run over or blown to bits by a tank, but if you manage to survive, just think about the bragging rights!

Vehicle Raid on Bravo

A favorite tactic of Control Point Bravos everywhere, vehicles are the way to roll when it comes to this US zone objective. The risk of seizing the control point on foot is enough to justify the expense of an LAV or Battle Tank, which can withstand the gunfire that pings from both sides of the highway. Rush into the control point, capture it, then leave the scene to avoid getting blown up by an RPG, drone rockets, or helicopter hovering overhead. If possible, have teammates join you; not only do you gain the benefit of a secondary machine gunner, but you also capture the control point more quickly.

Cover to Cover

Use the objects strewn across the highway—large pipes, jackknifed trucks, burnt cars—for cover against vehicles, snipers, and the occasional airstrike. Whether you're moving between control points or scrambling to a vantage point, minimize your chance of being nicked by an enemy by always hiding behind the nearest available cover.

Control Point Charlie

CAPTURE DIFFICULTY:

Coils and power boxes fill the electric substation in which Control Point Charlie is located **[C]**. Exploit a slight US advantage by rushing to Charlie when the round begins, securing it, and moving to Bravo. Beware of KPA operatives who flank Charlie by approaching from the nearby lake.

Nowhere to Hide

Although there's nowhere within the Control Point Charlie capture zone to hide, make the most of what's available by crouching against the sandbags by the trailer. You won't be shielded from all attacks, but it does provide enough cover to see you through a complete capture.

Walking on the Waterfront

Because approaching Control Point Charlie from the highway is dangerous, take the lovely detour along the lakeshore. Flank enemies holding the control point by crossing the highway near the KPA spawning ground and traveling along the water's edge to the electric substation. It's highly unlikely anybody will be guarding the rear approach; as such, lob cooked grenades or call in an airstrike, then go in for the capture.

An Electrifying Defense

Capturing Control Point Charlie from the sandbags by the trailer is a great tactic, though it's not the best defensive position. Instead, head over to the electric coils on the other side of the substation. Hide behind the coils and fire on enemies as they try capturing Charlie.

Drones Over Charlie

Drones are a great way to attack Control Point Charlie, particularly when you're on the KPA faction and have a harder time approaching the objective across the highway. It's more convenient, however, to deploy drones when playing on the US side because you can send out the remote-controlled contraptions from the isolated residential area up the highway. As KPA, hide in the bushes along the lakeshore and send drones into the electric substation at Charlie from the rear for a killer surprise.

Vantage Points

Fuel USA Store Rooftop

With a stellar view of Control Point Alpha in the gas station directly below and a peek over to Bravo on the open highway, the Fuel USA retail building is arguably the best vantage point **[VP.01]**. It's definitely the safest, at least when playing as the KPA because your spawning ground is just over the hill at the building's rear. Whether you're attacking or defending Alpha, this vantage point is essential. When playing on the US side, aim big: snatch this from the KPA and keep them from pushing on the objectives at the center of the zone.

Sniper's Mound

The elongated mound to the side of the Fuel USA store makes for decent sniping, though only when the nexus of the battle has shifted away from Control Point Alpha—if there are tons of vehicles in the gas station, this vantage point puts you too close to the action **[VP.02]**. Shadows cast by the trees provide a bit of camouflage, but otherwise you're easy to spot on the bare ground. Use this exposed hill to fire on US soldiers approaching Alpha and Bravo from the highway.

Highway Sign

The highest vantage point in the US zone is also one of the deadliest—for snipers and soldiers on the ground alike. Climb the ladder just outside of Control Point Charlie to get a great view of the highway **[VP.03]**. With so many vehicles on the road below, carry an RPG just in case. Also, be mindful of Buzzard drones and helicopters overhead that can wipe you off the map in an instant.

Shrub Bluff

Shrub Bluff is a rarity among vantage points: it has good lines of sight *and* is well-hidden. The bluff near Control Point Charlie features a number of shrubs in which you can crouch and look out onto the highway **[VP.04]**. Unless a enemy equips a pair of Thermal Goggles or walks in front of you, there's a good chance you'll remain undetected as you snipe.

CUL-DE-SAC

Cul-de-sac
Skybridge
School Bus
VP.03
VP.04
Yellow House
A
VP.02
B
Off-White House
VP.01
KPA Zone
VP.02
VP.03
Neutral Zone
Ramparts
VP.04
VP.05
Blue House
US Zone
Crashed Semi-Truck
VP.05
Blue House
VP.06
VP.01
B
A
Cul-de-sac
VP.03
Gas Station
B
VP.06
Blue House
VP.01
Fenced-In Supply Crates
A
VP.02
VP.04

The KPA's relentless assault on America has led them to the heart of this once-thriving residential area. Middle-class houses left charred and broken from fighting, cars and school buses tossed like garbage on the streets, and the sounds of children playing in backyards lost amid the whir of drones in search of a kill.

NEUTRAL ZONE

A maze-like urban battlefield that does double duty as an intense Team Deathmatch arena and fierce start to Ground Control, the neutral zone encompasses a large area that includes the smoldering gas station and several destroyed homes.

Close-quarters combat, drones, and devilish use of grenades and air strikes dominate the tactics. Rely on SMGs and mid-range rifles to do the dirty work, complementing your arsenal with deadly cluster and white phosphorous grenades intended to clear vital areas.

Key Locations

- Gas station, Control Point Alpha
- Blue house, Control Point Bravo
- Ramparts
- Crashed semi-truck

Control Point Alpha, within the smoking gas station, is significantly easier to capture than the wide-open Bravo, on the ground floor of a hollowed-out home. Multiple entrances—two doors, an open garage, and several windows—make capturing Control Point Bravo a serious test of skill.

Exploiting hiding spots is key in Team Deathmatch, as is utilizing corner spaces. Avoid open lines of sight favored by snipers, instead sticking to home interiors and backyards to hunt for kills.

Tactics

Control Point Alpha

CAPTURE DIFFICULTY:

Gas station and convenience store alike have been burnt to a crisp, leaving a blackened space for Control Point Alpha **[A]**. Capturing Alpha is easier than holding it, as hiding spots and fierce fighting both in and around the gas station make defending it a real challenge.

Counter Capture

Lie prone behind the cashier's counter inside the gas station to quickly capture Control Point Alpha. While it's not the safest spot, you can largely remain out of sight. This spot is particularly good if you're US, because you won't be harassed by teammates moving in through the back entrance. When playing as the KPA, lay down C4 at the back door before hiding behind the counter.

Full Throttle Hiding Spot

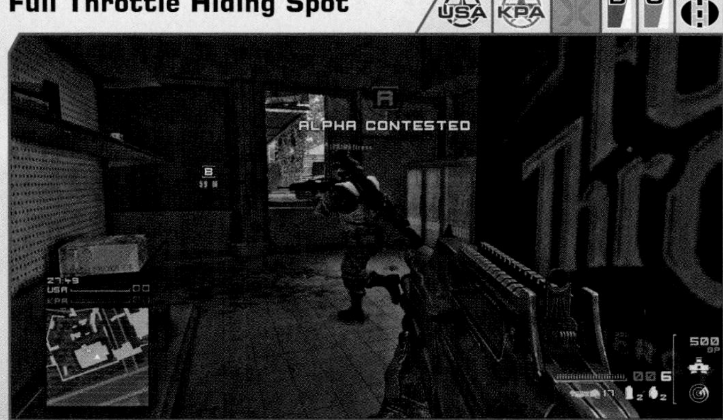

At the side entrance of the gas station on the KPA side is a Full Throttle vending machine. Press yourself against the wall between the vending machine and empty shelf to capture Alpha. This is a great spot to capture the control point when playing as the KPA because you don't have to worry about attacks from the side door.

Capturing Alpha between the Shelves

The most popular capture hiding spot lies between the two empty shelves in the center of the gas station. However, its popularity doesn't correlate to usefulness. This predictable spot is always searched by attacking enemies and you can be certain a grenade or two will be thrown your way. Coordinate with a teammate who can guard the entrances while you capture from this hiding spot.

Rooftop Grenade Delivery Service

Rather than entering the gas station at street level, attack it from above. Climb the ladder at the rear of the building to reach the hole in the roof that looks directly down to the cashier's counter. You can also access the roof by climbing the semi-truck and RV to the gas station awning, then jumping onto the convenience store. Drop cooked grenades into the store interior, then hop down to capture Alpha.

Backroom Surprise

A devious way of preventing US forces from contesting Control Point Alpha is to tuck yourself in the small hallway near the back door. From the shadowy recess near the door you can fill enemies rushing in to capture Alpha with bullets from an SMG or knock them back with a blast from a shotgun. Give yourself an extra edge by laying C4 at the door or chucking a white phosphorous grenade that kills on contact.

Dumpster Diving

This forward defensive position should be used only when Control Point Alpha is well secured and your team has put the pressure on the US. Crouch behind the dumpster away from the gas station on the US side. The nearby wall shields you from view, allowing you to remain undetected until US operatives run past the wall toward the gas station. From behind the dumpster, you can easily take enemies out and prevent them from ever reaching Alpha.

Denied Entry to Alpha

The small anteroom at the side entrance to the convenience store makes for a devious US defensive position. Cram yourself into the corner and kill any KPA soldiers that stream into the building. Unfortunately, C4 and area-of-effect grenades aren't wise in this location given the confined space.

Wall-to-Wall Defense

Similar to the forward defensive tactic used by the KPA involving the dumpster, when playing as the US you can pressure KPA forces attempting to make a push for Control Point Alpha. Press yourself against the wall of the house across from the gas station on the KPA side of the map and nail enemies as they emerge from the corner. As they run toward the convenience store, you should have no trouble mowing them down.

Drone Tactics

Because you lack access to vehicles, drones are your next best option for dishing out serious damage. Use the garage in the yellow house across from Control Point Alpha to launch drones. Aerial drones are better for attacking Alpha because you can fire at enemies through the hole in the gas station roof.

Control Point Bravo

CAPTURE DIFFICULTY: ★★★★★

Without question one of the toughest control points to capture and hold in any map, Bravo has plenty of avenues for an assault and few for defense **[B]**. Holding the control point is a matter of skill given the lack of defensive positions both in and around the two-story house.

Gutsy Ground Floor Assault

Several doors and windows make it difficult to determine the ideal street-level breach point to Control Point Bravo. So, take your pick and just run right in—sheer skill together with a little luck determines success. Equip an SMG or similar weapon with a high rate of fire that will enable you to quickly kill enemies as you secure the ground floor. Once you take the control point, drop a C4 charge in the living room and take a defensive position on the second floor.

Second Floor Intrusion

The best and most overlooked access point to the house containing Control Point Bravo is the backyard. A ladder leading up to the second floor grants entry to the house, allowing you to take Bravo from within rather than daring a direct push at street level. Of course, entering from the second floor simplifies only the approach, not the actual battle. You still need to hold the living room long enough to capture the control point.

Flanking the Fray

Instead of running straight toward the blue house containing Control Point Bravo, flank the attacking faction by walking around the small structure in the backyard near the edge of the map. With bullets whizzing about, you should be able to escape detection and attack from this alternative perspective.

Second Floor Stand

Defending Control Point Bravo from street level isn't feasible considering the ridiculous number of open doors and windows. As such, your best bet is to retreat to the second floor and mount a two-pronged defense. First, fire at enemies that approach the house using the windows. Should any make it inside, bounce cooked grenades down the stairs to get rid of them. If that's insufficient, return to the living room and flush them out with a burst of gunfire.

Drone Tactics

Although Wolverine gunfire and Buzzard rockets aren't nearly as powerful as a Battle Tank cannon, the ability to deploy drones from a distance offers a tactical advantage. Take to the roof of the blue-gray house across from Control Point Bravo to find a hidden deck. Drop down to it from the roof—there's no ladder access, which makes it much harder for enemies to find you. From here you can launch only aerial drones, but because they're great for attacking Bravo through the skylight looking into the control point, it's a limitation you can live with.

Vantage Points

Gas Station Rooftop

Without the threat of helicopters, taking aim from the gas station rooftops is a little more inviting. Nevertheless, there are still aerial drones and air strikes to consider. Use this vantage point to shoot enemies at Control Point Alpha through the hole in the roof **[VP.01]**. It's also effective for warding off attackers as they approach the gas station.

Catwalk, Blue House across from Control Point Bravo

From the second floor of the blue house containing Control Point Bravo, step onto a catwalk that stretches down the block for a great view of the neutral zone **[VP.02]**. Unfortunately, there's not much cover. Anticipate battles with snipers who have found similar spots in the houses on the other side of the map. Regularly check your back to avoid being ambushed by enemies who sneak into the house via the second floor access ladder.

Rooftop, Blue House across from Control Point Bravo

To avoid being ambushed while sniping on the catwalk, climb onto the roof for an alternate vantage point. Doing so trades one risk for another: you're more easily spotted against the dark shingles of the roof. Nevertheless, it provides an excellent view of the area surrounding Control Point Bravo, not to mention a clear line of sight to the other side of the map where you can snipe enemies well before they reach the vicinity of the control point **[VP.03]**.

Ramparts, Yellow House across from Control Point Alpha

Not much protects you from incoming bullets when standing on the ramparts near the gas station, yet that doesn't prevent this street-level vantage point from being noteworthy **[VP.04]**. While you're better off taking to the catwalks and roofs for longer periods of sniping, you can tag a few enemies running from the US side of the map to the two nearby control points.

Catwalk, Yellow House across from Control Point Alpha

This easily accessible walkway offers a good view of the gas station and street that stretches back into the US side of the map **[VP.05]**. US snipers using a similar catwalk on the other side of the map have a clear line of sight to your position when standing up here, so avoid marathon sniping sessions.

Rooftop, Yellow House across from Control Point Alpha

While the rooftop provides a better view of the neutral zone, it does so at great risk of being seen and shot. Jump from the nearby catwalk that runs the length of the street onto the roof, then lie prone to snipe enemies running between the two control points at the zone's center **[VP.06]**. Just be aware of snipers on the other side of the map, as well as the threat of drones and air strikes that can quickly silence your sniping.

KPA ZONE

Open houses make winning the KPA zone a tall order. Both Control Points Alpha and Bravo sit within houses with multiple access points, which act like revolving doors for possession: in comes one faction, out goes another.

Stopping this cycle largely depends on skill, although using hiding spots, vantage points, and drones can turn the tide to your team's favor. The shrunken battle perimeter adds to the pressure, though, because both factions spawn relatively close to each other.

Key Locations

- Yellow house, Control Point Alpha
- Off-white house, Control Point Bravo
- Skybridge
- School bus
- Cul-de-sac

There's no advantage in going for one control point over the other; instead, focus on capturing and holding one rather than dividing attention between the two. Exploit catwalks and ladders to sneak into each control point, because resistance is fiercest at ground level.

Tactics

Control Point Alpha

CAPTURE DIFFICULTY: ★★★★★

There's no way around it: capturing Control Point Alpha is tough **[A]**. The house in which it's located has several entrances and the lack of hiding spots leaves you vulnerable during capture. Holding Alpha comes down to skill and preventing enemies from ever entering the house by using vantage points to nail them at a distance.

Direct Assault on Alpha

Forming a squad of teammates to capture Alpha is the best direct assault tactic, because going it alone will likely result in your body sprawled on the floor like a discarded rag doll. Split up to cover the house's multiple access points, hurling cooked grenades into the house before entering. Watch the entrances as you collectively capture the point. Even if a few of your squad get picked off by the opposition, you should be able to succeed in taking Alpha.

Backdoor Capture Spot

Press your back against the debris piled against the stairs on the ground floor and face the rear of the house while capturing Control Point Alpha. While this leaves you open to attack from this back entrance, you're hidden from enemies entering the front of the house. Only having to deal with enemies streaming in through the rear is still tough, but at least gives you a fighting chance of capturing and holding Alpha.

Second Floor Windows

The windows on the second floor grant line of sight to the enemies streaming in through the back, as well as a view of the fight on the street in front. Nail enemies using a mid-range rifle like the M4 or SCAR-L while diligently checking the stairs for any attackers heading up the stairs to kill you. A C4 charge can help halt such an advance.

Skybridge from Hell

The short skybridge connecting Control Points Alpha and Bravo allows quick capture of both points. However, it's much easier said than done. With the battle raging on the street below, skipping across the skybridge to an easy capture is highly unlikely. Instead, expect to come under heavy gunfire. Use the skybridge not to launch an assault to capture one of the control points, but rather as a way of moving between the two when your team has control of both Alpha and Bravo.

Drone Tactics

There are few ideal drone deployment spots in the KPA zone, which leaves each faction's spawn point as a suitable option. When playing as the KPA, stay put in the backyards behind the houses lining the cul-de-sac at the edge of the map. Hang back at the opposite end of the map when playing as the US to launch drones toward the two control points. There's no roof access for aerial drones, which makes Wolverine and Rhino drones a good option for attacking Alpha and Bravo, both of which sit at street level.

Control Point Bravo

CAPTURE DIFFICULTY: ★★★★★

Like Control Point Alpha, Bravo **[B]** deserves its reputation as one of the trickiest control points in Cul-de-sac. Multiple access points, including the skybridge connecting it with Control Point Alpha, prevent easy occupation. Drones and explosives can make the difference in capturing Bravo, but holding it is all about skill.

Bravo Bum Rush

Control Point Bravo is so wide open that finding a decent spot to capture it is difficult. Having a teammate join you is advisable to speed the capture and boost your defenses. Use the small corner between the stairs to the second floor and the garage door to capture Bravo. Place C4 at the garage door and stand watch until you take the point. Don't stay here once you succeed—head upstairs to defend Bravo from a much safer vantage point.

Staircase Surprise

Crouch at the right angle turn in the stairs leading up to the second floor of the house and prime the shotgun attachment of your rifle (a quick-fire SMG works too). The moment an enemy runs up the stairs, blast him with your shotgun, preventing him from using the second floor windows as a vantage point against your team.

School Bus Shootout

The wheels on this school bus haven't gone 'round for quite some time, having made a permanent stop in the middle of the street between Control Points Alpha and Bravo. Seizing the inside of the bus is great for attacking enemies that run down the street on their way toward either control point. In particular, this spot is useful when playing as the US because it enables you to shoot down toward the KPA spawn point at the cul-de-sac down the street.

Sneaking through the Backyards

Tiptoeing through the backyard to reach the spawn point around the cul-de-sac down the street is an ideal tactic for cutting off KPA efforts to assail Control Points Alpha and Bravo. Of course, you're not likely to stay alive for long in the enemy's home turf. Call forth a cluster bomb or white phosphorous air strike to cripple the KPA where they spawn, ensuring that even after you've been killed, the opposition has to contend with a deadly area of effect weapon that serves as a distraction from the objectives up the street.

Vantage Points

Catwalk, Yellow House, Control Point Alpha

The catwalk that runs the length of the street in the KPA zone is much more dangerous now that the battle has shifted, making this a less useful vantage point **[VP.01]**. Still, there's limited value to be extracted from it. When playing as the US, take to the catwalk at the point closest to the gas station to shoot at KPA farther down the road near Control Points Alpha and Bravo. It's trickier to use as the KPA, though if you put enough pressure on the opposing faction you can use the catwalk to hit US soldiers as they emerge from their spawning grounds.

Rooftop, Yellow House, Control Point Alpha

With fewer vantage points in the KPA zone, the rooftop is a more viable sniping spot than it was during the battle for the neutral zone **[VP.02]**. Of course, you still have to worry about aerial drones shooting at you and air strikes taking you out from above. This spot can be potent when playing as the US, because it grants a limited view of the KPA spawning grounds in the cul-de-sac down the street.

Second Floor Windows, Yellow House, Control Point Alpha

The two rear windows on the second floor can be instrumental in defending Control Point Alpha from US soldiers attacking from the backyard **[VP.03]**. Drop C4 at the base of the stairs, then aim at enemies filtering past the fence at the lot's edge to the right. Even when playing as the US, you can use the windows overlooking the street at the front to defend Alpha and support teammates assaulting Bravo across the road.

Second Floor Windows, Off-White House, Control Point Bravo

You can use the windows on the second floor of the blue house in which Control Point Bravo lies to snipe enemies approaching from the street; however, it's of greatest use in sniping the KPA spawn point when playing as the US **[VP.04]**. Peer through the back windows to get at KPA soldiers spawning down the street.

US ZONE

Although the location of Control Points Alpha and Bravo differ, the same stalemate tactics define the US zone as they do the KPA zone on the opposite end of Cul-de-sac.

Tough to capture control points with multiple access points, enclosed spaces with corners tailor-made for ambushes, and vantage points that peer into spawn points and directly into each control point make maintaining possession of either Alpha or Bravo quite the feat.

Key Locations

- Fenced-in Supply Crates, Control Point Alpha
- Blue House near Control Point Alpha
- Blue House, Control Point Bravo
- Cul-de-sac

Pull from the same playbook as in the KPA zone: close-range weaponry, aerial drones to attack from a safe distance, and use of catwalks and ladders to avoid the clash at ground level in each of the houses. There are noticeably fewer hiding spots in the US zone than other areas of the map.

Tactics

Control Point Alpha

CAPTURE DIFFICULTY: ★★★★★

Resting in a backyard at the edge of the map rather than inside a house, Control Point Alpha is open from several angles **[A]**. This makes for straightforward capture, but difficult defense. Use the adjacent house to defend possession, simultaneously sniping at the other team spawning in the distance while maintaining an eye on Alpha directly below.

Capture Behind a Crate

USA KPA

Despite being outdoors, Control Point Alpha can be quickly and quietly captured behind any of the several crates stacked behind the fences. Crouch or lie prone while nabbing the control point, and drop C4 along the paths leading to your position. You can either hold your position or take to the nearby house to mount a defense.

Grenade Assault on Alpha

USA KPA

The best and easiest way to incite panic at Control Point Alpha is to chuck cooked grenades among the crates and fences. Whatever enemies survive will be forced out of hiding; shoot them as they seek a new hiding spot. Because defenders can't shoot through the fencing, use that to your advantage in a final push for control of Alpha by throwing a flash grenade and spraying bullets amid the confusion.

Holding Ground at Alpha

USA KPA

Mounting a defense from among the crates and fences of Control Point Alpha is tough. The inability to fire through the wire fencing means that you have to rely on explosives to hold attackers at bay. Move among the crates to keep enemies guessing as to your position, because it's likely that grenades will be hurled your way. Use your own explosives to defend the control point, detonating C4 when an enemy approaches the perimeter. Should C4 charges and cooked grenades fail, your last resort is to mow your opponent down with an SMG.

Blue House Defense

USA KPA

Defending Control Point Alpha on the ground is pretty tough because you can't shoot through the many fences; therefore, stationing yourself in the adjacent house is a great way to keep an eye on your prize without putting yourself in serious jeopardy. The back deck offers a good view of the control point, enabling you to snipe at intruders and throw grenades should they duck behind a crate. Drop C4 charges before heading into the house and detonate them from the deck whenever an enemy decides to stroll in.

Sneaking through the Backyards

Why concern yourself with defending Alpha when you can prevent the opposition from ever reaching it in the first place? Sneak through the backyards lining the cul-de-sac in the US zone to reach either faction's spawning ground. Camp out for a shoot out—while you're not likely to last long in enemy home turf, you can get in a few kills and distract them from the main objectives.

Control Point Bravo

CAPTURE DIFFICULTY:

There are multiple ways of capturing Control Point Bravo, located within the garage **[B]**. Unfortunately, this also makes it tough to defend. Set explosives to ward off attackers and take up defensive positions within the house to prevent the control point from switching hands.

Staircase Capture

Without a doubt the best place to capture Control Point Bravo is from the stairs inside the house. Chuck a C4 charge at the base of the staircase, then crouch midway up the steps to complete the capture. Should anybody come for you, detonate the charge and fire a few rounds from your gun.

Assailing the Garage

Control Point Bravo is hardly the ideal place for an assault given the two doors that grant full access to the garage. Nevertheless, it's possible to seize the control point in spite of the garage's open layout. Ideally with the backing of teammates, clear the garage and crouch behind the refrigerator and metal crate. Once you capture the point, drop C4 and head into the house to defend your new possession. Shoot approaching enemies from the windows on the second floor.

Second Floor Defense

Regardless of how you grab Bravo, defending it is a tricky task. The lack of cover and decent defensive positions on the ground floor makes a direct defense of the control point unattractive. Your best option is to use the windows on the second floor to shoot at enemies that approach the house. This distanced defense is safer, though more difficult. Plant C4 charges in the garage in case you can't snipe attackers from upstairs. In this sort of situation, you can run down the stairs, eliminate the invaders, then resume sniping on the second floor.

Drone Tactics

Drones work well in the fight for both Control Points Alpha and Bravo, enabling you to attack from a distance effectively. Ground drones—the rapid-fire Wolverine and hard-hitting Rhino—can quietly infiltrate the garage containing Bravo, as well as crates and wire fencing that surround Alpha. Aerial drones work too, though they're easily spotted and the layout of each control point makes it difficult to issue sneak attacks from above. When deploying drones, hang back at your team's spawn point. Nestle against a wall or inside a room such as the garage in the yellow house near the neutral zone to avoid being seen.

Vantage Points

Deck, Blue House adjacent to Control Point Alpha

Overlooking Control Point Alpha, the deck behind the blue house provides an ideal spot from which to guard Alpha. The angled roof blocks the line of sight from the house across the street, granting protection from sniper fire coming from behind **[VP.01]**. Not all corners of the control point are visible, however, and enemies can capture Alpha underneath covered sections of the control point.

Second Floor Windows, Blue House adjacent to Control Point Alpha

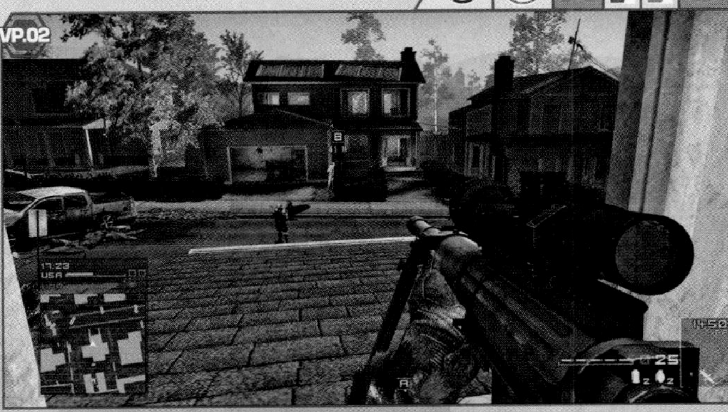

With the deck sufficiently covering Control Point Alpha in the back, use the second floor windows at the front of the house to engage enemies on the street **[VP.02]**. The ability to move between the windows and deck makes the second floor an attractive position, enabling you to monitor Alpha and support teammates moving to capture Bravo.

Rooftop, Blue House adjacent to Control Point Alpha

From the deck you can jump onto the roof for a great view of the US zone **[VP.03]**. Unfortunately, you're easy to spot against the slate gray roofing. Expect to get a lot of attention sniping from up here, whether it's enemy sniper fire from the house across the street, drones, or even a deadly air strike.

Catwalk, Blue House, Control Point Bravo

Attacking from higher ground is always tactically advantageous, and the catwalk that runs the length of the street in the US zone hands you that advantage on a platter **[VP.04]**. While it makes for poor sniping, the catwalk can be used to fire at enemies milling about on the street below.

Second Floor Windows, Blue House, Control Point Bravo

Peek out the windows on the second floor to watch the area surrounding Control Point Bravo **[VP.05]**. It's easiest to tag enemies that try entering the front of the house from the street, although you can do some damage from the back where US operatives are likely to enter the house by sneaking along the edge of map through the backyards.

Rooftop, Blue House, Control Point Bravo

Effective for either US or KPA players, the rooftop provides a clear view of the immediate area around Control Point Bravo **[VP.06]**. More importantly, though, it offers a line of sight to each faction's general spawn grounds. The risk of drone attacks and air strikes is worth the opportunity to put a bullet in a newly spawned enemy's head.

FARM

A picturesque snapshot of rural Americana shattered by the horrors of war, the Farm entertains rural combat between US and KPA forces across three zones. Each zone features a mix of expansive battlefields and interior spaces that make for fierce fighting.

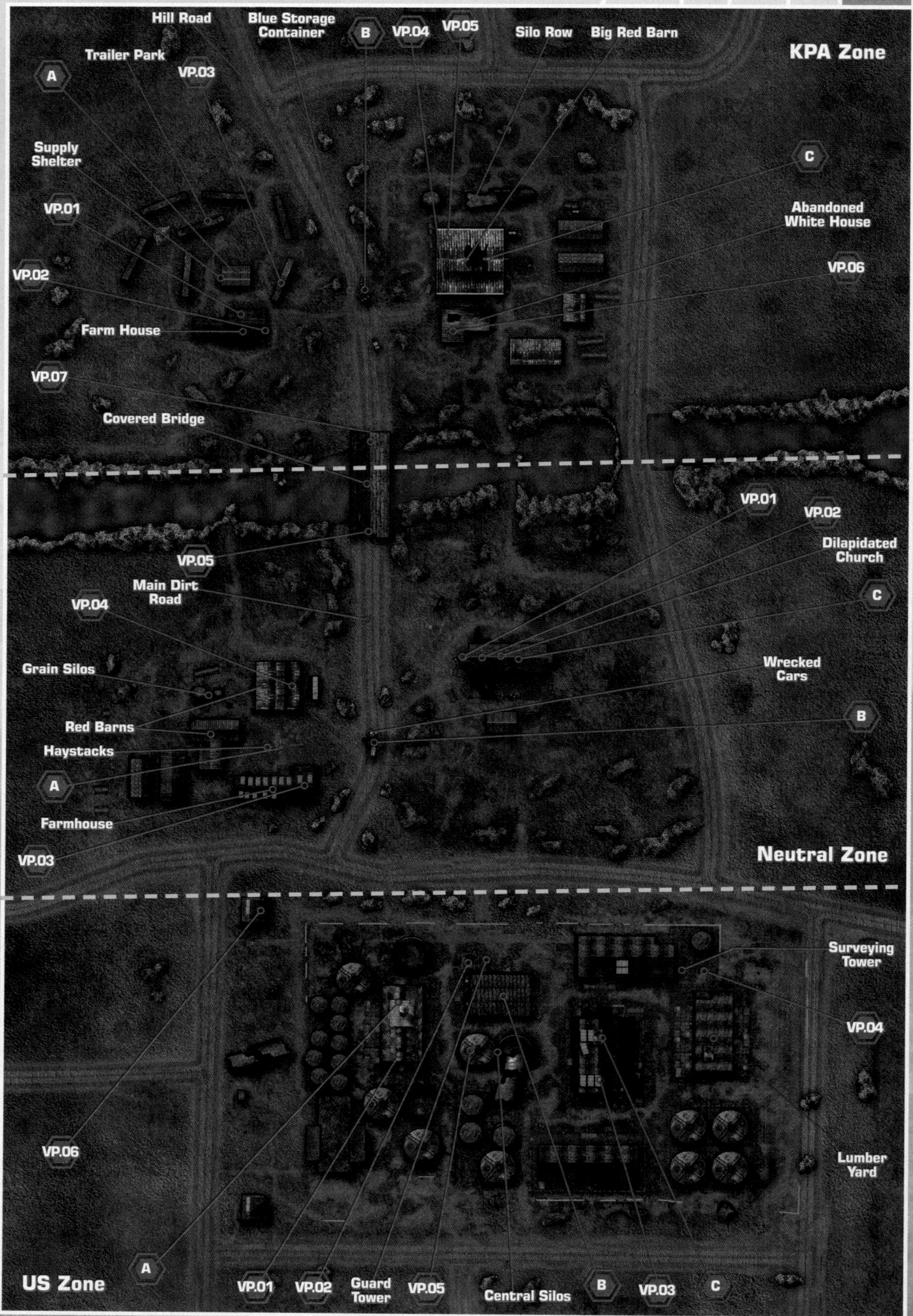

KPA Zone

Hill Road
Blue Storage Container
B
VP.04
VP.05
Silo Row
Big Red Barn
Trailer Park
VP.03
A
Supply Shelter
VP.01
C
Abandoned White House
VP.02
VP.06
Farm House
VP.07
Covered Bridge

Neutral Zone

VP.01
VP.02
Dilapidated Church
VP.05
Main Dirt Road
C
VP.04
Grain Silos
Wrecked Cars
B
Red Barns
Haystacks
A
Farmhouse
VP.03

US Zone

Surveying Tower
VP.04
VP.06
Lumber Yard
A
VP.01
VP.02
Guard Tower
VP.05
Central Silos
B
VP.03
C

NEUTRAL ZONE

The neutral zone hosts a bitter struggle between US and KPA forces for control over three control points situated near a farmhouse, church, and strategically significant dirt road.

US operatives have a slight advantage at Control Point Alpha due to the position of the US spawn point down the road. KPA forces must march a little farther to reach the control point. Yet, this negligible advantage doesn't prevent Control Point Alpha from being a hotly contested combat zone.

Key Locations

- Farmhouse
- Red barns
- Grain silos
- Haystacks
- Main dirt road
- Wrecked blue car
- Dilapidated church
- Covered bridge

Both factions should aim to seize Control Point Bravo as soon as the battle starts to avoid a bloody battle for possession on the open road. Vehicles are essential for attacking Bravo mid-battle, which in turn makes explosive weaponry—RPGs, grenades, even the Z-10 Chimera rocket-equipped helicopter and T-99 Battle Tank—a must for defending the control point.

Whereas the US benefits from closeness to Control Point Alpha, KPA forces have the advantage when it comes to Control Point Charlie. Make this a priority when playing as the KPA given the short distance from the spawn point and tactical significance of the steeple. Of course, you can bet on fierce resistance both in and surrounding the chapel.

Tactics

Control Point Alpha

CAPTURE DIFFICULTY: ★★★★★

Strategically nestled between a two-story farmhouse, towering grain silos, and a pair of lofty red barns, Control Point Alpha is all about close-quarters combat **[A]**. Although it offers some elevated vantage points for sniping enemies from afar, seizing and holding the control point requires urban-style fighting through the farmhouse and barn before a climatic push on the outdoor control point itself.

Flanking Control Point Alpha

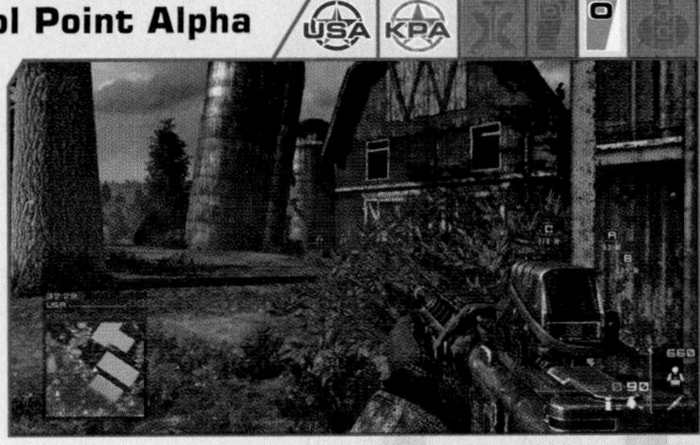

The path of least resistance to Control Point Alpha involves circumventing the pair of red barns and a two-story farmhouse surrounding the control point. Skirt around the farmhouse when playing as a US operative and approach the control point from the left. You're unlikely to run into any KPA resistance along this route given its close proximity to the US spawn point. As a KPA soldier, run to the right of the barn near the silos. US forces usually don't patrol this barn back alley, making it an easy inlet for a push on Control Point Alpha.

Farmhouse Assault

The farmhouse adjacent to Control Point Alpha provides good cover and a staging ground for a two-pronged tactical assault. Enter the house from the back door and you can proceed to the control point at ground level or run up the stairs to snipe the area clear. Coordinating a simultaneous attack on both floors is optimal, because it allows the team on the second floor to soften the area for ground forces to move in and capture Alpha. Lob in grenades to flush out any KPA camping amid the haystacks before seizing the control point.

Barnyard Push

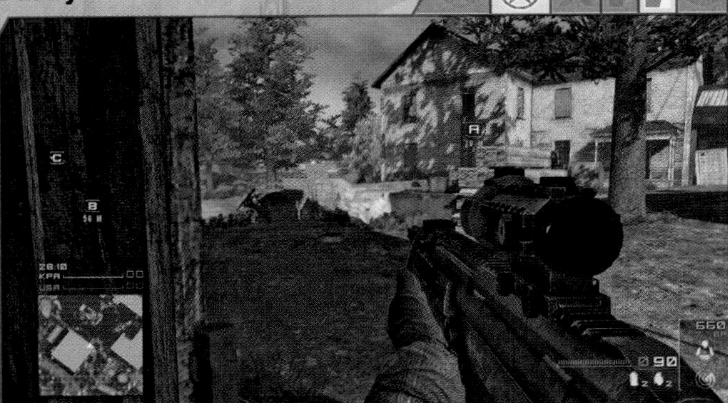

As a KPA soldier, stage an attack on Control Point Alpha using the open red barn towering over the control point. Aside from providing good cover, the loft overlooking Alpha allows you to coordinate with teammates who can rain down bullets as you rush in on foot. Eliminate US snipers in the farmhouse opposite the barn before attempting to seize the control point. Additionally, clear out any US forces hiding in the haystacks by hurling grenades.

Loft Lookout

Maintain watch over Control Point Alpha using the barn's loft window. Climb up to the loft from inside and crouch to survey the control point. Check your back frequently to avoid being ambushed by US operatives infiltrating the barn and climbing up to the loft.

Haystacks Hideaway

Use the element of surprise to nail enemies eager to capture Control Point Alpha by hiding away inside the checkpoint. Crouch into the cubbyhole in the corner and shoot unsuspecting opponents hoping to capture Alpha. Alternately, lie prone in the hay cart resting near the control point for a better view of approaching enemies. A point-blank blast with the shotgun attachment to your primary weapon is an effective way of holding your ground.

Holding Firm at the Farmhouse

Two floors of doors and open windows facing Control Point Alpha make the farmhouse an excellent defensive position. The more teammates holding the house, the better. Station yourself at either the ground level door across from the control point or on the second floor overlooking the area, both of which let you watch for activity and retreat to the farmhouse interior when you inevitably come under attack.

Shoot 'em Where They Spawn

When playing as the US, take advantage of the barn loft window facing the KPA spawn point. Climb up to the loft from the barn interior and lie prone on the hay bales stacked against the window to fire on KPA forces that appear. Another option is to leap from the top of the hay bales onto the barn rafters, where you can crouch and shoot at opponents who will no doubt express bewilderment as to how you scaled such heights.

Farmhouse Invasion

Expect a challenge holding the farmhouse when playing as the KPA due to its proximity to the US spawn point down the road. Still, it's ideal to make the farmhouse a forward defensive position as a means of preventing US forces from seizing Control Point Alpha. The second floor window provides an excellent opportunity to pop shots at spawning US forces. Before taking aim upstairs, arm the ground level door facing the US spawn point with C4 to prevent easy US infiltration.

Control Point Bravo

CAPTURE DIFFICULTY:

In the middle of the dusty road that runs between the farmstead and local church, Control Point Bravo is a dangerous testing ground for daring soldiers **[B]**. This exposed control point offers little cover, so taking it comes down to timing, teamwork, and vehicles.

Bravo Bravado

Dangerous, but direct—an all-out assault on Control Point Bravo isn't the best plan, though it's sufficient for seizing the area at the start of a match. Push fast and hard to take the control point, preferably with the aid of teammates who can watch for enemies and to speed the rate of capture. Lie prone against the blue car to remain out of snipers' sights as you capture the point. It offers little cover, but plenty of risk of aerial attack and snipers, so hightail it to a safer spot once you've nabbed the control point—after priming C4 charges to deter an assault, of course.

Vehicular Tactics

Your best bet for seizing Control Point Bravo is based on your ability to spawn vehicles. Rather than foolishly attempting a direct assault on foot, buckle into a Humvee, APC, or tank. Not only does spawning a vehicle get you to the area quickly, but you can remain in the vehicle while capturing the point. Cram a bunch of teammates into a Humvee and you can even increase the rate of capture. The one catch is that you're vulnerable to explosives, which can render your beloved ride nothing more than a charred chassis.

Control Point Charlie

CAPTURE DIFFICULTY: ★★★★★

The sheltered Control Point Charlie sits within the local church, which miraculously still stands after extensive bombardment by KPA air strikes and artillery blasts **[C]**. Seizing the control point is more difficult than holding it due to the church's easily defended points of entry. Aerial drones and helicopters are ideal for taking aim through the collapsed roof at forces guarding the interior. Rolling hills surrounding the church provide low cover for mid-range sniping, easing the march to the control point.

Church Perimeter Push

The boulders surrounding the church can be used to great effect in a push to take Control Point Charlie. Crouch behind the massive rocks on the church grounds to nail enemies at a distance. Positioning yourself near the rear of the church facing Control Points Alpha and Bravo is an equally viable tactic, enabling you to snipe into the fray. Better yet, sneak down the perimeter road along the back of the church to cut down your opponents where they spawn.

Deploying Drones

Send in drones through the church's blasted roof and crumbling exterior walls to soften up enemy defenses. The AQ-11 Buzzard was made for this job, allowing you to fly down through the gap in the roof to rain down rockets on unsuspecting defenders. You can also send in a MQ50 MG Wolverine on the ground and spray machine gun fire before stepping into the church to seize Control Point Charlie, although it doesn't carry quite the same element of surprise as the rocket-equipped Buzzard. Naturally, you need to camp out in a safe spot while piloting a drone. As the KPA, hide underneath the bridge near the spawn point. When playing as the US, hang back near the spawn point behind a boulder to stay out of a sniper's scope.

Church Interior

Upon seizing Control Point Charlie, your most immediate tactical option is to defend the inside of the dilapidated church. Hide beneath the wooden pallet angled against the wall to surprise enemies who rush in. A quick burst of gunfire is all it takes to teach an opponent that there's no such thing as an easily captured control point. Be careful, though, because aerial attack drones can sneak through the gaping hole in the roof, and ramps at each entry point enable ground drones to roll in with ease. Alternately, maintain watch over the church interior from the alcove opposite the main doors. From this enclosed location you can wait for enemies to enter the church, then emerge to pop a few shots.

Church Utility Shed

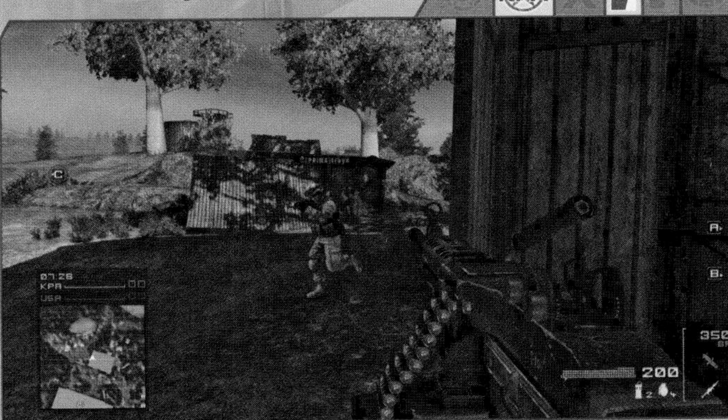

Despite its airy design, the utility shed adjacent to Control Point Charlie on the US side of the neutral zone can be useful in cutting off an assault on the church. Stand against the walls of the shed and shoot US attackers as they pass on their way the control point. Constantly check your side toward Control Point Bravo to avoid a flank attack.

Devilish Church Defense

Prevent US forces from claiming Control Point Charlie by setting C4 charges at the ramp leading into the church on the US side, then crouch against the stack of boards near the ramp, staying out of sight and protected from enemy fire. When US attackers run up the ramp, detonate the charges and pop up from cover to finish anyone left standing.

Vantage Points

Church Steeple

A sniper's dream, the church steeple offers a fantastic view of the neutral zone **[VP.01]**. Control Points Alpha and Bravo are clearly visible, making it ideal for picking off opponents at range. Unfortunately, you're easily identifiable when sniping here, and a well-guided Hellfire air strike or skilled use of a proximity launcher can take you out of commission. As such, maintain a low profile by crouching behind the waist-high railing and taking conservative shots.

Church Rooftop

A risky alternative to the steeple is crouching on the church's angled roof **[VP.02]**. While it's tricky to keep your footing given the steep angle, you're likely to catch enemies off guard by sniping from such an unlikely spot. KPA forces can also use the steeple as cover against US snipers. Saddle up against the steeple from the KPA side of the map and snipe down to the area encompassing Control Point Bravo.

Farmhouse, Second Story

The window facing Control Point Bravo on the second floor of the farmhouse provides a great view of the US side of the map **[VP.03]**. A clear sight line to Bravo makes this spot ideal for defending the control point or weakening the enemy's hold on it. Additionally, KPA troops can make good use of this forward vantage point to eliminate US operatives as they scamper across the hilly field and road below.

Rooftops

If you're really adventurous, eject yourself from a helicopter and use your parachute to drift onto the roof of the farmhouse or barn near Control Point Alpha for one killer and thoroughly unexpected sniping spot **[VP.04]**. Keep in mind that ejecting from a helicopter will draw attention and could broadcast your sniping intentions.

Covered Bridge

Climb onto the roof of the bridge near the KPA spawn point for an excellent view of Control Point Bravo and the front of the church **[VP.05]**. Given the bridge's distance from the main fighting, you can do serious damage with minimal risk of injury. Brave US operatives can sneak to the bridge and snipe at spawning KPA, although venturing this close to the enemy raises the risk of being riddled with bullets.

KPA ZONE

The portion of the farm that butts up against the hill has been utterly decimated by KPA forces. A creaky barn, two hollowed-out homes, and a grimy trailer park are all that remain of this once productive farm.

All three control points—Alpha inside a garbage-filled supply shelter located near the trailer park, Bravo on the open hill road, and Charlie situated within the big red barn—lie relatively close to the KPA spawn point, yet there are other tactical advantages for US attackers.

Key Locations

- Covered bridge
- Farmhouse, Control Point Alpha
- Supply shelter
- Trailer park
- Hill road
- Blue storage container
- Abandoned white house
- Big red barn
- Silo row

Assaulting Control Point Alpha is easier for US forces thanks to the layout of the adjacent farmhouse, which enables you to attack the supply shelter from cover. The farmhouse also makes staging a push for Control Point Bravo possible.

Much commotion occurs in the big red barn where Control Point Charlie is located. While enclosed, the expansive barn features several points of entry, including three doors and a blown-out roof. Both sides should anticipate a protracted battle for Charlie with tussles over Control Points Alpha and Bravo determining the victor.

Tactics

Control Point Alpha

CAPTURE DIFFICULTY: ★★★★★

It's hardly fine living in the residential complex that surrounds Control Point Alpha **[A]**. Dingy mobile homes and a two-story farmhouse in dire need of renovation sandwich the enclosed control point. The supply shelter containing the control point provides a tactical advantage for the US—a wall ends the line of sight from the KPA side, but there's a clear view into the shelter from the farmhouse on the US side.

Through the Farmhouse

The quickest route to Control Point Alpha for the US is directly through the two-story farmhouse. Rather than running and gunning to the control point, leap up the stairs to the second floor and eliminate any KPA opposition from the windows facing Alpha. Chucking grenades through the window into the open supply shelter is the most effective way of clearing the control point. Once you've softened up the area, head back to the ground floor and proceed to capture Alpha. Better yet, coordinate with your team to station someone on the second floor to cover your approach.

Circumventing the Farmhouse

Sidestepping the farmhouse at the edge of the map to reach Control Point Alpha takes more time, but avoids any intense fighting near the farmhouse. There's unlikely to be much resistance along the perimeter, making it relatively easier to pick off KPA soldiers while approaching Alpha.

CAUTION 조심하다

When playing as the US, resist the temptation to search for KPA operatives in the trailer park. There's no need to venture past the supply shelter—don't squander a tactical advantage on a brash assault. Stay behind the supply shelter and the area surrounding the farmhouse to prevent unnecessary casualties.

Trailer Park Charge

Seizing Control Point Alpha is more challenging when playing as KPA because of the wall that prevents you from looking into the supply shelter. The US has the upper hand with an obstructed line of sight into the supply shelter, though you can make an aggressive push through the trailer park to take the control point. Combine use of drones—crouch behind the boulders on the hill to remain hidden during drone deployment—and firearms suited for close-quarters combat such as the Diablo and Super-V SMGs in a push to Alpha.

Supply Shelter Campout

There's nowhere to hide while capturing Control Point Alpha, but the supply shelter's back wall provides a natural barrier that makes it much easier for US forces to grab the point than KPA. Use this to your advantage and crouch on top of the pile of garbage in the shelter's corner. From here, you can nail any KPA that run in and attempt to stop you—if they aren't blown to bits by the C4 you laid at each entrance, that is.

Supply Shelter Sortie

Control Point Alpha is tough to hold when playing as the KPA because it's so exposed. Be on high alert when moving into the supply shelter because US forces can hurl grenades and snipe at you from the farmhouse's second story. Your best bet is to coordinate an aggressive defense with teammates, leaving someone to guard the supply shelter and a small squad to engage US forces in the farmhouse as a distraction. Make sure to lay C4 charges at the shelter's two entrances to deter US operatives.

Farmhouse Defense

Holding the farmhouse is critical when playing as the US because it's your staging ground for seizing Control Point Alpha. Keeping it out of KPA hands means exploiting the second story windows that overlook the control point. Lob grenades and pop shots, ideally with a rifle such as the M4 or M16, to keep opponents at bay. Adding the shotgun attachment to your rifle is a great idea, just in case KPA soldiers break into the farmhouse and need to be put down quickly.

Knocking at the US's Backdoor

If you manage to take Control Point Alpha, your next objective is to seize the farmhouse. Rather than attempting a direct assault using the entrance across from the control point, flank US forces by going around the farmhouse to the right and entering from the side that faces the river. Evict the soldiers stationed inside, then take up guard on the second floor window facing the US spawn point at the riverbank. From here, you can snipe opponents as they spawn, effectively cutting off an attack on Control Point Alpha before it even begins.

Control Point Bravo

CAPTURE DIFFICULTY: ★★★★★

A host to hotly contested battles, Control Point Bravo is top among the most dangerous areas in the KPA zone **[B]**. Situated in the middle of the hill road that bisects the zone, it's best approached within the confines of an armored vehicle. Limited cover makes an on-foot assault unattractive, but not impossible.

On Foot

Capturing Bravo on foot is not the sanest tactical option, though it is feasible. The KPA have the advantage for seizing the control point at the start of match, but that edge quickly evaporates under a barrage of bullets once US forces arrive *en masse*. Approach the control point and scurry into the blue storage container where you can crouch or lie prone while capturing it. Chuck C4 at the entrance of the container to dispatch approaching enemies. Once you've captured the point, flee from the scene to avoid an air strike, grenades, or helicopter attacks.

Vehicular Tactics

Speedy and powerful—vehicles are the most effective means of capturing Control Point Bravo. Not only does spending Battle Points on a Humvee, APC, or tank enable you to roll into Bravo quickly, but it also affords you a little protection while you capture the control point. The Humvee obviously can't take much of a beating, but you can cram a bunch of teammates into a Humvee to increase the rate of capture. Better yet, have a teammate join you in the machine gunner seat to ward off RPG-equipped enemies and helicopters.

Control Point Charlie

CAPTURE DIFFICULTY: ★★★★★

The sounds of livestock are replaced by the rat-tat-tat-tat of gunfire in the big red barn that encases Control Point Charlie **[C]**. Holding this point is arguably more challenging than capturing it due to the barn's expansive interior. A gaping hole in the roof invites aerial drones and helicopter attacks, while the adjacent two-story white house makes a choice staging ground for a US assault.

Breaking into the White House

Similar to how the farmhouse across the hill road can be used to stage an attack on Control Point Alpha, the abandoned white house adjacent to the big red barn is useful in making a push for Control Point Charlie. Run through the ground floor to evade sniper fire on your way into the barn or head up to the exposed second floor to take a catwalk into the barn loft where you can fire on opponents guarding the control point below.

Silo Row Strategy

Although the KPA side of the barn doesn't have the benefit of a two-story house for mounting an attack, the row of silos provide good cover for an offensive push. Dart among the silos, including the one tipped on its side, to avoid incoming fire as you run to the backside of the barn.

Ground Assault on Big Red Barn

Regardless of which side you approach Control Point Charlie, taking it is a matter of winning the ground war inside the big red barn. Throw a flash grenade into the barn to daze opponents before running in to gun them down with a close- to mid-range weapon such as the Diablo or M4. Cooking a frag grenade or two is also effective for clearing the control point. Keep an eye on the loft to ensure that you're not shot at from on high. Avoid standing out in the open while taking the control point by hiding in the blue storage container in the corner. Be careful, though, because backing yourself into a corner makes you highly vulnerable to grenades.

Drone Assault on Big Red Barn

Take advantage of the hole in the barn roof by sending aerial drones to attack enemies guarding Control Point Charlie. While playing as the US, hide beneath the covered bridge near the spawn point or within the storage container sitting on the bridge. Your options are fewer as a KPA soldier; crouch behind a boulder on the hill by the spawn point.

The Helicopter Option

If you have the Battle Points, pilot a Z-10 Chimera attack helicopter to the gap in the barn roof and unload a barrage of rockets to obliterate enemies guarding the control point. Don't hover for long in one spot, though, or you're a prime target for RPG fire.

Flanking via Perimeter Road

While not the best tactical option if you want to storm Control Point Charlie, traveling the perimeter road enables you to circumvent the battle inside the big red barn and go right at the heart of the enemy: their spawn point. Use the gray barns in the distance for cover and snipe enemies from afar.

Big Red Barn Loft Defense

Although your first instinct is to take up a defensive position on the ground, the loft is an equally viable option. First, attacking from a high ground is always to your favor. Second, you're less likely to be flanked because you only need to monitor the barn floor and white house catwalk for enemy movement.

Rafter Surprise

You can surprise opponents by dropping onto the storage containers near the barn's entrance and firing from there. If you're willing to take the risk, you can walk onto the rafters that stretch into the middle of the barn. You're vulnerable from all angles and can't make a quick escape, but you're sure to rack up a couple kills courtesy of the element of surprise.

Vantage Points

Farmhouse, Second Story

Control Point Bravo and the big red barn are visible from the second story windows of the farmhouse, making this a good, though limited vantage point **[VP.01]**. It's particularly desirable when playing as the KPA because of the view it provides of the US spawn point; however, it's easier to reach when playing as the US.

Farmhouse Rooftop

If you're not up for fighting for control of the farmhouse, just parachute from a helicopter onto the roof **[VP.02]**. Snipe at enemies running between Control Points Bravo and Charlie with ease. Additionally, the roof provides an excellent view of the US spawn point when playing as the KPA. The drawback is that you're sure to draw attention abandoning a helicopter, plus the trajectory of your shots can be traced to the rooftop.

Mobile Home

While it's possible to climb onto three different mobile homes, only one provides a direct line of sight to Control Point Bravo. Unfortunately, there's no cover and you're completely exposed. Use this dangerous vantage point during those last-ditch efforts to defend Bravo from capture **[VP.03]**.

Barn Tower

The tower atop the big red barn is the highest point in the KPA zone and it's also one of the most dangerous vantage points **[VP.04]**. While it provides a spectacular view of the zone, it also has little in the way of cover, leaving you open to attacks from all angles.

Big Red Barn Roof

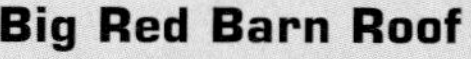

Instead of hopping down into the barn loft or climbing the nearby tower, head out onto the slanted roof itself and crouch for an effective vantage point **[VP.05]**. It's not without its drawbacks, though. You're extremely vulnerable to air strikes, helicopter fire, and drone attacks. Use this to nail a couple enemies, then move on before you're used to apply a fresh coat of red to the barn.

Abandoned White House, Second Floor

With the roof torn off, the second floor of the abandoned white house near Control Point Charlie makes for a decent vantage point **[VP.06]**. It overlooks the hill road leading up to Control Point Bravo and provides a limited view of the area in front of the barn. Use the ladder on the side of the house nearest the river when playing as the US to quickly climb to the second floor.

Covered Bridge

What the covered bridge lacks in terms of sight lines, it makes up for in relative safety **[VP.07]**. Compared with the other vantage points in the KPA zone, sniping from atop the bridge isn't all that dangerous when playing as the US. Of course, it's far from the action, which makes it less relevant. If you're brave, you can sneak onto the covered bridge when playing as the KPA and cut down US soldiers spawning farther up the river, although be prepared to make a hasty escape the moment you're discovered.

US ZONE

Storage buildings and silos dominate the US zone, defining the warehouse complex for which both factions bitterly fight. Unlike the barnyards and boulder-strewn fields of the neutral and KPA zones, this dense area features more aggressive combat.

The position of the KPA spawn point on the perimeter road so close to each of the three control points offers a natural advantage, though use of smart tactics can even the odds when playing on the US side. Skilled use of vehicles and hiding spots can push either faction to victory.

Key Locations

- Warehouse, Control Point Alpha
- Warehouse, Control Point Bravo
- Warehouse, Control Point Charlie
- Surveying tower
- Guard tower, Control Point Bravo
- Lumber yard
- Central silos

All three control points are located inside warehouses filled with nooks and crannies in which you can hide. Exploit these spaces to capture each point, then use aerial drones and helicopters to keep your opponents from taking them away.

In Team Deathmatch, the faction with the upper hand in close- to mid-range combat wins the day. As in Ground Control, focus on using hiding spots and nailing the opposing faction with vehicular attacks. When you're not manning a vehicle, seek cover inside the buildings that make up the warehouse complex. Avoid staying out in the open for long; dart between structures as you search for kills.

Tactics

Control Point Alpha

CAPTURE DIFFICULTY: ★★★★★

Storage containers stacked within the warehouse in which Control Point Alpha is located provide cover for capture, as well as solid defensive positions **[A]**. Although vehicles can't roll into the warehouse, they are useful in softening up resistance with machine gun and rocket fire. By combining use of vehicles, select hiding spots, and handheld explosives such as C4, Control Point Alpha can be captured and held amid fierce fighting.

Camping on the Storage Containers

Climb onto the storage containers littering the warehouse for an elevated position while seizing Control Point Alpha. The corner nearest the broken silo outside the warehouse is a decent spot, though scurrying across the wooden planks to the containers on the other side of the warehouse puts you in a superior position. Not only does the latter enable you to capture the control point, it also shields you from incoming KPA attackers when playing as the US. In Team Deathmatch, shoot at enemies as you move among the containers to keep the other team guessing.

Control Point Alpha Motorcade

Before launching a push to take Control Point Alpha on foot, mount a vehicular assault to soften up the opposition's defenses. Both the LAV and Battle Tank pack enough punch to open Alpha up for an attack, but you can also use drones for a quieter approach. When playing as the US, hang back at the spawn point to deploy drones. Either US or KPA forces can use the broken silo outside the perimeter wall near Control Point Alpha to launch drones. Lobbing cooked grenades is always a good idea before entering enclosed spaces too.

Back Door Defense

The rear entrance to Control Point Alpha provides a clear line of sight all the way to the US spawn point at the other end of the warehouse complex. Use this to your advantage when playing as KPA to defend Alpha. Plant C4 at the back door and tuck yourself into either corner to the side of the door. This enables you to monitor the front two entrances and stay out of sight from US forces advancing toward the rear. When they approach, detonate the C4 and step out to unload your clip.

Front Door Defense

Mirroring the KPA defensive tactic used to hold Control Point Alpha, when playing as the US, station yourself near the pair of entrances at the front of the warehouse to check for KPA attackers. Drop C4 at both doors, then position yourself in a corner or climb onto the storage containers. When KPA operatives try to enter the warehouse, blow them to bits with the C4 charges and finish them off with a burst of gunfire. SMGs excel in these close-up combat situations.

Control Point Bravo

CAPTURE DIFFICULTY:

Contained within a warehouse at the center of the US zone, Control Point Bravo is all about utilizing hiding spots among the storage containers to capture and hold **[B]**. When it comes to offense, explosives are your friend—nail the warehouse with grenades and vehicular attacks to clear the way for capture.

Explosives Assault on Bravo

Control Point Bravo is tough to hold because of the warehouse's open layout. Use this to your advantage by pummeling the control point with explosives. On foot, cook grenades and throw them inside to clear out any defenders. Flashbang grenades are also useful for disorienting enemies ahead of an interior assault. While you can't roll in to capture the control point, vehicles work well in softening up resistance, specifically the LAV and Battle Tank, both of which enable you to unload a barrage of bullets and cannon fire on Bravo.

Storage Container Cubbyhole

A great way to capture Control Point Bravo is to tuck yourself away in an L-shaped cubbyhole in the corner nearest the guard tower outside the warehouse. It recedes so far back from the center of the room that you're safe from vehicular attacks. You do have to be careful of grenades, which can kill you if you don't flee. Unfortunately, you're sure to face a firing squad as soon as you emerge from hiding, so be prepared to fight.

Blending in with the Storage Containers

Across from the L-shaped cubby inside Control Point Bravo is another useful hiding spot among the storage containers. Lie prone to hide in the small recess with a waist-high crate. As long as you stay prone and tuck yourself as far back against the containers as possible, enemies shouldn't be able to see you. While it's less hidden than the L-shaped cubby on the other side of the room, you can use this spot to both capture the control point and defend it by popping up to take shots at opponents.

Storage Container Ambush

Hop onto the stack of storage containers in the corner of the warehouse nearest Control Point Charlie. From here you can crouch or lie prone and guard the warehouse. Even though you aren't hidden, you're likely to go unnoticed. If an opponent enters the warehouse when you're trying to capture Bravo, hold your fire until you're certain you can kill them. Don't give away your position and die because of a poorly aimed shot.

;ontrol Point Charlie

;APTURE DIFFICULTY: ★★★★★

⁻he elongated rectangular warehouse in which Control Point Charlie ;its offers a multitude of hiding spots **[C]**. Use these nooks and ;rannies to quickly capture the control point, then take up any of a ıumber of defensive positions inside the warehouse. Pay attention o the hole in the roof, as it's an effective delivery point for explosive ıttacks.

Warehouse across from Control Point Charlie

A great way to soften up Control Point Charlie for a ground assault s to stage an nitial attack from the warehouse across the way. There's a clear line of sight into Control Point Charlie, enabling you to fire at defenders nside. Cook grenades and chuck them at an angle into the control point to flush out anyone hiding among the storage containers. If you have enough Battle Points for a LAV or Battle Tank, spraying machine gun fire or a hammering the control point with the tank's cannon is effective for clearing the spot.

Lumber Yard

Along the edge of the warehouse complex, the lumber yard provides a staging ground for an attack on Control Point Charlie. Particularly when playing on the US side, approach the control point via the lumber yard to avoid the battle raging near Control Point Bravo. The stacks of timber make for nice cover, enabling you to eliminate enemies from a short distance before moving in for the capture. In Team Deathmatch, use the stacks to rack up kills on US soldiers spawning down the road or to nail KPA moving between warehouses.

Raining Down Explosives on Control Point Charlie

Exploit the hole in the roof above Control Point Charlie by dropping explosives—grenades, C4 charges, rockets—to rattle defending enemies. Raining down machine gun fire from a Scout helicopter is good too, though rockets from a Buzzard drone or Z-10 Chimera are even better. A great spot for staying hidden while deploying drones is in the broken silo along the warehouse complex's outer wall near Control Point Alpha.

Capture Spots

Dart into a corner when capturing Control Point Charlie to keep a low profile. Either corner near the far door works; press yourself against the storage containers to hide yourself as much as possible. Consider laying a couple of C4 charges at the two entrances as insurance against attackers. Another clever capture spot is to jump onto the thin edge of the container against the perimeter-facing wall. Not only can you capture Charlie from here, but enemies won't necessarily look for you on top of the containers.

Defending Control Point Charlie

Remaining within the capture zone as a defensive tactic isn't the best idea because it's open to fierce attack. Instead, pull back into the other half of the warehouse and take a position among the storage containers facing Control Point Charlie. Against the far wall are a stack of containers you can crouch upon, although the shadowy space against the opposite wall is better. From here you can crouch between a container and wall, taking aim at any opponents who rush in to capture the control point.

Vantage Points

Warehouse Roof, Control Point Alpha

USA KPA

The warehouse rooftops aren't the safest sniping spots due to the lack of cover and accessibility, though KPA operatives should leverage the roof over Control Point Alpha **[VP.01]**. A direct line of sight into the US spawn point on one side and a clear view of the ground in front of the control point on the other makes it worth risking an air strike or helicopter attack to head up to the roof. Similar advantage is afforded when playing as the US. Take to the roof to fire on KPA soldiers as they spawn and pass through the breaks in the zone's perimeter wall.

Guard Tower, Control Point Bravo

USA KPA

When on the KPA side, the guard tower next to Control Point Bravo is an attractive prospect for its good views of the immediate area around Control Point Alpha and solid line of sight back to the US spawn point **[VP.02]**. It's also possible to hop from the guard tower onto the roof of the neighboring warehouse that contains Control Point Bravo—something to consider when playing as the US.

Warehouse Roof, Control Point Charlie

USA KPA

Make good use of the roof above Control Point Charlie when playing as the KPA to snipe at spawning US soldiers **[VP.03]**. Climbing up here is equally useful as a US soldier for nailing enemies attempting to approach Control Point Charlie. The main drawback—which applies to each of the rooftop vantage points—is exposure. Easy access via ladders to the roof combined with no cover puts you at high risk. Additionally, drones, helicopters, and air strikes can eliminate you quickly if you stay put too long.

Surveying Tower

USA KPA

For the best view of the US zone, climb up the surveying tower across from Control Point Charlie **[VP.04]**. This tall structure provides a full line of sight to the zone's most contested areas. You're vulnerable to air strikes, drone fire, and helicopter strikes, yet the tower's extreme height largely makes you out of reach of gunfire coming from the ground. It's possible to jump down to the pair of adjacent silos, although tactically it's an inferior position. As a sidenote, you can quickly leap from the survey tower in a bind by deploying your parachute.

Central Silos

USA KPA

The cluster of silos at the center of the US zone (near Control Point Bravo in Ground Control) are conveniently equipped with a ladder for easy access **[VP.05]**. Scramble up for a good view of the warehouse complex. While it's easy to take aim at enemies from this point, you're sure to attract attention due to the lack of cover.

Perimeter Guard Tower

USA KPA

One of the few spots that's of greater tactical use in Team Deathmatch than Ground Control, the corner guard tower at the zone's perimeter offers a limited view of the warehouse complex at the map's center **[VP.06]**. Silos prevent a full line of sight to your right, but you can still snipe at opponents running for cover among the warehouses.

GREEN ZONE

A pair of skyscrapers separate the remnants of a bustling American community complete with multi-story apartment buildings, car dealership, and a cheap fast food restaurant from the KPA-forced neighborhood with its Korean language signs staring down oppressively at empty streets. Such an intrusive act prompts both factions into an urban battle on the ground and in the skies.

NEUTRAL ZONE

Where American and Korean cultures clash, the neutral zone marks the boundary between the KPA-occupied half of the town and the abandoned US side. A fierce battle for control of the objectives on and under the highway determine on whose turf the fight continues.

When playing as the US, head right for Control Point Alpha under the highway. The opposite is true for KPA: aim to capture Control Point Charlie on the other side of the zone under the freeway once the match begins. With these secured, go for the win by taking Control Point Bravo at the center of the zone.

Key Locations

- Highway checkpoint, Control Point Alpha
- Guard tower
- Hooters billboard
- Twin skyscrapers
- Highway crater, Control Point Bravo
- Highway patrol tower
- Supply checkpoint, Control Point Charlie
- Billboard (KPA side)

Ground vehicles are helpful in applying pressure, yet it comes down to coordinating an infantry approach that can successfully capture and hold this bitterly fought control point. Sniping from billboards and guard towers supports a ground assault, as do helicopters and airstrikes.

Tactics

Control Point Alpha

CAPTURE DIFFICULTY: ★★★★★

A military checkpoint beneath the highway, Control Point Alpha features a number of useful vantage points and defensive positions [A]. When playing on the US side, take this objective early in a match and then push toward Bravo on the highway above.

Annexing Alpha

USA KPA

There's aren't any good hiding spots within Control Point Alpha's capture zone, which means seizing it is a matter of parking a vehicle on the road or clearing the area and executing a quick capture while crouched against a stack of cargo containers. As you approach the control point, lob cooked grenades to kill and disperse enemies defending the area. Use an SMG or LMG to quickly mow remaining forces down, then press against the cargo containers to shield yourself from incoming gunfire as you seize the control point.

Parking Under the Highway

USA KPA

Rev up a vehicle to instigate a speedy capture of Control Point Alpha. Park yourself (and teammates willing to join you to make the capture quicker) on the road that runs under the highway. Watch for RPG and other explosives attacks coming from within the control point, but more importantly, on the guard tower. Helicopters aren't useful for attacking or defending Alpha because it's sheltered by the highway.

Ramped Up

USA KPA

Bear down on Control Point Alpha from the highway above. Slide grenades down the concrete slope into the control point to rattle defenders, then inch down the ramp. Send a Wolverine anti-infantry drone down the ramp if you're worried about too much enemy resistance. Defend against an attack from the ramp by crouching underneath the road as it angles down toward Alpha. Because enemies will roll grenades to the street and won't expect you hiding at the side, shoot soldiers as they descend from the freeway unaware.

Bridge over Troubled Alpha

USA KPA

Instead of attacking Control Point Alpha from the ramp, assail it from the gap in the highway without ever setting foot on the ground. Hop past the two trucks at the edge of the highway onto the barriers that look down onto the control point. From here, fire on defenders and clear the way for your teammates to capture the objective. This is also a great defensive location. After seizing Alpha, run up the ramp, jump onto the concrete sides, and guard the area below.

Checkpoint Hostilities

The small checkpoint across the street from Control Point Alpha serves as a great KPA defensive position. Station yourself inside the square checkpoint after placing a C4 charge in the middle of the road, crouching behind the waist-high walls. Fire on US soldiers running toward Alpha, while saving the C4 for any vehicle that tries rolling through.

Control Point Bravo

CAPTURE DIFFICULTY: ★★★★★

A nexus for the battle in the Green Zone, Control Point Bravo has seen plenty of combat, as the crater in which it sits shows **[B]**. Banged up storage containers transform this seemingly exposed objective into a hotspot for close-quarters combat.

Crater Container Capture

You can capture Control Point Bravo from essentially anywhere within the crater, but the best spot is inside the banged up storage containers that run perpendicular to each other at the base. While you still have to contend with enemies who filter into the open containers from either end of the highway, you're protected from airstrikes, helicopters, and aerial drones. One nice thing about the containers is that they enable you to defend the control point as long as you can beat back enemies. Equip an LMG to ensure you don't run out of ammunition and quickly slaughter any foes who peek inside the containers.

Capture Under the Lip of the Highway

While the containers are your best bet for seizing Control Point Bravo, try the lip of the road at the edge of the crater. This partially hidden spot is frequently overlooked by enemies and provides cover from airstrikes and helicopter attacks. Defending from this position is trickier, though, because you have no easy route of escape.

Softening Up Bravo

Hammer Control Point Bravo with airstrikes and explosives to accomplish two things: kill as many defenders as possible and rattle the surviving enemies. While there's cover to be had in the containers at the base of the crater, a cooked grenade hurled through an opening can kill or at least flush out an enemy. The opposite is true when using an airstrike. Hail down Hellfire missiles and enemies will seek shelter, making it easy for you to run into the container with an SMG and mow them down.

Impact Zone Perimeter Tactics

Before heading into the crater to capture Bravo, attack from the perimeter to clear as many enemies from the area as possible. Grenades are helpful, although be careful to angle your throws properly—you don't want to accidentally throw a grenade and have it bounce off a raised bit of asphalt only to land at your feet. From a defensive perspective, the crater perimeter is useful too, particularly if your team possesses one of the other control points. This enables you to attack from the side of the highway that your faction holds without fear of getting flanked.

Skyscraper Shield

The only effective use for helicopters in the neutral zone is weaving between the twin skyscrapers while attacking enemies in the cratered Control Point Bravo. Although the cover provided by the containers means that helicopter fire won't always hit a target, it serves to spook enemies into tight hiding spaces where they're easily eliminated with a quick burst of fire from an SMG.

Furthermore, monitoring the stretches of highway on both sides of Bravo is best done from a helicopter.

Control Point Charlie

CAPTURE DIFFICULTY:

A near mirror image of Control Point Alpha, Charlie is riddled with supply crates and containers **[C]**. Vehicles won't work for capture, but use them when launching an assault or attempting to hold this objective.

Ground Contest for Charlie

Even though vehicles can't be used to capture Control Point Charlie, they're still great for attacking the area and putting pressure on defenders to give up the objective. Expect a ton of action on road that runs through Charlie. When you're defending, keep a RPG or Grenade Launcher attachment handy for use against vehicles that roll by. Better yet, drop C4 charges on the road that you can detonate while crouching among the crates.

Down from the Highway

Without the ability to call in airstrikes on Charlie or even attack from a helicopter, the alternative is to attack from the highway ramp. Identical to the tactic used at Control Point Alpha, slide down the ramp from the freeway above and fire at enemies defending Charlie. Defend the slope from attackers by squeezing into where it meets with the highway. Shoot enemies as they descend the ramp; they won't be expecting an attack from the side.

Elevated Defensive Spot

Take aim at enemies from the gap in the highway above Control Point Charlie. Similar to the tactic used at Control Point Alpha, jump onto the concrete sides of the highway to shoot down into Charlie. It's a superb defensive position too, enabling you to stay above the fray, yet still get a piece of the action by firing from above.

Bank Shot Grenades

The fence surrounding Control Point Charlie gives defenders an upper hand, but you can turn this disadvantage around by bouncing grenades off the concrete underside of the highway over the fence. From the base of the ramp that leads up to the highway, throw a grenade at the overpass to make it bounce up and over the fence, dropping right into the control point—that should catch the enemy by surprise.

Drones Near the Highway

Wolverine drones are good for attacking and defending Control Point Charlie because it's only accessible on foot. While there's always the risk of having your drones taken out by an EMP blast or deft melee hit, the machine gun is unbeatable when it comes to eliminating infantry. On the KPA side, hang back at the skyscrapers to avoid detection when deploying drones. When playing as the US, take shelter in the Montrose Car Dealership.

Vantage Points

Hooters Billboard

The Hooters billboard (remember that fine establishment from Borderlands?) looks down on Control Point Alpha **[VP.01]**. While it's decent for watching Alpha, it's actually better for monitoring the highway above and peeking over at Control Point Bravo farther down the road.

Guard Tower, Control Point Alpha

With the highway cutting off the view, the guard tower near Control Point Alpha is solely intended for keeping watch on this one objective **[VP.02]**. Because it's on the KPA side of the highway, you best utilize it when playing as this faction. If you favor an aggressive approach when playing as the US, push KPA forces back from Alpha by taking position in the guard tower and sniping them as they approach the highway.

Highway Patrol Tower

The highway patrol tower near Control Point Bravo isn't as great spot a sniping as it is for deploying drones and attacking helicopters ducking and bobbing between the two skyscrapers **[VP.03]**. Because the patrol tower is so close to the battle at Bravo, consider the risks before sending out a drone. When it comes to wielding a Proximity Launcher against a pesky helicopter, however, this vantage point can't be beat.

Fuel Systems Billboard

Set far back from the highway on the US side of the map, the Fuel Systems billboard offers a distant view of the action at Control Point Charlie **[VP.04]**. Only take position at this vantage point if you're confident in your sniping skills because the distance makes tagging enemies challenging.

Skyscrapers

The twin skyscrapers that tower over the Green Zone are inaccessible on foot, but that doesn't mean you can't use the rooftops for sniping. Spawn a helicopter and eject yourself, drifting onto the rooftops using your parachute **[VP.05]**. It's an expensive endeavor, to be sure, though you're rewarded with an insanely awesome view of the entire map. Plus, only a helicopter can attack you from such heights—talk about the ultimate sniping spot!

KPA ZONE

A sign for a dentist's office set it Korean type, a nail salon with a Korean banner outside—there's something perverse in the way the KPA has tried forcing their culture onto an American population that continues to resist their oppressive rule.

However, it's not easy fighting back. Routing the KPA from this outlying zone means winning the control points located in the park, military shelter, and auto shop. This is KPA turf, so expect fierce fighting at each objective.

Key Locations

- Gazebo, Control Point Alpha
- Park pond
- Guard tower
- Armory, Control Point Bravo
- Auto shop, Control Point Charlie
- Greg Bennett Design billboard
- Korean strip mall

Control Point Charlie is the easiest to defend thanks to a number of hiding spots and defensive positions. Alpha and Bravo are much harder to hold, particularly the former, which sits inside an open gazebo that's constantly under fire.

While vehicles can play a role in the KPA zone, they're less effective than in the other two sections of the map. Drones and helicopters are much more helpful, whereas clever infantry tactics ultimately determine who wins the round. Focus on using vantage points and hiding spots, using airstrikes to clear open spaces in the park, and plain ol' sharpshooting.

Tactics

Control Point Alpha

CAPTURE DIFFICULTY: ★★★★★

Instead of happy weddings and birthday parties, the gazebo containing Control Point Alpha marries guns and rockets in a battle for domination of the surrounding park **[A]**. The lack of cover makes Alpha tough to capture, but easy to defend.

Under the Table

This devious little hiding spot is the best place from which to capture Control Point Alpha. Crawl underneath the table and lie parallel to the outer gazebo wall to prevent your torso from sticking out. Don't plan on staying put, though. Enemies love throwing cooked grenades into the pavilion—an excellent tactic for killing those hiding in the gazebo.

Hiding by the Pond

Wade through the pond near Control Point Alpha to reach the foliage among the rocks. Hide in the greenery to take aim at enemies running through the park. Attach a silencer to your rifle to maintain a low profile while attacking from this position.

Drone Patrol

Use drones to attack and defend Control Point Alpha in the gazebo. After seizing the control point, leave a Wolverine drone on the wooden floor as an active threat to enemies seeking to nab Alpha. Launch rockets into the gazebo from a Buzzard to rattle enemies hiding inside. While the rockets won't deal much damage to infantry, they sure will get enemies scrambling out of hiding.

Defending Alpha

Defend the gazebo from a distance, rather than attempting to hold Control Point Alpha from inside. While there's sure to be vehicles milling about the park, take a defensive position among the boulders strewn about. This enables you to fire into the gazebo, as well as catch enemies approaching the control point from the interior of the map. Also, before taking up a defensive position, place a C4 charge inside the gazebo and detonate it if an enemy slips into the control point. Lastly, circling the gazebo in a LAV or tank is a great way of squashing interest in Control Point Alpha. The thought of engaging a tank is often enough to keep enemies from attempting to capture the control point.

Control Point Bravo

CAPTURE DIFFICULTY:

Unlike most centrally located objectives, Control Point Bravo has a wealth of hiding spots and defensive positions **[B]**. This prevents it from changing hands frequently, though it's still contested ground that's well worth fighting for. Holding this objective gives you an edge on taking Charlie across the street.

Bravo Blitz

Spam with cooked grenades, pummel it with a tank cannon, spray it with machine gun fire from a Wolverine drone—unload on Control Point Bravo before entering the armory on foot (vehicles can't be used for capture). The harder you hit it, the easier it is to capture. Because the armory is open at two sides, have teammates join you to quicken the capture once the armory has been cleared.

Corner Capture

Tuck yourself in the corner created by the stack of supply crates to capture Control Point Bravo relatively out of sight. It's a predictable hiding spot, so anticipate grenades being thrown your way. Think ahead and drop C4 charges at the two access points, which you can detonate when you suspect an enemy is approaching.

Crate Climbing

It's too bad you can't capture Control Point Bravo from on top of the crates, but at least you can mount a good defense looking down into the armory. Hop up the stacks and lie prone on the crate of your choice to guard the control point below. Alternately, use the nearby building rooftop and face toward the water to defend Bravo.

\wning Overlook

:limb on top of the rates, then hop om the rooftop f the adjacent uilding onto ne sheet metal wning above the rmory. There's gap to exploit s a defensive verwatch. Aim own into the armory to defend Control Point Bravo. Drop a C4 harge and keep grenades at the ready should any unsuspecting nemies try taking your control point.

Control Point Charlie

:APTURE DIFFICULTY: ★★★★★

he most defensible location in the KPA zone, Control Point Charlie ; set within the garage of an auto shop **[C]**. Access through the djoining office is a great way to infiltrate when playing on the KPA ide, whereas a back entrance is ideal for the US.

\uto Shop Assault

Volverine drones re your best friend vhen assailing the nterior of the auto hop that houses :ontrol Point :harlie. Send one f these puppies n to chew up nemies, then head nside yourself to eize the objective. Another approach involves spamming the auto hop office with grenades before entering the building. The two tactics ren't mutually exclusive and working with a teammate could enable ou to attempt both simultaneously.

)ffice Space

Hide in the ectangular alcove ocated on the treet side of the uto shop office o quietly capture :ontrol Point :harlie. It's the best iding spot in the uilding, even if it's he most obvious.

Hedge your bets by placing C4 charges at the doors: side door to blast approaching KPA, and garage access to take out US attackers.

Locking Down the Office

With US soldiers frequenting the garage access, cut them off as they're attempting to enter the auto shop office. Stand at either side of the doorway and blast them with a shotgun or spritz of bullets from an SMG. Augment your defense by placing a C4 charge on the other side of the door or chucking a WP Grenade to deny passage through the garage.

Flanking the Office

Although the back entrance is a great way to approach Control Point Charlie, flank defending KPA forces by entering from the side office door. Not only will it comes as a surprise to the KPA who stream into the control point via this entrance, but you can coordinate with teammates who can filter in through the back and make it a pincer assault.

Drones at the Water's Edge

One of the advantages granted to the KPA is the swath of territory away from the zone's center. While there's not much action among the strip mall shops, it's still tactically significant. Deploy drones from this area, sending them into any of the three control points at the map's center. This is a great place when sending drones into Charlie, in particular, because the auto shop is a short jaunt from the strip mall.

Vantage Points

Park Rocks

Lie prone on the large boulders scattered around the park for an unlikely vantage point **[VP.01]**. The shadows cast by the trees provide a sort of camouflage among the rocks that toys with enemy eyes. You still have to be careful, however, because you're not completely hidden and with vehicles milling about, you could quickly become toast.

Guard Tower

Useful for KPA when assaulting Control Point Alpha during the battle for the neutral zone, the guard tower along the park perimeter has its own value here in the KPA zone **[VP.02]**. Take aim at enemies fighting for control of Alpha while crouching against the waist-high guard rail. This is also a great position from which to fire explosives at vehicles patrolling the park.

Armory Rooftop, Control Point Bravo

Climbing the stacks of crates inside the armory at Control Point Bravo is a great defense tactic, though scaling the rooftop is an even better one **[VP.03]**. While you can't see into Bravo below from the roof (there is a gap in the connected sheet metal awning over the control point, however), the view of Alpha in the park and Charlie inside the auto shop is solid.

Auto Shop Rooftop, Control Point Charlie

Rather than being useful as a defensive position for Control Point Charlie, the auto shop roof serves well during an attack on neighboring Bravo inside the armory **[VP.04]**. Scale the ladder at the back of the building to access the roof, being mindful that you're exposed to airstrikes and helicopters while up here.

Greg Bennett Design Billboard

Located right outside the auto shop office, the Greg Bennett Design billboard provides a nice line of sight through Control Points Bravo and Charlie, as well as parts of the park near Alpha **[VP.05]**. Because both Bravo and Charlie are covered and alternate vantage points offer a better view of the park, opt for this spot if others have already been taken.

US ZONE

A commercial district complete with a car dealership, gas station, fast food joint, and row of apartment buildings at the perimeter, the US zone was once a bustling community. Now it's an urban battlefield fought on rooftops, billboard catwalks, and on the open streets.

Controlling the rooftops and billboards is key to success, which incidentally gives the US an edge. Fast access to the Fuel USA convenience store rooftop at Control Point Alpha and the Fuel Systems billboard near Charlie enables sniping of KPA as they try attacking the objectives at the map's center.

Key Locations

- Fuel USA gas station
- Fuel USA convenience store, Control Point Alpha
- Apartment complexes
- The Diablo billboard
- Boarded-up fast food restaurant
- Abandoned truck, Control Point Bravo
- Montrose car dealership, Control Point Charlie
- Fuel Systems billboard

With such a clear US advantage at Control Point Alpha, devoting energy to the other two control points is preferable. Smart tactics at the exposed objective at Bravo and a hardy defense of Charlie inside the Montrose car dealership can overcome the built-in US edge.

Tactics

Control Point Alpha

CAPTURE DIFFICULTY:

Located inside the Fuel USA convenience store, Control Point Alpha favors the US **[A]**. Rear access enables you to quickly enter the building, and the rooftop vantage point works against KPA who spawn farther away near the highway.

Control Point Cash Grab

Cash in on the hiding spot behind the counter inside the Fuel USA convenience store to capture Control Point Alpha out of sight. Lie prone to take the objective, then dart to a defensible position to avoid getting blown to pieces by a grenade purposefully thrown behind the counter to clean out the hiding spot.

Stocking the Shelves

The empty shelves inside the Fuel USA convenience store provide a nice bit of cover from gunfire coming from the gas station when capturing Alpha. Because the approaching US forces can see behind the shelves when entering through the back of the store, hiding behind them isn't advisable when playing as the KPA.

Flanking Fuel USA

Just because the US have easy access to Control Point Alpha from the back of the Fuel USA convenience store doesn't mean you should accept it. When playing as the KPA, be aggressive and flank the rear entrance to take defending US soldiers by surprise. This is a great approach when sending in a drone too.

Back Entrance Choke Point

Deny the US their advantage at Control Point Alpha by aggressively guarding the convenience store. Stand at either side of the back entrance and blast any approaching US soldier with the shotgun or burst of SMG fire. Alternately, station a Wolverine drone at the door to mow down US operatives as they enter the building.

Side Entrance Choke Point

KPA have two main options when it comes to infiltrating Control Point Alpha: a direct assault through the front of the convenience store or sneak in through the side entrance. Cut off the latter by camping out by the side door with a shotgun or SMG and nailing any KPA soldiers who walk in.

Drone Tactics

Rely on a Wolverine anti-infantry drone to do your dirty work in clearing Control Point Alpha. Sending a drone in to clear the convenience store before capturing the objective is a decent plan, although stationing a Wolverine in the store to defend Alpha is an even better approach. When playing as the US, hang back along the row of apartment buildings behind the Fuel USA building, whereas KPA should sit against the boarded-up fast food restaurant to deploy drones. If you're having difficulty defeating a drone guarding the convenience store, chuck an EMP grenade to disable the contraption.

Control Point Bravo

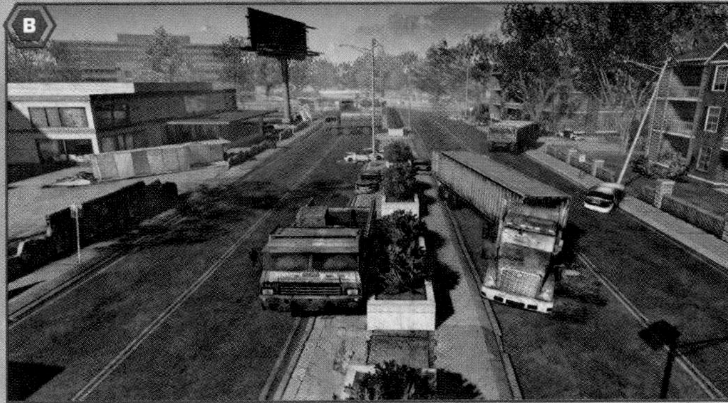

CAPTURE DIFFICULTY: ★★★★★

Although Control Point Bravo sits on the open road that runs past the car dealership and fast food joint, there's no taking it from behind the driver's seat **[B]**. Instead, it's all about pounding the area with airstrikes and capturing it while hidden in the nearby bushes.

Bushwhacking

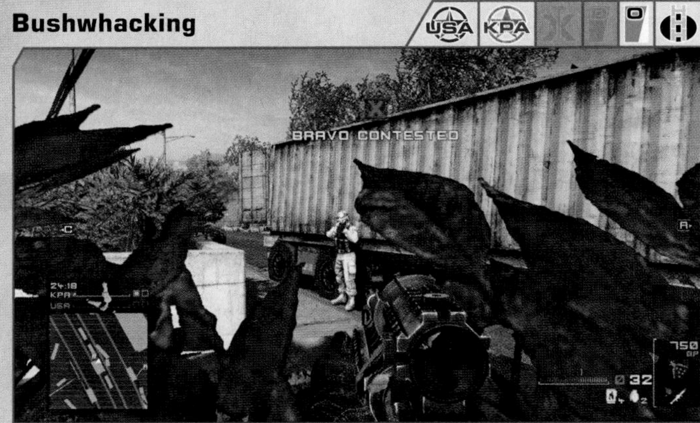

A most unlikely hiding spot, lie prone in the shrubs planted in the rectangular containers decorating Control Point Bravo. Although enemies can spot you by name (your profile name appears whenever an enemy passes their firing reticle over you), you essentially blend in with the shrubbery. It's unwise to stay here once you've captured Bravo, so head into the truck to hold ground or take to a vantage point to safely snipe enemies.

On the Open Truck Bed

Flaunt your skill by seizing Control Point Bravo out in the open. Leap into the open truck bed nearest the boarded-up fast food joint to capture Bravo. You have to be one brave soldier to pull off this move, though, because there's no cover in the bed of the truck, leaving you highly vulnerable to airstrikes, snipers, and generally any other type of attack you can think of. That said, if you and a few teammates manage to flood the capture zone, the risk of attack is countered by how quickly you'll seize the objective.

Semi-Hidden in the Trailer

If parading out in the open as helicopters fly above isn't your thing, hide inside the abandoned truck trailer for a guarded capture of Control Point Bravo. As you're seizing the objective, considering deploying a Buzzard or Rhino drone to attack the vehicles patrolling the street outside. You're vulnerable while controlling the drone, but because the greatest threats are attacks coming from vehicles, act aggressively and take them out before they snuff you. If you don't want to brave a drone deployment, purchase a RPG and fire at vehicles from inside the trailer.

Automotive Hold

Even if you can't capture Control Point Bravo from inside one, vehicles are still useful for securing the area. Rev up an LAV or Battle Tank after seizing the control point to patrol the road and scare prospective attackers out of approaching your territory.

Control Point Charlie

CAPTURE DIFFICULTY: ★★★★★

The expansive Montrose car dealership offers an array of hiding spots and vantage points, though Control Point Charlie is limited to a small area on the showroom floor at street level **[C]**. Defense is more important than offense—because it's easy to capture the objective once inside, whoever can best defend the building and prevent enemy infiltration wins.

Showroom Strike

Attacking Control Point Charlie inside the car dealerships is a harrowing prospect: you don't know where enemies are positioned inside the building, grenades won't reach the mezzanine, and C4 on the showroom floor could end your assault prematurely. As such, take a cautious approach by doing a UAV Sweep or sending in a Parrot to pinpoint enemy locations. Don't waste grenades—if the opposition is smart, they won't be on the showroom floor and grenades won't hit them. Instead, run inside and take cover behind the cars or rush up the stairs to clear the mezzanine. When playing as the US, it's easier to enter the dealership from the KPA side because you can access the stairs more quickly than if you enter from the front doors.

:apture Spots

here's plenty of over to be had ehind the trashed ars parked in ne Montrose car ealership, though ne question ; finding the ght one for the tuation. Figure ut from which irection your enemies are firing and take shelter behind the car pposite their position. Staying on the showroom floor is not an option nce you've wrapped up Control Point Charlie, so head up the stairs nd wrest control of the mezzanine from the opposition so as to stage defense of the control point below.

)rone Models Now in Stock

/hy not add to the ollection of wheels n the showroom oor with your own ersonal drone? ;end a Wolverine nti-infantry drone nto the floor to liminate enemies ttempting to ake Control 'oint Charlie. A ground drone won't be effective when attacking the lealership because your enemies are likely smart enough to defend ne control from the mezzanine. As such, send in a Buzzard to scare nem away with rockets. Even though the Buzzard won't kill them, ney'll be distracted or forced to move, which gives you cover to run nto the building and seize Charlie.

/lezzanine Patrol

)efending Control Point Charlie from the showroom floor puts you t risk of getting tagged by an attacker, so fire down at enemies nfiltrating the dealership from the mezzanine. Not only do you have ne advantage of looking down on your enemy, but the interior of the uilding is shadowy, giving you an edge over your enemy who will be oming in from the bright outside. Combine shots from a mid-range un such as the trusty M4 with cooked grenades to clear the howroom floor. If you want to be really dastardly, drop a WP Grenade n the floor to prevent anyone from approaching Charlie.

Vantage Points

The Diablo Billboard

Also useful during the battle for Control Points Alpha and Bravo in the neutral zone, the Diablo billboard near the abandoned fast food place offers a fantastic view of the US zone **[VP.01]**. Superb lines of sight to the Fuel USA gas station, Control Point Bravo on the open road, and the rooftop of the Montrose car dealership housing Control Point Charlie make it one of the most attractive sniping spots on the map.

> **CAUTION 조심하다**
>
> **While it's possible to jump from one side of a billboard to the other, it's extremely dangerous. Miss the jump and you tumble to the concrete below. Avoid the risk of death entirely by sticking to the side of the billboard with ladder access.**

Fuel USA Rooftop, Control Point Alpha

Seizing this sniping spot is critical to maintaining possession of Control Point Alpha in the interior of the Fuel USA store **[VP.02]**. The US have a built-in advantage when it comes to this vantage point because the ladder up to the rooftop is at the back of the building, which is a short walk from the US spawning ground. Still, make an effort when on the KPA side to grab this spot and use it to prevent spawning US soldiers from taking Alpha.

Montrose Car Dealership Second Floor Windows, Control Point Charlie

Enter the offices away from the mezzanine inside the Montrose car dealership to access windows that look out onto the street below **[VP.03]**. Maintaining watch over Control Point Bravo is a plus, but more importantly you can tag enemies trying to enter the dealership from any of the windows. When playing for the KPA, use the front windows to take shots at US soldiers running from their spawning ground near the apartments up the road.

Montrose Car Dealership Rooftop, Control Point Charlie

You might think that the rooftop of the Montrose car dealership is superior to the second floor windows as a vantage point, but surprisingly, it's a mixed bag **[VP.04]**. While the view is better—your sight is not limited by windowpanes and walls—you're susceptible to airstrikes, helicopter attacks, and snipers who can clearly see you sticking out like a sore thumb on the bare rooftop.

Fuel Systems Billboard

Another great vantage point, the Fuel Systems billboard near the Montrose car dealership containing Control Point Charlie enables you to fire on enemies moving among all three objectives **[VP.05]**. Because it's farther from the Fuel USA store, this billboard is a good position from which to counter snipers on that building's rooftop.

Apartment Rooftop

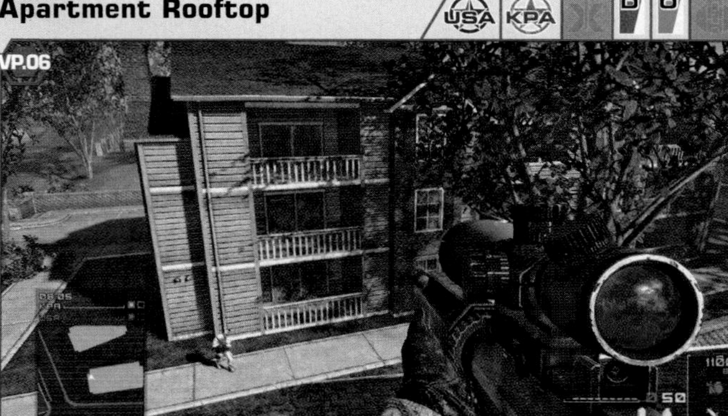

The apartment complex across from the Montrose car dealership doesn't offer ground access to the roof, but you're welcome to parachute out of a helicopter and land on top for a great view of the US zone **[VP.06]**. When playing as the US, crouch on the side closest to your team's spawning ground to partially shield yourself from view. Conversely, look down on spawning US soldiers when playing as KPA by lying prone on the side facing the other apartment buildings.

LOWLANDS

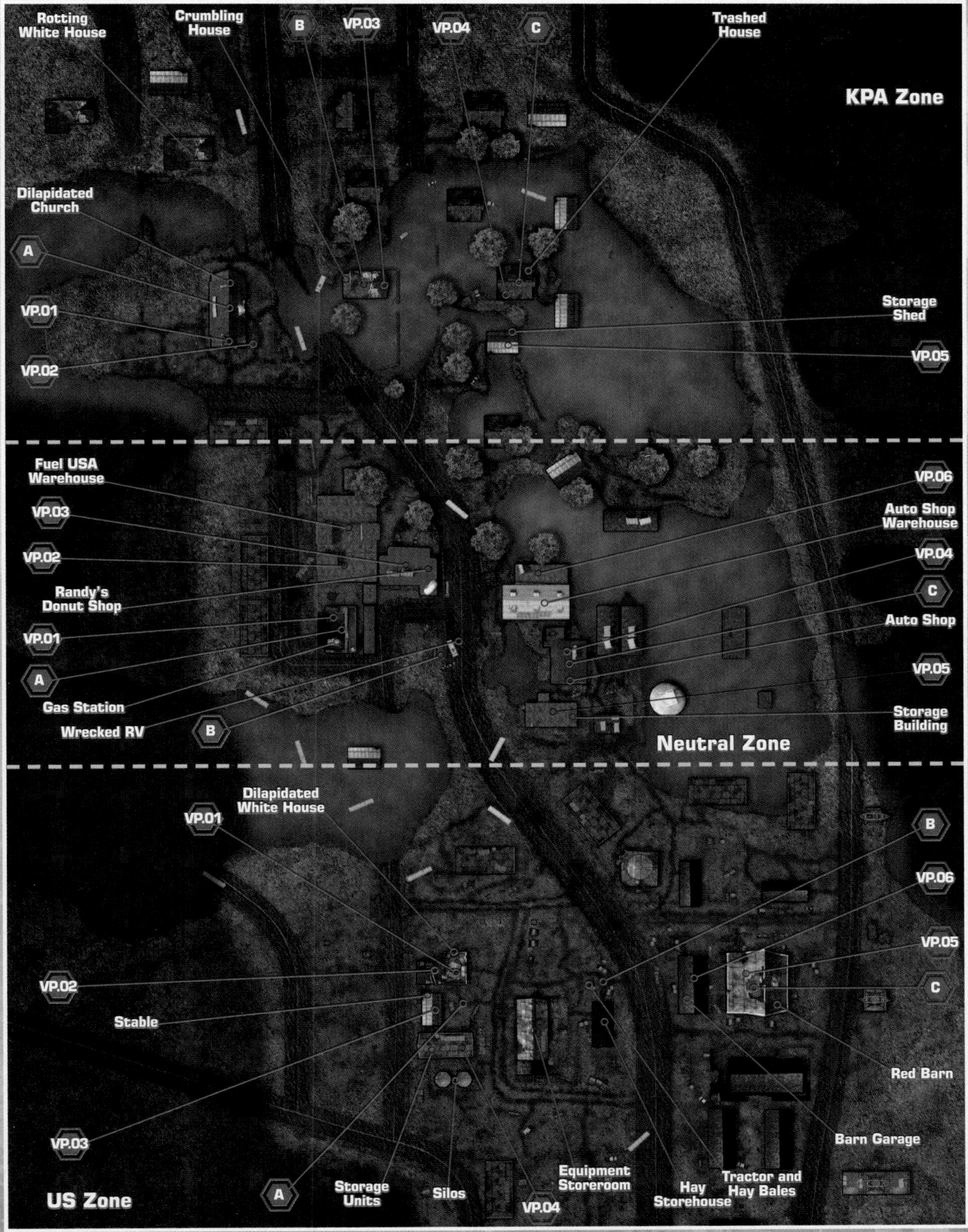

Rotting White House
Crumbling House
B
VP.03
VP.04
C
Trashed House
KPA Zone
Dilapidated Church
A
VP.01
VP.02
Storage Shed
VP.05

Fuel USA Warehouse
VP.03
VP.02
Randy's Donut Shop
VP.01
A
Gas Station
Wrecked RV
B
VP.06
Auto Shop Warehouse
VP.04
C
Auto Shop
VP.05
Storage Building
Neutral Zone

Dilapidated White House
VP.01
VP.02
Stable
VP.03
US Zone
A
Storage Units
Silos
VP.04
Equipment Storeroom
Hay Storehouse
Tractor and Hay Bales
Barn Garage
Red Barn
B
VP.06
VP.05
C

A vicious KPA attack on the local dam has left the rural Lowlands a flooded wasteland. Abandoned homes, businesses, and community centers rot in the fetid water as KPA and US forces battle for control of this flat expanse of land.

NEUTRAL ZONE

Previously the center of rural commerce in the Lowlands, the neutral zone now sees gunfire exchanges around Randy's Donut Shop, the local automotive shop, and the gas station. These retail locations add an urban feel to this rural map.

Much of the action centers on the gas station and Randy's Donut Shop during Team Deathmatch, as well as Ground Control where Control Point Alpha is hotly contested. KPA forces have a slight advantage in accessing Alpha because they spawn relatively close to the building.

Key Locations

- Gas station, Control Point Alpha
- Randy's Donut Shop
- Fuel USA Warehouse
- Wrecked RV, Control Point Bravo
- Auto shop, Control Point Charlie
- Auto shop warehouse
- Storage building

It's an even game at Control Point Bravo where vehicles dominate the battle. Both helicopters and tanks make the difference in holding this contentious area.

When it comes to Control Point Charlie and the assorted buildings near the US zone, drones and close-quarters combat tactics rule the battlefield. Careful sniping to keep enemies at bay and smart use of close-range weapons are needed to hold this side of the map.

Tactics

Control Point Alpha

CAPTURE DIFFICULTY: ★★★★★

KPA forces have the jump on Control Point Alpha, given the close proximity of their spawning ground, yet that doesn't make for an automatic win. Clever use of the gas station rooftop and smart defenses at each of the building's access points is essential for holding Alpha **[A]**.

Convenient Counter Capture

Hide behind the cash counter at the front of the gas station to easily capture Control Point Alpha from behind cover. You're vulnerable to attacks launched through the skylight, but won't be spotted by enemies shooting into the building at street level.

Skylight Carnage

Opponents defending Control Point Alpha expect an attack to come from either the front or back of the gas station; they're not anticipating an attack from above, which is exactly why climbing onto the roof and dumping grenades through the skylight is a superb battle plan for taking Alpha. Launching rockets from an Apache or Buzzard drone also works, as does a Hellfire air strike. Whatever the weapon, attacking via the skylight is unexpected and effective.

Skylight Defense

Rather than leaving the skylight unguarded for attackers to use, why not turn the tables and use it to your advantage as a defender? Head up to the roof and peek down at Control Point Alpha through the skylight. Drop a C4 charge or even a white phosphorous grenade to deter attackers. Should opponents decide to invade the building, all you have to do is aim through the open skylight to secure the control point.

Back Room Surprise

The long hallway connecting the back door of the gas station to the cash counter in the front is a great place to defend Control Point Alpha from infiltrators. Press against the right side of the door and use an SMG or shotgun attachment to shoot enemies who run into the building.

Side Room Surprise

KPA soldiers love streaming into the gas station from the side entrance because it's a quick beeline from their spawning ground up the road. Stop them in their tracks by hiding on either side of the door and shooting them with an SMG or shotgun as they enter.

Control Point Bravo

CAPTURE DIFFICULTY:

There's no nuance involved in capturing Control Point Bravo. Surrounded by a wrecked RV and abandoned tank trailer, this wide-open objective calls for aggressive vehicular tactics **[B]**.

Brazen Bravo Capture

Assailing Control Point Bravo in an LAV or Battle Tank should be your top priority, but if you're running low on Battle Points or already failed in an effort to seize the objective using a vehicle, an on-foot approach is your last resort. Do your best to remain out of sight from vehicles patrolling the open road. Stick to the perimeter of the control point—press against the wrecked RV or tank trailer depending on where the gunfire is most intense—and avoid getting caught in the fight. With such little cover, you're likely to lose long before you finish capturing the control point.

Driving into Bravo

No doubt about it, driving into Control Point Bravo is the best way to capture and hold this tough objective. Naturally, you're strongest in a Battle Tank, although an LAV is a good alternative. At the start of the battle, a Humvee can get you and a few buddies to the control point quickly, but its lack of armor means that one blast from a tank or a well-aimed RPG will take you out of commission. An Apache can soften up the control point, particularly if the opposing faction has a bunch of Battle Tanks guarding the road.

Dumpster Defense

Don't even think about defending Bravo anywhere near the control point perimeter without a vehicle; instead, hide inside the dumpster across the street and protect your possession by destroying vehicles attempting to seize the objective. An RPG is essential here, although Hellfire air strikes and grenades are useful too.

Control Point Charlie

CAPTURE DIFFICULTY:

Although Control Point Charlie lies inside the dark abandoned auto repair shop, it takes more than skilled close-quarters combat to capture **[C]**. The open garage allows vehicles to fire directly into the control point, which means dealing with enemy motors is as crucial to capturing and holding Charlie as clearing the interior on foot.

Crouching Soldier, Hidden Capture

It's so dark inside the auto shop garage that you almost don't need a hiding spot. Crouch in a corner or behind a car to quietly capture Charlie. Make sure you're out of sight and away from the open garage door, where vehicles are sure to be pummeling the control point with gunfire. You can stick around inside and kill any enemies that try taking Charlie, although a safer plan is to exit the garage and take a defensive position in the adjoining office or warehouse rooftop to prevent enemies from even entering the building.

Applying Pressure with Vehicles

While it's not possible to capture Control Point Charlie in a vehicle, apply pressure to enemies defending the objective by hammering the garage with an LAV, Battle Tank, or even a helicopter. Coordinate with teammates who can run in to capture the control point once you've sufficiently softened the resistance.

Deploying Ground Drones

Wolverine and Rhino drones are effective for infiltrating Control Point Charlie because they can sneak into the dark garage and take out defenders preoccupied with avoiding cannon blasts from a Battle Tank or skirting away from cooked grenades. Deploy drones from behind the auto shop warehouse where there's not much action.

Side Room Surprise

KPA soldiers are likely to access Control Point Charlie from the side office. Prevent them from reaching the garage and capturing Charlie by hiding near the door and shooting them with an SMG or shotgun as they run through.

Back Room Defense

US operatives love running into the auto shop from the rear entrance in hopes of avoiding the battle raging in front of the building. Check them at the door when playing as the KPA by hiding by the doorway. When a US soldier heads through the door, a quick nick from a shotgun or burst of fire from an SMG takes him out of commission.

Vantage Points

Gas Station Rooftop, Control Point Alpha

You can use the gas station rooftop for sniping enemies approaching Control Point Alpha, but it's best for picking off enemies attempting to seize the control point from inside the building **[VP.01]**. Drop grenades and fire your gun through the skylight to dispatch attackers. This is a particularly good spot when playing as the US, because solar panels block KPA sniper fire from the adjacent warehouse roof.

Warehouse Rooftop adjacent to Gas Station

KPA snipers should relish the warehouse adjacent to Control Point Alpha **[VP.02]**. Not only is it a quick jaunt from the KPA spawning ground, but it provides a killer line of sight to the roof over Alpha. Alternately, much like the warehouse on the opposite side of the street near the auto shop, climb up here when playing as the US to kill KPA soldiers as they spawn.

Randy's Donut Shop Rooftop

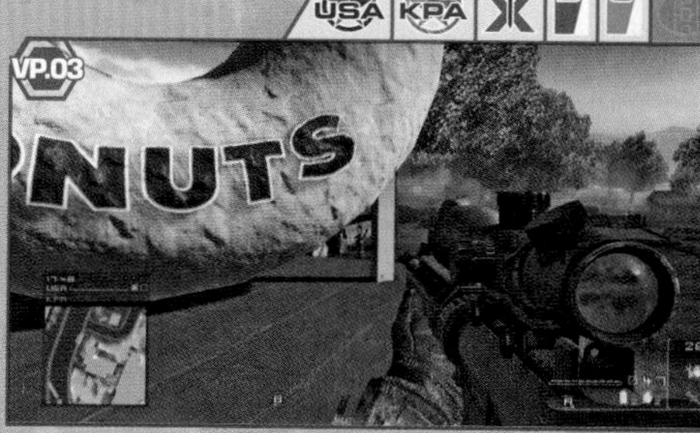

The thin, flat awning over the gas pumps provides a means of reaching the roof of Randy's Donuts—you can only access the roof by hopping from the gas station to the awning to the shop—but it's a dangerous vantage point to be used with extreme caution **[VP.03]**. Hide behind the massive plastic donut because you're easily targeted elsewhere on the flat roof.

Auto Shop Rooftop, Control Point Charlie

Scale the auto shop roof to fire rockets and summon air strikes on vehicles attacking the garage below. The rooftop is also a great sniping spot, offering a clear line of sight at Control Point Bravo and inside the gas station at Control Point Alpha **[VP.04]**. The only drawback is the lack of cover, which leaves you susceptible to other snipers and air strikes.

Storage Building Rooftop next to Auto Shop

The small storage building next to the auto shop takes some fancy footwork on the tire stacks to reach the rooftops **[VP.05]**. There's no cover on the roof, which leaves you open to enemy attacks—snipers on the auto shop warehouse are of particular concern—but if you're having difficulty firing RPGs at pesky vehicles assailing Charlie, then it's worth scaling to get an elevated perspective.

Warehouse Rooftop adjacent to Auto Shop

Although the warehouse sits next to the auto shop, sniping from the roof does little to defend Control Point Charlie. Instead, it offers only a limited view of the neutral zone that faces toward the KPA spawning ground **[VP.06]**. As such, it's a great spot for US snipers to take aim at spawning KPA soldiers, particularly because you can take cover behind a photovoltaic panel near the front of the building. Picking KPA off can indirectly help efforts to defend the control points, but it's best used in Team Deathmatch.

KPA ZONE

The KPA zone spans the residential area of the Lowlands with its bombed-out houses and crumbling church. These structures punctuate the flat, flooded expanse that offers little cover for soldiers of either faction.

Combat centers on vehicles pounding each other on the dry road that bisects the map, as well as fierce indoor gunfights. Close-quarters combat is the focus, although the church offers spectacular vantage points for the keen sniper.

Focus on the ground game to achieve victory, aggressively pushing on each of the control points on foot. While vehicles and sniping are effective for softening an area for capture, it's ultimately skilled close-range fighting that determines success.

Use hiding spots in the church to capture and hold Control Point Alpha. Coordinate with teammates to attack Bravo and Charlie, which require more daring tactics due to their open design. As the KPA, aim to take the church first, then attack Bravo. When playing as the US, taking the church is more difficult, which makes Bravo and Charlie attractive alternatives.

Key Locations

- Dilapidated church, Control Point Alpha
- Rotting white house
- Crumbling house, Control Point Bravo
- Trashed house, Control Point Charlie
- Storage shed

Tactics

Control Point Alpha

CAPTURE DIFFICULTY: 

Towering over the saturated Lowlands, the local parish church has fallen to pieces as a result of relentless KPA bombardment. The steeple remains intact for sniping, while the chapel hosts a battle for domination over the area with a slight advantage given to the KPA given the proximity of their spawning ground **[A]**.

Cool Church Capture Spot

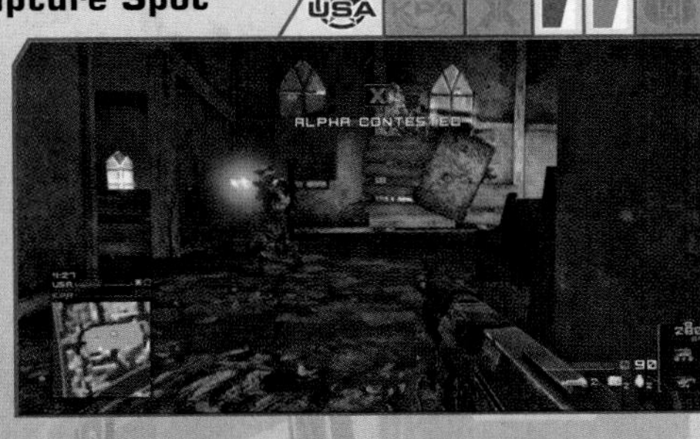

Upon entering from the back of the church on the US side of the map, crouch or lie prone behind the set of tipped-over refrigerators to capture Control Point Alpha. From here you don't have to worry about getting attacked from behind because KPA forces almost always enter the church from the opposite entrance; additionally, the refrigerators provide cover from KPA attacks. Once you've captured Alpha, however, move to a more secure defensive position such as the cloakroom at the front of the church or attic.

Particle Board Capture Spot

Enter the church from the front when playing as the KPA to take advantage of a well-guarded capture spot. Particle board provide cover from incoming US gunfire near the center of the chapel as you grab the control point. Should enemies move through the church, you can fire at them from behind cover as they walk by. Move to a more secure defensive position once you've captured Alpha, such as the small room at the back of the church or attic looking down on the pews.

CAUTION 조심하다

Resist the temptation use the gaping hole in the side of the church as an access point. Not only does entering from the side put you at risk of being attacked from inside the church on both sides, but you're also exposed to attacks from Control Point Bravo.

Hiding in the Pews

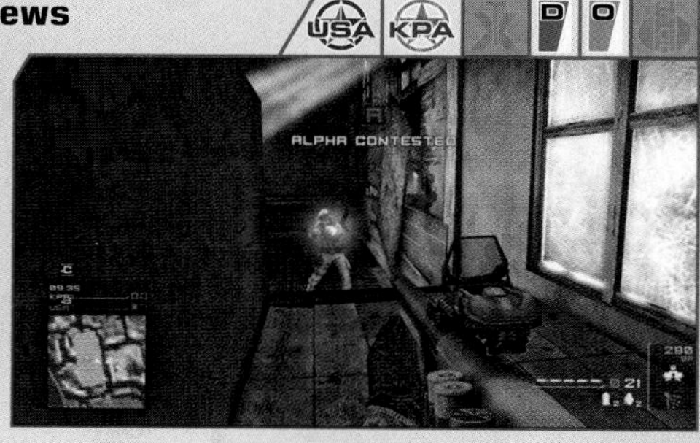

Rather than racing across the chapel floor out in the open, move through the church along the far wall. Ramps and particle boards nailed to the floor grant covered passage when moving back and forth through the building. While not ideal, it's possible to capture Alpha from this spot while monitoring either the front or back entrance for enemies.

Brimstone and Helicopter Fire

The massive hole in the side of the church grants an opportunity to attack Control Point Alpha from the air. Launch a Buzzard drone from the rotting white house near the KPA spawning ground and pummel the inside of the chapel with rockets. Better still, lift off in a helicopter and rain down bullets and rockets to soften the control point for teammates on the ground to capture.

Greeting KPA at the Door

Prevent KPA soldiers from taking Control Point Alpha by greeting them at the church's front door with an SMG or shotgun. Stand on either side of the doorway and gun any KPA operative foolish enough waltz by. Unfortunately, you can't use the debris at the side of the room for cover, but you should be able to remain hidden by pressing against the side of the door.

Back Door Confessions

Hide behind the stacks of timber in the back room to catch invading US soldiers by surprise. Because enemies are unlikely to suspect an attack immediately upon entering the church, you can pop up and fire a burst from an SMG for a quick kill. It's also a good way to defend access to the church steeple because the ladder is on the opposite side of the small room.

Gunfire from Above

Access to the church attic, which overlooks the chapel on both sides, is granted via the ladder in the center of the vaulted room. While the view is limited because you can only peer down to the center of the chapel from either side of the attic, it's difficult for enemies on the ground to fire back; moreover, it's a great position from which to drop white phosphorous grenades that are sure to keep enemies away, but won't affect you up in the attic. Be aware that drones and helicopters can attack from the side opening. Tuck into a corner should you come under fire from outside.

Control Point Bravo

CAPTURE DIFFICULTY: 

The faction in possession of Control Point Alpha has the upper hand with regards to Bravo. Launching an assault on the open control point is much easier when you own the church because of the ability to fire on Bravo from the steeple and deck **[B]**. Approaching Bravo from the opposite direction near Charlie is much more difficult and not recommended.

Holy War

Without question, the best plan for taking Control Point Bravo involves the dilapidated church. Controlling this building dramatically improves your chances of taking Bravo because you can coordinate an assault from church vantage points, then maintain guard over the control point once it has been captured. In this sense, Control Points Alpha and Bravo can be seen as linked, and a winning battle plan involves securing both locations using the steeple and deck overwatches, combined with aerial drone and helicopter deployments. This is a solid plan when on the KPA side, given the close spawning ground and shelled white house from which you can launch drones.

Capture Spots

There aren't any great hiding spots in the remains of this crumbling two-story house, but squeezing under the stairs and crouching by the refrigerator in the opposite corner can provide a bit of cover. Your chances for success improve if your team holds Control Point Alpha; otherwise, expect to come under heavy fire while attempting to capture Bravo from these semi-hiding spots.

Shaky Second Floor Defense

Defending Control Point Bravo is tough without access to the church steeple and deck, but a weak defense can be mounted on the crumbling second floor. Crouch to maintain as low a profile as possible, then scan the area around the building for enemies. Placing C4 charges at the base of the building can discourage capture, although your main concern should be eliminating snipers in the church.

Stopping Vehicles in Their Tracks

Although it's not recommended that you approach Control Point Bravo from Charlie, the road that runs between the two objectives sees a lot of action. Vehicles are unlikely to fire into the flooded yard surrounding Bravo because a wall shields the objective from view, which makes this unassuming area a cunning stage from which to attack vehicles on foot. Purchase an RPG to blast tanks that roll by, and chuck C4 onto the center of the road, detonating the charges as vehicles drive over them. You can even call in Hellfire missile strikes from behind the wall without worrying about retaliation from vehicles that can't enter the submerged backyard.

Control Point Charlie

CAPTURE DIFFICULTY: ★★★★★

Although Control Point Charlie sits inside a house, its position in the very center of the living room means you can't capture it from the sides of the room, making capture and defense difficult **[C]**. Neither faction has a clear advantage here, and control is sure to switch hands frequently during the course of the battle.

Gunplay in the Living Room

Fling a flashbang, toss a cooked frag grenade, then enter guns blazing—this three-step tactical plan lets you capture Control Point Charlie with minimal fuss. While it's always critical to clear an interior control point to avoid enemies contesting control, it's of particular importance for Charlie because there's no good cover. Any enemy who enters the room can gun you down with ease. Work with teammates to flood the living room, quickly take Charlie, then defend it from the second floor. As the US, flank the KPA by going around to the back of the house to stifle resistance during capture.

Sending in Drones

Send in a Wolverine or Rhino to clear Control Point Charlie ahead of a push on the house. Ground drones aren't a good option for the KPA, although it's perfectly feasible when playing as the US because you can deploy them from underneath the adjacent shed or farther away at the US spawning ground.

Shooting from the Second Floor Windows

The best way to defend Control Point Charlie involves camping out by the windows on the second floor. Not only do you get a great view of the road separating Control Points Bravo and Charlie—useful for attacking vehicles with RPGs, airburst launcher, and air strikes—it also affords a peek toward the KPA spawning ground at the edge of the zone.

Side Door Defense

Along with sniping spawning KPA soldiers from the second floor windows, the other tactic for stopping a KPA advance on Control Point Charlie involves guarding the door at the side of the trashed house. Stand at either side of the doorway and blast unsuspecting KPA operatives with a shotgun or few quick rounds from an SMG as they walk by.

Vantage Points

Church Steeple

No question about it, the church steeple is the best vantage point in the KPA zone **[VP.01]**. Its usefulness, however, is limited by the fact that you must control the church. If you're not in possession of Control Point Alpha inside the church, you're out of luck when it comes to exploiting this elevated overwatch. Fully exploit this prime vantage point for both defending Alpha and attacking and guarding Bravo when playing as either faction.

Church Deck

The second-best vantage point in the KPA zone goes to the church deck, which is located a level down from the steeple (in fact, accessing the steeple requires stepping onto the exterior deck) **[VP.02]**. Unfortunately, there's no cover and so you're at high risk of opposing sniper fire, drones, and helicopter fire.

Destroyed House Rooftop, Control Point Bravo

If standing on the crumbling second floor wasn't risky enough for you, try jumping onto the roof **[VP.03]**. Sure, you might find your body slumped on the ground mere moments after climbing up to the rooftop, but the view of the surrounding area is great. You might even be able to rack up a couple kills before that inevitable sniper's bullet, drone rocket, helicopter fire, or air strike arrives.

Second Floor Windows, Trashed House, Control Point Charlie

Whether for firing rockets at vehicles on the road or deterring enemies from launching an attack on Charlie on the floor below, the windows on the second floor of the trashed house provide a phenomenal vantage point so long as you maintain control of Control Point Charlie **[VP.04]**. Using these windows is critical to defending control of Charlie. Watch the shed rooftop across from the house for snipers.

Shed Rooftop across from Control Point Charlie

US forces have the advantage in firing from the shed rooftop directly across from Control Point Charlie **[VP.05]**. This overwatch is highly exposed, particularly to snipers positioned by the second floor windows, which counters its usefulness in attacking Charlie. Beware of air strikes when venturing up here.

US ZONE

Tractors and hay bales line the side of the road that runs through the US zone. The enormous red barn and surrounding storehouses, garages, and silos provide a network of structures from which to attack and defend each control point.

Control Points Alpha and Bravo are found outdoors, the former requiring an on-foot approach, while the latter can and should be taken from the driver's seat of a LAV or Battle Tank. Both objectives are tough to capture and hold, particularly because neither faction has a clear advantage.

Key Locations

- Dilapidated white house
- Stable, Control Point Alpha
- Storage units
- Silos
- Tractor and hay bales, Control Point Bravo
- Hay storehouse
- Equipment storeroom
- Red barn, Control Point Charlie
- Barn garage

Control Point Charlie is a different matter, situated inside the big red barn on the opposite side of the road. Packed with nooks and hiding spots, the interior hosts dangerous close-range gunfighting. The rooftop is just as active with sniping, drones, and even helicopters attacking through a gash that grants a view into the barn.

Tactics

Control Point Alpha

CAPTURE DIFFICULTY:

Unlike Bravo situated on the side of the road, Control Point Alpha can't be easily captured in a vehicle. Instead, this outdoor objective has to be taken on foot **[A]**. Exploit vantage points overlooking the area to defend it once you succeed in wresting control.

Capturing Alpha Out in the Open

Call in an air strike to clear the area before approaching Control Point Alpha. Grenades work too, though issuing a Hellfire air strike is a more aggressive tactic that should rattle enemies defending Alpha. Once you capture the control point, drop a white phosphorous grenade to prevent opponents from retaking the objective while you settle into a defensive position in the nearby dilapidated house or on the warehouse rooftops.

Dumpster Diving

The blue dumpster in the middle of Control Point Alpha makes a great capture hiding spot. Crouch inside the bin to take Alpha. While it's better to head into the nearby house to defend Alpha from an elevated vantage point, staying in the dumpster ensures that enemies can't capture the control point, but merely contest it. Of course, once they discover your location, expect a short fight.

Leaning Against the Wall

Jump inside the blue container against the stable to capture Control Point Alpha away from sight. You aren't completely hidden when crouched in the container, but enemies often ignore it and check the dumpster first. Move into the house once the control point has been taken to settle into a more defensible position.

Defending from the Dilapidated House

Capturing Control Point Alpha is one thing; defending it is another. Without any defensible positions on the ground, you're left to garrison in the adjacent house. Head up to the second floor, which has been blasted in a KPA attack, and guard the control point using a mid-range M16. Because there's no roof, watch for air strikes and drones that can nix you from your six.

Warehouse Drone Deployments

Hide in one of the empty warehouses away from the action to deploy drones that can help clear the way for teammates to run in and capture Control Point Alpha. Launch a Buzzard to fire rockets on the control point or send out a Wolverine to distract enemies with machine gun fire as teammates overrun the control point.

Control Point Bravo

CAPTURE DIFFICULTY:

Seated on the shoulder of the road that runs through Lowlands, Bravo is best captured and held behind the wheel **[B]**. While it's possible to mount an attack on foot, the lack of cover and overbearing presence of vehicles make it inadvisable.

Vehicles for Victory

Spawn an LAV or Battle Tank to roll in and grab Control Point Bravo. Pass on the Humvee, which can't withstand a tank blast or even last long under fire from an LAV. The goal is to move in quickly to capture the control point, then pull out to avoid getting hit by an RPG, air strike, or rockets from a Buzzard drone or Apache helicopter.

Taking Bravo on Foot

If you plan on risking Bravo on foot, stay away from the road. Aside from being bombarded by cannons and mounted machine guns, stepping onto the road puts you at risk of being run over. Crouch against the hay bales and attempt to nab Bravo from the outside. Equip an RPG to deter vehicles from engaging you in combat.

Control Point Charlie

CAPTURE DIFFICULTY: ★★★★★

Filled with all sorts of crates, containers, and dark corners, Control Point Charlie is a challenging fight **[C]**. Combine explosives with close-quarters gun combat to seize control. A tear in the roof invites aerial drones and helicopter attacks, while the adjacent warehouse makes for good sniping.

Ground Assault on Charlie

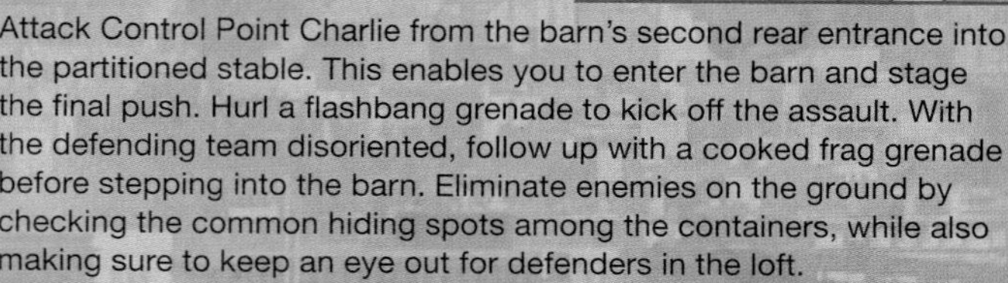

Attack Control Point Charlie from the barn's second rear entrance into the partitioned stable. This enables you to enter the barn and stage the final push. Hurl a flashbang grenade to kick off the assault. With the defending team disoriented, follow up with a cooked frag grenade before stepping into the barn. Eliminate enemies on the ground by checking the common hiding spots among the containers, while also making sure to keep an eye out for defenders in the loft.

Red Container Capture Spot

Tuck yourself into the corner with the stack of red storage containers directly under the loft to capture Control Point Charlie out of sight. While it's not completely hidden, you're largely out of sight and should be able to seize the point before getting into much trouble. Take to the loft once you've finished capturing Charlie to avoid getting flushed out with grenades.

Blue Container Hiding Spot

This devious little hiding spot is always overlooked. Hide yourself in the crack between the blue container and waist-high barrier to capture Charlie. It's not a good idea to stay here once Charlie has been seized, so climb up to the loft to defend the control point from above.

Barn Loft Stronghold

Defend Control Point Charlie from the loft overlooking the interior of the barn. Not only does the loft provide an elevated perspective that gives you an edge in combat, but you're safer in the loft than fighting on the ground. You still have to worry about drones and helicopters firing through the hole in the roof, though.

Rafter Surprise

Surprise enemies by shooting from the barn rafters. From the loft accessible from either the ladder inside the barn or outside on the roof, inch onto the narrow beams that run the width of the barn. Drop onto the containers on the floor below for an alternative defensive position that's just about as effective. You're highly vulnerable to gunfire, but the element of surprise will keep you safe long enough to kill any enemies before they spot you.

Drone Assault on Charlie

Insert a Buzzard drone through the tear in the barn roof to wreak havoc on defenders inside. A Parrot can relay useful information on the location of enemies hiding within the barn, but it's better to be aggressive and send in a Buzzard to attack straightaway. Even better, send the Buzzard in as a distraction while teammates infiltrate the barn.

The Helicopter Option

Helicopters aren't generally the best vehicle for use in Lowlands given the generous cover provided by trees in the outlying zones; however, an Apache is unbeatable for blasting the interior of the barn with rockets. Aim through the hole in the roof and unload. Don't hover in one spot for long to avoid getting tagged with an RPG or the proximity launcher.

Vantage Points

Second Floor, Dilapidated House

Access the second floor of the dilapidated white house via the exterior ladder near Control Point Alpha or from the staircase inside the house **[VP.01]**. What it lacks in cover, the house makes up for in its excellent view of the area encompassing Control Point Alpha. Be cautious of air strikes and drones as you defend Alpha on the ground below.

Dilapidated House Rooftop

Shimmy onto the remains of the white house's roof using a pair of steel girders linking it with the top of the stable **[VP.02]**. You need to first climb onto the stable from the second floor of the house. Because you can cover Control Point Alpha effectively from the second floor of the house, the only advantage afforded by scaling the roof is the element of surprise.

Stable Rooftop, Control Point Alpha

Connected to the second floor of the dilapidated white house via a set of steel girders, the stable overlooking Control Point Alpha isn't the safest vantage point **[VP.03]**. While it provides a great view of the land surrounding the control point, the lack of cover and unobstructed skies make it a prime target for air strikes and drones.

Storage Units Rooftop

Encircle Control Point Alpha from above by walking from the second floor of the dilapidated house to the stable and onto the storage units rooftops **[VP.04]**. Avoid drawing attention to yourself by engaging enemies on the ground at Alpha and instead take aim at enemies farther in the distance by lying prone on the roof. Attract the ire of attacking enemies and you can be sure an air strike will come your way.

Barn Rooftop, Control Point Charlie

Climb onto the rooftop using the loft access from within the barn or the exterior ladder on the side of the building **[VP.05]**. Despite being a target for air strikes and drone attacks, the roof is a great vantage point with clear lines of sight to the area in front of the barn and parts of Control Point Bravo.

Garage Rooftop, Control Point Charlie

Walk to the garage rooftop via the catwalk from the adjoining barn roof to take a shaded sniping position under the tree **[VP.06]**. Purchase a pair of thermal goggles to identify enemy heat signatures through the leaves. Opponents can't easily spot you sniping from the shade, and the central location enables you to see a large slice of the US zone.

SUBURB

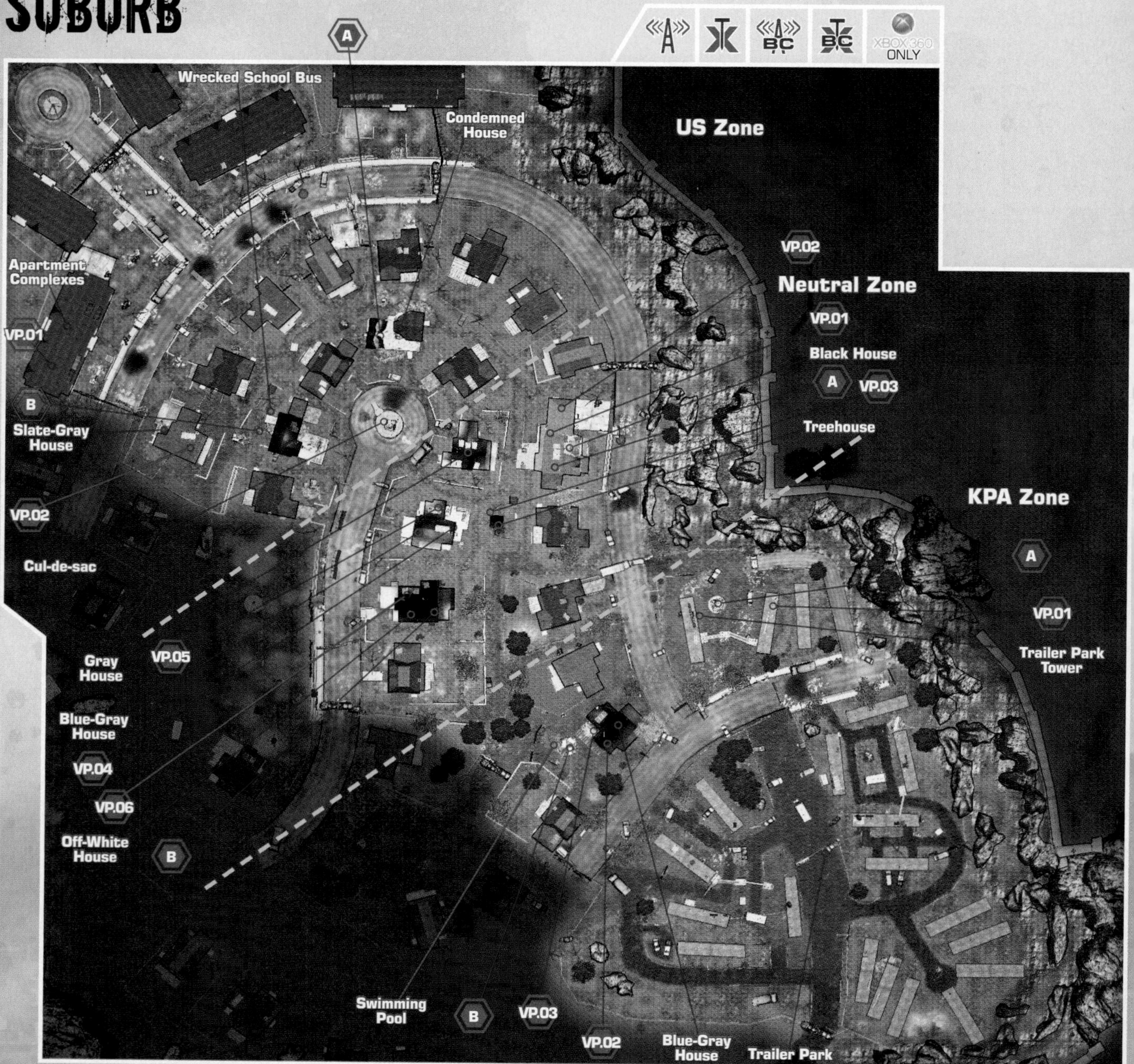

Xbox 360 Only

Wrecked School Bus
Condemned House
US Zone
Apartment Complexes
VP.01
VP.02
Neutral Zone
VP.01
Black House
A
VP.03
B
Slate-Gray House
Treehouse
VP.02
KPA Zone
Cul-de-sac
A
VP.01
Trailer Park Tower
Gray House
VP.05
Blue-Gray House
VP.04
VP.06
Off-White House
B
Swimming Pool
B
VP.03
VP.02
Blue-Gray House
Trailer Park
A

The once idyllic Suburb used to be filled with the sounds of kids playing in backyards and dogs barking at the mail's daily arrival, but now it's a tattered neighborhood defined by an eerie silence broken only by the gunfire and groans of fighting KPA and US soldiers.

NEUTRAL ZONE

Tightly packed homes create a maze of backyards and side spaces ideal for close-quarters combat. Sniping is possible in the neutral zone, yet the focus is squarely on close-range gunfights in which the fastest shooter survives.

Both Control Points Alpha and Bravo sit indoor at street level, which emphasizes the need for aggressive assault tactics including prolific use of grenades—flashbang and frag—and guns such as the SMG or shotgun capable of quickly eliminating enemies.

Key Locations

- Black house, Control Point Alpha
- Gray house near Control Point Alpha
- Treehouse
- Off-white house, Control Point Bravo
- Blue house near Control Point Bravo

Sniping makes more sense in Team Deathmatch than Ground Control, where much of the action resides in and around the two indoor control points. The rooftops aren't the ideal vantage point during Team Deathmatch rounds, so opt for the treehouse or second floor windows of any of the houses.

Tactics

Control Point Alpha

CAPTURE DIFFICULTY: ★★★★★

Looking as though it were pulled from the set of "Leave It to Beaver," the house in which Control Point Alpha is found bears no semblance to that happy-go-lucky domain **[A]**. On the contrary, close-range gunfights fill the hallways and sniping from the second floor windows keep visitors away.

Home Invasion

Flashbang grenades are your friend when attacking Control Point Alpha. Roll a flashbang into the kitchen to disorient enemies guarding the room, then rush in with your SMG primed to finish them as they confusedly stumble around. Coordinating a pincer attack with teammates entering the house from the rear and/or sides increases your chances for success. Also, note possible snipers at the second floor windows. Hurl a cooked frag grenade upstairs to get them moving, following up with a few shots from an SMG.

Backyard Push

Use the gray house next to the house containing Control Point Alpha as a staging ground for a push on Alpha when playing as the US. From the second floor windows and exterior deck, you can fire on Alpha and lob grenades using the airburst launcher. Approach slowly by using the waist-high brick wall separating the two houses. While you have to be careful of shots coming from the second floor, the bricks will keep you safe from gunfire originating from street level.

If You Can't Take the Heat

The L-shaped counter separating the kitchen from the dining room makes an excellent capture spot. Lie prone during capture to remain out of sight, then stand back up to take a defensive position elsewhere in the house, such as by the windows on the second floor.

Once Upon a Mattress

One of the easiest ways to nab Control Point Alpha and defend it on the KPA side is to hide behind the mattress near the stairs. Because US soldiers will flood into the house from the backyard, you're largely protected from an assault. Should any US forces move past the mattress, you can tag them with an SMG.

Second Floor Stand

Lay a C4 charge by the stairs and aim at enemies advancing toward the house from the windows on the second floor. Naturally, position yourself toward the enemy's side of the map; if you're KPA, aim away from the setting sun into the backyard, whereas US ought to look out over the front yard and street. Instead of a sniper rifle, use a mid-range firearm like the M16 for faster shooting without too much loss in power.

Side Room Defense

Enemies often try entering from the side of the house through the garage, so guard this entrance as well as the front and back doors. Catch opponents by surprise by hiding in the shadows of the small cloakroom leading out to the side of the house. Equip a shotgun attachment or SMG to quickly eliminate anybody who passes through.

Forward Defenses

The US can prepare an attack from the gray house near Control Point Alpha. When playing as the KPA, aggressively pursue it as a forward defensive point. Use the brick wall that separates the two houses in the backyard to push against US forces inside the gray house. Hurl grenades inside to incite chaos, then enter the house to clear it. With the two-story building secured, you can prevent US operatives from attacking Alpha by firing from the second floor windows toward their spawning ground.

Control Point Bravo

CAPTURE DIFFICULTY:

Similar to Control Point Alpha with its two-story floorplan and multiple access points, Control Point Bravo's house offers tactical challenges and opportunities alike **[B]**. The second floor is critical to success: you can keep enemies from ever entering the house and guard the control point in the living room by way of the protected staircase.

Breaking into the Off-White House

Attacking Control Point Bravo at street level is a bit of a mad plan—the sheer number of open windows and doors leaves you vulnerable from multiple angles, and the lack of cover makes it tough to capture the control point safely. So try a sneaky second floor infiltration. Climb either of the ladders on the front and back of the house after lobbing a frag grenade into the windows. Once inside, roll a flashbang down the stairs to disorient defenders. Run down and gun them, then seize the control point before heading back upstairs to defend your new territory.

Chill Capture by the Refrigerator

Lying prone behind the tipped-over refrigerator in the living room barely counts as a hiding spot, but it's as good as it gets in Control Point Bravo. The sparse interior makes this the best place to capture Bravo, but retreat to a more defensible position once the control point is yours.

Second Floor Defense

The second floor windows are the best way of protecting Control Point Bravo; shoot approaching enemies long before they reach the doors. KPA can aim from the front side of the house facing the US spawning ground at the apartment complexes up the street. Peer out the back windows when playing as the US to kill KPA operatives approaching from Control Point Alpha. If enemies manage to infiltrate the ground floor, use the stairs to drop cooked grenades into the living room before heading down to secure the control point.

Drone Tactics

Ground drones are useful in the neutral zone because both Control Points Alpha and Bravo sit at street level, affording access to Wolverine and Rhino attack drones. Aerial drones are highly effective too, particularly for launching Buzzard rockets through skylights onto unsuspecting enemies below. The key is to find a safe deployment spot. Staying at your faction's spawning ground is always a good idea, though there are other locations to consider. Climb into the treehouse to launch aerial drones, or hide inside either of the empty homes near the control points to cut the distance ground drones have to travel.

A Roof Over Your Head

The lack of vehicles doesn't mean you can flit about the neutral zone without worry; on the contrary, the threat of air strikes, drone rockets, and sniper fire is real. Use vacant houses for cover as you move between control points. Another option is to stick to the perimeter of the zone, edging along to avoid detection from enemies fighting in the center of the map.

Vantage Points

Second Floor Windows, Black House, Control Point Alpha

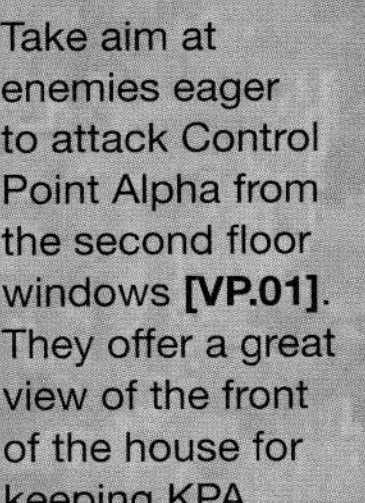

Take aim at enemies eager to attack Control Point Alpha from the second floor windows **[VP.01]**. They offer a great view of the front of the house for keeping KPA soldiers away, and they're essential for preventing US incursions when playing as KPA. Back windows facing the US spawning ground let you to shoot at enemies long before they reach the backyard.

Rooftop, Black House, Control Point Alpha

The rooftop is a risky proposition: you're vulnerable to air strikes and Buzzard rockets, and you cast a silhouette when standing or crouching **[VP.02]**. Light from the setting sun makes you visible from a considerable distance. Take to the rooftop only if you've routed KPA forces from the house and are aggressively keeping them at bay, or if you're playing as KPA and have control of the gray house as a buffer against US snipers.

Treehouse

Despite being centrally located in the neutral zone, the treehouse is often ignored in the fight over Control Points Alpha and Bravo **[VP.03]**. It makes for decent sniping—ladder access ensures that you're warned of any approaching enemies—but it's even better for deploying drones. Crouch to avoid being seen and let loose a Buzzard to shower enemies with rockets.

Second Floor Windows, Blue House near Control Point Bravo

Between Control Points Alpha and Bravo, the blue-gray house affords a fantastic vantage point overlooking either area **[VP.04]**. The second floor windows coupled with an exterior deck can be used to great effect, aiding a forward defensive position when playing as the KPA or bolstering an aggressive US assault on Alpha. Mid-range rifles such as the M16 often work better than the long-range M110.

Rooftop, Blue-Gray House near Control Point Bravo

Climbing onto the rooftop isn't the wisest of battle plans, but it can be helpful in a pinch **[VP.05]**. Your silhouette makes you a prime target when standing or crouching on the roof—similar to the situation at Control Point Alpha. Still, lying prone and sniping into the house at Alpha can be useful.

Second Floor Windows, Off-White House, Control Point Bravo

KPA snipers should marry the front-facing windows on the second floor because of the phenomenal view they provide of the US spawning ground at the apartment complexes up the road **[VP.06]**. Killing US soldiers as they spawn is a great way of maintaining control over Bravo—if you can seize it in the first place. When playing as the US, the second floor windows are not quite as useful, but peering out the back provides a decent perspective toward Control Point Alpha.

KPA ZONE

At the edge of the well-to-do Suburb sits a low-income trailer park that serves as a base for KPA operations. From here, the US can keep up the pressure to drive the enemy from their homeland. For the KPA, it's do or die.

Highly exposed control points with little in the way of cover make gaining the upper hand a tremendously difficult task. Skill and coordination define a winning strategy more than clever hiding spots in tough KPA zone.

Key Locations

- Trailer park
- Trailer park tower, Control Point Alpha
- Swimming pool, Control Point Bravo
- Blue-gray house at Control Point Bravo

Although the KPA spawn close to the wide-open objective at Control Point Alpha, the total lack of cover makes the area practically indefensible. As such, turning this negligible advantage into a tangible possession requires forward defenses best implemented with cooperative teammates.

US forces can break through minimal defenses at Control Point Alpha, but then must deal with incensed KPA operatives that spawn mere steps away in the heart of the trailer park.

Control Point Bravo is comparatively more approachable, though lack of cover makes maintaining possession challenging. Leveraging the nearby blue-gray house to keep the vicinity clear is critical to success.

Tactics

Control Point Alpha

CAPTURE DIFFICULTY: ★★★★★

No cover, no hiding spots—Control Point Alpha requires superior skill to capture, and creative defensive tactics to hold **[A]**. While the inability to hunker down and defend Alpha in a traditional manner makes it a daunting objective, it also makes it a prized possession.

Capturing Alpha Out in the Open

It's said that the best defense is an aggressive offense and that's doubly true for Control Point Alpha. Your best shot at taking this ephemeral objective involves an explosives blitz and coordinated infiltration. Blast the base of the tower with an air strike and hurl grenades as you approach on foot. If you can rush in with teammates by your side, all the better—the capture will be speedier and safer than doing it solo.

Owning the Trailer Park

Although neither faction has an advantage when it comes to the layout of the control point itself, the KPA spawn deep within the trailer park. Maintaining an iron grip of control over the trailer park is essential to mounting a successful bid for Alpha. Disallow US infiltration by taking to the rooftops of the homes and shooting soldiers on sight. C4 charges at the front of the trailer park can be a good deterrent.

Defending from the Trailer Rooftops

Exposing yourself to sniper fire and air strikes atop the trailer rooftops wouldn't normally be advisable, but given the complete lack of defensible positions at Control Point Alpha you have to make do with what you're given. The KPA have the clear advantage in using the trailers given the close proximity of their spawning grounds, yet it's possible when playing as the US to mount an aggressive push to keep the KPA at bay from the trailer rooftops. Keep moving while standing on the rooftops to avoid snipers and incoming air strikes.

Drone Deployment

Drones won't win Alpha, though they can be instrumental in supporting your efforts to capture and hold the control point. Launching a drone on the KPA side is easy: once you spawn at the back of the trailer park, find a spot behind a home and deploy an Buzzard capable of raining down rockets. Sending out Buzzards is an equally viable tactic when playing as the US, though finding a suitable deployment spot is trickier. The backyards near the neutral zone are your best bet.

Control Point Bravo

CAPTURE DIFFICULTY: ★★★★★

Comparatively more approachable than Control Point Alpha, Bravo is exposed at the backyard swimming pool and requires fierce fighting for capture **[B]**. Fortunately, the nearby blue-gray house affords defensive tactical options that make holding the control point possible—tough, but possible.

Splashy Assault on Bravo

Softening up the area is must before assailing Bravo, and bombarding the control point with explosives does the trick. Call in an air strike, hammer the area with rockets from a Buzzard drone, or cause defending enemies to scatter with a few cooked grenades. With the area clear, rush in and crouch by the swimming pool on the side closest to the fence to capture the control point. Avoid the temptation to stand on the swimming pool because it draws more attention to yourself.

Particle Board Hiding Spot

Hide behind the slab of particle board angled against the fence to defend Bravo. At the first sign of an approaching enemy, slink out from behind and fire a few rounds to preserve your faction's domination over the control point. Augment your defenses by planting C4 charges around the swimming pool.

Garden Shed Stronghold

Tuck yourself in the corner between the garden shed and perimeter fence to defend Control Point Bravo from advancing enemies. Particularly useful when playing as the KPA, this slightly protected position allows you to pop out from behind cover and shoot opponents who try to nab Bravo. It's trickier to use as the US, because the KPA tend to approach Bravo after spawning in the trailer park down the road.

Blue-Gray House Garrison

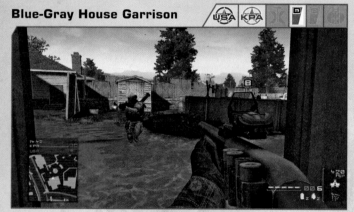

Whether you opt to fire from the second floor windows, outdoor deck, or the ground floor, there's no better way to hold Bravo than by using the house as a stronghold. This is especially true when playing as the KPA because US forces will overrun the control point via the house if you don't maintain a hold on it. On the US side, taking control of the house is much easier; however, be mindful that crafty KPA operatives can flank you by entering the front of the house.

Vantage Points

Rooftops, Trailer Park Homes surrounding Control Point Alpha

The trailer homes that encircle Control Point Alpha aren't ideal as an overwatch, but given the sparse landscape there's little else to exploit as a vantage point **[VP.01]**. Step onto the rooftops with a mid-range rifle—pass on the M110 sniper rifle because you're not going for distance—and patrol the flooded ground around the control point. Don't hesitate to drop behind the trailers if you're taking significant damage. Recover, then mount a counteroffensive.

Second Floor Windows, Blue-Gray House over Control Point Bravo

Keep an eye on Control Point Bravo from the second floor windows in the nearby house **[VP.02]**. Drop a C4 charge at the base of the stairs to cover your tail, then camp out near the windows to guard the control point below. You don't have to just use your gun—chuck cooked grenades to send enemies running or even call in an air strike to clear the area.

Deck, Blue-Gray House over Control Point Bravo

Reserve the deck for close battles where exposing yourself to attack is less a concern than potentially losing Control Point Bravo to the enemy. The deck provides no cover, so use it for emergency situations and duck inside the house to maintain watch over Bravo once things quiet down **[VP.03]**.

US ZONE

A testament to the chaos and carnage of warfare, the US zone is a mess of destroyed homes, blasted backyards, and charred vehicles resting in the empty streets.

The condemned house holding Control Point Alpha offers several capture hiding spots amid the rumble. While difficult to defend, it offers some tactical possibilities for the attacker.

Key Locations

- Cul-de-sac
- Condemned house, Control Point Alpha
- Wrecked school bus, Control Point Bravo
- Slate gray house across from Control Point Bravo
- Apartment complexes

Control Point Bravo is even less inviting. The wrecked school bus that juts out from the two-story house provides a unique defensive spot, although seizing the barren control point for the purpose of defending it is a tough task. Use air strikes and aerial drones to clear the area before going in on foot.

Tactics

Control Point Alpha

CAPTURE DIFFICULTY: ★★★★★

The bombed house in which Control Point Alpha sits has already seen more than its fair share of fighting **[A]**. A sunken second floor, crumbling walls, and deteriorating roof leave few options for defending this condemned property.

Condemned House Cleaning Crew

More than broken furniture and disintegrating walls need cleaning in this house—enemies nestled within the bombed-out remains should be routed with grenades and gunfire. Cook grenades and roll them under the sunken second floor to clear any enemies hiding underneath. Do the same for the hiding hole near the garage at the back of the house. Alternately, switch to an SMG and spray bullets as you walk through the house in the wake of the grenade blasts.

Sneaky Capture Under the Sunken Floor

Although the alcove created by the sunken second floor is a predictable hiding spot, capturing Control Point Alpha from there is still recommended. Grenades thrown into the house are your primary concern, so be prepared to flee as soon as they hit.

Defense from the Sunken Second Floor

Guarding Control Point Alpha from the sinking second story seems an obvious tactic—and it is. For the US it's an unwise move because KPA forces have a clear line of sight when approaching from the cul-de-sac and will quickly eradicate you. Instead, use it when playing as the KPA to watch for US soldiers entering through the back. You won't have much time to kill an invader, though, so use an SMG to finish the job quickly.

Cul-de-sac Shootout

The lack of vantage points makes sniping difficult in the US zone, though there are creative alternatives if you're itching for long-distance combat. Rather than taking to an elevated overwatch, lie prone next to the tower in the cul-de-sac to aim at enemies running about the condemned house at Control Point Alpha. It's not the safest spot—particularly when playing as the US given the nearby KPA spawning ground—but it's a surprisingly viable position.

Drones in the Apartment Complex

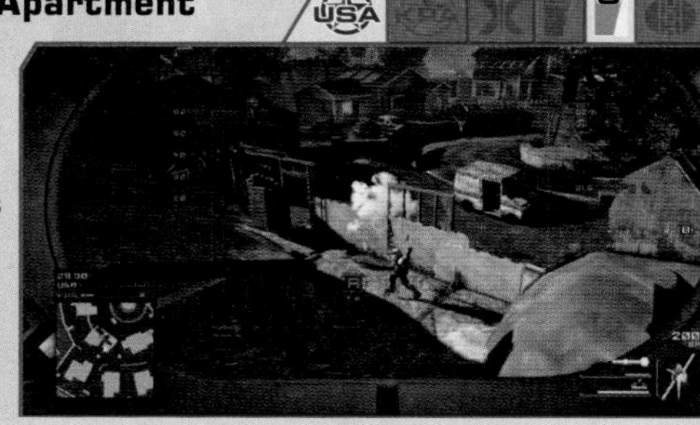

Your greatest asset when playing as a US soldier are the apartment buildings bordering the faction's spawning ground. From the complex stairwells, you can launch aerial drones to raid Control Points Alpha and Bravo, as well as snipe enemies running between the two objectives. Because the buildings are set along the edge of the map, you're unlikely to see KPA opposition sneak back here, which ensures a safe and secure drone deployment zone.

Control Point Bravo

CAPTURE DIFFICULTY: ★★★★★

Control Point Bravo serves as the last stop for the unfortunate passengers on the school bus smashed into the side of the boarded-up house **[B]**. It makes for a decent defensive position, though, in an otherwise barren control point.

Blitz on Bravo

Air strikes are the most effective weapon for clearing the backyard in which Bravo is located. The expansive yard renders grenades less useful because enemies can run away from the blast. Instead, focus on calling in a Hellfire strike and running in to capture the point once the backyard has been cleared. Drones can also be handy, particularly when playing as the US because you can deploy them from the apartments up the road.

Backyard Corner Capture

The corner with the tree is the most reasonable capture spot in the sparse backyard. While the tree doesn't completely shield you from gunfire, it offers at least some protection. However, seizing Bravo requires keeping enemies at bay. Depending on which faction you're playing, monitor the edge of the backyard for US activity, or the sides for approaching KPA soldiers.

Hitting a Brick Wall

Although Control Point Bravo lacks cover, the brick wall outlining the backyard can be used to mount an attack on the control point when playing as the US, or to defend possession as a KPA soldier. The US definitely has the advantage in using this wall, particularly if coordinated with a teammate firing down into Bravo from the rooftop of the blue-gray house. This combination attack makes it difficult for KPA forces to defend the backyard from behind the brick wall.

School Bus Defense

Lying prone on the floor of the school bus gives you a decent view of backyard and allows you to maintain a low profile; however, this predictable defensive position is sure to attract grenades. Aim quickly and accurately to take out enemies before they come within grenade-throwing range. Additionally, because the school bus is accessible from the front of the house, beware of flank attacks.

It's Coming from Inside the House!

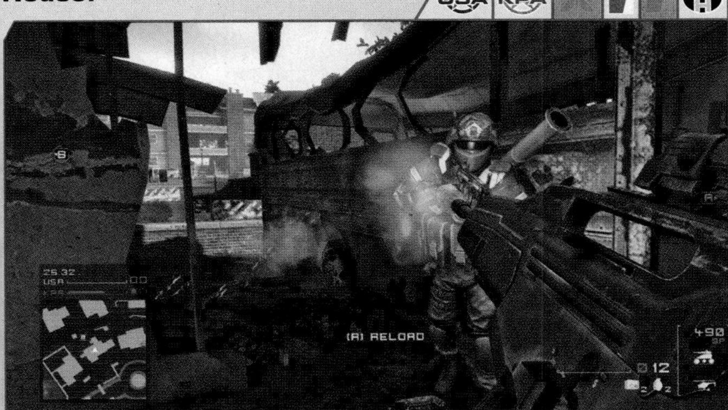

It's a shame you can't capture Bravo from inside the house, because it provides good cover from air strikes and hides you from approaching enemies. Press yourself to the interior wall and peek out at the backyard to guard Bravo. This is a particularly good position because you can watch the front of the house too.

Vantage Points

Apartment Complex Stairways

Reserved primarily for for US soldiers—trying to reach this area while playing as the KPA is practically suicide—the apartment complex stairways trade line of sight for safety. You can't see much from this limited vantage point, but you're unlikely to see much action so close to the US spawning ground. Use this overwatch position to snipe at enemies moving between Control Points Alpha and Bravo **[VP.01]**.

Rooftop, Slate Gray House near Control Point Bravo

The US zone's best and most active vantage point is also one of the most visible and dangerous. While the slate gray house across from Control Point Bravo offers a great view of the backyard objective, it also makes you an easy target standing out on the open rooftop **[VP.02]**. Fortunately, the lack of other vantage points means you don't have to worry about snipers so much as fighters taking aim from the ground below.

APPENDICES

The following charts reveal how all of the Ranks and Unlocks become available during the Multiplayer game, as well as every Achievement/Trophy that can be acquired. Happy hunting!

APPENDIX 1: DEFAULT UNLOCKS

These are the items and abilities that are available at Rank 0, when you first begin:

Unlockable	Primary Type	Specific Type
M4	Weapons	Assault Rifle
M249	Weapons	LMG
PWS Diablo	Weapons	SMG
M110	Weapons	Sniper Rifle
Ground Assault Drone	Special Weapons	Drones
RPG	Special Weapons	Launcher
Hellfire	Special Weapons	Air Strike
Flak Jacket	Special Weapons	Equipment
EMP Grenade	Special Explosive	—
Flashbang	Special Explosive	—
Humvee	Vehicles	—
Light Armor Vehicle	Vehicles	—

Unlockable	Primary Type	Specific Type
Littlebird: Scout Helicopter	Vehicles	—
Fist Full	Ability	Infantry
Tactical Reload	Ability	Infantry
Quickdraw	Ability	Infantry
Straight from the Hip	Ability	Infantry
Drone Be Gone!	Ability	Infantry
Thick Skin	Ability	Infantry
Now That's a Knife	Ability	Infantry
Full Tank	Ability	Vehicle
Gyro	Ability	Vehicle
Faster Reload	Ability	Vehicle
Big Stick	Ability	Vehicle

APPENDIX 2: RANKS AND UNLOCKS

This chart reveals the Ranks (AKA "Levels") that you can attain during weeks of Multiplayer matches. Each Rank has a title, the required XP (experience) to reach each Rank, and the total XP accrued. Then there's the type of ability, weapon, or equipment you reach, and the specific prize.

Rank	Rank Title	Exp Required	Total Exp	Unlock Type	Unlock
1	Private	0	0	Default Loadouts/Unlocks	Default Loadouts/Unlocks
2	Private First Class I	200	200	Vehicle	Tank
3	Private First Class II	1,800	2,000	Assault Rifle 2	ACR
4	Private First Class III	3,000	5,000	Equipment	Personal UAV
5	Lance Corporal I	3,000	8,000	Infantry Ability	Penny Pincher
6	Lance Corporal II	3,000	11,000	Drone 2	Recon Drone, Clan Tags
7	Lance Corporal III	4,000	15,000	Playlists	Battle Commander
8	Corporal I	4,000	19,000	Infantry Ability	My Buddy
9	Corporal II	4,000	23,000	SMG 2	Super-V
10	Corporal III	4,000	27,000	Custom Vehicle Loadouts	Humvee Loadout
11	Sergeant I	4,000	31,000	Vehicle Ability	Coated
12	Sergeant II	5,000	36,000	Vehicle	Attack Heli
13	Sergeant III	5,000	41,000	Infantry Ability	Grizzled
14	Staff Sergeant I	5,000	46,000	Assault Rifle 3	SCAR-L

Rank	Rank Title	Exp Required	Total Exp	Unlock Type	Unlock
15	Staff Sergeant II	5,000	51,000	Custom Vehicle Loadouts	LAV Loadout
16	Staff Sergeant III	5,000	56,000	Custom Infantry Loadouts	Custom Infantry Loadouts +1
17	Gunnery Sergeant I	6,000	62,000	Air Strike 2	White Phosphorus Bomb
18	Gunnery Sergeant II	6,000	68,000	Infantry Ability	Grave Robber
19	Gunnery Sergeant III	6,000	74,000	Sniper Rifle 2	M200
20	Master Sergeant I	6,000	80,000	Vehicle Ability	Ejection Seat
21	Master Sergeant II	6,000	86,000	Drone 3	Anti-Tank Drone
22	Master Sergeant III	7,000	93,000	Custom Vehicle Loadouts	Tank Loadout
23	First Sergeant I	7,000	100,000	Infantry Ability	Ghost
24	First Sergeant II	7,000	107,000	Special Explosive 3	C4
25	First Sergeant III	7,000	114,000	Ability Point	Infantry Ability Point +1
26	Master Gunnery Sergent I	7,000	121,000	Infantry Ability	Steady Aim
27	Master Gunnery Sergent II	8,000	129,000	Assault Rifle 4	M16
28	Master Gunnery Sergent III	8,000	137,000	Drone 4	Air Assault Drone
29	Sergeant Major I	8,000	145,000	Custom Vehicle Loadouts	Littlebird Loadout
30	Sergeant Major II	8,000	153,000	Infantry Ability	Boomer
31	Sergeant Major III	8,000	161,000	Launcher 2	Proximity Launcher
32	Second Lieutenant I	9,000	170,000	LMG 2	SCAR MG
33	Second Lieutenant II	9,000	179,000	Vehicle Ability	Speed Boost
34	Second Lieutenant III	9,000	188,000	Infantry Ability	Crater-to-Order
35	First Lieutenant I	9,000	197,000	Custom Infantry Loadouts	Custom Infantry Loadouts +1
36	First Lieutenant II	9,000	206,000	Equipment	Resupply
37	First Lieutenant III	9,000	215,000	Custom Vehicle Loadouts	Apache Loadout
38	Captain I	10,000	225,000	Infantry Ability	Utility Belt
39	Captain II	10,000	235,000	—	
40	Captain III	15,000	250,000	Assault Rifle 5	T3AK

Rank	Rank Title	Exp Required	Total Exp	Unlock Type	Unlock
41	Major I	15,000	265,000	Vehicle Ability	Missile Defense
42	Major II	15,000	280,000	Infantry Ability	Blastwave
43	Major III	15,000	295,000	Special Explosive 3	WP Grenade
44	Lieutenant Colonel I	15,000	310,000	Air Strike 3	Cluster Bomb
45	Lieutenant Colonel II	17,500	327,500	—	
46	Lieutenant Colonel III	17,500	345,000	Assault Rifle 6	XM10
47	Colonel I	17,500	362,500	Infantry Ability	Quick Healer
48	Colonel II	17,500	380,000	Vehicle Ability	Monkey Wrench
49	Colonel III	17,500	397,500	Equipment	Thermal Goggles
50	1-Star General I	22,500	420,000	Ability Point	Vehicle Ability Point +1
51	1-Star General II	20,000	440,000	—	
52	1-Star General III	20,000	460,000	—	
53	1-Star General IV	20,000	480,000	—	
54	1-Star General V	20,000	500,000	—	
55	2-Star General I	25,000	525,000	Weapon Camo	Chrome
56	2-Star General II	25,000	550,000	—	
57	2-Star General III	25,000	575,000	—	
58	2-Star General IV	25,000	600,000	—	
59	2-Star General V	25,000	625,000	—	
60	3-Star General I	30,000	655,000	Weapon Camo	Gold
61	3-Star General II	30,000	685,000	—	
62	3-Star General III	30,000	715,000	—	
63	3-Star General IV	30,000	745,000	—	
64	3-Star General V	30,000	775,000	—	
65	4-Star General I	35,000	810,000	Weapon Camo	Viper
66	4-Star General II	35,000	845,000	—	
67	4-Star General III	35,000	880,000	—	
68	4-Star General IV	35,000	915,000	—	
69	4-Star General V	35,000	950,000	—	
70	5-Star General I	40,000	990,000	Weapon Camo	Perses
71	5-Star General II	40,000	1,030,000	—	

Rank	Rank Title	Exp Required	Total Exp	Unlock Type	Unlock
72	5-Star General III	40,000	1,070,000	—	
73	5-Star General IV	40,000	1,110,000	—	
74	5-Star General V	40,000	1,150,000	—	
75	Supreme Leader	50,000	1,200,000	Weapon Camo	I <3 My Gun

APPENDIX 3: ACHIEVEMENTS AND TROPHIES

The following reveals every Achievement/Trophy available, and how they are acquired.

Name	Mode	Description	X360/PC Points	PS3 Trophy	PS3 Points	Secret?
Why We Fight	SP	Complete Chapter 1 in the Single Player Campaign	10	Bronze	15	
Freedom	SP	Complete Chapter 2 in the Single Player Campaign	10	Bronze	15	
Fire Sale	SP	Complete Chapter 3 in the Single Player Campaign	10	Bronze	15	
The Wall	SP	Complete Chapter 4 in the Single Player Campaign	10	Bronze	15	
Heartland	SP	Complete Chapter 5 in the Single Player Campaign	10	Bronze	15	
Overwatch	SP	Complete Chapter 6 in the Single Player Campaign	10	Bronze	15	
Golden Gate	SP	Complete Chapter 7 in the Single Player Campaign	10	Silver	30	Yes
Why We Fight—Guerrilla	SP	Complete Chapter 1 on the Hardest Difficulty in the Single Player Campaign	25	Bronze	15	
Freedom—Guerrilla	SP	Complete Chapter 2 on the Hardest Difficulty in the Single Player Campaign	25	Bronze	15	
Fire Sale—Guerrilla	SP	Complete Chapter 3 on the Hardest Difficulty in the Single Player Campaign	25	Bronze	15	
The Wall—Guerrilla	SP	Complete Chapter 4 on the Hardest Difficulty in the Single Player Campaign	25	Bronze	15	
Heartland—Guerrilla	SP	Complete Chapter 5 on the Hardest Difficulty in the Single Player Campaign	25	Bronze	15	
Overwatch—Guerrilla	SP	Complete Chapter 6 on the Hardest Difficulty in the Single Player Campaign	25	Silver	30	
Golden Gate—Guerrilla	SP	Complete Chapter 7 on the Hardest Difficulty in the Single Player Campaign	25	Silver	30	Yes
Iron Man—Why We Fight	SP	Complete Chapter 1 in the Single Player Campaign without dying or restarting a checkpoint	25	Bronze	15	
Iron Man—Freedom	SP	Complete Chapter 2 in the Single Player Campaign without dying or restarting a checkpoint	25	Bronze	15	
Iron Man—Fire Sale	SP	Complete Chapter 3 in the Single Player Campaign without dying or restarting a checkpoint	25	Bronze	15	
Iron Man—The Wall	SP	Complete Chapter 4 in the Single Player Campaign without dying or restarting a checkpoint	25	Bronze	15	
Iron Man—Heartland	SP	Complete Chapter 5 in the Single Player Campaign without dying or restarting a checkpoint	25	Bronze	15	
Iron Man—Overwatch	SP	Complete Chapter 6 in the Single Player Campaign without dying or restarting a checkpoint	25	Silver	30	
Iron Man—Golden Gate	SP	Complete Chapter 7 in the Single Player Campaign without dying or restarting a checkpoint	25	Silver	30	Yes

Name	Mode	Description	X360/PC Points	PS3 Trophy	PS3 Points	Secret?
Archivist	SP	Find 30 of 61 news pick-ups in the Single Player Campaign	10	Bronze	15	
Historian	SP	Find all 61 news pick-ups in the Single Player Campaign	30	Gold	90	
Pistol Whipped	SP	Kill 25 enemies with a pistol in Chapter 1: Why We Fight	10	Bronze	15	
Give Him the Stick	SP	Kill 25 enemies with melee attacks in Chapter 1: Why We Fight	10	Bronze	15	
Welcome to Freedom	SP	Talk at least once to each inhabitant of Oasis in Chapter 2: Freedom	10	Bronze	15	
Good Use of Cover	SP	Destroy the first sentry tower without taking any damage in Chapter 2: Freedom	10	Bronze	15	
Mercy	SP	Kill 5 enemies while they are on fire in Chapter 3: Fire Sale	10	Bronze	15	
Let 'em Burn	SP	Don't kill any of the enemies that are on fire in Chapter 3: Fire Sale	10	Bronze	15	
David Rejected	SP	Complete the street section without Goliath taking any damage in Chapter 4: The Wall	10	Bronze	15	Yes
Fatal and Tragic	SP	Jump off the Golden Gate Bridge in Chapter 7: Golden Gate	10	Bronze	15	Yes
Chronicler	SP	Find the first of 61 news pick-ups	10	Bronze	15	
Stairway to Heaven	SP	From the front door of the church, make it to the crow's nest in 240 seconds in Chapter 5: Heartland	10	Bronze	15	
Speed Demon	SP	Hijack the tankers in less than 8 minutes in one life in Chapter 6: Overwatch	10	Bronze	15	
Safer Skies	SP	Destroy all the SAM trucks in the level in Chapter 6: Overwatch	10	Bronze	15	
Wilhelm's Nightmare	SP	Kill 10 enemies in the helicopter fly-in in Chapter 7: Golden Gate	10	Bronze	15	Yes
Soft Targets	SP	Destroy all vehicles using the UAV in Chapter 7: Golden Gate	10	Bronze	15	Yes
Single Player Totals			**600**		**705**	
Weapon Expert	MP	Complete an expert challenge for any weapon in Multiplayer	25	Bronze	15	
Drone Expert	MP	Complete an expert challenge for any drone in Multiplayer	25	Bronze	15	
Vehicle Expert	MP	Complete an expert challenge for any vehicle in Multiplayer	25	Bronze	15	
Expert of War	MP	Complete all challenges for weapons, drones, vehicles, and modes in Multiplayer	100	Gold	90	
Over the Hill	MP	Reach experience level 50 in Multiplayer	50	Silver	30	
Squad Commander *	MP	Enter a public match as the Party Leader of a 4-player Minimum Party in Multiplayer	20	Bronze	15	
Medal of Honor *	MP	Win a public match as the Party Leader of a Party in Multiplayer	20	Bronze	15	
Full Boat *	MP	Enter a public match in a Party with 16 players in Multiplayer	30	Silver	30	
3-Star Threat	MP	Become a 3-Star threat in a Battle Commander public match	30	Silver	30	
5-Star Threat	MP	Become a 5-Star threat in a Battle Commander public match	75	Gold	90	
Multiplayer Totals			**400**		**345**	
Grand Totals			**1,000**		**1,050**	
Platinum Trophy (PS3 only)	SP/MP	Complete all other trophies for *Homefront*	–	**Platinum**		
Tea Party (PC Only)	MP	For Steam users only – Successfully examined 5 enemy corpses				

* Console Only